D1255724

# FIGHTING JOE HOOKER

JOSEPH HOOKER, MAJOR GENERAL

# *Fighting Joe*
# Hooker

by
Walter H. Hebert

•

**The Bobbs-Merrill Company**
*Publishers*
Indianapolis • New York

*First Edition*

*To my father*

# FOREWORD

ON THE twenty-sixth of January 1863 a weary and disheartened President sat by the long, low conference table in the White House study. His attempt to keep the Southern states in the Union by military force, which had once seemed so certain of success, now appeared to be well on the road to failure. The Confederacy had gained a wide edge in the last two months of fighting. In the East the Army of the Potomac was still demoralized from the disaster of Fredericksburg which climaxed a long succession of Union reverses; even a minor expedition into North Carolina had just been repulsed. In the West the year-end battle of Stone's River, proclaimed as a great Federal victory, was now recognized as an indecisive contest. The attempt to capture Vicksburg, Mississippi, via Chickasaw Bluffs had been beaten back, the advanced Union base at Holly Springs, Mississippi, destroyed, and Galveston, Texas, retaken by the Confederates. Desertion was whittling down the effective force of the armies, and the ranks could not be filled since volunteering had practically ceased.

Home-front support of the war was crumbling from dejection over the reverses in the field and the unanticipated length of the struggle. In the President's own Northwest resolutions were being proposed in the state legislatures to acknowledge the Confederacy, to seek an armistice, or to call a convention of all the states to compromise the sectional struggle. Even the prominent New York Republican editor, Horace Greeley, was advocating foreign mediation to terminate it. The war administration had received a vote of no confidence in the mid-term elections, and a radical committee from the Senate had just tried to force the resignation of the Secretary of State. The Copperheads were riding high! Was the union of these states perpetual after all? Would the nation ever regain its solidarity and emerge from this tragic period?

Abraham Lincoln turned to the job at hand. He had just appointed a new commander to the Army of the Potomac—that ill-fated body buffeted by poor leadership and by the seemingly invincible infantry from Virginia, the Carolinas, Georgia, Tennessee, the Gulf states and faraway Texas. No other Federal army was more important to the preservation of the Union, yet none was so sadly in need of reorganization and a strong hand to direct it. When the colonies made their bid for independence the occasion produced a man to inspire their little army to victory; if the present crisis were to bring forth such a leader, he must appear soon or it would be too late.

Sadly the President must have reflected on the nearness of disaster and the responsibility he had just conferred on Major General Joseph Hooker. Could this man overcome the Army of Northern Virginia and bring back belief in final victory, or would he lead his men to another crushing defeat—perhaps the last the shaken North could endure? The new commander was unquestionably a fighter and as popular with the soldiers as anyone available, but he possessed troubling weaknesses—weaknesses which Lincoln well knew and which could not be glossed over. The President must compose a letter to supplement the official appointment blending his faith and his doubts in such a way as to apprise Hooker of his feelings without rebuking him. The wide shoulders hunched over the long table and from the pen of Abraham Lincoln came a two-page letter of such sincerity and purpose that many today consider it one of the foremost examples of his simple literary genius. It is safe to say that no commanding general ever received at the time of his appointment a message more forthright and penetrating from the head of his government.

"EXECUTIVE MANSION
"WASHINGTON, January 26, 1863.
"MAJOR GENERAL HOOKER:
"GENERAL
"I have placed you at the head of the Army of the Potomac. Of course I have done this upon what appear to me to be sufficient reasons. And yet I think it best for you to know that there are some things in regard to which, I am not quite satisfied with you. I believe you to be a brave and skilful soldier, which, of course, I like. I also believe you do not mix politics with your profession, in which you are right. You have confidence in yourself, which is a valuable, if not an indispensable quality. You are ambitious, which, within reasonable limits, does good rather than harm. But I think that during Gen. Burnside's command of the Army, you have taken counsel of your ambition, and thwarted him as much as you could, in which you did a great wrong to the country, and to a most meritorious and honorable brother officer. I have heard, in such way as to believe it, of your recently saying that both the Army and the Government needed a Dictator. Of course it was not *for* this, but in spite of it, that I have given you the command. Only those generals, who gain successes, can

set up dictators. What I now ask of you is military success, and I will risk the dictatorship. The government will support you to the utmost of its ability, which is neither more nor less than it has done and will do for all commanders. I much fear that the spirit which you have aided to infuse into the Army, of criticizing their Commander, and withholding confidence from him, will now turn upon you. I shall assist you as far as I can, to put it down. Neither you, nor Napoleon, if he were alive again, could get any good out of an army, while such a spirit prevails in it.

"And now, beware of rashness.—Beware of rashness, but with energy, and sleepless vigilance, go forward, and give us victories.

"Yours very truly

"A. LINCOLN"

Thousands of books and monographs have been written covering the important and even the inconsequential facts of Abraham Lincoln's life, but what about the recipient of this famous letter? Was he deserving of the praise and guilty of the sins accredited to him? How did he take so unusual a message, and how did he make use of his opportunity? How well did Lincoln know his man?

# CONTENTS

# LIST OF ILLUSTRATIONS

# MAPS

# FIGHTING JOE HOOKER

## CHAPTER I

## THE EARLY TRAINING OF A FIGHTER

IN A COMFORTABLE home on the main street of Hadley, Massachusetts, an anxious father waited as his wife gave birth to their fourth child. So far three daughters had resulted from their union; this time they must have a son. For one hundred and twenty-five years an uninterrupted line of Joseph Hookers had participated in the westward expansion of Massachusetts. Starting from Wenham, just north of Salem where the founder of the line had arrived from England in 1689, the family had reached the Connecticut River in the course of four generations. It was now November 13, 1814. The tired mother was delivered of her burden and a sound, healthy boy was gratefully received by the Joseph Hookers of Hadley. The infant was straightway christened Joseph, the fifth of a line of farmers, prominent landowners, town officials and warriors to bear their traditional family name.

The first Joseph Hooker had advanced from commoner to freeholder, prospering as the years passed and becoming a surveyor of highways. His son moved on to Westford, where he spent the productive years of his life as a successful farmer and landowner. The third Joseph Hooker took part in the French and Indian War and then settled in Greenwich. From here he led the minutemen of the village to Cambridge in April of '75 and went on to become a captain in George Washington's Continental Army. After the war considerable real estate was amassed by the captain and his sons, the third of whom was named Joseph. This son was not too fortunate with his property holdings and after the death of his first wife moved on to Hadley on the Connecticut River for the fresh start our forefathers could always make in the west. Here he purchased a lot and buildings facing West Street, a thoroughfare where the town's most magnificent elms shaded pleasant homes. He soon married Mary Seymour of Hadley and started the family which was to conclude with this fourth child, Joseph, destined to become one of the most controversial figures of the Civil War.[1]

For three years the little boy enjoyed the roomy house and ample grounds on West Street, but his father's declining fortunes brought on the sale of the property and the removal of the family to a rented dwelling on Middle Street. The War of 1812 had occasioned financial disaster to the Hookers. Their drygoods business was hard hit and the family was ever after hampered by insufficient funds. The father took a job as purchaser of cattle for market, but never got back on his feet financially. He seemed whipped by his business reverses, and only the resolution and courage of Mary Hooker kept the family going. The three daughters and, in due time, Joe took every opportunity to earn money at odd jobs. Joe gathered floodwood for fuel from the banks of the Connecticut, gleaned scatterings left by harvesters in the fields of broomcorn, drove the neighbors' cows to pasture and did any farm work within his grasp. These activities interfered considerably with the games of boyhood, but those he found time for he played with energy and great pleasure. Joe was slender, lithe, alert, graceful and vigorous in all his movements. At One Old Cat, a forerunner of baseball, he was expert; catching was his specialty. The town historian testifies that Joe crowded the plate to such an extent he seemed to receive the ball before the batter (who probably was using an out-of-service ax handle) could swing. This aggressiveness was a characteristic which he was to retain all his life and was to earn for him on the field of battle, in years to come, the title of "Fighting Joe." Busy as he was, there was still time occasionally to rob a fruit orchard with a friend or to practice marksmanship with the small rifle his father had given him.

Mr. Hooker was away from home much of the time, leaving the control and direction of Joe to the mother and the three sisters, who were respectively eight, six and three years older than their brother. Mary Hooker proved to be the kind of woman who overcomes adversity, and she exerted a stimulating influence upon her family. She was determined that the children should receive a good education and they were sent, one after the other, to the Hopkins Academy in Hadley where the Reverend Daniel Huntington served as principal. Originally this institution had been a free school, but the loss of its invested endowment had necessitated the charge of an annual fee of $12 per student. When it came time for Joseph to enroll, his tuition was paid with funds he earned from setting hairpin-shaped wires into thin hardwood boards used in the home wool-spinning occupation of the day.[2]

The academy was a three-story brick building erected in 1817. To the students it seemed the most imposing structure in the world.[3] Young Joseph was doubtlessly impressed, but this did not inhibit his interest in a good time nor cause him to devote all his hours to study. His most distinguished academic performances occurred in public speaking. He possessed a full-toned, flexible, well-modulated voice which lent itself well to the stirring speeches of Patrick Henry, the redheaded Virginia radical.[4] Thirty years later the "peace, peace—but there is no peace" phrase of the colonial orator was to take on a new and terrible meaning, and the young man of Hopkins Academy would be in the midst of the storm.

There is some evidence that Mary Hooker wished her son to prepare for the ministry,[5] but by heredity Joseph was better fitted to take up the sword than the cross. In addition to his grandfather, who had attained distinction in the War for Independence, there had been Great-Uncle John who fought for King George in the Louisburg expedition of 1744-1745; there was Uncle John Hooker at Saratoga when Burgoyne surrendered; and there was the ever-present influence of Uncle Ben who had served five years in the Continental Army before following his brother to Hadley in 1810.[6] According to a boyhood chum, Joe never had ambition to enter either field. He was a regular attendant at church and Sunday school and he had taken the pledge when the temperance reformation passed through Hadley, but this action had been prompted more by illness following a drinking bout at a friend's cider mill than by any firm conviction on the subject. He was much taken with history and read constantly about the world's great generals and their campaigns, but his chief interest was in getting more education with the view of later studying law.[7]

It had looked as though there would be little opportunity for Joseph to go to college—money was still scarce—but Mary Hooker was determined that her boy should have a chance to take full advantage of his quick mind and resolute nature. Fortunately one of Joseph's teachers, Giles C. Kellogg, became deeply interested and suggested, since funds were not available for further schooling, that an attempt should be made to get the boy into West Point Military Academy. Kellogg, with the aid of a lawyer friend, induced Congressman George Grinnell from the Hadley district to secure an appointment for Joseph.[8] He then helped the boy to pass the entrance examinations and in June of 1833, at the age of eighteen, Joseph left his pleasant home for the military school on the Hudson. It was a sad parting for mother and son, for their relationship had been an affectionate one.

On July first Plebe Joseph Hooker began his four-year course of study and discipline—discipline of the mind and of the body—with sufficient relaxation for purposes of health. The barracks were ill-arranged and lacked even the usual conveniences of the day. Three or four cadets were huddled into rooms adequate for two at most. The food was plain, undress-clothing simple, and the hours regular.[9]

The rigid life of the Academy agreed with the cadet from Hadley and he returned home on furloughs in the best of health, cutting quite a figure in his gray coat, gilt buttons and white trousers.[10] In appearance he was as manly as any young soldier attending the "Point." Tall, well-proportioned, with light brown hair, a ruddy complexion, regular features and large blue eyes, he was familiarly known around town as "the beautiful cadet."[11] This title most certainly brought protests from Joe, but he possessed enough vanity to appreciate such recognition even though he could not outwardly accept it.

The allurement of his uniform and his amiable manners also contributed toward his position as the most welcome escort in young Hadley society. These vacations were marked with pleasant reunions of the Hooker family. The sisters had married successful business and professional men and had drifted away from the town, but they returned home regularly for summer visits.[12]

The curriculum at the Military Academy was well within Hooker's comprehension and he applied himself with zeal and industry. "He was quick to learn, original in applying what he learned, and critical of the ideas and facts taught him."[13] Critical assertiveness in the young cadet was not limited to the classroom but expressed itself in contacts with his fellow cadets. A constant source of friction arose from the discussion of the slavery question between the zealous Southern boys and the more outspoken of the Yankee cadets. Joseph Hooker was a stanch member of the latter group and forcefully defended John Quincy Adams of his native state who was then fighting in Congress for the right to introduce antislavery petitions.

In his senior year he was examined on civil and military engineering, ethics, rhetoric, constitutional law and artillery and infantry tactics.[14] He ranked well above the average in final grades, but in his four years of training he had acquired enough demerit marks to bring his standing down to twenty-ninth in a class of fifty. The customary grounds for demerits—violations of post rules, lack of proper respect for superiors, inattentiveness in class, etc.—undoubtedly brought on many of Joe's black marks, but he was independent, outspoken, quick to take offense, and it is certain that these contributed their share to the total.

Competition in the class of 1837 was keen, twenty-two of the graduates later distinguishing themselves in the Union and Confederate Armies. No. 1 was Henry W. Benham of Connecticut who was to handle Hooker's pontoon bridge at Chancellorsville; No. 22, William H. French, and No. 24, John Sedgwick, were also to serve him in important commands at the peak of his career. Other classmates destined to prominence in the Union Army were Israel Vogdes and Edward D. Townsend. The list of those who fought for the Confederacy was even more imposing, including Braxton Bragg, Jubal A. Early, John C. Pemberton, Arnold Elzey, William H. T. Walker and Robert H. Chilton.[15] Of more importance to Hooker's subsequent military career was the acquaintance formed with three underclassmen: Henry Wager Halleck of New York, William Tecumseh Sherman of Ohio and George Henry Thomas of Virginia.

Upon graduating Hooker was commissioned a second lieutenant in the 1st Artillery, a position for which his training was inadequate. Although four months of the school year were devoted to field maneuvers of the battery, mortar practice and target firing, procedure was governed by Lallemand's text and the regulations adopted by the West Point Board of Officers in 1825. A new textbook of artillery tactics embracing the latest improvements of other nations had been needed for some time.[16]

July of 1837 was an opportune time to graduate from West Point, for an active field of operations existed in Florida. There the Seminole Indians, under the leadership of Osceola, had repudiated a treaty which provided for their migration to the West. The massacre of a United States major and his detail of 100 soldiers indicated that the repudiation was not to be taken lightly. A strong force would be needed if the Indians were to be deprived of their birthright.[17] Although at this time our military force in Florida already numbered 3,599 men[18] under the command of General Thomas S. Jessup, by the last of October large numbers of regular troops began to arrive as reinforcements.

Among the newcomers were nine companies, 387 men of the 1st Artillery commanded by Lieutenant Colonel B. K. Pierce.[19] Included in F Company was Lieutenant Joseph Hooker. They moved down the east coast in barges to a point northeast of Lake Okeechobee where they established Fort Pierce. The command was first assigned to the transfer of supplies from the main base, two hundred miles up the coast to Fort Pierce, and to Fort Jupiter forty miles farther south. Continual skirmishes were fought with small bands of warriors in the interior, but the Indians were elusive and few casualties resulted.[20] The regiment's most important expedition came in March 1838, when a detachment went out with the 4th Artillery and the Tennessee Volunteers to hunt the Indians in the Everglades. It was slow progress through the difficult, wet country. The Indians were adept at disappearing into the swamps, and very little was accomplished.[21] There is no evidence to indicate the nature of the work to which Lieutenant Hooker was assigned within the regiment or whether he distinguished himself in these frequent sallies against the Indians.

By April 30, 1838, active operations had ceased. Osceola had been captured through treachery and the Indians were temporarily subdued. General Jessup had gladly given over the command to Brigadier General Zachary Taylor, late of the 1st Regular Infantry. Now the Cherokees in Georgia, Alabama, North Carolina and Tennessee were taking their turn at repudiating treaties with the "Great White Father," and four regiments of artillery were ordered to march into southeastern Tennessee. The 1st Artillery was part of the strong force collected under General Winfield Scott. The Indians in quick time decided to move west of the Mississippi[22]—thus ending the need for troops in this area.

In July 1838 Hooker's regiment was withdrawn from the Cherokee country to serve on the Canadian border. Many citizens along our northern frontier were aiding disaffected Canadians in an attempt to overthrow their government, thereby violating United States treaty obligations to England. The 1st Artillery was scattered at posts along the border from Big Sodus Bay, New York, on Lake Ontario, to Houlton, Maine.[23] Joseph Hooker's company was posted at Swanton in the northwestern tip of Vermont. Here he received his first promotion, becoming a first lieutenant on November 1, 1838, at a salary of $546 a year.

Meanwhile, a more serious border outbreak had occurred over territory on our northeastern border. The international boundary in this region had been established only vaguely by the Treaty of Paris in 1783, and no commission as yet had been able to settle the line. Timber cutters from Maine and New Brunswick were constantly crossing axes over the valuable virgin timber in the "disputed territory." It was too great a prize to relinquish without a fight, and the rival governors had called out their militia and appealed to their respective government to support their claims. President Van Buren sent General Scott to dissuade both Maine and New Brunswick from further aggression until another commission could take a try at solving the difficult question. Half of the 1st Artillery was drawn over to Hancock Barracks at Houlton, Maine, near the center of bitterest feeling, so as to be on hand should Scott fail in his mission. The General did not fail, but it seemed expedient to concentrate more regulars on the Maine border, and by 1840 eight companies of the 1st Artillery, including Joseph Hooker, were available to help keep the eager State-of-Mainers under control.[24]

On July 1, 1841, four years after graduation, at the age of twenty-six Lieutenant Hooker returned to West Point for a three-month interlude as adjutant of the Military Academy. The fact that he was chosen for this responsible position would indicate that his record had been satisfactory, for there were many other graduates of higher class-standing available. The advancement was one of position only, not of rank, but was undoubtedly welcome, for it was in a field which was of interest to Hooker. He was ambitious to get ahead in his chosen profession, and the company duties of a lieutenant were not such as to afford him a chance for distinction in the near future. He realized that staff work at West Point would give him experience in military administration and perhaps lead to association with higher officers whose recommendations might be of value. His short stay at the Academy started him in the work he was to follow for the next ten years.

In October Hooker was called back to Maine as adjutant of his regiment. The 1st Artillery was concentrated in Military Department No. 6 under Brigadier General Eustis and, later, Colonel I. B. Crane.[25] For four years the Adjutant journeyed between headquarters at Portsmouth, New Hampshire, and posts at which the 1st Artillery was stationed throughout New England, preparing all orders, making all reports and returns, keeping all records and rosters, and carrying on the administrative correspondence for his regiment. A description of him at the time of an inspection trip to Fort Adams, at Newport, Rhode Island, has been recorded by an unusually good observer:

"It was about this time that Lieut. Joe Hooker came to the Fort, on a visit. What a handsome fellow he was! tall, straight, wavy light hair, blue eyes and a complexion a woman would envy, polished in manner, the perfection of grace in every movement, and with all, the courtesy of manner we attribute to the old time gentleman. He was somewhat effeminate in freshness of complexion and color perhaps, but his figure was robust, and of good muscular development. He was simply elegant, and certainly one of the handsomest men the Army ever produced. . . ."[26]

Any young blade would have found Newport interesting at this time, and Hooker made it a point to inspect there as often and for as prolonged periods as possible. The town stood upon its traditions of colonial grandeur. It was celebrated for old, influential families and its beautiful and charming maidens. In the summer, during the resort season, many of the "best" Southern families added to its gaiety and color.[27] It is surprising that Lieutenant Hooker's eligibility did not lead to a permanent alliance with one of the attractive, wealthy girls of the town, but no record remains that he came even close to losing his freedom to pursue a good time, a freedom he cherished and was to retain for many years to come. Any home-loving instincts he may have possessed were apparently satisfied during the frequent visits with his family. They had now forsaken Hadley for Watertown, New York, where the two eldest daughters and their husbands were prospering. The parents were living with the daughters, and Joseph usually made his headquarters at the home of his sister Mary, reputed to be the most beautiful girl ever to settle in Watertown.[28]

The New England sojourn came to an end when trouble arose in the Southwest. This brought about a gradual shifting of the army in that direction. The 1st Artillery was transferred to the Western Division, comprising the Mississippi Valley, the Indian Territory and the Gulf states, then commanded by General Edmund P. Gaines. The regiment was posted along the Gulf Coast and headquarters were set up in Pensacola in September of 1845.[29] Here Hooker served not only as adjutant of the 1st Artillery but in the more responsible capacity of assistant adjutant general of all troops in Pensacola Harbor and the 1st Military Department of the Western Division.[30] Within a year, however, the Lieutenant was petitioning for a leave of absence from his regiment. Stirring events along the Rio Grande gave promise of glory and a chance for quick advancement.

War with Mexico had been brewing ever since the normal westward movement of the American people had brought about a joint Congressional proposal for the annexation of Texas on March 1, 1845. This had been viewed by Mexico as an act tantamount to war. She still considered the vast area of Texas a part of the Republic and appeared ready for hostilities, doing little to resume normal relations with the United States. James K. Polk had just come to the Presidency on an expansionist platform which had demanded "Reoccupation of Oregon and reannexation of Texas." Neither, however, represented the new President's real ambition. California was the prize he sought. This territory could be acquired only through purchase or conquest from Mexico. There was little chance that the determined Polk would allow such difficulties to deter him. Frontier eagerness for more land and a little fighting helped to make a conflict fairly certain.

Mexico obliged by committing several overt acts. An attack on two companies of United States dragoons by a Mexican force in the disputed area between the Nueces River and the Rio Grande furnished Polk with the justification he desired for forcing the issue. A war message was sent by him to Congress, and on May 13, 1846, it was declared that by the act of the Republic of Mexico a state of war existed between that government and the United States.

War was welcomed by the Mississippi Valley, Texas and the Southern expansionists in the Democratic party, while the Whigs and most of the northern spokesmen were afraid of the ramifications concerning the extension-of-slavery question which might result from a successful war. The legislature of Massachusetts went so far as to call it a war of conquest —a war to strengthen the slave power. Joseph Hooker, although a faithful son of Massachusetts, did not concur with the official attitude of his native state and looked upon the war as a great personal opportunity.[31] While he awaited his leave of absence at Pensacola news arrived of the battles of Palo Alto and Resaca de la Palma near Brownsville which had been fought and won early in the month of May by Zachary Taylor's army on disputed soil. For two months longer Hooker impatiently cooled his heels at Pensacola before the good news came of his appointment to the staff of General Persifor F. Smith as brigade commissary.[32]

Smith was a slightly round-shouldered man with blue eyes, a sandy mustache and sandy hair. He was a Princeton graduate, a lawyer, a simple, scholarly, unassuming man[33] who was to prove himself one of the few capable generals of the war. He was far from ignorant of military service, having distinguished himself with a volunteer regiment in the Seminole war. Polk had first made him colonel of a new regiment called the Mounted Rifles and had then promoted him to the rank of brigadier.

By the time Hooker made his way to Smith's headquarters along the Rio Grande the army had been reinforced by hundreds of poorly disciplined volunteers and several politically appointed generals whose military experience had for the most part been limited to heading parades on the Fourth of July. One of these was Thomas Lyon Hamer, a prominent Democrat from Ohio. He had raised the 1st Ohio Volunteers and had been commissioned a brigadier general by President Polk. Despite his lack of military experience he was a man of strength and sound judgment.[34] To compensate for Hamer's shortcomings, Lieutenant Hooker was transferred to his headquarters to serve as chief of staff. This was an unfortunate change for Hooker, for Smith distinguished himself throughout the war while Hamer was destined to fight only one battle.

On August nineteenth Taylor began his invasion of Mexico and a month later his army of 6,000 men, half regulars and half volunteers, was before the town of Monterey where the Mexican forces under General Ampudia had decided to make a stand. In the operations which started on September 20, 1846, Hamer's brigade was stationed with Taylor's main force in front of the citadel of the town. The rest of the army under General W. J. Worth went off to attack the Mexicans' left flank and seize their line of communications along the Saltillo road. On the twenty-first Taylor advanced toward the town. Hooker directed Hamer's volunteers into battle. He was accompanied by the commanding general, as well as his immediate superior, which was a guarantee that his action in battle would not go unnoticed, but did not help the volunteers to overcome the murderous Mexican artillery fire. Hamer's men could not make progress nor were Taylor's other brigades much more successful. They did get within the town but by five in the afternoon had to withdraw. Along with them went a future President of the United States, Lieutenant Ulysses S. Grant, and the only President the Confederate States were to have, Colonel Jefferson Davis. The men fought with great gallantry but their generals had sent them blindly against a maze of fortifications and well-defended, narrow streets.[35]

The next day Taylor rested his men; there was little else he could do. The Mexicans should have attacked, but Worth had meanwhile won substantial success to their left and rear, which made their leader timid. When Ampudia abandoned his outer works on the twenty-third Taylor again advanced. Once more fierce street-to-street fighting profited the American army little except casualties, and Taylor again drew back. Worth, however, had turned the tide of battle, and his entrance into the

its barrage on the hill. At eight in the morning Hooker advanced with the Voltiguers, Worth's storming party and the 9th and 15th regiments. The outlying breastworks were captured and the parapet enclosing the crest of the hill reached. Here a halt had to be called since those detailed to bring the scaling ladders had failed to keep up. The men covered themselves in a ditch and behind rocks while the Mexicans, afraid even to expose a hand, fired high and did no damage. Hooker went back in search of the ladders and met most of Quitman's division and half of Worth's coming up.

At the bottom of the hill he found Gideon Pillow in great misery, wounded in the foot and temporarily disabled. As soon as he had hurried the ladders on their way he asked his general for permission to take a regiment to attack well over to their left. Pillow was more than willing for his brilliant adjutant to do anything to carry the hill and told him to use any regiment he could find. With the 6th Infantry of Worth's division Hooker made an attempt but found the ascent too difficult. He then returned to the troops in front of the wall just in time to see the Voltiguers go over the barricade.[61] Quitman's storming party of Marines and regulars under General P. F. Smith, who were attacking on the road east of Chapultepec near the city, soon did likewise and Quitman organized the pursuit toward the city. At the western outskirts he was stopped, but Scott meanwhile had sent all his remaining troops around to the northwestern gate. Under General Worth they fought from house to house and by 6:00 P.M. were in the city. That night Santa Anna withdrew from the capital and at 7:00 A.M. on September fourteenth the American flag flew from the palace. That day some of the natives engaged in sniping activities but by night the situation was in hand and United States Marines were patrolling the halls of the Montezumas.[62]

The war was now over for most of the United States forces, although minor military operations continued in Mexico for half a year. Hooker had won all the glory he could have wished. His actions at the storming of Chapultepec merited his third brevet of the war, that of lieutenant colonel. Scott mentioned him prominently in his report on the capture of Mexico,[63] and Pillow testified that he was distinguished throughout this action by his extraordinary activity, energy and gallantry.[64] He had also acquired a knowledge of the problems involved in the handling of 2,500 to 3,000 soldiers under battle conditions and an understanding of the personalities of those men who were to work with or against him in a greater struggle fifteen years later.

The months after the fall of Mexico City were pleasant ones for Joseph Hooker. His affable ways, good manners and commanding appearance made him a great favorite with the Spanish ladies of the capital. They called him "el capitan hermoso" or "el buen mozo" and found his company very entertaining.[65] He was popular also with his fellow officers and got into difficulty only when an argument arose between rabid Northern and Southern sympathizers. Then his habit of talking vigorously, tying up facts with invectives, made him an outstandingly successful exponent of the views of his section, particularly of his native state, which was continually castigated for her lukewarm support of the war.[66]

To keep alive the traditions of the Mexican War 160 officers of the United States Army, among them Joseph Hooker, organized the Aztec Club on October 13, 1847.[67] In line with this activity were trips to the recent battlefields. The campaign was fought and refought, an educational exercise of great value to the ambitious Lieutenant Colonel.

On December 13, 1847, Hooker once more transferred his staff affiliation. This time he went with Brigadier General Caleb Cushing of Massachusetts, who had recently arrived with fresh troops to reinforce the army of occupation. Cushing was one of the few Northern statesmen to support Polk. He had organized a regiment of volunteers with his own money and had been made a brigadier general for his trouble. He was a strict disciplinarian but lacked experience in military affairs.[68] Once again Hooker was of great value in covering up for one of Polk's political appointments.

Even before the capture of Mexico City two prominent generals, to promote their own selfish interests, had started a movement to destroy Scott's prestige. In this effort they were ably abetted by President Polk. They were Generals Pillow and Worth. Their reports on the battle of Contreras, San Antonio and Churubusco belittled and ridiculed Scott's direction. They went even further, sending private accounts, which appeared in the newspapers, unfavorable to the Commanding General. When Scott somewhat petulantly called them to account he was met with defiance and insubordination. Finally he made formal charges against them and they were put under technical arrest. Polk, without investigating, parried by removing Scott from the command, promoting Worth, and releasing both of the defendants from arrest.

A court of inquiry met in the middle of March 1848 to investigate the Scott vs. Pillow controversy. On March twenty-third and twenty-seventh and on April eleventh and thirteenth Hooker testified for General Pillow. Although his testimony was not critical of Scott, as some have stated, it was very important in substantiating Pillow's side of the major issues of the trial. It was at least important enough to earn for the promising young officer the enmity of the Commanding General, an unfortunate augury for the future.

The court dragged on in Mexico City until the end of April, then adjourned to meet in the States. Finally, on June twenty-third, it found that no further proceedings against Pillow were called for in the interest of the public service. The President heartily agreed with the court's decision.[69]

Hooker's letters home to his family in Watertown and a letter to Mr. Kellogg of Hadley, who was responsible for his West Point career, indicate that he thoroughly enjoyed his two years in Mexico. He wrote that his health had been excellent at all times—not even a headache bothered him. His only complaint was of the occasional shortage of rations, but he said that a mule's rib was as sweet a morsel as he had ever tasted.[70] Nevertheless, he was ready to go home. Sometime in the spring of 1848, after the ratification of a treaty of peace, he came back to the States. He returned with as proud a record as anyone: He had been brevetted three times for gallantry in action; had engaged in the two most important campaigns of the war; had been an important member of the staffs of six different generals. Also he returned with a firm belief in fate and destiny—that strong minds and brave hearts control their own fortunes. Untiring in energy and unacquainted with fatigue, he had been a good campaigner.[71] His self-confidence had received a justifiable boost and his reputation as a straight-out fighter had been established.

The summer was devoted to visits in Watertown and Hadley where he was royally feted. On September thirteenth he took over the duties of adjutant general of the 6th Military Department, commanded by General Twiggs. This department included Iowa, Illinois and parts of Wisconsin and Missouri. Two regiments of infantry and five companies of dragoons were posted at Jefferson Barracks in St. Louis and at the forts within the departmental area.[72] Hooker was not interested in this appointment and did not last there long enough to get acquainted. He had his eye on far more interesting and exciting country at that time—the newly acquired West Coast. In November 1848 came word of the assignment he coveted, that of adjutant general of the Pacific Division.

## CHAPTER II

## CIVIL INTERLUDE IN CALIFORNIA AND OREGON

SHORTLY after the holiday season Hooker left New York for the long trip to Sonoma, headquarters of the Pacific Division. Travel to California was popular that winter. Each month thousands of folk of all description were starting west, activated by a wild, unreasoning enthusiasm for the almost year-old discovery of gold in John A. Sutter's millrace. They scattered out over the cross-country trails; they shipped by way of Nicaragua and Panama, and they sailed around the Horn.

There is no evidence that Hooker had been bitten by the goldbug, but he was interested in this new western country and wanted to reach California as soon as possible. He therefore chose the quickest route, via the Isthmus of Panama. By the end of January he had landed at Aspinwall and had made the short trip to Panama City on the Pacific. Here on February 1, 1849, he boarded the Pacific Mail Steamship Company's *California* along with his superior, General Persifor F. Smith, other army officers and an eager, intemperate boatload of Forty-Niners.[1]

The trip was historic in that the *California* was making her first voyage, becoming the first American steam-driven boat to reach California. At San Diego Hooker left his companions in order to do detached duty with a Federal commission assigned to fix the borderline between California and Mexico.[2] In four months the work was accomplished and he set off on the S. S. *Panama* for his California post. The *Panama* was another of the Pacific Mail's steam side-wheelers and was also making her first voyage.

The Colonel reached San Francisco June 4, 1849,[3] and proceeded on to Sonoma which was located a few miles above the northern end of the bay. He moved into a house on the southwest corner of the plaza with General Smith, Major Philip Kearny and Captain George Stoneman.[4] His arrival relieved Lieutenant William T. Sherman who had held the post of adjutant general temporarily at Smith's request.[5] Sonoma was a town typical of old Mexican California, with a historic background. Here the California Bear Flag had first been raised on June 14, 1846, when a small group of settlers forced the surrender of the Mexican garrison. Included among the buildings around the plaza were the Franciscan

Mission, San Francisco de Solano; the Sonoma barracks built of adobe by the Mexican General, Mariano Guadalupe Vallejo; and the Blue Wing Tavern, one of the first inns established in northern California.[6]

In 1849 the old town had become the center of military affairs for the entire coast since it was from headquarters at this point that General Smith administered his Pacific Division. Within the division were Departments No. 10 (California) and No. 11 (Oregon). The California Department was commanded by General Bennett Riley with headquarters at Monterey. In the absence of organized civil government, General Riley was acting as governor of California. A regiment of infantry with complements of artillery and dragoons was scattered about the territory from the Sacramento Valley down to San Diego. The Oregon Department was directly under Smith's supervision and a regiment of mounted rifles and artillery was on hand to maintain order on behalf of the United States.[7]

As Colonel Hooker's duties might take him to any point in this military division, he was presented with the opportunity of studying the whole West Coast. This he was to do with an eye toward picking out a likely spot to settle upon should he decide to give up his career in the army and try to make his fortune in this new country. General Smith and his staff started immediately to investigate the enormous territory which was their new military responsibility. First came a two-months tour of the gold mines to the northeast;[8] next a trip was made to the Oregon Department; and, finally, Hooker left with General Smith to complete the circuit heading south. They went to San Diego by boat and then took an 840-mile ride in a roundabout fashion visiting all points of interest in the southern part of California and picking out sites for future army posts.[9]

After completing inspection of the division, Colonel Hooker found himself facing a protracted stay at Sonoma. His duties soon proved too routine for his adventurous spirit, and army life fast lost its charm. The Indians in the immediate territory showed little inclination to go on the warpath and were primarily an administrative problem. Hooker was of the opinion that they were more in need of protection than the settlers. He recommended to General Bennett Riley, referring to a proposed expedition to Clear Lake seventy-odd miles north of Sonoma, that citizens should be forbidden to bring away Indian captives or prisoners, pointing out that if this were permitted the expedition would develop into little more than a servant-gathering foray.[10]

The discrepancy between set pay of the officers and soldiers of the army and the inflated scale of civilian wages in California was a major cause of dissatisfaction at the post. Whereas a common soldier might, with extra-duty pay, make $14 per month, a laborer expected $16 per day. Hooker's salary fell far short of the wage received by any capable domestic servant.[11] Discontent and frequent resignations from army service were inevitable.

Idleness led Hooker along the usual path to the devil's workshop. In this case the devil was holding forth at the Blue Wing Tavern where poker and whisky were available to all comers. Guests ranged from the bandits Joaquin Murieta and "Three-Fingered Jack" to ex-Governor Pico and almost all army men stationed in the vicinity.[12] An authority states that Hooker was a total abstainer from drink at the time he left West Point,[13] but apparently this aloofness had been overcome. The handsome Colonel became a regular at the Blue Wing.

Although now thirty-six years of age he had not acquired a wife during his most eligible days and was not hindered by family responsibilities. He was to enter upon a period of bad habits and excesses—known to pioneers in California as "going to the dogs"—which would impair his health and his business character.[14] This reputation was to plague him in all the years to come. Peacetime army life had become too restraining for him and he applied for a two-year leave of absence, which was granted on November 24, 1851. Envisioning himself as the master of a profitable rancho, the Colonel had acquired title to 550 fertile acres near what is now Agua Caliente, a few miles north and west of Sonoma.[15] The rancho had been part of the large holdings of General Vallejo and was in that country between the Sonoma and Napa mountain ranges known as the "Valley of the Moon."[16] Tradition had it that, because the mountain ranges held back the mists rolling in from the ocean, the light of the moon was never obscured in this valley. More important, however, was the fact that the land was fertile.

Hooker's first moves were to build a home and to put some of his land under cultivation. A modest house of four rooms was erected from finished lumber brought around the Horn, and ten acres of the broad, level land were planted in grapes. From time to time more acres were turned into vineyards, but either the soil was unsuitable or the neophyte farmer was too unskilled in the cultivation of his crop, for the wine proved unpalatable. Potatoes were no more successful, being inferior to those grown on the coast.[17]

Hooker then turned to the natural resources of his land. Through his army friends he secured a contract to supply cordwood from his extensive stand of timber for the Benicia Arsenal and the Presidio at San Francisco. Men were hired to do the cutting, leaving the Colonel free to amuse himself at the Blue Wing, to stage elaborate fiestas at his rancho and to hunt in the wilder northern parts of the valley.[18] On one of these hunting trips he came close to a premature end. A sudden encounter with a bear brought forth an ineffective shot from his rifle and a more skillful charge from the bear. Man and beast rolled down the side of a canyon and Hooker, badly mauled, wound up in the limbs of a redwood tree from which he was extricated by a searching party.[19]

He also found entertainment at weekly meetings of the young army officers at the near-by rancho called "the Rendezvous." Here Pedro Curillo, a wrinkled Spanish miser, generously threw open his ranch house to any guests who were willing to pay handsomely for amusement. The native wines in the cellar were old and tasty, and the card games were hotly contested.[20]

An unfortunate evening with the cards on January 3, 1853, led Hooker into his first legal entanglement. On that date he signed a note which read: "I acknowledge my indebtedness to Mr. Nevill to be $485, which I promise to satisfy at my earliest convenience, say three months from date."[21] Mr. Nevill almost immediately signed the note over to a Mr. Thomas Nugent of Sonoma County who had little concern for Hooker's "earliest convenience." He wanted prompt payment and made repeated requests for it. Hooker just as repeatedly refused, and Nugent asked the District Court to grant him a judgment. The County Clerk complied with a summons and in due time the Sheriff served it on Hooker. He pleaded that he was not on January third or at any other time indebted to Mr. Nevill for $485, as the note was tendered without any consideration; that it was given for money lost in a game of cards and he was therefore not bound to pay. It was common knowledge at that time that a gambling note was not collectible in the courts, and it would appear that Nugent was trying to force Hooker into a settlement which would enable the Colonel to avoid unfavorable publicity.

Hooker either was not in a position to make a settlement or cared nothing about publicity, for in November the suit was still open and came before Judge E. W. McKinstry for a hearing. Hooker retained William Ross as counsel and waived a trial by jury. The case was settled abruptly. Attorney Ross put Nugent on the stand and forced him to admit that he had known the note was for a "debt of honor." The judge immediately dismissed the case on the ground that the note was made out for an illegal consideration. Nugent was assessed court costs of $88.25, and the innocent Nevill was fined for contempt when he flared up at Hooker's refusal to meet the note. The Colonel suffered only the probable loss of future gambling credit.[22]

Meanwhile, the cordwood business had been taking care of his more modest expenditures. The price exacted per cord was $15, and the cost of cutting and hauling was roughly $6, leaving a profit of $9, plus the asset of many cleared acres. This enterprise was not without its complications, however, for in 1854 Peter H. Albertson sued him for $1,200 and attached fourteen yoke of oxen while awaiting settlement. Albertson was aggrieved because he had been promised $3,000 for transporting Hooker's wood down the bay but had been able to collect only $1,800. Hooker's defense was that some of the wood had not been hauled, that the scow had been so badly handled she leaked, her stays and masts were loose and her two yawl boats lost. The court compromised, ordering him to pay $802. Then a woodcutter, one James Hallock, started suit for $295 for back wages; evidently Hooker paid up, for the suit was soon dismissed.[23]

As his leave of absence ran out he resigned from the army on February 21, 1853. This proved to be an error, in light of the coming war, but was one committed at this time by many officers who were later to become top-ranking Union generals. At the same time he took steps to confirm his title to the rancho. He filed before the Federal Land Commission and received acknowledgment of his ownership of the property, less any liens legally accrued against it.[24]

Hooker's next venture was in public office. He ran for Sonoma County Road Overseer and was elected. This whetted his appetite for local politics and in the summer of 1853 he ran on the Democratic ticket for State Assemblyman. His running mate was Lindsay Carson, brother of Kit Carson, and the opposition, or Settlers Ticket, put up James Bennett and Judge Robert Hopkins, respected and well-known residents. The strong Settlers slate was fought to a standstill by the popular Colonel, and the vote resulted in a tie.

A runoff was scheduled for October twenty-ninth, and the candidates went back to their constituency with a new appeal for support. In order to drum up more votes in the western end of the county, Bennett raised the issue of moving the courthouse from Sonoma, on the eastern edge of the county, to Santa Rosa, more centrally located. This maneuver gained the support of the communities of Petaluma and Sebastopol, and Hooker and Carson were licked by thirteen votes. The defeated candidates immediately raised the old American political hue and cry, "We were robbed," and claimed that voters had been imported by the Settlers ticket.

When in time Bennett had seen to it that a bill was passed in the California legislature for removal of the courthouse to Santa Rosa, Hooker's adherents said it would never be moved, law or no law! The change was arranged, however, when the Santa Rosa boys got to "Peg Leg" Menefee, the County Clerk, and at three o'clock one morning the county records were spirited off by mule wagon.[25]

Once legal title had been acquired to the rancho, Hooker began to consider selling out. The responsibility of making the land pay grew tiresome to his restless disposition,[26] and an option to purchase the property was given to a neighboring settler. Subsequently, George E. Watriss of San Francisco, who liked the springs, wild game and trees on the rancho, expressed a desire to buy the property as soon as the existing option expired. On its expiration Hooker went to San Francisco and sold out to Watriss who took over also three liens, at two percent monthly interest, attached to the property.[27]

As we have seen, several of his business dealings resulted in legal difficulties, and there quite probably were other defaults not aired in the courts. There is a story to the effect that he borrowed money from Henry W. Halleck and William T. Sherman, at this time prominent in San Francisco business life. He supposedly went to their respective offices one Saturday to make payment on the loans but found them closed and by Monday morning his money was gone.[28] The story may be true; unquestionably both Halleck and Sherman evinced a dislike of Hooker during the war. In General Sherman's *Memoirs* there is but one mention of Hooker in California, despite the fact that they served together for several months on General Smith's staff. In 1864 General Halleck was to write to Sherman:

"He [Hooker] is aware that I know some things about his character and conduct in California, and, fearing that I may use that information against him, he seeks to ward off its effect by making it appear that I am his personal enemy, am jealous of him, etc."[29]

Failure as a farmer did not cause Hooker to leave Sonoma; indeed, by arrangement with Watriss he continued to occupy his little cottage while the new owner built for himself a substantial stone house on the property.[30] Hooker again became interested in politics in 1857 and helped promote the candidacy of John B. Weller for governor. Weller was his friend and fellow worker on the California-Mexico boundary line. The campaign was successful, and in January 1858 he went over to Sacramento to attend Weller's inaugural ball.[31]

In the spring of 1858 he received a worth-while political plum. He was appointed Superintendent of Military Roads in Oregon. The exact means by which he came into this good fortune is not clear. It was quite possibly connected with the upheaval which occurred in Democratic politics on the coast in 1857. David C. Broderick was elected senator from California and took over much patronage and power from the senior senator William M. Gwin.[32] Joseph Hooker was to be associated with the Broderick faction in the next election and may have been on the bandwagon at this date.

At any rate, this was a line of work where his ability to command men could be utilized and it presented an opportunity to re-establish his personal reputation and fortune. Congress had recently appropriated $60,000 for the completion of a military road from Scottsburg, Oregon, to the California state line.[33] By the early summer of 1858 a large force of men and teams was strung along the road from Roseburg on toward the south with the Colonel in charge.[34] By winter the road was finished and for some time was known as the "Hooker Road." The *Oregon Statesman* gave "Much praise . . . to the Superintendent of the work, Col. Hooker, for the energy and faithfulness which he has devoted to it, and for the excellent manner in which the work has been performed."[35]

In the early part of 1859 he was back in California where he was made a colonel in the State Militia[36]—another stride in the right direction. Thus in the late '50's he was emerging from the low estate to which he had fallen and for which his residence in California has been chiefly remembered. News of the death of his devoted mother in early 1857 may have caused him to take stock of himself. A military road was being projected from Astoria to Salem, Oregon, and in the latter part of the year he was back on the job,[37] not only investigating this project but examining possible lines for a road along the eastern shore of Puget Sound in Washington Territory.[38]

In addition to road-construction activities, Hooker had become intensely interested in Oregon state Democratic politics. In 1858 the Democratic party in Oregon had begun to split: on the one side were the

National Democrats led by General Joe Lane, who supported the Buchanan administration and were proslavery, on the other the Oregon Democrats, or "Salem clique," who were interested in sidetracking Lane, getting control of the Federal patronage and pushing Stephen A. Douglas of Illinois as the national leader of the party. This latter group was headed by Asahel Bush, editor of the *Oregon Statesman*, LaFayette Grover, candidate for Congress, and Colonel J. W. Nesmith, the Superintendent of Indian Affairs in Oregon. Nesmith was a man of keen and ready wit, of great plainness of speech, and was a warm friend or a bitter enemy.[39] Hooker happened to be on the best of terms with him and strung along with his faction, exerting influence in its behalf.

Oregon was in the process of electing delegates to the National Democratic Convention of 1860. The delegates were to be chosen at a meeting held at Eugene on November 16, 1859, but Hooker's trip to Puget Sound kept him from attending. The meeting was a failure as far as the Douglas faction was concerned; in fact, as Hooker said, ". . . it made a damned ass of itself."[40] He expressed this opinion when the delegates were finally instructed to nominate General Lane for the Presidency—only after the Douglas men, led by LaFayette Grover, had withdrawn. The action of the Grover group did not please Hooker either, for it committed them to the nominee of the National Democratic Convention in April regardless of whom he turned out to be. Hooker said that Grover needed a guardian and that the "atrocities" of the Buchanan administration had not been sufficiently aired. The Colonel was no mean· surveyor of the national political field.

"The Administration and the thousand and one aspirants for the nomination are moving heaven and earth to defeat Douglas. If they should succeed they defeat the ablest man in the party and what is more, *they defeat themselves*. The Republicans know it and they have joined in the hue and cry against Douglas. Whether he sinks or swims his bitterest enemies must admit that he is of the stuff of which heroes are made. The office he is seeking can add no luster to his fame."[41]

The intraparty strife in Oregon continued throughout 1860 as Lane was nominated for Vice-President on the Breckinridge Democratic ticket and Douglas was placed by the Salem clique in the local race for presidential electors. For the approaching state senatorial election in October Colonel Nesmith, who had been in Oregon since 1843, was chosen leader of the state Douglas Democratic ticket. There is some testimony that Joseph Hooker was suggested as a possibility for the other senatorial vacancy.[42] This would no doubt have been very welcome to him but almost certainly would have ended in failure, for by October it was clear that an alliance would have to be made with some other political group to assure even Nesmith's election. Edward Dickinson Baker, a Californian by adoption, had moved to Oregon in February 1860 to head the Republican ticket at the request of party members there. Nesmith and Baker joined forces and succeeded in defeating the Lane entries for the two places in the Senate.[43]

The victory of Nesmith assured Hooker a political appointment on the coast. The plum agreed upon was the chairmanship of the Boundary Commission about to be selected for marking the state line of California and Utah, although his first choice was the position of Superintendent of Indian Affairs for Oregon. If Baker took advantage of his friendship with the President-elect, Abraham Lincoln of Illinois, Hooker believed that this more lucrative position could be secured for him.[44]

Meanwhile he returned to California to await his expected appointment and to continue his militia activities, but he did not return to the same state he had left three months before. As the misguided representatives of each section steered the nation into civil war, California too, remote as she was from the capital, seethed with dissension between the unionist and secessionist elements. Lincoln's victory in the state and the nation had fanned the local fires of disunion. Agitation was reawakened for a Pacific Republic. It became a real possibility, but the unionist element in the California legislature triumphed and Leland Stanford, a stanch Republican, was elected governor.[45]

As the Cotton States withdrew from the rest of the nation, Hooker, with a background of at least four generations of New England ancestors and a political tie-up with the Douglas Democrats, found no difficulty in determining where his sympathies lay. In early 1861, a man of action bent on putting his recognized abilities to full use, he gathered a regiment of Union volunteers under his wing and drilled them in the evolutions of the day, until he learned that California regiments would not be accepted for enlistment in the East. Service in the Pacific or Mountain Departments had no attraction for the Colonel; he realized that military reputations could be made only in those areas where the fight would be to a finish.

An offer of his personal services to the Commander of the United

States Army, General Winfield Scott, brought no response. This was extremely discouraging; Hooker ardently believed it his duty to make use at this time of the education his country had given him and of the experience he had gained in the Mexican campaigns. It was an opportunity that any military man, particularly a fighter, would welcome, and to Hooker it offered also a chance for a fresh start in life.

Out of funds, as was his custom, he was unable to manage a trip to Washington where he could seek an appointment with good chance of success. Disheartened by his fate, he drifted one day into Chapman's, the great rendezvous in San Francisco for food, drink and flow of soul. Seated at the table in the corner which Billy Chapman reserved for his friends, he was approached by the proprietor, who noted his downcast appearance.

"What's the matter, Captain?" asked Billy.

"I was wishing," replied Hooker, "that I was in the East. I'm a West Pointer, as you know, a trained soldier. I could be of use in this struggle, but here I am tied down to a ranch in California, merely because I lack funds to clear off some little debts and pay my expenses to Washington."

"How much would you need?" inquired Billy.

After a moment's reflection Hooker said he thought $700 would be enough. Chapman went to his safe and returned with a big roll of bills.

"Here's a thousand, Captain. Take it and go to the front. I wish I could go with you—but I am not quite willing to be a private, and they wouldn't give a commission to a faro dealer. The steamer sails day after tomorrow. I'll be at the wharf to see you off, and you needn't buy any liquor or cigars to keep you cheerful on the way. There will be a few necessaries of that sort in your stateroom."[46]

Hooker accepted the $1,000, whether as gift or loan no record remains. Time was short to make the next boat, and the Colonel busied himself settling his affairs and preparing for his first journey east in twelve years. In the midst of his preparation he received the following gratifying note:

"SAN FRANCISCO
"May 18, 1861

"Col. J. Hooker—Sir: We, the undersigned officers of the California State Militia, having heard with regret of your intended departure for the Eastern States cannot allow you to leave our shores without expressing appreciation of your worth as a gentleman and a soldier and of your successful efforts to increase the efficiency of the militia of our State. We therefore beg that you will meet us at a dinner, to be given at the American Exchange, on Monday evening next."[47]

Surprisingly enough, the first name on the long list of signers was that of Henry W. Halleck, Brigadier General in the State Militia.

Hooker needed all available time to prepare for his departure and was forced to refuse the invitation in a note on May twentieth in which he said:

"I go, gentlemen, to tender my services to the Federal government with a will and a purpose; to seek an opportunity to prove my faith in, and devotion to the Union of all the States, and to find a place, however humble, among those who have taken up arms to defend it."[48]

The San Francisco *Evening Bulletin* on May 21, 1861, records that Hooker left that day on the steamer *St. Louis* for Panama, adding: "He was invited . . . to eat a complimentary dinner last evening, but with many thanks the Colonel wisely declined."[49] Why it was a "wise" move the writer does not dwell upon; quite likely he felt that the celebration would have made Hooker miss the boat!

# THE FIRST COMMAND

THE LONG trip to the East Coast was completed without incident and Hooker hurried to make his bid for a commission. His first action was to get in touch with his friends and acquaintances in Congress, realizing that they could do much for him in this heyday of political military appointments. First he sent a letter to Senator Nesmith asking him to do what he could "in any quarter."[1] Next he held a conference with Senator Baker in New York which resulted in this letter to the President:

> "FT. SCHUYLER
> "June 16th
>
> "SIR
> "Colonel Joseph Hooker has just arrived from the Pacific Coast and will wait on you in person.
> "He desires to draw his sword for the country. He is an educated soldier. The history of the Mexican War is filled with battles in which he bore distinguished and honorable part. No regular officer of his rank won more renown, and no man of any rank showed more gallantry. His testimonials are of the very highest order. I have known him well and add mine. You cannot rely too much on his capacity as a soldier and his loyalty as a man.
>
> > "truly yours
> > "E. D. BAKER"[2]

This testimonial should have been effective, for Baker was an old and trusted friend of Abraham Lincoln since early Springfield days.

After a few days in New York Hooker went on to Washington where his credentials were delivered to the White House. He next looked up the congressional delegation from his native state of Massachusetts. In a conversation with Senator Charles Sumner of this group he showed great enthusiasm, stating that if he were given the colonelcy of a regiment he would come to the command of the army and take Richmond.[3]

This self-confidence was nurtured by the tremendous military confusion about the capital and the presence of politically officered regiments everywhere. Old comrades, once outranked by Hooker, were being commissioned daily. Across the river was the fast-growing Federal Army commanded by Irvin McDowell, who was behind him in the Adjutant General's Department at the time of his resignation; there was William Tecumseh Sherman, a subordinate staff officer at Sonoma, now in command of a brigade; also Ambrose E. Burnside, William B. Franklin and Israel B. Richardson, all of lower rank in the Mexican War, now colonels commanding brigades.

It was to be expected that Hooker, sure of his ability, would soon convince himself it would be foolish not to hold out for a command more imposing than that of a regiment. Thus, when he was asked by Governor Andrew of Massachusetts to accept the colonelcy of an "Old Bay State" regiment stationed in Washington, he declined on the ground that his position and experience entitled him to a higher grade.[4]

Meanwhile, no response of any kind had been received from the White House or the War Department. His credentials had come to the attention of the President, who was deluged with similar requests bearing political indorsements, and the papers had been sent on in routine fashion to General Joseph Mansfield, Commander of the Department of Washington, with the following letter:

"MY DEAR SIR:

"The inclosed papers of Colonel Joseph Hooker speak for themselves. He desires to have the command of a regiment. Ought he to have it, and can it be done, and how?

"Please consult General Scott, and say if he and you would like Colonel Hooker to have a command.

"Yours very truly
"A. LINCOLN"[5]

This was the end of the line, however, for Hooker's credentials. They had run into safe storage—General Winfield Scott, Commander of the Federal armies. The General had not forgotten Hooker's damaging testimony back in March and April of 1848, and the credentials were neatly pigeonholed.

When in mid-July the "On-to-Richmond" enthusiasts had pushed General McDowell into making a move against the Confederate Army at Manassas Junction, Virginia, Hooker rode out of Washington along with several thousand assorted spectators to see the show. Critical by nature, embittered by the War Department's silence, he was quite possibly one of the very few who questioned the ultimate success of the Federal advance. There is no record of the vantage point from which he watched the Union debacle of First Bull Run on July twenty-first, but it can be assumed that his trained eye and alert mind grasped the tactical dispositions within range.

A few days later, by now thoroughly discouraged in his quest for an appointment and contemptuous of the generalship displayed at Bull Run,[6] he went with George Cadwallader, upon whose staff he had served in Mexico, to the White House. He was presented to Abraham Lincoln as "Captain" Hooker. The President acknowledged the introduction and as his tall form began to turn away, Hooker spoke out.

"Mr. President, I was introduced to you as Captain Hooker. I am, or was, Lieutenant Colonel Hooker of the Regular Army. When this war broke out I was at home in California, and hastened to make a tender of my services to the Government; but my relation to General Scott, or some other impediment, stands in the way, and I now see no chance of making my military knowledge and experience useful. I am about to return, but before going I was anxious to pay my respects to you, Sir, and to express my wish for your personal welfare, and for your success in putting down the rebellion. And while I am about it, Mr. President, I want to say one thing more, and that is, that I was at the battle of Bull Run the other day, and it is neither vanity or boasting in me to declare that I am a damned sight better General than you, Sir, had on that field."[7]

This forthright statement of self-confidence brought a quick, searching glance from the President to gauge what manner of man confronted him. Impressed, Lincoln seized Hooker's hand and asked him to sit down. One story led to another and finally the President rose, placed his hand on Hooker's shoulder and said:

"Colonel—not Lieutenant Colonel—Hooker, stay. I have use for you and a regiment for you to command."[8]

Lincoln was to comment later of this meeting:

". . . his eye was steady and clear—his manner not half so confident as his words, and altogether he had the air of a man of sense and intelligence, who thoroughly believed in himself and who would at least try to make his words good."[9]

Meanwhile, Hooker's political friends had been busy, and upon investigation the President learned that he was being pushed for an assignment more imposing than that of regiment commander. On July 31, 1861, the names of eleven men were sent to the Senate as nominees for the commission of brigadier general in the United States Volunteers. Fifth on the list was Joseph Hooker of California, recommended by the Massachusetts delegation in Congress. Noteworthy among these nominations were the names of U. S. Grant of Illinois; Colonels Samuel Heintzelman and W. B. Franklin, veterans of the Bull Run affair; E. D. Baker, Senator from Oregon; and J. A. McClernand, Representative from Illinois.[10] On August third Hooker's nomination was confirmed; the commission was signed August sixth but was predated to May 17, 1861.[11] At last the Government was beginning to catch up with his estimate of his own ability!

A total of thirty-four volunteer brigadier generals were appointed during the summer of '61 and all thirty-four of the commissions were dated May seventeenth. This created a nice problem of relative rank! The *Official Army Register for September, 1861*, published by order of the Secretary of War, gave Hooker fifteenth position out of the thirty-four (two places ahead of Grant). The net result was that he became the thirty-second ranking general in the army. Ahead of him were four regular major generals (Scott, McClellan, Frémont and Halleck), four volunteer major generals, nine regular brigadiers, and fourteen volunteer brigadiers commissioned with him.[12]

The new Brigadier was straightway scheduled for one of the twelve brigades then forming in the vicinity of Washington.[13] General George B. McClellan, who had only recently been called in to save the capital, was now at the head of the Military Division of the Potomac. He was at this time only thirty-five years old (twelve years Hooker's junior). He had been graduated at the head of his class at West Point, 1846, and was twice brevetted for gallantry in Mexico. Retirement to civil life was followed by notable success as vice-president of the Illinois Central Railroad and later as president of the Eastern Division of the Ohio and Mississippi Railroad. Nine days after the fall of Fort Sumter he had been commissioned a major general of Volunteers. His dashing success against a small band of Confederates in western Virginia, along with his handsome appearance, unquestioned engineering ability and gift of leadership, offset his relative youth and pointed to him as the man of the hour. He was immediately called the "Young Napoleon of the West"—a doubtful advantage. His job was a difficult one. Official Washington, the local

## WHITE OAK SWAMP

This tangled morass lay in the path of McClellan's forces in the great "change-of-base" movement in June 1862.

GENERAL
GEORGE B. McCLELLAN

GENERAL A. E. BURNSIDE

EDWIN M. STANTON,
SECRETARY OF WAR

GENERAL
HENRY WAGER HALLECK

citizens, the disorganized army and even McClellan himself were panic-stricken over the possibility of an invasion by the enemy. After the rueful experience of Bull Run many felt certain that the Confederate chieftains, Joe Johnston and Beauregard, were about to descend upon the capital and drive all before them.

McClellan was exerting superhuman efforts to organize the deranged Union forces and to fortify the approaches to Washington. He was also contributing considerably to the general alarm by indulging his fatal weakness of overestimating the strength of the enemy. On August sixteenth he wrote that he was outnumbered three or four to one.[14] The facts, however, were that the Confederate forces at Bull Run had numbered 35,000, and during the month of August only ten regiments—or around 6,000 men—were added.[15] McClellan later admitted that he had had 37,000 effectives on August first and 59,000 by the end of the month.[16] Almost all estimates of the Federal forces in Washington give a higher figure. In justice to McClellan it should be mentioned that many of his so-called "effectives" were raw recruits, newly formed into brigades, or demoralized "veterans" of one battle. The Confederates, on the other hand, had retained their organization after the battle. They had come north fully expecting to sweep the foe from the field, and they had done it. They little realized upon how slim a margin the fate of battle had turned.

McClellan had placed eight of his brigades on the Virginia side of the Potomac, covering all approaches to Washington in the event of a direct attack. Another brigade was placed so as to guard the Potomac crossings for a distance of forty miles northwest of the city. The other three brigades were to be held in reserve behind Washington in good supporting distance of the advanced forces and ready to march to the aid of the regiments on the upper Potomac.[17]

The brigade assigned to Hooker was one of those in reserve and was composed of four volunteer regiments:

1. *The 1st Massachusetts* had been engaged at Blackburn's Ford in the preliminaries to Bull Run and had performed creditably though not under heavy fire. During the battle it had been stationed on the left and had not seen action. It was one of several regiments which added to the general confusion by wearing gray uniforms.[18]

2. *The 11th Massachusetts* recruited in Boston had behaved miserably at Bull Run. The officers could not prevail upon the men to

fight and, although they were in a position to distinguish themselves, they had failed. Casualties were light.[19]

3. *The 2nd New Hampshire* had fought hard in the early stages of the battle and had hung on as well as most when the tide began to turn. Their Colonel had been wounded but General Ambrose E. Burnside, their brigade commander, stayed with them and kept them steady.[20]

4. *The 28th Pennsylvania* had missed the fight.

When Hooker arrived at the brigade rendezvous at Bladensburg, a suburb northeast of Washington and outside the District of Columbia, none of his regiments had assembled. He did not even possess a uniform! On the morning of August ninth the 2nd New Hampshire came in and was directed to its camp on a pleasant knoll west of the town.[21] The other three regiments were all on hand within a few days and settled down to an active camp life under the observant eye of the new Brigadier.

Bladensburg, in addition to being famous for its springs, was a spot of considerable historical interest. On August 24, 1814, a battle had been fought there between 3,000 English regulars and 7,500 American volunteers. The volunteers had run shamefully and opened the way for the British to sack the public buildings of Washington. Bladensburg had also been a favorite locale for dueling after Congress had made this sport a penal offense in the District of Columbia. Among famous encounters, there was that on March 22, 1820, in which Commodore Decatur was killed by Captain Barron.[22]

Camp life suited Hooker. He was burdened with no family responsibilities and worries. He had known no real home life since leaving Hadley twenty-eight years before; during this period his parents had passed away and his sisters had married and were raising families of their own. He was free to pursue his military career wholeheartedly. It is safe to say that he was as happy now as at any time of his life: he was facing a fresh start, the prospect of a good fight and an opportunity for glory!

Hooker wisely enforced strict discipline upon his apprentice soldiery. Officers as well as men were drilled in marching, the manual of arms, the use of the bayonet[23] and target shooting. Drilling was held both before and after breakfast, topped off with a dress parade in the late afternoon. The soldiers were forbidden to leave camp without the signed permission of a colonel; the use of a countersign was rigidly enforced and the roads were well guarded. In addition to the general routine the men worked on the fortifications near Bladensburg which were designed to protect Washington from approach down the main road from Baltimore or from along the Baltimore and Ohio Railway track.[24]

Whereas he believed in requiring rigid observance of every proper regulation, Hooker made himself accessible to officers and men who had complaints to air or favors to ask. He also took care that his brigade received its rightful share of rations, clothing and other supplies. He early struck upon the right balance of discipline and paternalism which marks those generals who gain the good will of their men.

McClellan has seldom been given due credit for his contribution toward winning the war, but even his detractors laud him for his organization of the Army of the Potomac. In this work Hooker was a worthy lieutenant. On August twenty-seventh his well-organized brigade was rewarded with an opportunity to demonstrate its discipline and drill before McClellan and his staff. Two days later President Lincoln, Secretary of State Seward and Secretary of the Navy Welles came out to review it at what had become known as Camp Union.[25]

Twice during the encampment here the "long roll" was beaten and the brigade fell to arms on rumor that the Confederates were at last advancing. Each time the rumor proved false and could be traced in part to the uneasiness of McClellan, the skittishness of the advanced pickets and scouts in Virginia and the impossibility of obtaining reliable information from the predominately secessionist area along the Potomac.

In September the brigade was strengthened by the addition of the 1st Michigan Volunteers which had seen some service at Bull Run. Hooker assigned to it the duty of guarding the Washington branch of the Baltimore and Ohio Railway from Annapolis Junction to Bladensburg.[26] About this time the 2nd New Hampshire received a batch of recruits from back home and the regiment's old smoothbores were exchanged for Springfield rifled muskets.[27] The 1st Massachusetts had even better luck—it was detached for active duty. The enemy had been busy in lower Maryland recruiting men and smuggling supplies across the Potomac;[28] Hooker was instructed to send a regiment to investigate and he chose the 1st Massachusetts. After three weeks of scouting Colonel Robert Cowdin reported back to Hooker that the secessionist sympathy of that part of Maryland had not been exaggerated nor had the treasonable activities taking place there been overestimated.[29]

McClellan had adopted the plan of forming his brigades into divisions just as soon as they were organized, disciplined and instructed. On

October eleventh Hooker was promoted to the leadership of a division, receiving authority over General Daniel Sickles' "Excelsior" brigade (the 70th, 71st, 72nd, 73rd and 74th New York).[30] In addition to the two brigades of infantry, the division was to be composed of eight companies of the 3rd Indiana Cavalry and a battery of the 1st United States Artillery. This meant that approximately 10,000 men were to be under Hooker's command,[31] or nearly one-third more men than Scott had marched into the city of Mexico.

Thus by the autumn of '61 Hooker's fortunes had progressed even more than the ambitious General could have dared hope. He had come to Washington seeking one regiment and had already acquired ten!

## CHAPTER IV

# IN LOWER MARYLAND

THE ELEMENT of luck, which plays so large a part in man's destiny, was now working overtime in Hooker's favor. Whereas he had been appointed to a division command more recently than any other general in the Army of the Potomac, he was almost immediately sent off on a responsible mission. The Southerners had been active on the Virginia side of the lower Potomac, where they had erected batteries in an attempt to interfere with transit on the broad river highway to Washington. There was also the possibility that the enemy might try to seize the poorly defended Maryland shore south of the capital. To forestall this and to curb the smuggling, recruiting and other secessionist activities there, Hooker's division was ordered to proceed to Budd's Ferry, Maryland, opposite the main Confederate batteries at Evansport and Shipping Point, Virginia. He was to dispose his command so as to keep the river open and to protect the vessels on it and was to report by "special expressman" once a day upon anything of interest.[1]

This mission pleased him mightily for it gave him something of an independent command. Although he was instructed to report to McClellan daily, he would be almost forty-five miles from the Commanding General's headquarters. He had been in the "Old Army" long enough to know all about the desirability of getting out from under "rank" as much as possible; throughout the war he was to show marked agility in avoiding the shadow of higher-ranking officers. It would also give him an opportunity to demonstrate on a large scale the military administrative "know-how" gained in his ten years of adjutant's work.

McClellan's opinion of Hooker at this time is not recorded but three months earlier Lincoln had asked "Little Mac" what he thought of Hooker and had been told that although he had been a good officer in Mexico common report indicated he had "fallen" in California.[2] This was certainly true during the middle 1850's, but Hooker had pulled himself together in the last few years in the West and his actions since coming back east had shown he was still a good officer. The judicious administration of his brigade in camp was not, however, the reason he was chosen for the lower Maryland job, nor was it an indication of McClel-

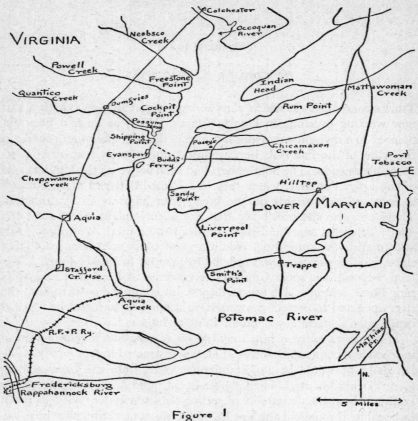

Figure 1
The Lower Potomac Region

lan's good will.  It is more likely that his force was chosen because it was closest to the area to be occupied.

By late October the main force of the Federal Army (seven divisions) was posted on the Virginia side of the Potomac opposite Washington. Two divisions were upriver at strategic points and one was in reserve.[3] The total force had grown to almost 100,000 men,[4] and now even McClellan felt secure from an attack on Washington.

One setback had been experienced, however, known as the disaster of Ball's Bluff.  On October twentieth 1,800 Federals under Hooker's late political associate, Edward D. Baker, Senator from Oregon, had been caught upriver on the Virginia side of the Potomac and slaughtered. Baker and approximately 1,000 soldiers were casualties.

Perhaps the most important result of the Ball's Bluff affair was the formation in December 1861 of a Joint Congressional Committee on the Conduct of the War. This committee was appointed to ascertain the causes for the disaster and to look into any future military movements which seemed to need investigation. The committee consisted of four leaders of the radical Republican bloc—Senator Ben Wade of Ohio, Chairman, Senator Zach Chandler of Michigan, Representative G. W. Julian of Indiana and Representative John Covode of Pennsylvania; two members who were War Democrats, Senator Andrew Johnson of Tennessee and Representative M. F. Odell of New York; and one who could be classed as a conservative Republican, Representative D. W. Gooch of Massachusetts. Johnson later resigned to become military governor of his native state, but the others hung on for the balance of the war.[5]

The committee early assumed the character of an antiadministration organ and became more radical as the war progressed.[6] It worked over the Army of the Potomac to a fare-you-well, and the customary penalty for military failure consisted of a hearing before the grim body. This, as we shall see, was an embarrassment spared Joseph Hooker who, within a year, was to become the Committee's favorite son.

His division, with the exception of the 1st Michigan which had been permanently detached, reached the lower Maryland region the last week in October. Headquarters were located six miles northeast of Budd's Ferry, and the troops were posted in all important locations in the western half of Charles County. The General aggressively took hold of the situation along the lower Potomac. A depot of supplies was established at Rum Point Landing on Mattawoman Creek. Here substantial warehouses and a good-sized wharf were built, and later a warehouse was added at Liverpool Point on the Potomac.[7] Telegraphic communication was established with McClellan's headquarters, and a complement of aeronautic equipment for observation was installed.

Hooker immediately conferred with the Commanding Officer of Naval Forces on the Potomac about the advisability of erecting earthworks on Indian Head, north of headquarters. He believed that from this point it would be possible to establish batteries which might prevent the enemy from further fortifying the Virginia shore, one and one-half miles away. The engineers' reports were favorable, and work was begun at once.[8] Another battery was planned for Budd's Ferry to protect that point and to be so situated as to intercept the Confederate steamer *Page* which had been annoying commerce on the river and which was now moored in the mouth of Quantico Creek.

On October twenty-eighth Hooker made out his first report of action. The occasion hardly merited a report, but the General wrote it up in lengthy fashion. He was to continue to report in this manner almost every day while on his detached command. At about three in the afternoon a steamer going to Washington was fired upon by a hitherto undisclosed battery. The boat, however, continued on her way without mishap. Hooker detailed the slight affair and lamented that he had been unable to scout the other side of the river personally; that for this reason he had little idea of the force opposed to him; yet he "was satisfied that the enemy expected an assault more than they intended to give one."[9]

Concurrent with his move to lower Maryland came the retirement of the seventy-five-year-old Lieutenant General Winfield Scott and the succession of Major General George B. McClellan to the command of the Army of the United States.[10] This gave McClellan direction of all the armies in the field and had the effect of sidetracking his attention from the possibility of active operations along the Potomac.[11]

Hooker did not have any such diversion and was aching for an opportunity to distinguish himself. In a letter to McClellan in early November he tried to promote such an opportunity, saying that it would be impossible to silence the enemy's batteries, which were being improved daily, from his side of the river. He wanted to make a surprise night attack with his entire division, embarking on the high ground north of Quantico Creek known as Possum Nose; by morning the position could be entrenched against 30,000 attackers, and the field artillery would force the enemy to abandon their guns. He suggested this move "with great confidence, for the reason that [he felt] no doubt of its absolute and complete success."[12]

McClellan replied that he would take the proposal into serious consideration, but he wisely requested full information as to the ground, the approaches, the character of the landing, and every material point relating to the matter.[13] From what we are learning today of the difficulties involved in forcing a beachhead and the exhaustive preparation necessary for such a maneuver, it was probably all to the good for Hooker's subsequent military career that his commander "cooled off" his suggestion.

A proposal of this kind might have come from any general as confident and aggressive as Hooker. Rash as it was, the plan should not be criticized too severely. The war was young; with the exception of McDowell at Bull Run, no Federal general had commanded 10,000 men in any kind of attack. The ability to direct successfully so large a force in the field could come only with experience. Fortunate, indeed, were the Union generals who gained the experience gradually; those who rose to the top in the early stages of the war were not around at the finish.

Although denied this chance to make a bold stroke, Hooker was at least reaping some personal benefit from his independent command. General Sickles was in Washington at the time and wrote him that public attention was concentrated on his attempts to open the Potomac. He added: "The President spoke warmly and enthusiastically of you. . . ."[14] Hooker did not share concern about the blocking of the river. He had developed great disdain for the Confederate batteries, believing them no real threat to navigation, and reporting that small boats were perfectly safe to pass. "They are as likely to be struck by lightning as by rebel shot."[15] His only regret was that the Confederate force on the opposite shore showed no sign of attacking.[16]

In event the enemy should decide to make a raid, the division was ordered to concentrate in a more advantageous defensive position. The brigades were placed along the Potomac just out of reach of the Confederate batteries—the 1st near Budd's Ferry and the 2nd at Sandy Point. One regiment was to guard the landing on Mattawoman Creek, and the cavalry was to police the interior. The flotilla was to protect the possible landing points above and below.[17] Headquarters were also moved nearer the Potomac to Budd's Ferry where the 1st Massachusetts was camped and Hooker had spent much of his time. The 1st had named its camp "Hooker," but the General preferred to call the new location "Camp Baker" in honor of his late friend.

His service of information had been a failure up to this point. On November eighth he had reported that all was quiet and that the enemy had apparently reduced forces. This was pretty much pure conjecture, for no means had been found of estimating accurately the number of troops on the opposite shore. The General had to admit that his attempts to elicit such information from the country people near by were unavailing; nor could he obtain reliable news from the agents he employed. So far intelligence of the enemy had been gained from a study of the campfires on the Virginia shore—not an altogether satisfactory index.[18]

The observation balloon assigned to the division, which should have been a help to him, had been handicapped by bad weather. It was operated by Professor T. S. C. Lowe, who introduced the service to the Federal Army. The General was slow to give his approval to this means of obtaining information. He had never seen a balloon in use and considered the service impractical. Still, he and his subordinates were interested enough to spend much time watching the *Constitution* go up on practice flights. As many as three men at one time could make the customary ascension of 1,000 feet. By the end of the month Hooker had lost patience and wrote that the history of the balloon was one of accidents and failures; but within a week he had become so enthusiastic that he took a trip himself. This reversal of attitude was probably due to the completion of an excellent aerial map showing the enemy's position;[19] in addition, it was determined that the enemy had been strengthened by new regiments and batteries about Cockpit Point.[20]

Whenever the weather permitted the men were drilled long and hard. Hooker continually preached discipline and attempted to win the confidence of his officers. In comparison with the rest of the army the division had a low rate of sickness, only four percent being laid up in the middle of winter. This was due in part to the discipline maintained by the General and to the excellent hospital set up at headquarters by Medical Director Charles Tripler.

In an effort to spare the teams the exhaustion of pulling heavy army wagons through long miles of mud, land communication with Washington was forbidden except via horseback. Future provisioning was to be by steamer exclusively, plus only the land haul necessary to reach camp from the landing. Brigade hospitals were established in a move to end transfer of the sick to Washington, which had been inconvenient and had led to prolonged absence on the part of both officers and men.[21]

The only operation of note accompanying these administrative changes was a reconnaissance into Virginia by Colonel Charles K. Graham with 400 men of the 74th New York. With the aid of a cutter from the Potomac Flotilla they crossed to Mathias Point. They met no resistance, found no guns mounted in the earthworks, burned a few houses, and returned.[22] The expedition was without Hooker's authority or knowledge and it did not please him that any one of his officers should take the initiative in making the first move of the division into Virginia. As no misfortune had resulted he decided not to censure Graham;

in the future, however, no operations were to be projected without his sanction.[23] General McClellan was not so forgiving; he ordered Colonel Graham put under arrest.[24]

The troops were not without entertainment. There were many visitors from back home—civic delegations bringing gifts, speeches and prayer sessions. At any time a bored soldier could wander down to the river and watch the Confederate batteries fruitlessly bang away at a passing schooner or oyster boat. Since the ship channel was nearer the Virginia side, large vessels could hardly risk the passage, but boats of light draft could keep well over toward the Maryland shore and pass in safety. Only one vessel was hit during the time Hooker's men were in lower Maryland. Thanksgiving was celebrated religiously, as might have been expected, and an entertainment for Hooker and his staff was put on by the 1st Massachusetts.[25]

His division was the smallest in the army at this time, but on November twenty-eighth a third brigade was added, the "Jersey Blues" (5th, 6th, 7th and 8th New Jersey Volunteers) under Colonel Samuel H. Starr, 4,000 strong. They had missed Bull Run, arriving in Washington in September. They came into camp along Chicamaxen Creek the first week in December.[26] Other organizational changes consisted of the addition of Smith's and Bunting's New York batteries and the detachment of Battery E of the 1st Artillery.[27]

This strengthening of Hooker's division did not mean that the Commanding General was at last getting ready to move. On the contrary, he had decided that nothing worth-while could be accomplished in the face of winter's cold, rain and mud. A long wait was to be the lot of the eager army.

As the cold weather approached the men delayed erecting winter quarters because of persistent rumors that the division was to be sent to Charleston, South Carolina, or farther south. Finally, wet, blustery weather forced the need of protection, and spacious, comfortable log huts were built.[28]

The winter of 1861-1862 was an unpleasant one in lower Maryland. The weather became sharp and bracing and on January sixth the Potomac froze over, cutting off supplies from Washington. Rain began four days later and soon the temperature was up and the country roads became trenches of bottomless mud.[29] Freeze and thaw alternated the balance of the winter.

Military defense of the lower Potomac was only part of Hooker's assignment. The secessionist activity of the citizens in his territory was another problem. The government was exerting every effort to stamp out disloyal conduct and he co-operated in full. At the time of the Maryland state elections Lincoln, wishing to make sure that no one interfered with the turnout of Union sympathizers, directed McClellan to detach military forces to supervise the various polling places and see that "fair play" prevailed.[30] Hooker complied in his area by sending out his cavalry and arresting Perry Davis, the secessionist candidate for the legislature.[31] The troops apparently performed their task, for on the day after election he reported that the balloting was conducted quietly and "a much larger Union vote was polled than anticipated."[32] He might have added that a much smaller antiadministration vote was polled than had been expected because of various devices he employed, such as the dispatch on election day of a full company of Indiana troopers to break up a political barbecue held by Southern sympathizers at the White Horse Tavern.

The noted special agent, Colonel Lafayette C. Baker, spent the early winter leading raids into lower Maryland under the jurisdiction of the Department of State.[33] He could always count on Hooker for a detail to aid him in routing out what he termed "traitors." After one expedition he wrote the General thanking him for his help. "Mr. Seward is much gratified at the promptness with which you responded to the orders given to me. . . ."[34] Hooker independently sent out several expeditions to search for arms and interrupt illicit traffic.[35] The 3rd Indiana Cavalry devoted almost its entire time to breaking up the regular passage of mail and supplies from Baltimore to Richmond. Mail between these points proceeded just as regularly after the start of hostilities as before, the only difference being that it was no longer carried by United States officials. The service was well protected and difficult to stop. The Federal gunboats were helpless to check the passage of small Confederate boats at night, and the cavalry finally took to picketing the river with its own small craft, receiving Hooker's praise as his "horse marines."[36]

Arrests and oaths of allegiance were not too effective. The following note indicates pretty well the attitude of the stanch Southern sympathizers:

"DEAR MISS STUART

"I am very sorry that I have not been able to send the gray flannel which you requested me to purchase for you, but I was not so situated at the time as to comply with your request but when the next boat comes over I will send the newspapers, the tea and flannels, or anything else I can procure which will be useful the other side of the water. I expect my father home before long. If however he takes forty oaths of allegiance he cannot prevent my shipping what I please, that is without he is much sharper than I have ever known him to be before, therefore know that it will give me the greatest pleasure to serve you at any time.

> "Very respectfully
> "SOPHIE ASHTON DENT

"PROSPECT HILL, March 24th 1862."[37]

This note fell into the hands of the 3rd Indiana Cavalry. Mr. Dent had just been released from arrest.

One of Hooker's first acts in lower Maryland had been to arrest Timothy Posey, his wife, a son, R. Harrison Posey, and a daughter. They were sent to Washington but received paroles and were released, to return to their plantation one mile inland from the river. Apparently Hooker became reconciled to the Poseys, for he wrote Simon Cameron, Secretary of War, in January '62, asking for the return of the papers taken from Posey at the time of his incarceration. He also allowed Mr. Posey the generous fee of $5.00 per day for use of his large front room for division court-martial proceedings—a steady source of income since the Board met with great regularity.[38] There is evidence that even this bit of good will was a mistake. The soldiers greatly enjoyed the companionship of the Posey family, but it was later discovered that the womenfolk were in the habit of signaling across the river—by mirror during the day and by lantern at night.[39] In addition, a roomer in their house, Philip H. Linton, was found to be carrying on a clandestine mail arrangement with the Evans family, notorious secessionists of Evansport, directly across the river.[40]

Runaway slaves created another difficult administrative problem. McClellan had issued an order for their return by all commanding officers. Hooker co-operated to the extent of granting permits to slaveowners to visit his camps, to search for their property and take possession of it without interference.[41] He had little interest in the slavery question and definitely no abolitionist leanings. The war to him was one to preserve the Union. To follow his orders and the Rules and Articles of War was more important to him at this time than to follow the party wishes of the rising radical Republican bloc that was attempting to take over the administration of the war. Senator Charles Sumner went after Hooker with a sharp stick when he found that the General was granting slave-owners permission to enter his camps. This was brought out before the Joint Committee on the Conduct of the War which held a short hearing in April 1862 on the return of runaway slaves. General Sickles testified that Hooker had let slaveowners into his camps and also that the Congressional enactment of an Article of War "making it a penal offense for officers to surrender fugitive slaves" had never been communicated to his brigade through division headquarters.[42] But, as Hooker said to his friend Senator Nesmith, "What the hell do they expect an officer to do?"[43] If the officer disobeyed orders he faced a court-martial, and if he obeyed them he must face the unreasonable and powerful radicals.

The protection of slave property and the return of "contraband" was really an impossible job in view of the attitude of the New England and New York regiments in the division. An anecdote illustrates the situation and indicates that Hooker's co-operation with the slaveowners was not wholehearted. A party of owners rode up to him, reported that several of their slaves were in the camp of one of his Massachusetts regiments and demanded their surrender per McClellan's order. Hooker replied, "Yes, I have seen the order, and yonder is the Massachusetts camp. And if your slaves are there and choose to go with you, and the Massachusetts boys are content, I have no objections. But if they refuse and a row occurs over there, I fear you will get into the guardhouse—the same as any other marauders." The slaveowners asked, "But, General Hooker, are you not going to apprehend our slaves for us?" Hooker answered, "Why, bless my soul, no. I am Brigadier General United States Volunteers, and no nigger catcher. I was born and bred in New England."[44]

This incident is reported by a soldier who later became quartermaster of the Jersey brigade. He apparently could not resist touching it up a bit, as "bless my soul" is not a phrase characteristic of Hooker's vocabulary.

In addition to complaints over runaway slaves, Hooker was bombarded with claims for payment for hogs, sheep, turkeys, corn, fodder, straw, shingles and fencing allegedly appropriated by his men. Many of these claims were just, and payment was authorized, but many were the work of opportunists.[45]

A grave problem concerned the smuggling of whisky to the restless troops. Army sutlers and merchants in the vicinity were the greatest offenders. A plot was unearthed to bring in whisky put up in oyster cans.[46] Hooker was even importuned by a Major De Venoge of New

York for permission to install a French eating establishment which would stock the best champagne.[47] Smuggling of whisky to the commissioned officers was not a problem since the government supplied every brigade commissary with barrels of spirits for officers' use.[48]

The General's personal habits have been the subject of much debate. His close followers were ever ready to testify that they had never seen him take a drink, but current nonpartisan opinion held otherwise. Eventually a parody was developed on the popular war tune hit "Marching Along." The lines

> McClellan's our leader,
> He's gallant and strong

were replaced by

> Joe Hooker's our leader,
> He takes his whisky strong.

The General should not be taken to task too sternly; many of his colleagues had similar or even better-developed tastes for liquor. An observer remarked that when certain officers fell in battle it was doubtful whether the cause was a bullet or a flask.[49] Colonel Baker of the Secret Service, who seems to have had his nose in almost everything, devotes much space to the "disgraceful but well-known prevalence of intemperance in the army."[50]

The voracious thirst of Hooker's men was responsible for most of the disciplinary problems in the division. The Hooker Papers are full of court-martial proceedings instigated because of misdemeanors committed by intoxicated soldiers. On December 2, 1861, riotous drunken soldiers of the 26th Pennsylvania were cutting up in Port Tobacco, and twenty-one were arrested. On January 13, 1862, a lieutenant colonel was charged with taking a bottle of brandy from the medical stores to entertain a member of Hooker's staff. A few days later a messenger of Hooker's was called a "God-damn son-of-a-bitch" and struck in the face by the Colonel of the 26th Pennsylvania; each claimed the other was drunk. Next a captain was accused of retaining liquor for his own use after having been ordered to destroy it.[51] And so it went during the winter of '62, to reach a climax in the grand riot of the 71st New York on March first.

That afternoon the regiment staged a review which was witnessed and applauded by General Hooker. It seemed a good occasion for a spree. The drinking started in the early evening in the tent of Lieutenant Colonel Potter and picked up steam as the hours passed, unhindered by the presence of several ladies. As the party left the tent they passed that of Colonel Hall and stopped to drop some insulting remarks. This brought forth a group of Hall supporters and a free-for-all fight started in which most of the regiment engaged as "Hall sympathizers" or "Potter men." Several were badly injured. The real cause of the riot was the long-standing antipathy between the Colonel and the Lieutenant Colonel and the rather even division of the regiment into factions behind them. Charges had been preferred against both in the early winter and they were awaiting court-martial. Their immediate commander, General Sickles, was disgusted and recommended to Hooker that both be barred from camp and the regiment made a battalion under its major and combined with the 70th New York.[52]

The many charges of "conduct unbecoming to an officer and a gentleman" and the oft-recurring offense of playing cards on the Sabbath kept the court-martial busy a good part of the time.[53] There were other disciplinary problems which never reached the court-martial stage, one of which is of interest since it involved General Sickles, the second in command. On the march to Charles County it had been ordered that all ambulances were to be left in Washington except one per regiment. The 1st Brigade abided by this order but Sickles' men, who were comparatively undisciplined, like their commander, took all the ambulances they could find. According to Hooker, they had used them for "lazy soldiers, officers' and women's trunks and knapsacks to such an extent as to lead one to fear that if they reached camp at all, it would be with crippled horses and broken down ambulances. . . ."

Sickles protested this accusation to McClellan, and in Hooker's reply to the Commanding General occurred one of those biting criticisms for which he became noted: "In my official intercourse with veteran politicians suddenly raised to high military rank, I have found it necessary to observe their correspondence with especial circumspection."[54] He continued to be extremely critical of Sickles, writing to Senator Nesmith that he would come up to Washington if "I had anyone to leave my command with, except Sickles, with whom I would expect to have it dishonored in less than 12 hours after leaving."[55] In light of the fact that Sickles later became one of Hooker's few boosters of high rank, it may be assumed that these communications were kept confidential. It was growing evident that unless Hooker soon bridled his sharp tongue with caution his army career would be a stormy one.

The organization of Hooker's division was far from satisfactory. The First Brigade was without a brigadier until February 21, 1862, nearly five months after its organization. Colonel Cowdin of the 1st Massachusetts had held the position. When a brigadier was assigned he proved to be a martinet and a troublemaker. He was Henry M. Naglee, a West Pointer, successful San Francisco businessman and good friend of McClellan. One of his first edicts was that his men must build a new dungeon for transgressors in his command. It was to be "without a crack or an opening, so that it will be perfectly dark." The soldiers obliged literally by not even cutting an entrance into the log structure! Within a month Naglee's private letters were calling his superior inefficient and slow and saying that he was too strong for Hooker, that Hooker realized it and was therefore very envious of him.[56] So in this early stage of the war Hooker was the subject of criticism from a subordinate, an offense of which he himself was to be guilty continually in days to come.

Naglee was nettled when late in February Hooker denied his request for a thirty-six-hour leave of absence to go to Washington. He wrote ominously that he would let the matter drop but would keep the denied application for future reference by himself and his friends.[57] In March he did go up to Washington but a dispute arose with Hooker over the leave.

The Second Brigade had General Sickles in command—but not often. He had been a Congressman from New York and had been authorized by Lincoln on May 18, 1861, to raise a brigade for service in the field. His nomination as brigadier general had never been confirmed by the Senate. The Congressman had been an outspoken and uncompromising Democrat before the war. The controlling radical Republican bloc in the Senate questioned the advisability of entrusting the command of so many Federal troops to an "otherwise-minded" man. Unscrupulous partisans and a few newspapers feared that "troops raised by Sickles or other Democrats would march over to Jeff Davis in the first battle in which they were engaged."[58] He spent a great part of his time in Washington pushing his confirmation. He had asked Hooker to give him letters to Senator Williams of Massachusetts, who opposed him, and to Senator Nesmith of Oregon.[59]

On March eighteenth General Hooker heard that the Senate had negatived Sickles' appointment and the President had therefore revoked it.[60] He immediately asked for a competent man to lead the Excelsiors and was informed that he might designate an officer to receive the command and the rank of brigadier general. Hooker's choice was Colonel Nelson Taylor of the 72nd New York, who was forthwith given the command, but the Brigadier's commission was never issued. Sickles protested Hooker's order on the score that even though he was no longer a brigadier general he was nevertheless the senior colonel in the Brigade and could not rightfully be replaced by a junior colonel. He said he would obey but would appeal to McClellan.[61] Evidently the appeal was of no avail for Taylor took command and Sickles went back to Washington again to plead his case.

The Third Brigade was also lacking a brigadier; Colonel Samuel H. Starr of the 5th New Jersey was in command during the entire stay in lower Maryland. Furthermore, it was not until January twenty-third that Hooker was assigned a division chief of artillery—Major Jonathan Wainwright.

The year 1862 opened with Hooker still trying to figure out some way to make a forward move. On Friday, January tenth, he went up to Washington for an interview with McClellan. The essence of the interview is not certain, but succeeding correspondence indicates that he had probably gone to propose some aggressive move across the river.[62] Further evidence of his intentions are found in a report to him at that time from Lieutenant R. H. Wyman, commanding the Potomac Flotilla. Wyman gave his strength as eleven steamers, capable of carrying only 1,000 men in addition to their crews. He suggested, however, that by towing launches and barges many more troops could be transported across the Potomac; deep water would allow the vessels to get close in to the Virginia shore at Cockpit Point, Evansport and Mathias Point.

On January twentieth Hooker received a welcome request from McClellan to make a stroke against the enemy's batteries, if nothing more than just to spike the guns or throw them into the river. McClellan asked what Hooker's views were on the feasibility of the project, the number of batteries and troops needed, and the possibility of a demonstration at Aquia Creek.[63]

On January twenty-seventh Hooker was ready to put his thoughts on paper. He proposed to open up with an attack by one of his brigades at Aquia Creek in order to inspire confidence within his command, to break up the enemy's depot of supplies and to threaten Confederate communications with Richmond. This attack was to be followed the next morning with an assault by two regiments on the batteries across from headquarters. The purpose was merely to destroy the batteries, not to give battle. On the third day as much of the division as could be transported would land in the vicinity of Powell Creek or Neabsco Creek, advance on the Colchester Road and take the Confederate batteries on the Occoquan in reverse.

This modest proposal thus called for three separate landings by troops who had no experience in co-ordinating separate attacks and who, in many cases, were completely innocent of any actual battle experience. Hooker admitted that he was not acquainted with the views and intentions of the Commanding General, that the expedition would require great secrecy, dispatch and resolution, and that the enemy would have all the advantage in position; yet he believed himself justified in recommending it. As an afterthought he added: ". . . another division will be required for this service, and should be landing nearby at the same time."[64]

On the same day that Hooker submitted his plan of attack to McClellan, Abraham Lincoln issued his General War Order No. 1, which made it clear that the President had not abdicated his power as Commander in Chief of the Army and Navy. It was ordered "that the 22nd day of February, 1862, be the day for a general movement of the land and naval forces of the United States against the insurgent forces. . . ."[65] The Army of the Potomac particularly was to be ready to move from the vicinity of Washington on that day, and the Commanding General was to be held fully responsible for prompt execution of the order. This was a direct expression of the administration's dissatisfaction with McClellan's delay in assuming the offensive and was issued without consultation with him. It came shortly after Edwin M. Stanton had succeeded Simon Cameron as Secretary of War.

McClellan, who had just recovered from a serious illness, was much taken aback by this directive, as he favored a plan of advance he had been working on for some time. His design was to attack Richmond by way of the lower Chesapeake Bay using Urbana on the Rappahannock or Fortress Monroe as a base. The impossibility of collecting the necessary water transportation by February twenty-second meant that his plan would have to be abandoned if the President's order were to hold. McClellan immediately presented his ideas to Lincoln, but the President disapproved and issued his Special War Order No. 1 which called for a direct overland attack by the Army of the Potomac to seize the line of communication between Richmond and the main Confederate army at Centreville, twenty-five miles southwest of Washington.[66]

McClellan continued to demur and on February third set up the arguments for his plan in a letter to the Secretary of War. It had the desired effect. The President submitted to McClellan against his better judgment. While waiting to accumulate the necessary transportation, McClellan was glad to authorize Hooker to make his try at silencing the enemy's batteries on the lower Potomac. Lincoln was anxious that the Potomac be cleared before the main body of the army was removed from the Washington area. Hooker received permission to go ahead primarily as a concession to the wishes of the President; McClellan had doubts as to the probabilities of success.

The expedition authorized was not so elaborate as Hooker had recommended, and it was necessary to revise the plan accordingly. Now the attack was to be made at Cockpit Point by 4,000 men. From there the troops would march south destroying the batteries at Shipping Point and Evansport.[67] Preparations were made daily, extra attention being given to the bayonet and skirmish drill, and the musicians were ordered to drop their instruments and practice ambulance routine.[68] The attack was first scheduled for the night of February fifteenth, but on this day the necessary boats had not arrived and Hooker did not feel that his junior officers were ready.[69] A week passed and he still felt unable to move, whereupon McClellan offered him the support of the ironclad steamer *Ericsson* and an additional 10,000 to 15,000 men.[70] Thus a rare opportunity was presented to Hooker to lead an attacking force of two divisions.

Unfortunately, however, he had waited too long to strike, for on the twenty-seventh he received a wire from McClellan to make no move until he had received further orders.[71] This was due to a report McClellan had had from General John G. Barnard, Chief of Engineers. After a careful reconnaissance, Barnard had come to the conclusion that the operation, if attempted, would require three divisions and should be commanded by McClellan in person. The landing where proposed was too hazardous since the ground was not known.[72] He even predicted that the result of the expedition might be the capture of Hooker instead of the batteries.[73]

Hooker was naturally chagrined at this turn of fortune which cheated him of the opportunity he had been striving for, but he took his disappointment with good grace, remarking only upon the lack of secrecy with which the venture had been handled. On February fifth he had attended an evening reception at the White House[74] and on the twenty-second had again visited the capital.[75] He was impressed by the loose talk indulged in by men of high rank on both occasions. He was later to be even more impressed with the impossibility of secrecy in the vicinity of Washington.

In early March the enemy became very active, and kept huge fires burning in certain localities both day and night. The meaning of this activity became plain on the afternoon of Sunday the ninth. About noon an unusual amount of black smoke was noticed over the Confederate works. The Federal gunboat *Anacostia*, while making a reconnaissance, threw a heavy fire into the enemy positions and drew no response. To the astonishment of the onlookers in Hooker's division, it was then observed that the Confederates were leaving. For two hours or more explosions were heard, indicating that much gunpowder was being destroyed. Great fires flared up and the whole Virginia shore for miles back seemed in a terrific uproar. The Confederate steamer *Page* and two schooners were also fired.

About three o'clock in the afternoon the *Anacostia* crept over to the Virginia shore, landed two boatloads of sailors and marines, and in fifteen minutes the Stars and Stripes were floating over the abandoned batteries north of Quantico Creek. Men from the 1st Massachusetts, intent upon sharing the glory, crossed in small boats and hoisted the colors on the south side of the Quantico.

Hooker's headquarters were soon crowded with officers of the division and great excitement prevailed.[76] Orders were sent out for 500 men from the Jersey Brigade and the same number from the 1st or old Hooker Brigade to go over at sunrise the next morning to examine the ground and to bring off anything of value left by the enemy. The Jersey boys were directed to Cockpit Point and the others to Shipping Point.[77]

The lucky men who were picked to make this investigation found that the big guns which had threatened them all winter had been spiked. Some of the guns had been constructed entirely of wood. Many suspicious-looking "graves" were found and when they were opened good tools, new tents, mess kits and packages of clothing were exhumed. Trophies were brought back ranging from bloodhound pups to Underwood's Boston pickles.[78] On the eleventh Hooker reported that the batteries at Cockpit Point had been entirely destroyed and the guns tumbled down the banks of the Potomac for salvage at a later date. Within a few days the guns at Shipping Point had received the same treatment.[79]

On the thirteenth, in compliance with the President's General War Order No. 2, which dictated that that part of the Army of the Potomac intended for active operations should be divided into four army corps, McClellan notified Hooker that in the future his division would be a part of the First Corps, commanded by General Irvin McDowell. This order was almost immediately changed and Hooker's regiments were assigned to the Third Corps under Brigadier General Samuel P. Heintzelman.[80] This shift is unexplained but it was important to Hooker: the Third Corps was to be placed in a position where much glory could be won whereas most of the First Corps would miss the spring battles altogether.

Heintzelman was a man small in stature, with a stern, rather unkempt appearance, a full beard and long, thin hair. He was a Pennsylvanian, nine years Hooker's senior, and like him a West Pointer. In the Mexican War he had reached the rank of major. He had been severely wounded at Bull Run while commanding a division. A lack of initiative was to prevent him from advancing very high in the Army and he was to be one of the early leaders shelved midway in the struggle.[81]

This General War Order of the President contributed considerably to McClellan's difficulties, for it arbitrarily divided his active force into four corps and placed at the head of them men whom he would not have chosen. They were Irvin McDowell, Edwin V. Sumner, Samuel P. Heintzelman and Erasmus D. Keyes.[82] The radical members of the Committee on the Conduct of the War had been foremost in urging this arrangement upon Lincoln. They had become even more determined when they found out that McClellan did not favor it.[83] Hooker did not suffer; there is little chance he would have been chosen by the Commanding General for a position of such responsibility. He had neither the seniority nor the close friendship and confidence of McClellan which were enjoyed by several other generals of equal rank.

The week after the Confederate withdrawal, detachments were sent over to the Virginia side to scout and to test the enemy pickets around Aquia and Dumfries.[84] Hooker, of course, wished to cross his whole division and push the Confederates back at least to the Rappahannock River.[85] General Heintzelman, his new corps commander, gave him an order to do this on the eighteenth,[86] and he made feverish plans to get across the "infernal river," but the next day McClellan wired him that his force was too small to venture as far as Fredericksburg.[87] The Confederate command unquestionably feared such a move,[88] but McClellan was not interested in actively following up the enemy withdrawal from the Potomac.

The Commanding General was busy at the time hastening his plans for the great move to the lower Chesapeake. His main interest in Hooker's division was in arranging for its departure and replacing it in lower Maryland with a force large enough to police this no longer threatened area.

The President's War Order No. 3 had taken the burden of the command of all the Federal armies away from McClellan, leaving him only the Army of the Potomac. The excuse was that McClellan was about to take the field personally. This was undoubtedly a wise order, but it was unfortunate that McClellan was to receive the news through the public press. It was evident that relations between the General and the War Department were far from satisfactory and that he might meet similar embarrassment at any time.

## CHAPTER V

## YORKTOWN AND WILLIAMSBURG

THE BEST method of approach to Richmond from a military point of view has been a controversial subject ever since the Confederacy, for political reasons, established its capital in the "old Dominion State." The overland route approved by Lincoln and Stanton had one great advantage—it would keep the Army of the Potomac directly between Washington and the Army of Northern Virginia. Yet the disadvantages were many: this advance would cross numerous rivers, difficult obstacles in the path of the army; the most direct route would pass through the hazardous Wilderness region south of the Rappahannock; and the nearer the Federal Army came to Richmond the longer would be the line of supply to be protected.

The approach to Richmond up the Peninsula between the York and James Rivers, as introduced by McClellan, would take advantage of the possession of the coastal waters by the Federal Navy and the established base at Fortress Monroe at the tip of the Peninsula; it would shorten the vulnerable line of supply, would bring the army closer to Richmond before encountering substantial resistance, and would pin down the Confederate Forces to defensive strategy in order to protect their capital. The main disadvantages were that a substantial force would need to be left in front of Washington to guard against Confederate raids, and the route would pass through swampy, unhealthful territory. McDowell, Pope, Burnside, Hooker, Meade and Grant were all to fail to reach their goal via the overland way. On the other hand, McClellan, following his plan, was at least to see the church spires of Richmond. When finally Grant did achieve victory, he, too, was operating from a river base.

Hooker opposed the water route at the time, but he had not been given an opportunity to speak his mind at the council of division commanders called by Lincoln on March eighth to deliberate on the alternatives. His views were not aired only because he was not notified of the meeting. His subordinate, General Naglee, had engineered the gathering to secure backing for the plan of his good friend, McClellan. Naglee had a double purpose in keeping Hooker away: first, to eliminate a dissenting voice, and second, to make a place for himself in the meeting on

74

the trumped-up excuse that he was Hooker's representative, the latter being indisposed. The division commanders voted eight to four for the water route despite the fact that both Lincoln and Stanton attended the meeting and favored the overland advance. Three of the "nays" came from Generals McDowell, Sumner and Heintzelman; three of the four corps commanders foisted on McClellan were opposed to the type of campaign they were to conduct.[1]

At any rate, in April 1862 the water route was to be given a try. The retreat of the enemy from in front of Washington fixed Fortress Monroe as the base. Urbana, Virginia, McClellan's alternative starting point, was now covered by the new Confederate position. The movement by water of an army of over 100,000 men with full equipment to a base nearly 200 miles away was a stupendous undertaking. Probably no Federal officer other than McClellan possessed the military administrative ability necessary to organize such a venture. In all, 400 steam vessels and sailing craft were used. The movement began on March seventeenth and took a little more than a month to complete.[2]

Hooker's division was one of the last scheduled to leave. In early April superfluous baggage was sent to Washington, shelter tents were issued and temporary piers were erected. On the fourth, orders were issued to the infantry and artillery to pack up and move to the transports waiting in the Potomac.[3] The cavalry was left behind to police lower Maryland.

The "Jersey Blues" embarked at Rum Point and got away in a storm on Sunday night the sixth, arriving at Hampton Roads without mishap at 4:00 P.M. the next day. They then went up the York River to Ship Point on Cheeseman's Creek, six miles below Yorktown.[4]

The 1st Brigade, or old Hooker brigade, left on the forenoon of the seventh from Budd's Ferry and at the mouth of the Potomac ran into a severe northeaster. The boats hove to and were held up for three days waiting out the storm, detained from reaching their destination at Ship Point until the eleventh and twelfth.[5] While coaling at Fortress Monroe the morning of the eleventh the *South America*, on which two regiments were aboard, had to shove off in a hurry when the dreaded Confederate *Merrimac* was seen steaming down from Norfolk. The sturdy little *Monitor* and the frigate *Minnesota* went out to stand in her way, but the big ironclad didn't mean business and after a few long-range shots turned back.[6]

The "Excelsior" brigade left Liverpool Point on the ninth but had proceeded only as far as Port Tobacco when a snowstorm delayed its pas-

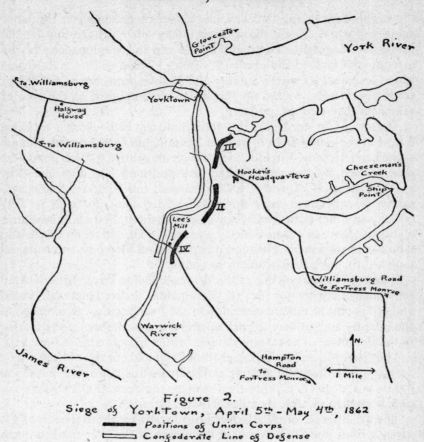

Figure 2.
Siege of Yorktown, April 5th - May 4th, 1862
▬▬▬▬ Positions of Union Corps
▭▭▭▭ Confederate Line of Defense

sage. Ship Point wasn't reached until the twelfth. The disgruntled leaders of the 71st New York—Colonel Hall and Lieutenant Colonel Potter—asked to be released from arrest so that they might accompany their regiment. Hooker approved, but only with the proviso that they travel in separate boats.[7]

The move by water was far from enjoyable. The division used sixteen steamers for men and supplies and seven schooners for the artillery horses.[8] There was little concern for comfort or cleanliness, and the bad weather they encountered doubled the journey's length for many of the boats. Food ran short and many men were seasick.

The landing on Cheeseman's Creek was an exciting place. Steamers and sailing vessels filled with stores and munitions of war came in, unloaded and hurried back for more. Piles of shot and shell, commissary and quartermaster supplies, and rows of army wagons were everywhere. Laborers and soldiers hustled about the wharf serving as longshoremen. As soon as Hooker's division was united it moved away from this busy spot to a camp near the headwaters of Cheeseman's Creek, four miles distant.[9]

That part of the Army of the Potomac which had preceded the division had already been brought to a standstill by the Confederate line of fortifications running across the peninsula, along the Warwick River and the defenses at Yorktown. Here General John Bankhead Magruder, the cagey Southerner, barred the way.

McClellan had encountered one disappointment after another arising from uncertain support in Washington and his inborn caution. He had planned to turn this advanced Confederate line by using the Navy to destroy the water batteries at Yorktown and Gloucester Point. Then the Federal First Corps was to land up the York River past the Confederate left, making a hasty retreat inevitable. This sensible plan miscarried when Flag Officer Goldsborough decided he did not have a naval force sufficient to accomplish the mission, and when Abraham Lincoln, yielding to his own fears and the bad counsel of his Secretary of War, temporarily detached the First Corps from McClellan's command.[10]

The harried Commanding General then had to decide between an attempt to break the opposing line by vigorous frontal attack or to lay siege to Yorktown. The latter choice was more to his taste, and after a weak attack against the James River end, siege operations were begun.[11] Batteries and redoubts were established along the whole front, particularly before Yorktown. At this point a parallel was opened a mile from the enemy fortifications. Into the parallel filed part of Hooker's old brigade on April sixteenth to take its part in the siege. The rest of the division camped under cover of a thick wood nearly a mile to the rear on fields where General George Washington's Continentals spent the month of October 1781.[12]

Heintzelman's Third Corps, to which Hooker's division had been attached, was on the extreme right of the Federal line. Fitz-John Porter's division was on Hooker's right and Charles S. Hamilton's on his left. General Hooker had been concerned about his position within the corps. Almost his last act before leaving Maryland was to inquire whether or not he ranked General Porter. He believed that he did, for, although their commissions bore the same date, his had been confirmed first by the Senate. The matter was important: in the event Heintzelman should be incapacitated in the impending battles the ranking general—Hooker or Porter—would automatically succeed to the corps command, at least temporarily. The disappointing information came back from General Seth Williams, McClellan's Adjutant General, that Porter stood above Hooker on the Army Register.[13] Thus Hooker was only the third-ranking officer in the corps—a not too enviable position in view of the semi-independent command he had just left in lower Maryland.

His new headquarters were on the left of the Williamsburg Road in an advanced position well within cannon shot of the enemy. Lowe's balloon had tagged along and ascended near headquarters almost every day, drawing considerable fire but obtaining worth-while information.[14]

Hooker kept an active eye on his advanced troops and constantly reported to McClellan any changes in their position. He also found it necessary to warn the Commanding General that a more perfect understanding should be reached over the dispositions for night defenses if a catastrophe were to be avoided.[15] This was prompted by a brisk skirmish between two regiments of the Third Corps (not belonging to Hooker) who were quicker to fire than to ascertain whether they were firing on foe or friend.

The men took turns working in the trenches, along the approaches and on the roads. Most of the work was done at night and was very exhausting. It was so grueling that a special whisky ration was dealt out to the trench parties. The ration came through regular channels—brigade quartermaster to regimental quartermasters to company captains. Along the way it became considerably diluted as officers filled their own canteens and then made good the "quantity" of whisky allotted to their men by adding water. Finally one night a long-legged private of the 2nd New Hampshire, grimy with smoke and dirt from long hours in the trenches, strode up to Hooker with his dipper of whisky and asked his general to sample it. The potion could not have been subjected to a better test! Hooker took a mouthful, blew it out and threw the dipper into the brush, damning the thieves who doctored his men's whisky. The next trench party received its spirits directly from the General's headquarters.[16]

Disciplinary problems continued to annoy Hooker. General Naglee, second in command in the division and his only brigadier, was ordered under arrest. When Colonel Taylor, with the 2nd Brigade, had proceeded to the camp site assigned him, he found Naglee's brigade there. Naglee refused to move or to make room for the "Excelsiors." "I'll be damned if I'll be crowded," he said. He added that the regulations allowed him a specified ground, that he now had only about one-third of that space and he would not be satisfied with one-sixth. In a huff Naglee took it upon himself to order Taylor to camp in the rear.[17] Hooker was eager to get rid of Naglee, anyway, and this seemed a good time, but McClellan believed that his friend was being "pushed around" and brusquely asked Hooker to give reasons why the arrest was necessary.[18] Regardless of whether his explanation was satisfactory the General won his point, for Naglee was "sent to afflict some other command."[19]

One of the most competent but as yet unheralded generals to wear the Federal blue was then assigned to the 1st Brigade: Cuvier Grover. He was a State-of-Mainer, fourth in his class at West Point (1850), and a career man in the "Old Army." At the outbreak of the war he had been on frontier duty in New Mexico. He refused to surrender to the Confederate authorities there and marched his command to safety on the Missouri River. His commission of brigadier general was less than a month old when he was assigned to Hooker.[20] He was a younger brother of LaFayette Grover, Hooker's co-worker in the Oregon Democratic Party.

No sooner had the 1st Brigade command been altered than the leader of the 3rd Brigade got out of line. Charges were brought against Colonel Samuel Starr of "conduct prejudicial to good order and military discipline" and of "conduct unbecoming an officer and a gentleman." He had ridden past the sentinel, refusing to give the countersign and using abusive language. Later on the same afternoon he rode his horse into a detail of the 74th New York and struck a private with his sword, calling him a "God-damned son-of-a-bitch."[21]

A few days later Starr was rewarded for this bit of waywardness by being remanded to the command of his regiment, the 5th New Jersey. Brigadier General Francis E. Patterson was assigned to Hooker to take over the "New Jersey Blues."[22] He was a son of Robert Patterson, the Federal general in the Shenandoah Valley who, in July 1861, permitted the Confederate force on his front to give him the slip and to unite with Beauregard against McDowell at Bull Run. The son proved to be a chip off the old block. His chief virtue was that he was undeniably easygoing and pleasant.[23]

Another problem was the shortage of men to handle the twenty-two guns.[24] Hooker had to issue a call for volunteers.

Meanwhile, the 11th and part of the 1st Massachusetts had distinguished themselves with a successful sortie against an enemy lunette projecting in front of Hooker's position. In the early hours of April twenty-sixth General Grover had personally led them against the enemy. They destroyed the lunette, scouted around a bit and came back under fire with a loss of only eighteen men. McClellan was clutching at anything resembling a favorable action to report to Secretary of War Stanton and wrote up this affair handsomely. That they were Hooker's troops did not get into the dispatch.[25]

Work on the approaches to Yorktown was completed the first few days in May, and the batteries were all set to demolish the opposing works. Hooker had about 7,950 men ready to take advantage of any breach on his front. (Fifteen hundred men were at work on the Yorktown and Hampton Road and 725 were on guard duty at Ship Point.)[26] On the night of May third the enemy started a heavy fire which fell full on Hooker's force. The 4th New York Battery happened to be in an exposed position only 800 yards in front of one of the main Confederate redoubts. Hooker flew into a rage when he discovered the situation and ordered the battery back, exclaiming to its commander, "My God! Can't I find anyone to carry out an order intelligently?"[27]

The heavy bombardment continued until the early hours of the next morning, then suddenly ceased. As dawn came on the suspicion grew that Magruder had withdrawn, leaving the Union gunners an empty target for their siege batteries. Heintzelman went up in Lowe's balloon and found that the enemy's works were deserted—a fitting end to a needless siege.[28] But worse than that, thirty precious days had been lost, time sorely needed by the Confederates to concentrate their forces.

Pursuit was started immediately by General Stoneman's cavalry, and Hooker was ordered to follow in support along the Yorktown and Williamsburg Road. The General was impatient to get started but the men had to be called in from their scattered positions. Busy as he was, he found time to write a short prophetic letter to his friend Nesmith in Washington. He mentioned the evacuation of Yorktown and expressed confidence that he had the best division in the army. The general tone of the letter was not encouraging, however, and it ended: "The Army of the Potomac will be the death of some of us."[29]

By 1:00 P.M. the division was on its way, getting ahead at a good pace with straggling almost negligible. The foremost of the pursuers had met up with what was then considered a barbarous method of waging war— the land mine. Torpedoes had been planted along the road under the direction of Confederate General Gabriel Rains (Hooker's brother staff officer in 1847), and several soldiers had been blown up. Soon, however, unexploded mines were located and marked with red flags or guarded by sentries.[30]

In the late afternoon numbers of wounded Federal cavalrymen were encountered. Governor Sprague of Rhode Island, who had been with the advance, rode up to Hooker and told him that General Stoneman had struck the Confederate rear guard near Williamsburg.[31] Hooker galloped to the front to see how he could best support the cavalry and found that the enemy was located in a big earth redoubt, commanding the road, from which it was delivering a steady fire.

When the General returned to his troops he noted that General W. F. Smith's division of the Fourth Corps was filing into the Yorktown-Williamsburg Road at the Halfway House, ahead of his own division. His 1st Brigade was necessarily halted and the division closed up, while the General applied to his corps commander Heintzelman, for permission to cross over to a parallel road a mile away which ran from Hampton through Lee's Mill to Williamsburg.[32] The permission was granted and at dark the division columned left at an old brick church and passed over to its new line of approach, but by that time three hours had been lost.

A heavy rain had settled down in the late afternoon and by ten at night the water was knee-deep in the rutted roads. About three miles from Williamsburg Hooker decided that the pursuit must be abandoned for the night and the exhausted men fell out, many for the last bivouac.

At daylight on May fifth the division renewed its march through a region of large trees and thick underbrush. The rain continued but the water-soaked soldiers moved forward with spirit. The column was halted at the edge of a forest and Hooker went forth to reconnoiter. One-third of a mile away at the junction of the Williamsburg-to-Hampton and Williamsburg-to-Yorktown roads was the imposing earthwork he had observed the afternoon before. It was embrasured for cannon and manned by several fieldpieces. It seemed to be flanked on either side by a series of redoubts extending beyond the range of view. Between the forest and the main enemy line were numerous rifle pits. Be-

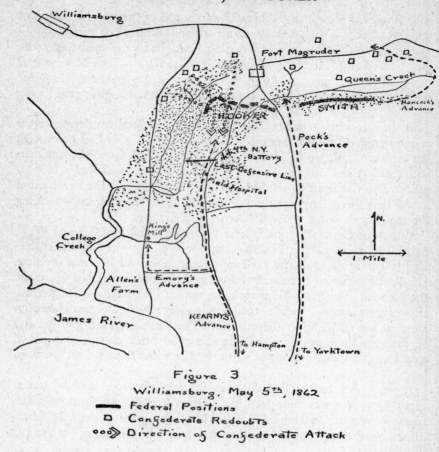

Figure 3
Williamsburg, May 5th, 1862
━━━ Federal Positions
☐ Confederate Redoubts
ooo⟩ Direction of Confederate Attack

The code used in all maps to indicate the size of a general's command is as follows: Brigade Commander—Hooker; Division Commander—HOOKER; Corps Commander—HOOKER; Army Commander—HOOKER.

yond the earthwork (which was known as Fort Magruder) and several miles to the west could be seen the venerable spires of Williamsburg.

Here was the opportunity Hooker had been waiting for since the previous autumn—a chance to hurl his well-drilled division at the enemy. What was even better luck, no superior was at hand to cramp his plans or claim credit for whatever success might be attained. As he said in his Official Report, "Being in pursuit of a retreating army, I deemed it my duty to lose no time in making the disposition of my forces to attack, regardless of their number and position. . . ."[33] He might have added "and regardless of the enemy's number and position," since he had no knowledge of how strongly defended the Confederate line might be that morning. He reasoned that even if he did not capture whatever force the enemy had in front of him, he would at least hold it while the other near-by divisions came to his support.[34]

Whereas almost any other general in the Army of the Potomac at this time would have hesitated when confronted with such a problem, Hooker had long chafed at McClellan's conservatism and believed that aggressive action was needed. The private soldier, who was sure the war would soon be over, agreed with him. At this point Hooker appears to be a needed counterbalance to the hesitant Commanding General.

In short order he was ready to advance and General Grover, whose brigade was first in the line of march, was ordered to send out several companies as skirmishers. At 7:30 A.M. part of the 1st Massachusetts went to the left of the road and part of the 2nd New Hampshire to the right.[35] They were instructed to engage the enemy in the rifle pits and the gunners and sharpshooters in the big earthen fort. While the skirmishers were working their way through an obstruction of felled trees the other companies of these regiments were halted under cover. The 11th Massachusetts and 26th Pennsylvania were held in reserve and then directed to form on the right of the 2nd New Hampshire. They were to advance as skirmishers and try to reach the Yorktown Road, where it was presumed they would find a supporting division.[36]

While Hooker was waiting for his artillery to arrive his skirmishers engaged in a long-distance sharpshooting contest and did well. Webber's 1st U. S. Battery soon came up and Hooker directed Major Wainwright to place two guns in the road and the other four in a field on the right. However, before a single piece could be fired the cannoneers and drivers were scattered by a concentrated fire from the fort and a sunken redoubt on its left. Chief of Artillery Wainwright had to call for volunteers to man the deserted guns and the officers and men of Osborn's 1st New York Battery rushed out to take over. Shamed by this turn of events, Captain Webber finally persuaded a handful of his men to return to their guns. Captain Bramhall's 6th New York Battery then unlimbered its five guns on the right and the enemy's fort was silenced in a half-hour.[37]

On Hooker's left the clearing between the forest and the enemy's works petered out making a surprise approach possible on this flank. Two regiments of the Jersey Blues (the 6th and 7th) under General Patterson were sent to extend the left of the 1st Brigade. The 5th New Jersey was detached personally by General Hooker to support the advanced batteries.[38]

By nine in the morning the Excelsior Brigade arrived, with the exception of one regiment (the 71st New York) and one battery. A small company in this brigade brought up two rapid-firing guns, even then technically known as machine guns but referred to by the soldiers as "corn poppers" or "coffee grinders." Fifty-eight-caliber cartridges were poured into a hopper on top of the mantling and the gun was fired by means of a crank on the side. The barrel was set on a swivel and could cover a large sweep of territory.[39]

Now the entire division was at Hooker's call. The General and his staff went out into the clearing during a heavy rain to get a better view of the uncertain ground to their left. Lieutenant Miles McAlester of the Engineers was sent to reconnoiter the enemy redoubts in that direction and to find out whether a suitable opportunity presented itself for carrying the works by assault.[40] The General calmly sat his horse amid the steady fire of Confederate sharpshooters—a habit he was to carry on throughout the war and one which endeared him to his men but was of little other practical value. Eventually a bullet found his horse and Hooker dismounted to examine the wound. He then rearranged his artillery and went back into the protection of the woods.[41]

By 10:30 Lieutenant McAlester was back with the word that it might be possible to get around the enemy's right.[42] This was the news Hooker wanted to hear, but increased musketry fire from the direction of the Jersey brigades made him hesitate. Glimpses of large bodies of enemy infantry massing toward the Federal left made it seem likely that defensive maneuver might be in order first.

Patterson had already become aware of his danger and had called up his 8th New Jersey to form on his extreme left. Grover in veteran style had shifted the 1st Massachusetts over close to the Jersey brigade. The shrill Rebel yell announced the enemy's intentions; they came on with a rush. Hooker's men held steadily to their work. When the 1st Massachusetts, which had been skirmishing most of the morning, ran out of ammunition, the 72nd New York went up to take its place, followed by the 70th New York at eleven o'clock. The position held by the 72nd was subjected to a hot fire from a field battery, and Hooker ordered

THE FIRST TO FALL

Confederate dead on the Hagerstown Pike, the men who first received Hooker's attack at Antietam.

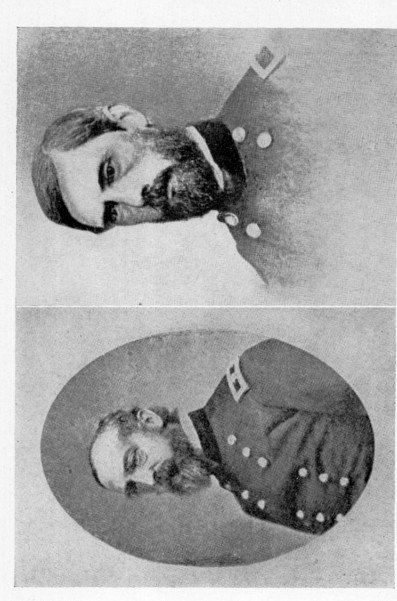

GENERAL GEORGE G. MEADE          GENERAL JOHN F. REYNOLDS

General Grover, who commanded that part of the line, either to silence it or take it. The Excelsior regiment advanced but was forced to retire, losing heavily.[43]

Word came from the 11th Massachusetts and 26th Pennsylvania, on the right, that they had reached the Yorktown Road. Colonel Blaisdell of the 11th was told to take command and to proceed cautiously up the road. No sign, however, was discovered of any supporting division.[44] This prompted Hooker to send a note to Heintzelman suggesting that one be provided. It gave a fair picture of the situation. Hooker said, "I have had a hard contest all the morning, but do not despair of success. My men are hard at work, but a good deal exhausted. It is reported to me that my communication with you by the Yorktown Road is clear of the enemy. Batteries, cavalry, and infantry can take post by the side of mine to whip the enemy."[45] The Third Corps Commander was not found and the suggestion went unheeded by General Sumner of the Second Corps who did read it. He had been delegated the command of the pursuit and was, therefore, over Hooker's division as well as his own corps.

By 1:00 P.M. the action on the left had grown to such proportions that there was no longer any question but that Hooker had ventured into a full-sized battle and not the offensive type he would have chosen. The men in gray kept coming at his left and center with impetuosity and seemingly overwhelming numbers. The only remaining regiments in reserve, the 73rd and 74th New York, had to be sent in to face the repeated attacks.[46] Lieutenant Abbott, one of Hooker's aides, was sent to hurry the last available reinforcement in the division, Smith's 4th New York Battery.

Captain Smith had reported to Hooker in the middle of the morning that his battery was blocked by a forage train, and the General had replied, "Well, Captain, I don't think you'll be needed, but get up as soon as possible."[47] This optimistic view was no longer justified and when Captain Smith came up with his battery in the early afternoon he found General Hooker in the middle of Hampton Road about 200 yards past the field hospital, seated on his white horse without aide or orderly in sight. The General asked, "Where are you going, Captain?" and was answered, "To the front." "My God," said Hooker, "there is no front! Can you go in battery here?"[48] This was not exactly true. The infantry was still clinging desperately to its position, but there were many holes.

Under Hooker's supervision the 4th New York prepared for action on a three-foot bank alongside the road. The guns were double-shotted with canister and trained on the advancing Confederates. At the first round Hooker's horse reared and jumped over the bank, falling on him. Muddy but uninjured, he remounted and in desperation rode off to order the 11th Massachusetts and 26th Pennsylvania to return from the Yorktown Road and help withstand the increased pressure.[49] The 2nd New Hampshire was also drawn over farther to the left, but the line was becoming untenable and the 5th New Jersey and 2nd New Hampshire were overcome by a strong enfilading fire. They had to retreat and the batteries before Fort Magruder which had been so effective had to be abandoned. Four of the guns were later captured; the rest were so deeply mired they couldn't be carried off.[50]

As this catastrophe occurred on the right of the fighting front, word came from Colonel Taylor that the 70th and 72nd New York were using cartridges from the boxes of the fallen. As the supply train was not up, there was no other recourse. The 11th Massachusetts had moved promptly from the right and went in to help General Patterson who was steadily losing ground. Their smoothbore Springfield muskets, with a cartridge of three buckshot and a large musket ball, were momentarily effective.[51] The 26th Pennsylvania was still off somewhere on the Yorktown Road.

Now all the reserves had been thrown in and the men began to realize that they were beaten. The Jerseymen were driven back almost to the road and the Excelsiors fell back in confusion. As the men began to break, Hooker ordered a line of cavalrymen to form across Hampton Road and to cut down any unwounded soldiers intent on retreating.[52] With the aid of General Heintzelman, who had at last come upon the field to see what his 2nd Division was doing,[53] Hooker and Grover formed a second defensive line about a half-mile to the rear, running east and west from the road. Here the 4th New York Battery continued to throw canister at the advancing Confederates and, according to General Grover, "contributed more toward sustaining our position than anything else. . . ."[54] The most rugged characters in the defeated regiments fought hand-to-hand against superior numbers while Hooker rode up and down exhorting his men to stand—and Heintzelman rallied the regimental musicians. He gathered up the scattered bands and ordered: "Play! Play! It's all you're good for. Play, damn it! Play some marching tune! Play 'Yankee Doodle,' or any doodle you can think of, only play something."[55]  Hooker in his report, however, very courteously acknowledged Heintzelman's aid and counsel.

Of even more value in preventing a rout was the assurance that at last reinforcements were near.  About three o'clock in the afternoon[56] the dashing one-armed Phil Kearny came up with his brigade of Michiganders under Hiram Berry and two regiments of New Yorkers under David Birney.[57]  Heintzelman had told Kearny to report to Hooker, thinking that Hooker was the senior general.  Hooker put Berry's brigade in on the left side of the road and Birney's men on the right.  When these immediate dispositions had been made, Kearny turned to him and said, "I think I rank you," and Hooker replied, "Certainly, General, you do."[58]  Kearny then took charge of the counterattack as was perfectly proper.

Berry and Birney immediately advanced, the Confederate attack was stalled, Hooker's battered divisions were relieved and the Federals regained part of their former ground.  The rain ceased as evening approached and the firing died down.  The Confederate leaders were satisfied to call it quits; they had done their job well!

While Kearny made his effort on the main front Heintzelman had sent General Emory and the cavalry, a battery and three regiments of the 3rd Division infantry on a flanking move to the Confederate right.  Emory pulled up short of his goal believing that he was too weak to accomplish anything.[59]

Hooker's men reorganized their brigade formations and went into camp in the woods.  Blazing fires were built to warm and cheer the tired, hungry and drenched warriors.  The wounded were removed from the field hospital farther in the rear.  The casualties had been very heavy, almost entirely suffered while the division fought alone.  In the 1st Brigade there were 253 killed, wounded and missing, while the Excelsior regiments were terribly decimated, 772 failing to answer roll call, 330 in the 70th New York alone; the New Jersey men lost 526 and the Artillery 24.  This made a total of 1,575 men—20 percent of the division.[60]  Heintzelman felt that it was so badly used up it would be undependable if attacked the next day.[61]

This was the roughest fight any division of the Army of the Potomac had experienced to date.  Though the losses were severe, they were not unreasonable considering the two-to-one superiority in man power enjoyed by the enemy until Kearny arrived.  Hooker later claimed that he had faced the whole Confederate Army of the Peninsula,[62] but in reality he opposed only six brigades under General James E. Longstreet.

Yet, was it necessary that his force should have been allowed to make such a heavy sacrifice? The General unqualifiedly said no. To quote his report:

"History will not be believed when it is told that the noble officers and men of my division were permitted to carry on this unequal struggle from morning until night unaided in the presence of more than 30,000 of their comrades with arms in their hands; nevertheless it is true."[63]

While Hooker stood at bay during the morning, General Smith's division went into line of battle well to the right of the Yorktown Road and stayed there unopposed most of the day. At 1:00 P.M. General John J. Peck's brigade of Couch's division advanced up the road to the position held by the 26th Pennsylvania. After several ineffective attempts to find Hooker, Peck went ahead on his own, engaging the enemy on the right of the road. Losses of 124 in the entire brigade would not indicate that he was seriously involved.[64]

On the extreme right of the Federal position General Hancock advanced at noon with five regiments and a battery on the east end of the series of Confederate redoubts. By mid-afternoon he had occupied several abandoned fortifications and was in an admirable flanking position from which to throw artillery fire into Fort Magruder. His superior general, W. F. Smith, had promised to support him but at this juncture General Sumner, commander of the entire field, ordered Hancock to return to his former position. Hancock stalled until shortly after five in the afternoon when the enemy advanced on him, making immediate retirement impossible. A Confederate brigade attacked his guns which were supported by infantry, and the enemy was fearfully cut up while the Federals lost but 95 men and held their ground.[65]

The balance of Couch's division and Casey's division reached the battlefield by nightfall but were not engaged. General Hooker's statement that 30,000 comrades were available to help him is essentially true. The four divisions which eventually reached the field totaled approximately that number and all except Kearny could have been up by noon. It is interesting to note that although Kearny was the last to leave Yorktown he was the first to reach Hooker in his hour of need.

The explanation for Hooker's being allowed to wage a private fight lies in the misunderstanding of the state of affairs by the top-ranking generals. McClellan was fourteen miles away superintending the embarkation of his divisions which were to advance by way of the York River to West Point, and he didn't get to the scene of battle until 5:00 P.M., though still in time to claim a bit of credit for stemming the retreat.[66] General Sumner, who was in command of the pursuit, never realized what was going on. Hooker later testified before the Congressional Committee that Sumner could have advanced through the enemy lines on his (Hooker's) right without losing ten men.[67] This was, of course, a rare exaggeration. He was naturally curious why Sumner hadn't followed his suggestion of the morning to advance on the Yorktown Road or at least sent him support from Smith's idle division.

The mystery was cleared up a few days later by General Kearny who asked Sumner point-blank. It seems that the old soldier believed the attack on Hooker was merely a feint and that the enemy really intended to break through well to Hooker's right, that he had frustrated this possibility by his concentration to the right of the Yorktown Road, and that when the enemy had seen these dispositions he dared not attack.[68] This explanation would make it seem that McClellan was justified in his distrust of at least one of the corps commanders thrust upon him. It appears that the Confederate intentions were merely to defend their wagon train from too rapid pursuit. They had no thought of attacking until the brigade commanders on their right saw an opportunity to overwhelm the Union left. Hancock's threatening position on their left was all that brought on an attack there. Otherwise, they would have been content to remain on the defensive. As pursuers, it was really up to the Federals to push the fighting.

As usual, both sides claimed the victory. Since no appreciable amount of ground was gained by either side, and since the Federals suffered the greater number of casualties—2,200 as against 1,600—and the Confederates successfully accomplished their purpose of delaying the pursuit, it would seem that the battle of Williamsburg should rightfully appear in the victory column of the South.

Hooker's battle was unnecessary, as it later developed. The Confederate position could have been turned on the Union right where Hancock attacked. McClellan in his original report to Stanton focused his attention on Hancock's skirmish and said little about Hooker's and Kearny's battle. The two fighting brigadiers never forgave this slight, even though McClellan later took steps to make a correction.[69]

In a conversation with Lieutenant Colonel Mott of the 5th New

Jersey shortly after the battle, Hooker discussed the peculiar original report of the Commanding General. He finally summed things up by saying, ". . . Mott, it seems to me you and I, and your Jersey Blues and the Excelsior Brigade were not at Williamsburg at all! Hancock did the business."[70]

In a letter to Nesmith written about the same time he attempted to set the Senator right as to McClellan. "He is not only not a soldier, but he does not know what soldiership is. . . . He is no more of a man than Mc-Dowell."[71] A few days later he warned Nesmith that McClellan ". . . is an infant among soldiers" and added: "Form no opinion of what you read in the newspapers. They and the wires are under [McClellan's] control, hence the flattery, etc. The blazoning about the bayonet charge of Hancock is all stuff."[72]

McClellan's lack of appreciation at this time undoubtedly had a good bit to do with Hooker's severe criticism of "little Mac's" leadership on the Peninsula. When the campaign was being reviewed by the Committee on the Conduct of the War, Hooker testified that if the pursuit had not been abandoned after Williamsburg they could have gone into Richmond by the second day after the battle without another gun having been fired.[73] This is another example of the exaggerations in which he frequently indulged.

Kearny also was an accomplished critic. In a letter to his friend, Cortlandt Parker, five days after his battle, he referred to McClellan as ". . . a dirty, sneaking traitor," and to Heintzelman as an "old fool." His remarks on Hooker are revealing as an evaluation of character: "Hooker has been beaten because he did not know his mind; I have full evidence by the field over which he fought; that he wanted to take the enemy's works but did not even think that he could do it"[74]—an interesting critique in view of what was to happen at Chancellorsville.

The Northern papers were not to overlook Hooker's end of the business. Whereas the early reports all followed McClellan's original dispatch emphasizing Hancock's engagement, by May ninth most papers carried the account of an army correspondent who said, "General Hooker's division bore the great brunt of the battle and fought most valiantly throughout, though greatly overpowered by numbers. . . ."[75] On the sixteenth the New York *Tribune* even printed Hooker's plea for help to Heintzelman which Sumner had ignored.

Hooker had little cause for dissatisfaction. His early boast that he would come to the head of the Army began to take on some weight. He had at least fought this army's first battle. The reputation of a "fighting" general was being attached to his name. The story of his calmly sitting his big white horse named "Colonel" in the face of heavy fire would be often retold. A typesetter on a New York newspaper titled a story on the desperate going before Williamsburg: "Fighting—Joe Hooker." Popular fancy seized this unintentional coupling of words and "Fighting Joe" became the sobriquet which Hooker would bear throughout the rest of his days.

This account of the derivation of his nickname has been the accepted story, and it is supported by a wealth of detail concerning the incident, but it is still not altogether satisfactory. The typesetter involved purportedly worked for the New York *Courier and Enquirer*, but by 1862 this paper had been swallowed up by the New York *World*. The sobriquet does not appear in any issue of the *World* immediately after the battle of Williamsburg or any other battle on the Peninsula. The same is true of all other papers of that period which the author has been able to examine. "Fighting Joe" does not appear in common usage for four months after Williamsburg. A reasonable conclusion is that in some spontaneous manner it was applied to Hooker after Williamsburg and was revived popularly as his aggressive leadership guided his command into one desperate fight after another.[76]

Regardless of how or when Hooker received the name of "Fighting Joe," it stuck—much to the General's lifelong disgust. He continually rebuffed those who so referred to him. His plea to the press was:

"Don't call me Fighting Joe, for that name has done and is doing me incalculable injury. It makes a portion of the public think that I am a hot headed, furious young fellow, accustomed to making furious and needless dashes at the enemy."[77]

## CHAPTER VI

# ON THE OFFENSIVE ALONG THE CHICKAHOMINY

IF NOTHING else, the hard fight of Hooker's men earned them a rest. They were not called upon to pursue their opponents, who had moved off again toward Richmond, but were allowed to stay in camp. The 1st Brigade was given the honor of acting as Provost Guard in Williamsburg, and General Grover was appointed military governor. Burial details were set to work at once and wherever possible brigade burial grounds were established.[1] The wounded were housed in the college buildings and churches until they had improved sufficiently to make the trip to the hospital steamers *Daniel Webster* and *Commodore*, anchored at Ship Point.[2]

Williamsburg was the oldest incorporated town in Virginia and long its seat of colonial government. It occupied slightly elevated land midway between the James and the York. The streets were regularly laid out at right angles. The public buildings and private mansions were of architectural elegance.[3]

Grover's brigade camped in a field near William and Mary College, the alma mater of four good Democratic Presidents—Jefferson, Madison, Monroe and Tyler. Classes were not in session since the faculty and student body had long since gone off to war. The townspeople were pronounced in their secessionist sympathies but the military occupation was without unfortunate incident.

Hooker was busy reorganizing his shattered division. Many promotions had to be made due to the high officer casualty rate: nineteen had been killed, sixty-seven wounded, and two were missing.[4] The Colonel of the 6th New Jersey had been killed, the commander of the 70th New York wounded and captured; the leaders of the 26th Pennsylvania and the 7th and 8th New Jersey were wounded. The major who had succeeded to the command of the 8th New Jersey had been killed.[5] In the division artillery Bramhall and Webber possessed enough guns between them for one battery only. These were given to Bramhall, and Webber was sent back to Yorktown for a new battery of twelve-pounders.[6]

The regulation reports on the battle came in from almost all brigade and regimental commanders by May tenth, and Hooker wrote up his own report for General Heintzelman.[7] In addition he issued an order

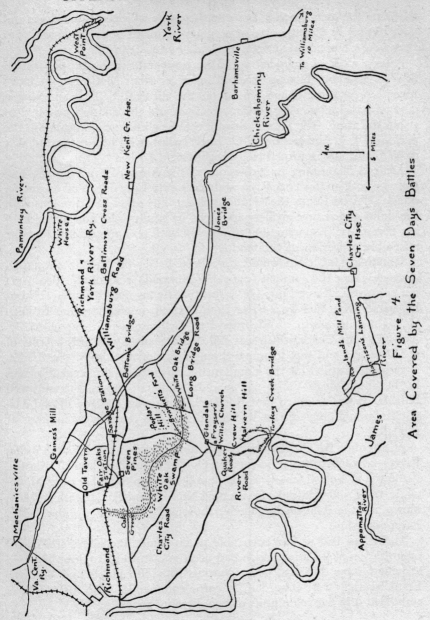

Figure 4.
Area Covered by the Seven Days Battles

thanking the men for their bravery; they were whipped three times and didn't know it. For the sake of accuracy he might better have said that they were whipped three times and didn't know it twice!

After a week of recuperation in the comparatively healthful location of Williamsburg, Hooker received an order from McClellan to move toward New Kent Court House on the fifteenth.[8] That morning a cavalry detachment relieved Grover's men and the division marched to rejoin the army. The Second Brigade set out with a new brigadier in the person of J. J. Abercrombie;[9] Colonel Taylor, who had commanded it at Williamsburg, returned to his regiment.

After Williamsburg four divisions of the Army of the Potomac had gone by boat up the York River and had successfully driven off an enemy attack at West Point, their landing place. The other five divisions with the trains and reserve artillery advanced by land up the northern side of the Peninsula. The marching troops met with no opposition except the miserable condition of the roads.

Whether McClellan would have been better off had he chosen to advance along the James River (or Richmond) side of the Peninsula is a controversial question. He claims that he favored this approach but his hands were tied by a letter from Stanton instructing him to keep his right wing north of Richmond to facilitate a junction with McDowell's First Corps, which was still theoretically a part of the Army of the Potomac and was to move through Fredericksburg.[10] The Union strategy also called for the simultaneous advance of three small armies in the Shenandoah Valley region under Generals Banks, Frémont and Shields. It was designed that this force along with McDowell and McClellan would converge on Richmond and end the war by summer at the latest.

At any rate, McClellan's army was now north of the Chickahominy River—a treacherous stream forty feet wide at low water and all over the Peninsula at high water—with Richmond safely on the other side. Meanwhile, the Confederates had evacuated Norfolk and Portsmouth and had blown up the *Merrimac*, thereby thoroughly opening up the James River approach.

McClellan had at last been able to do something about the corps-organization of his army which had been so disturbing to him. His two stanchest supporters had been Generals Fitz-John Porter and William Franklin; they were rewarded by corps commands. The infantry was reshuffled into five main units of two divisions each:

Second Corps: Sumner (Divisions of Sedgwick and Richardson)
Third Corps: Heintzelman (Divisions of Kearny and Hooker)
Fourth Corps: Keyes (Divisions of Couch and Casey)
Fifth Corps: Porter (Divisions of Morrell and Sykes)
Sixth Corps: Franklin (Divisions of W. F. Smith and Slocum)

A heavy rain fell the first day of Hooker's march to rejoin the army, but he was able to advance sixteen miles along the difficult roads. The next day New Kent Court House was reached and two days later the division moved on to Baltimore Cross Roads where they encamped for four days of heavy and continuous rain.[11] The weather was so bitter that McClellan, on the advice of the Medical Director of the Army, ordered an extra ration of one gill of whisky served daily to everyone.[12] On the twenty-third of May Hooker's division marched for Bottom's Bridge where it took position with the rest of the army on the north bank of the Chickahominy River.

On the next day the right wing of the army seized Mechanicsville six miles north of Richmond, while the left wing crossed the river and dislodged the enemy at Seven Pines, eight miles east of the city. Hooker's division supported the advance to Seven Pines, occupying some rifle pits and placing artillery in position. That night, however, it was recalled to the north side of the river.

On that same evening General McClellan received the bad news that the President had again postponed McDowell's supporting move. The great Confederate chieftain, Stonewall Jackson, was at that time threatening Washington with rapid marching and stern fighting in the Shenandoah Valley, completely neutralizing the value of the Federal forces in the valley. This made the administration uneasy—too uneasy to let go of McDowell's troops. It left Little Mac up in the air. He either had to keep all of his army north of the river to connect with McDowell and mark time until he arrived, or he had to divide his forces, leaving part to meet McDowell and the balance to advance on Richmond. He chose the latter strategy, even though he realized its danger.

On Sunday May twenty-fifth, the 1st and 3rd Brigades of Hooker's division again crossed the Chickahominy and marched south to Poplar Hill where they camped on the extreme left wing of the army. The Excelsior brigade was temporarily held at Bottom's Bridge where it had been joined by Daniel Sickles, its original commander. His fight for his brigadier general's star had finally succeeded, though by a close shave; on the thirteenth the Senate had confirmed it by a vote of 19-18.

General Abercrombie, who had not had time even to get acquainted with the Excelsiors, was reassigned elsewhere.¹³

At Poplar Hill the division remained for a week on fairly high ground surrounded by swampy country, the Chickahominy on one side and the great White Oak Swamp on the other. Rain fell heavily every day except one, and the health of the troops began to suffer severely from the continual exposure. Hooker could not count on more than 7,000 men available at any one time.

The Army of the Potomac engaged in continual reconnaissance in the direction of Richmond, remaining in its straddling position across the treacherous river. Two corps were now on the south side: Keyes had Casey's division three-fourths of a mile in front of Seven Pines with Couch in support; Heintzelman had Kearny's division at Savage Station and Hooker at Poplar Hill. Thus two-fifths of McClellan's army was on the same side of the river as the entire Confederate force, whose strength was unknown and grossly overestimated.

A terrible storm began on the afternoon of the thirtieth which further split the army as the river rose and almost completely carried away the connecting bridges. Mid-afternoon of the next day Hooker heard the rumble of artillery fire from the west, and soon orders came from corps headquarters to move part of his command toward the firing. The 5th and 6th regiments of Jersey Blues moved off to the Williamsburg Road about 3:30 P.M., followed by the Excelsior Brigade and Bramhall's and Osborn's batteries. The other two New Jersey regiments were detailed to guard the depot of supplies at Bottom's Bridge while the 1st Brigade was left to hold the division camp site at Poplar Hill.¹⁴ At Burnt Chimneys many fugitive Federal soldiers were encountered, and the troops were forced to halt. Colonel Starr, who commanded the New Jersey regiments in the absence of General Patterson,¹⁵ finally got started again but only by forcing his way through with bayonet and saber.¹⁶

General Hooker went on ahead to see what was up and found that the enemy had overrun Casey's division in front of Seven Pines on the Williamsburg Road and by six in the evening had pushed back the rest of Keyes' corps and two of Kearny's brigades well beyond this point. A disaster on the Union left wing had been averted only when General Sumner, redeeming his lapse at Williamsburg, had quickly crossed his corps over the Chickahominy to appear on the Confederate left flank and check their advance. The battle was then dying down, and it was certain that Hooker's men could not go into action until the next day.

At dusk they encamped behind the right flank of the Union rifle pits, straddling the Williamsburg Road.

At seven the next morning, Sunday, June second, Hooker advanced his available infantry regiments through the defensive line assumed by Keyes' corps at nightfall the previous day. His batteries were too mired down to join the movement but he was determined to show the mettle of his men and to demonstrate how a beleaguered comrade should be relieved. When a swamp was encountered and one of Casey's brigadiers told Hooker that his men could never get through it, the General replied, "Get out of the way. I have two regiments here that can go anywhere."[17] This was the type of expression that would endear any general to his troops. It was played up in the heroic battle accounts of the press.

The Jersey boys, with Hooker in the lead, ran into the enemy in a wooded position between the Williamsburg Road and the Richmond and York River Railway. They became rather heavily involved and he sent all his staff officers back to hurry up the Excelsiors. Sickles' men, however, had been detached from the column. General Heintzelman had sent them farther to the left and they were now advancing in the face of opposition on both sides of the Williamsburg Road.

Hooker, now reduced to the immediate command of but two regiments, enlisted the help of one of Kearny's brigades[18] and, by his own account after an hour's skirmish and a bayonet charge the enemy was thrown into wild confusion and fled. "At this moment," he says, "chivalry and rebellion presented a deplorable picture."[19] General Cadmus M. Wilcox, who commanded the two Confederate brigades opposed to Hooker and Sickles, spoils this account considerably by claiming that he retired in good order after receiving a command to do so, in writing, from his superior, General D. H. Hill.[20] This interpretation agrees more closely with the facts. Incidentally, the regiments under Wilcox happened to be part of the force that had driven Hooker's men at Williamsburg.

Firing ended along the entire field by noon. Sumner, who had also advanced a division, had met about the same reception as Hooker. The Jersey brigade had suffered seventy-four casualties and the Excelsiors seventy-nine. Six more officers had been wounded. This was the extent of Hooker's participation in the battle of Seven Pines or Fair Oaks. In his official report he was very warm in praise of the officers and men in the New Jersey regiments whom he was with continually, and he did not forget to commend the good work of Sickles and the 2nd Brigade.

The two-day battle had been far from decisive, and once more both sides claimed a stirring victory. The Confederacy gained a bit of ground but retired from it in less than twenty-four hours; it also suffered the greater number of casualties—6,134 as against 5,031.[21] The Union had foiled its opponent's objective, which had been to crush the exposed wing south of the Chickahominy. The wounding of Joe Johnston brought about what was perhaps the most important outcome of the battle—the accession of Robert E. Lee to the command of the Confederate forces. The battle was the biggest affair on the eastern front to date. Only Shiloh, fought two months before along the Tennessee River, had surpassed it in number of casualties. Hooker had played a small part but one for which he was gifted. Attack! This suited his temperament and allowed him to take advantage of his ability to inspire men to follow him. Let the engineers and McClellan worry about lines of defense and siege operations!

A few hours after his skirmish on June first, Hooker went over to Kearny's headquarters and discussed the possibility of proceeding straight into Richmond. It was an interesting meeting between the two most aggressive generals of the entire Army of the Potomac. While Hooker sat his horse talking excitedly, Kearny stood at his tent fly in short sleeves with a red bandana about his neck, gesturing violently with his one arm.[22] Both were incredulous at McClellan's failure to order a strong push toward Richmond by the three corps then on the south side of the Chickahominy. Each was by now entirely out of sympathy with his commander's "slows." Nine months later Hooker was to testify before the Committee on the Conduct of the War that a strong advance at this time would have taken Richmond.[23]

On the afternoon of the second he advanced with the Excelsiors and the two New Jersey regiments to the ground held by Casey at the start of the battle, recovering one Union gun and seizing many Confederate accouterments of war. At five o'clock he reported to Heintzelman that in front of Casey's old entrenchments was a swamp with two roads skirting it, one of which led to the railroad and the other to the James. He had gone up both roads for some distance without incident. It appeared from the information brought in that the enemy had stationed a regiment of cavalry and a brigade of infantry beyond these roads.[24] Hooker said in his testimony that his reconnaissance work had been stopped by a telegram from McClellan: "General Hooker will return from his brilliant reconnaissance. We cannot afford to lose his division." The General was insulted and later assured the Congressional Committee that he had no "expection" of being lost.[25] That night he brought most of his advanced regiments back to a point behind Casey's lines since the stench of dead horses prohibited a more advanced position.

The next day Grover's brigade came up from Poplar Hill and relieved the Excelsiors in the advanced works. The entire division was kept under arms, and no fires were permitted. The pickets engaged in much skittish shooting, adding to the state of alarm. Despite Hooker's talk with Kearny about the desirability of marching straight into Richmond, his actions indicated that he realized the enemy could not be taken lightly. The men were continually warned to be on the alert and no chances were taken of being caught by another impetuous attack such as Casey had suffered.

On the fourth Hooker felt more confident of his ability to hold his front-line position and relaxed precautions, allowing the men time to cremate the dead horses and to bury the many casualties of the battle fought three days before.[26] The position was thoroughly entrenched, Casey's old works were completed and new redoubts were built on the left by Kearny's division and on the right by Sumner's corps. Hooker was now confident, as usual, of his ability to hold the line. He told McClellan: "I can hold my position against one hundred thousand men."[27]

Nevertheless, the picket lines were too close for comfort. Skirmishing went on continually and repeated forays were made. Two brigades were always kept on duty, one on picket and one in the trenches, while the third brigade rested in camp. These duties were rotated, but the constant strain of the enemy shellfire, the severe storms, and the unhealthful sanitary conditions swelled the sick call to alarming proportions.[28] As one soldier put it, "We could not get a breath of fresh air, a drink of good water, or a sound night's rest."[29] A ration of whisky was served both morning and night to neutralize malaria and keep up morale.[30] There was little indication that the missionary work of last winter's Temperance League had been of lasting success.

Hooker's headquarters near the village of Fair Oaks were identified by a blue flag in imitation of the plain red flag which Kearny had adopted. For identification Kearny had also provided his soldiers with red patches to wear on their coats.[31] This was to be the beginning of the corps and division-badge plan which Hooker would popularize the following year.

From the tallest trees in the vicinity could be seen the spires of Richmond, a constant reminder of "so near and yet so far." Newsboys from the capital city of the Confederacy rubbed it in by regularly slipping into the lines with the latest editions of local papers.

During the month of June the army was stalemated in its unfortunate position, part on one side and part on the other side of the Chickahominy. The promise of reinforcements and the bad weather gave McClellan an excuse to mark time. Bridges were completed to connect the two wings, and entrenchments were strengthened. General Jeb Stuart of the Confederacy brightened an otherwise dull period with a successful cavalry raid around both wings.

There were many dispatches between McClellan and Stanton about reinforcement, authority over possible reinforcement and the co-operation of the administration. McClellan was outspoken and but slightly concealed his distrust. Stanton replied in the pretty forms of the day, protesting his friendship and trying to hide his lack of confidence and his intrigue against the general. In one unfortunate dispatch McClellan went on record as saying that he was opposed by 200,000 men. This was based on so-called "intelligence" reports. Any service of information which more than doubled the numbers of an antagonist would be an almost insurmountable handicap to a general and particularly so to one of naturally cautious instincts.

Nevertheless, reinforcements did arrive and McClellan did get control of the troops at Fortress Monroe as he had wished. Nine regiments were to come from this base and McCall's division of McDowell's corps arrived from Washington. Hooker naturally had no part in the haggling that went on between army headquarters and Washington, but he profited by the reinforcements from Fortress Monroe. The 3rd Brigade received the 2nd New York and the 1st Brigade the 16th Massachusetts. This latter regiment came up with full ranks and new uniforms, and General Grover wasted no time in testing its enthusiasm for fighting. On the eighteenth, along with a section of Bramhall's battery, it was sent to sound out the position and strength of the enemy on the right of Hooker's division between the Williamsburg Road and the railway. The 16th Massachusetts dashed forward, chasing the enemy pickets before them and stopping only when it encountered the main Confederate line. It withdrew when General Hooker gave the order. Its baptism of fire had caused fifty-nine casualties. The desired information was gained.

On the nineteenth Franklin's corps had been moved to the south side of the Chickahominy preparatory to an advance by the left wing of the entire army, now totaling about 115,000 men.[32] Only Porter's corps was

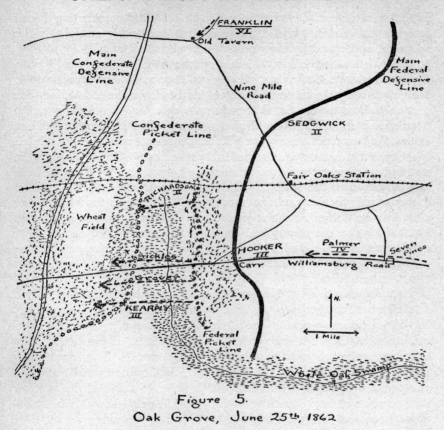

Figure 5.
Oak Grove, June 25th, 1862

still on the north side. McClellan was at last ready to drive the enemy back into the main line of works about Richmond. Franklin was to attack at Old Tavern, supported by the Second and Third Corps. On the evening of the twenty-fourth Sumner and Heintzelman were ordered to advance their picket lines as a preliminary move.[33] Since this would provoke a hot contest, the move necessarily was to be in force. At 8:30 P.M. Heintzelman sent for Hooker and outlined to him his part in the program.[34] It sounded fine. At last they were on the way to Richmond!

Early the next morning Hooker had Grover and Sickles place their entire brigades behind the picket line while the Jersey Blues, now under Colonel Joseph B. Carr of the 2nd New York,[35] were placed in reserve in the main defensive works. It was to be the third consecutive day of intermittent rain, but the skirmishers went out briskly at eight in the morning, undaunted by the gloomy forest ahead of them.

Sickles advanced on both sides of the Williamsburg Road with Grover to his left. Grover became engaged at once and Hooker rode up to see how fiercely the enemy was determined to hold the picket line. He met an officer of the 1st Massachusetts who had received a bullet through his mouth and could give no intelligible information. Then out of the forest came a captured Rebel lieutenant who jauntily saluted the General, a courtesy he immediately returned.[36] Grover's men were not finding their opponents in a retreating humor, and Hooker sent back to the reserve for the 5th New Jersey to help push the attack.

Apparently Sickles was also meeting stiff resistance for he had not closed up on Grover's right as planned. Hooker rode over to investigate and found that the enemy had concentrated a heavy fire on the right of the 2nd Brigade, and Sickles' attack was in grave danger of being completely checked. Hooker called up the 7th New Jersey to form on the threatened flank.

Then in unison all of Hooker's line, with Kearny in support on his left, advanced farther into the woods. At about eleven in the morning, Hooker came into possession of a telegram addressed to General Heintzelman from General Marcy of McClellan's staff: "If possible quickly withdraw your forces to your works of defense."[37] This completely baffled the General but had to be obeyed. Sickles too thought it was a mistake, for when he received Hooker's order to fall back he sent an aide to remonstrate. In answer Hooker could only show Marcy's telegram.[38] Sickles' brigade then fell back to the morning's picket line. Before Grover could be ordered back General Heintzelman came up and advised Hooker to let the rest of his men keep their positions if they could since McClellan was expected shortly and might possibly countermand the order. A fortunate lull in the battle occurred, and the advanced troops were allowed to hold on.

At one o'clock the Commanding General arrived and, after learning of the morning's success of the Third Corps, ordered the advance continued. Sickles' men were sent again into the forest with the 2nd New York in support. Heintzelman helped out by advancing a section of the corps reserve artillery under Captain De Russy. They opened with canister along the Williamsburg Road and, according to Hooker, "literally swept the jungle of rebels."[39] Palmer's brigade of the Fourth Corps then came up to support the batteries and to relieve Sickles who had suffered heavily.

During this time McClellan and his staff, with Heintzelman and Hooker, had been watching the battle's progress under a severe fire. An observer not friendly to Little Mac had to admit that everyone ducked except the Commanding General.[40] McClellan was well satisfied: an advanced position had been gained and it seemed to be securely held. His satisfaction, however, was short-lived, for at five o'clock he had to leave the field hurriedly in response to a telegram from his right wing. It said that the enemy was concentrating on the other side of the river, an indication that an aggressive move was in the air and that Robert E. Lee was not going to permit his new command to be slowly strangled in the defenses of Richmond.

Heintzelman's advanced line remained stable the rest of the day except for a sudden attack on the right of Kearny's brigade and Hooker's 5th New Jersey. That night, the twenty-fifth, Palmer's brigade took over all the positions which Hooker's men had won and they were permitted to withdraw to their camps.

The success of this reconnaissance or attempt to advance the Union picket line, known as the Battle of Oak Grove, is subject to argument. General Heintzelman, of course, claimed that it was a complete success and that the objective was attained. General Ambrose R. Wright of the Confederacy, whose brigade directly opposed Hooker, maintained that there was not one word of truth in the Federal claims.[41] The casualties were in favor of the Confederacy; the Federals had lost 626 men (half of the total belonging to Hooker), while the enemy's losses were but 441.

Hooker was well pleased with the work of his command, particularly the 1st Massachusetts which had gone forward through great natural obstacles in an unknown forest swamp and had fought courageously against an almost unseen enemy. He had much praise also for the skill of Sickles and Grover.[42] General McClellan, however, once more saw fit to give major credit to the men who had come to Hooker's support, namely De Russy's artillerists.[43] General Heintzelman was determined to give his subordinate his due and called attention to the "gallantry and good judgement displayed by General Hooker."[44]

This battle of Oak Grove has been almost forgotten in the annals of the Army of the Potomac, but it greatly enhanced the fighting reputation of Hooker and his division. It happened to be fought on the first day of that period which has become known as the Seven Days Battles, but it should not be considered as any part of that campaign. It did not alter in any way Lee's determination to go through with the offensive which he had planned and which was now gathering momentum.

Oak Grove closed the offensive phase of McClellan's Peninsula campaign and is a good point to note the contribution made by Hooker's division. The Army of the Potomac had fought two full-sized battles, Williamsburg and Fair Oaks, and many engagements, most notably the siege of Yorktown, West Point, Hanover Court House and Oak Grove. Casualties under fire ranged from 9,000 to 10,000; Hooker's division had lost an estimated 2,300 men, or about 25 percent of the total Federal casualties[45]—a very unbalanced loss for one of eleven divisions united in a common effort!

## CHAPTER VII

# THE CHANGE OF BASE

THE DAY after the engagement at Oak Grove, Hooker's men idled in their camps discussing the rumor that Stonewall Jackson, with his Army of the Shenandoah Valley, was on his way to join Lee and strike their comrades in blue across the river. In the late afternoon the rumble of artillery in the north verified this rumor. In the evening Hooker received a telegram from McClellan stating that the right wing of the army had been hotly engaged by the enemy in large force near Mechanicsville but had been successful. Hooker was to give the men the message that Porter had "whipped 'em on the right."[1]

Though this was literally correct—Porter had inflicted heavy losses on the Confederate opening attack—the force of Jackson's valley troops was yet to be felt. The retreat to the James River, which so quickly followed McClellan's pronouncement, made "Porter's whipped 'em on the right" a cry of derision in Hooker's division whenever an optimistic bulletin was received from headquarters.[2]

The next day, June twenty-seventh, was a day of concern to General Hooker. Although he was to claim that the portion of the army on the south side of the Chickahominy should have marched right into Richmond while Lee was north of it, at this time his dispatches to Heintzelman clearly indicate that he was concerned about a possible enemy advance on his front.[3]

The bothersome General Magruder was in charge opposite him and was again at work hoaxing his opponents, causing his 25,000 effectives between the main force of the Federals and Richmond to appear at least triple their true number. Hooker was taken in by the constant fusilades and the threatening artillery fire to the extent of calling for three brigades as reinforcements. His picket line was repeatedly broken and had to be re-formed. Fortunately, a brigade of Couch's division was serving with him and could be blamed for the front-line disorder.[4]

Meanwhile, north of the river General Porter's corps, with the assistance of one of Franklin's divisions, was putting up a determined fight at Gaines's Mill against greatly superior numbers. Jackson's men had made an unquestionable entrance on the stage and, with the majority of Lee's army, exerted sufficient pressure to force Porter to retire across the Chickahominy after dark. McClellan had been prepared to move his entire army to the south side of the river if this seemed advisable. As far back as June eighteenth he had made arrangements to change his base from White House on the York River to Harrison's Landing on the James. Lee's tactics compelled it, and the great "change of base" movement was on. It has been rudely termed a "retreat" by most critics.

The base of supplies was destroyed, the bridges over the river were burned as soon as Porter was across, the Fourth Corps was ordered back to cover the passage of the wagon trains to the James. Heintzelman was sent for on the night of the twenty-seventh and informed that his corps would help protect the movement from interference by the enemy on the Williamsburg Road. When he passed the word to Hooker and Kearny the two brigadiers exploded. The thought of retreat without the test of a general battle was too much, particularly for Kearny. In haste they rode over to McClellan's headquarters where Kearny insisted on being permitted to march into Richmond and at least rescue the 14,000 prisoners there, returning if he could not hold on. Hooker, who was Kearny's junior in rashness as well as rank, agreed that this could be done but suggested that another division should go along as support. Heintzelman also lent his voice to the proposal, but McClellan coldly refused. Kearny then gave the Commanding General as thorough a verbal beating as was possible short of inciting a court-martial.[5]

McClellan was undoubtedly sound in refusing to allow such an advance to be made by only two divisions; it was not his disposition to risk a larger force in a spectacular move the outcome of which was so unpredictable. Most critics are of the opinion that a determined advance toward Richmond at this time would have so upset Lee's plan of campaign that McClellan could have regained the position and prestige lost in the past few days, even though the actual capture of the Confederate capital was not possible.

On the twenty-eighth Hooker's men began to hear rumors that McClellan had given up, but the brigades continued to man the trenches in rotation, as had been the custom before the engagement of Oak Grove. In a thick fog early on the morning of the twenty-ninth Grover's brigade relieved the New Jersey boys up front and found that the artillery had already been withdrawn. Soon the pickets were called in and they were ordered to abandon the works. They were assembled in the Williamsburg Road and marched off after the rest of the division away from their objective. As they went through their camps they could see details busy slashing tents, burning supplies and pouring food stores on the ground. Hooker's men were thus introduced to the orgy of destruction and confusion which necessarily accompanies a retreating army.[6]

The General would long remember what he considered the needless loss of property. McClellan was slow—that was bad enough—but that he should order his large, well-equipped army to fall back without a fight to the finish was more than he could comprehend. In deep gloom he marched his men almost to Savage Station where Sumner and Franklin had halted their withdrawal to cover the retreat of the rest of the army across White Oak Swamp. Here Heintzelman placed his corps in line across the Williamsburg Road with Hooker's division on the right and Kearny on the left. By 11:00 A.M. the pursuing Confederates caught up and a lively artillery duel began. Hooker's men waited for the infantry attack, which all expected, but the enemy seemed to be concentrating on the right where the Second Corps was placed. At three in the afternoon Hooker was ordered to fall back to defend Savage Station since it was reported that the Confederates had already repaired a bridge over the Chickahominy and were advancing.[7] While Hooker was once more retiring his brigades, Heintzelman decided that Sumner and Franklin didn't need his help and he started his whole division across White Oak Swamp. This somewhat precipitate withdrawal prevented Hooker's men from taking part in the successful Union defensive action at Savage Station in the late afternoon. Turning to the south, they followed Kearny's division across the swamp at Brackett's Ford as night fell. By ten in the evening the corps had reached camp at the junction of the Brackett's Ford Road and the Charles City Road.

At daylight on Monday the thirtieth, Heintzelman informed Hooker that they were to defend the withdrawal of the trains and artillery down the Quaker Road which ran north and south from the Long Bridge Road to the James River. Kearny and Hooker mounted their horses and proceeded to reconnoiter what they both believed might be a decisive battleground. Less than a mile to the southeast on the Charles City Road they came to the important intersection of Glendale. Here they turned south down the Quaker Road passing Frayser's Farm and Willis Church. Noting that a road coming from the enemy's direction entered Quaker Road just north of the church, Hooker decided to post his division so as to prevent any interference along this route. Kearny agreed to form on Hooker's right.

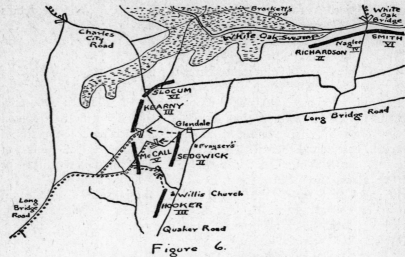

Figure 6.
Glendale, June 30, 1862

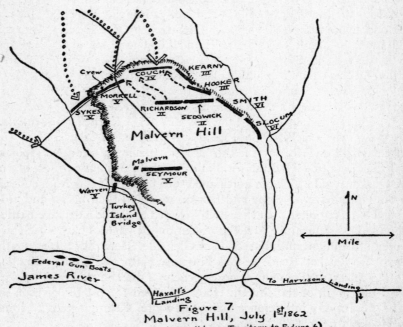

Figure 7.
Malvern Hill, July 1st 1862

(Figure 7 represents contiguous Territory to Figure 6)

━━━━ Federal Defensive Positions
ooo⟹ Confederate Attacks
--➤ Federal Counter-attacks

Apparently after this decision had been made Heintzelman found that General Slocum's division of the Sixth Corps had taken a good defensive position just north of him which covered any possible approach by the enemy from Brackett's Ford or the Charles City Road. He then decided to form his line on Slocum's left. Kearny was put in position connecting with Slocum, but Hooker's men had already moved back to the Quaker Road. Since General McCall conveniently brought up his division of the Fifth Corps at this time, he was placed on Kearny's left thus separating the two divisions of the Third Corps. Hooker was now several hundred yards to the left and rear of McCall.[8]

By noon the battle line had been formed, obstructions placed on the roads of approach, and the three advanced divisions (Slocum, Kearny and McCall) were in readiness to throw back any attempt to pierce the Federal line of retreat. Meanwhile Hooker had stationed his men in front of the Quaker Road with Grover's brigade on the right, Carr in the center and the Excelsiors on the left. The batteries had been sent on to the James River according to directions from headquarters.[9]

Hooker now had time to check the positions of the adjoining divisions. To his surprise, on his right he found Sedgwick's division of Sumner's corps occupying the cleared field where he thought Kearny was to be. He next discovered that McCall was on his right front. This was his first knowledge that Sedgwick and McCall were on the field and his first realization that he was not in the advanced line. He still was well posted, however, to defend the Quaker Road and decided to keep his men where they were, in the shade of the forest adjoining the road. A stream of army wagons rattled continuously down the road in the rear hurrying to escape the converging columns of Confederate infantry which were momentarily expected.

Just after noon the enemy on the other side of the swamp to the northeast began a heavy cannonading against the Federal force which was holding the White Oak bridge area. About 2:30 artillery fire broke out on the Charles City Road where Slocum blocked the way. Hooker rode out to discuss the impending attack with General McCall and to speculate on the failure of the Confederate infantry to show up.[10] The speculation was cut short for at three o'clock McCall's pickets were driven in and soon the enemy appeared in force down the Long Bridge Road. In the absence of anyone in supreme command on the field, McCall was left to face the superior numbers of the enemy almost alone until about 5:00 when a strong attack pierced his lines and his left brigade retreated in disorder. Two brigades of Sedgwick's division and Hooker's

16th Massachusetts stopped the momentum of the Confederate drive[11] and diverted it northward against Kearny.[12]

In the early evening Hooker ordered out the 1st Massachusetts and the 26th Pennsylvania to clear away the remaining Confederates on their front. The 1st Massachusetts unfortunately worked themselves into a pocket of enemy troops and only the ability of General Grover, who advanced with them, prevented their capture.

The rest of Hooker's division was not threatened although at one point Sickles sent word to Hooker that the foe was preparing to turn his left. This situation failed to develop, for he soon suggested to Hooker the possibility of advancing his brigade on the enemy's right flank.[13]

By nightfall the Confederates held a major part of the battlefield known as Glendale or Frayser's Farm, but they had failed to break through to the Quaker Road. The Union trains were now safely by and the army was no longer in danger of being divided. It was a sad day for General Robert E. Lee, who never again was to have so favorable an opportunity to wreck the Army of the Potomac. The resistance of McCall's division, plus the efforts of the supporting brigades, had been important; but of even greater consequence had been the failure of Lee's subordinates to co-ordinate their attack. Hooker had not been a decisive factor in the fight, his losses amounting to only 192 men, but he was to receive praise long denied him by McClellan.[14] Generals Sumner and Heintzelman also were to give him foremost credit for saving the day.[15] His efforts might have been spectacular had he believed it feasible to follow Sickles' suggestion and thrown his two inactive brigades on the right flank of the played-out Confederate advance. He chose, however, to follow his orders, which were to cover the Quaker Road.

That night Hooker held his position until the rest of the army had left for Malvern Hill where McClellan was next to resist the enemy's push. It was a sleepless night, for the cries of the wounded rent the air, and soon after daylight the division took up the march down the Quaker Road. On arriving at Malvern Hill Hooker met one of Heintzelman's staff officers who directed him to place his division on the right center of the defensive line. Kearny was on his immediate left and Sumner's corps occupied his right and rear.[16] By ten that morning he was ready for anything, with Grover's brigade on the right, Carr on the left and Sickles in reserve behind Grover. Two batteries were placed on a rise slightly to the rear and the other two batteries were held in reserve.[17]

Hooker was really in a first-class defensible position. The ground sloped gradually away from him down to Western Run in the direction from which the enemy would come. If he were attacked he could not lack support, as almost the entire army had formed in close order on both sides of him and in plain sight on Malvern Hill or the adjoining Crew's Hill.

In the late morning the advance guard of the enemy appeared in the woods along the Quaker Road and brought a battery into the field at the base of the rise of ground across the creek opposite Hooker's front. The fire was too accurate for comfort, the first shot landing almost in the midst of a group of officers conversing with the General. Captain Beam, commanding the 2nd New Jersey Battery, was killed. Hooker immediately had the battery wheeled into position and the enemy was sent back into the woods on the gallop.[18]

Other enemy guns were soon placed in position and artillery skirmishing continued at a range of 1,500 yards without further effect as far as Hooker was concerned.[19] Meanwhile, the infantry enjoyed comparative rest and a cool breeze that counteracted the summer heat. The men took turns piling the undergrowth into a breastwork and running to a clear cool spring back up the hill.[20] Realizing how favorable their position was, they were eager for the enemy to try their mettle.

On the Union left artillery fire had been heavier and finally at about five o'clock the Confederate infantry there sprang to the attack. The massed Federal artillery created a slaughter pen on the slopes of Crew Hill and the entrenched Union infantry was not seriously threatened. Repeated attacks to the left of Hooker caused General Fitz-John Porter, who had charge of the defense, to send to Heintzelman for a brigade in case the seemingly hopeless but valiant enemy efforts pierced the foremost line. Heintzelman relayed the order to Hooker, and Sickles' brigade was sent at sunset to the left center where they relieved three of Couch's regiments in the front line. Sickles' efforts in repelling the final attack cost him sixty-nine men.[21]

By nightfall the Confederate piecemeal attacks had been thoroughly crushed. Casualties were severe and their last attempt to destroy McClellan's army had ended in failure. Lee had permitted part of his army to destroy themselves against an impregnable position.

Hooker played a minor part in the battle but this did not hurt him as far as publicity was concerned. The New York *Times* had delegated a correspondent to stick with his division, the word having got around that where Hooker was the fighting was fiercest. The correspondent had to make a good story and reported that the Excelsiors and Jersey Blues fought with so much courage and determination that they decided the fate of the battle and of the Army of the Potomac.[22] This was pure hokum but helped to develop the reputation of Hooker's as the "Fighting Division."[23]

The newspapers were spending big money on coverage of the war, and the correspondents were expected to produce something interesting every day.[24] This was responsible for many of the excessively heroic accounts of generals with "newspaper appeal." The generous extension of hospitality to a correspondent who would "plug" hard for the donor was often the foundation of such publicity. Hooker soon appreciated and took advantage of this practice. All his early efforts in the war were recorded in the pages of a favorable press.

Despite the sound thrashing which had just been inflicted upon the enemy at Malvern Hill, McClellan believed it wise to retire eight miles farther to Harrison's Landing along the James River where the gunboats and supplies were ready at hand.[25] At three o'clock in the morning of July second Hooker's old brigade and the Jersey Blues continued the retreat southward in a heavy rain. It was the most difficult march of all, for the men finally realized that they were not engaged in a great tactical operation which would end in a quick turn on the pursuer but that they were hurrying to the shelter of the gunboats. This was an open admission of the loss of the campaign despite their recent successes.

Sickles' brigade, which had been detached from Hooker during the battle, also left the front in the early hours of the morning and reported to him at Harrison's Landing. The division occupied an area on the left center of the Union position where the enemy would most likely attack if he saw fit to repeat the Malvern Hill experience. The Union camp around the landing was thoroughly entrenched, the front being a line roughly five miles long on heights two miles from the river. The left and right wings were retarded and based on creeks flowing into the James.[26] Lee, of course, pursued the Federals from Malvern Hill, but a few days of hovering around their new defensive position convinced him that it would be foolish to attack McClellan again. Most of the Southern army returned to the vicinity of Richmond, leaving cavalry patrols to watch the enemy.

Several days after their arrival at the James River position Hooker's men moved into a permanent camp on a slight elevation west of Rowland's Mill Pond. After the defensive works had been completed the soldiers' duties were light, consisting only of an occasional review or round of picketing. The season was excessively hot, however, and the camp was a sand oven almost without tree or bush. Flies were an extreme annoyance to both man and horse. The animals did so poorly because of their constant stomping and moving about that they might as well have been engaged in an active campaign. The pond near by furnished relief, however, and wells were dug for pure drinking and cooking water.[27]

On the Fourth of July the Commanding General ordered a salute fired at noon from the headquarters of each army corps, followed by the playing of national airs. That afternoon he rode around assuring the soldiers that everything was all right, that reinforcements were on the way, and that they were all to enjoy the rest they had earned. On Tuesday the eighth, President Lincoln came down to see about the condition of the army and with McClellan, Hooker and other generals rode through the camps. He was greeted enthusiastically by the men, and the bands played "Hail the Chief."[28] Another visitor was George Wilkes, editor and proprietor of the New York *Spirit of the Times.* He had known Hooker before the war and on this visit he spent much time at his headquarters where Phil Kearny joined them in denouncing McClellan. *The Spirit of the Times,* which styled itself "The American Gentleman's Newspaper, A Chronicle of the Turf, Field, Sports, Literature and the Stage," was very hard on Little Mac thereafter.[29]

In his spare time Hooker made out reports on the recent battles, one of which led to a many-worded controversy. The rush of McCall's routed brigade through his lines at Glendale had nettled the General considerably and he took the opportunity, in his report on that battle, to castigate McCall's men unmercifully.

"Meanwhile the enemy's attack had grown in force and violence and and after an ineffectual effort to resist it, the whole of McCall's division was completely routed, and many of the fugitives rushed down the road on which my right was resting, while officers took to the cleared fields, and broke through my lines, from one end of them to the other, and actually fired on and killed some of my men as they passed. Conduct more disgraceful was never witnessed on a field of battle. At first I was apprehensive that the effect would be disastrous on my command, and was no little relieved when this herd of human beings had passed my lines."[30]

McCall had suffered the inconvenience of being captured that afternoon, but four months later when he heard of this slander of his men's honor he began to collect testimony to refute it. Hooker finally changed his report, giving as his reason the good work of McCall's men at a later battle, but he never admitted that his original report was in error.[31]

As usual, he was concerned about his personal advancement. The Senate had been promoting corps commanders of the Army of the Potomac and he had hope of being jumped to a major general of Volunteers. He had been told by McClellan that he was being recommended for such a promotion and that he might possibly be placed in command of a corps. This stirred his all-consuming ambition and also led him to soften temporarily his criticism of McClellan. In a letter to Senator Nesmith he declared that McClellan had suffered severely because of the shortcomings of his corps commanders—the very ones who were now being promoted. Hooker was bitter about it: ". . . if these officers are still to be imposed upon him [McClellan] God help him and this army. . . . I will sooner dig potatoes or cut down trees than belong to any army in which all these officers exercise commands." He grew even warmer as he wrote on. "If I cannot be placed upon the same footing of other officers of the Army the sooner I quit it the better. I will not fight their battles for them with the doors to promotion closed on me." Letters on the same subject were dispatched to several other senators.[32]

Only one reorganizational problem worried him and this was the skeleton appearance of the Excelsior regiments. He believed that for the good of the service the five regiments should be reduced to two and he recommended this to General Heintzelman, who approved. McClellan, however, felt that this should clear through Sickles, the organizer of the brigade. Sickles was away on recruiting service and when consulted later asked that consolidation be postponed because he was sure he could fill his regiments.[33]

General Patterson had returned to take over his Jersey Blues and on July ninth the 115th Pennsylvania was added to his brigade. Considerable friction had arisen in Patterson's absence. Colonel Starr of the 5th New Jersey had protested to Hooker that the Brigade Quartermaster and Surgeon were undermining his discipline.[34] There is no indication that Hooker prosecuted the case and the Quartermaster was later to write very kindly of the General.[35]

A few cases of discipline arose, most important of which were the arrests of Captain Webber, of the Artillery, and Lieutenant Colonel Van Dyke, commanding the 26th Pennsylvania. The artillerist had appeared in the camp of Fitz-John Porter in a state of gross intoxication and was locked up.[36] On the bright side was the apparent settlement of the Hall-

Potter feud. On June eighteenth when Colonel Hall was called upon to mention officers of worth in his regiment, H. L. Potter headed the list. General Sickles recommended both of them highly.

Social life at Harrison's Landing was not forgotten—at least by the officers. Generals Kearny and Sickles were confirmed party-givers and possessed more means to entertain than many of their colleagues. At one affair attended by a number of generals and their staff officers, it is reported that Hooker and his friend Kearny were foremost when the whisky and wine were turned out.[37] Perhaps one of these celebrations was occasioned by the promotion of the two fighting brigadiers to the rank of major general of Volunteers. Hooker's appointment was received the last week of July and was dated July fourth. It was subsequently dated back to May fifth in recognition of the Battle of Williamsburg.[38]

The officers and men of his division celebrated his promotion on August first. The musicians were assembled en masse at headquarters and played patriotic airs. The Chief Commissary had placed 200 candles in the branches of surrounding trees, the effect of which when lighted was said to be "surpassingly beautiful."[39]

The month of July was a quiet one for the Army of the Potomac. It was not disturbed by Lee until the last day of the month when he posted a group of batteries on the south side of the James River opposite the Federals. In the early hours of August first a cannonading began, directed at the camps and the shipping at the landing. The Federal gunboats before long succeeded in driving off the enemy batteries and McClellan subsequently seized Coggin's Point whence the fire had come.[40]

Meanwhile he had been forwarding to Washington his usual pleas for reinforcements and had been expounding on the James River as the true base of operations for the advance on Richmond. On July thirtieth General Henry Halleck, who had recently been placed in supreme command of all Federal armies in the field, wired McClellan that the enemy was reported to be evacuating Richmond and suggested that a force be sent out to check the accuracy of this.[41] McClellan straightway chose Hooker's division to do the checking. Fighting Joe had been impatient for a fight for some time. According to a reporter on the New York *Herald,* "He felt that something should be done to show the world that we have got a live army on the Peninsula."[42] Hooker believed that Malvern Hill could be retaken despite its strength and had submitted a plan to headquarters.

For the venture Hooker was also to have at his disposal some of Pleasonton's cavalry and two batteries of horse artillery. It was to be a surprise advance at night by a circuitous route approaching the enemy in the rear. The expedition set out from camp on the late afternoon of August second, but the guides furnished proved unusually incompetent and progress was so slow that Hooker realized it would be impossible to surprise the enemy by daybreak. With admirable forbearance he decided to return his force to camp.[43]

Two days later the project was tried again on a larger scale. Sedgwick's division of the Second Corps and all of Pleasonton's brigade of cavalry were this time included in the party which followed Hooker from camp in the late afternoon. The cavalry took the lead with the horse batteries, Hooker's division and Sedgwick's men in that order. This time there was no mistake about the roads taken. The people encountered along the route were held temporarily to keep them from passing on word of the expedition, and Hooker issued strict orders against the use of fires or the making of any loud noises.[44]

The approach to Malvern Hill was up a back way leading into the Quaker Road just north of Willis Church.[45] At 11:00 P.M. Hooker called a four-hour halt as they were nearing the church. Just before sunrise the advance headed back south on the Quaker Road stirring up the Confederate pickets. The Federals followed in quick pursuit up the slope leading to Malvern Hill. The enemy artillery was on the alert, however, and proceeded to open up effectively on the men approaching their rear. The surprise had not been so complete as Hooker had hoped for. He nervously sat his favorite white horse on the road near the Crew House directing his batteries and placing his infantry—Grover on the right and the Excelsiors (again under Colonel Taylor) on the left.

Apparently his plan was for Patterson to take the 3rd Brigade well to the right to close the River Road, thus trapping the Confederate force on the hill. But Patterson was indisposed that morning. According to the Reverend Warren H. Cudworth, Chaplain of the 1st Massachusetts, he had "admitted an enemy into his mouth which had stolen away his brains."[46] This Shakespearian reflection on Patterson's inability to handle his liquor is substantiated by Colonel Carr's report which, although deleted from the *Official Records,* is among the Hooker Papers. Colonel Carr refers to Patterson's erratic commands and disappearance from the field after the vicinity of Malvern Hill was reached. By the time Hooker had relieved Patterson and put Carr in command of the Jersey Brigade it was too late to cut off the Confederates. It is doubtful that it could have been done, anyway, for the enemy force, consisting of a battery and a regiment of cavalry, did not tarry long in the trap.

At any rate, Hooker easily took over his objective, Malvern Hill, and the cavalry was sent off to capture the stragglers. Most of Sedgwick's division was held in the rear to guard the approaches from Glendale and the north.[47] McClellan and his staff came up at noon and spent the rest of the day riding around the scene of the last battle of the "Seven Days" with Joseph Hooker.[48] The soldiers busied themselves by throwing up superficial defenses in case the enemy returned in force and by repairing the Turkey Creek Bridge on the direct route to Harrison's Landing. Well pleased with Hooker's direction of the expedition, McClellan ordered up to his support two brigades of infantry under General Abercrombie.

When Lee received reports from his cavalry on Hooker's recapture of Malvern Hill he dispatched three divisions to checkmate what might be a dangerous move by the cautious McClellan. On August sixth these divisions drove in Hooker's pickets and the stage was set for a second battle of Malvern Hill the following day. But it was not to be. McClellan had received orders from General Halleck on the morning of the fourth to remove the Army of the Potomac from the Peninsula and to take it to Aquia Creek. He had protested bitterly against this serious mistake and hoped that if he showed some sign of life the order would be rescinded. When he got back to headquarters he wired Hooker that other dispositions were being made to support him.[49] The war administration refused to reconsider the withdrawal order, and McClellan was curtly told to follow instructions. The night of the sixth Hooker's force was recalled and he returned from another promising venture without the satisfaction of a real test of strength. Total casualties in his biggest command up to that date were 7 killed, 35 wounded and 11 missing.[50]

Before the Congressional Committee on the Conduct of the War, Hooker told a story (which cannot be substantiated) to the effect that he went to McClellan on the Sunday after he had received orders to abandon Harrison's Landing and urged him to attack Richmond with the force then on hand; if he were unsuccessful it would probably cost him his head, but he "might as well die for an old sheep as for a lamb." By Hooker's account an order was issued to the entire army to be ready to move at two the next afternoon but the order was countermanded before then.[51]

McClellan went ahead with his preparations to leave the Peninsula—a move which brought joy not only to those conducting the war in Washington but also to General Lee. Lee was struggling with the problem of how to keep enough force at hand to hold McClellan and still release enough men to overpower a new Federal army under General John Pope organized from the scattered units serving in the Shenandoah Valley and around Washington. McClellan's departure would simplify the problem. The obvious strategy would be to take the Army of Northern Virginia up to whip Pope before McClellan could reinforce him.

The Federal sick and wounded were sent off by steamer and the Fifth Corps began the great withdrawal on August fourteenth. The next day the Third Corps left its James River camp, marching west to Charles City Court House unmolested. On the sixteenth they turned north, stopping just short of Jones Bridge across the Chickahominy. A long march the next day brought them to their old stamping ground, the Williamsburg Road. There was a short stop just past Williamsburg where the division had received its baptism of fire three months before. Yorktown was reached the nineteenth. Two days later Hooker's men began the water trip back to northern Virginia.[52]

Fighting Joe left the Peninsula with the honors he coveted. He had established himself before the country and to the satisfaction of most of his superiors and to all of his men as a fighting officer, capable of handling at least a division in battle. Heintzelman, his immediate superior, could not say too much for his ability. McClellan had reported very favorably on his work at Oak Grove and Glendale and his reconnaissance to Malvern Hill. Still, McClellan leaves the impression that he was afraid of Hooker's rashness. To quote a staff officer: "Let Hooker go where he will, he invariably meets the enemy, and always in superior force."[53]

One of Hooker's admirers serving in his division pulled out all the stops:

"Hooker . . . was always present on the field, alert and vigilant, conspicuously mounted on a white horse—with flashing eyes, florid face, and high shirt collar, that soon wilted down when we got engaged—but as cool and collected under fire as if directing a parade or a picnic. . . . He always seemed to know exactly what to do and when to do it. . . ."[54]

According to a reporter of the New York *Times* Hooker's men were proud of his reputation and so attached to him they would follow him anywhere.[55]

The press back home reacted to his work on the Peninsula in lighter vein:

"Hooker's military genius and accomplishments together with his bravery and good looks, ought to secure for him one of the noblest and handsomest of the loyal daughters of the land."[56]

## CHAPTER VIII

## SECOND BULL RUN

ON AUGUST 23, 1862, the fleet bearing Hooker's veterans of the Peninsula anchored in the Potomac River off Aquia Creek. It had been intended that the division would disembark here and then march to the aid of Pope's Army of Virginia, but after some delay orders were changed and the fleet went on up the river to Alexandria. The next morning the troops made camp three miles west of the town where they waited their turn to clamber aboard the cars which would take them down the Orange and Alexandria Railway to a juncture with Pope.[1]

Colonel Hermann Haupt, in charge of railway transportation, met Hooker and they agreed that the division would leave that evening, if possible.[2] The General decided to spend the day in Washington, however, and when Haupt had completed his arrangements for transporting the Hooker division he could not find its commander.[3] A wire to P. H. Watson, the Assistant Secretary of War, asked him to locate Hooker. Watson replied that he would send to Willard's Hotel to see whether or not Hooker were there but if he did not turn up within an hour Haupt should put the second-in-command in charge of the movement. Watson added this advice: "Be patient as possible with the generals. Some of them will trouble you more than they will the enemy."[4] These words were unnecessarily rough on Hooker, whose work had been outstanding on the Peninsula, but they had application in other cases. Hooker's absence plus inefficient loading in the available cars caused delays which held back the departure of the last brigade until the twenty-sixth,[5] but by that evening all the regiments had reached Warrenton Junction.[6]

General John Pope had been brought from the West, where he had won several minor victories, and was placed over generals who were his superior in age, experience and qualifications. He was handsome, dashing and soldierly and had bravely told all and sundry what he intended to do to the enemy,[7] but he had not fared too well to date. He had taken one of the overland routes to Richmond, using the Orange and Alexandria Railway as his supply line. On August ninth Stonewall Jackson had checked his advance in the fierce battle of Cedar Mountain. A week later Jackson was joined by part of Lee's army which was no longer

needed before Richmond to watch McClellan. Pope, fearing the odds
were against him, retreated behind the Rappahannock River. Lee, who
had by now assumed the command, then indulged in his favorite offensive maneuver of turning his enemy's position: he sent Jackson's men on
a wide flanking movement aimed at getting around the Federal right.

Only a few hours after Hooker's 3rd Brigade passed through Manassas
Junction Jackson's men broke the railroad at this point, completing their
turning movement and landing themselves fully in the Federal rear. Pope
then determined to abandon his position along the Rappahannock, to
throw his whole force in between Lee and Jackson, and to crush Jackson
before Lee could reach the field. At this time Pope's army of three corps
under Franz Sigel, Nathaniel Banks and Irwin McDowell had been joined
by Reynolds' division, Heintzelman's and Porter's corps from the Peninsula, and Reno's corps from the North Carolina coastal operations.

To cut off Jackson most of the available force was sent off toward
Gainesville, but Hooker's division was chosen for the more immediate
job of flushing the great Stonewall out of Manassas Junction and of
restoring railway connections with the balance of McClellan's troops sup-

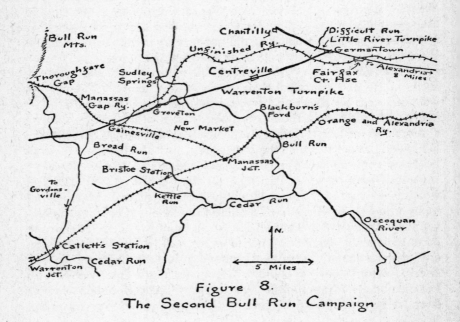

Figure 8.
The Second Bull Run Campaign

posedly hurrying from Alexandria.[8] This was a venture to Hooker's satisfaction. On the Peninsula he hadn't had a chance to oppose the highly
touted Confederate chieftain; there was no doubt in his mind who
would come out winner in a fair contest between his fighting division
and Jackson's boys in butternut.

The division started out in the early morning of August twenty-
seventh[9] accompanied by two and one-half regiments of Kearny's men
under General John C. Robinson.[10] The column moved toward the
northeast minus the divisional artillery, their horses and wagons, and with
only forty rounds of ammunition per man. Little equipment had arrived
from Alexandria, and even the field and staff officers were afoot. The day
was hot, but Hooker and Pope, who had remained with this small frac-
tion of his army, pushed the march rapidly along the railway and the dirt
road paralleling it. At Catlett's Station the lack of artillery was remedied
when two batteries from other units reported to Hooker.[11]

By noon the enemy outposts and a section of artillery were encountered, but skirmishers cleared the way. About two o'clock Kettle Run
was crossed and the enemy found in force. Line of battle was formed
with Grover's brigade on the right side of the railroad and Carr with four
of his regiments astride it. General Hooker personally detached Carr's
other two regiments, the 6th and 7th New Jersey, and advanced with
them, deploying to the left where a slight rise offered a vantage point.
Robinson's regiments also went to the left where they supported the two
Federal batteries. The Excelsiors formed behind Carr and went forward
with him protecting his flanks. Grover was stopped by the enemy's dispositions but the 2nd and 3rd Brigades, assisted by a battery which
Hooker advanced, did the business. After an hour's fighting the Confederates retired in good order having inflicted 300 casualties on Hooker's
determined division.[12]

Grover's brigade led the pursuit through the enemy's abandoned position capturing many wounded. A show of strength on the far side of
Broad Run and lack of Federal ammunition caused a halt at dusk. That
night a brilliant glow from the east made it apparent that the Confederate raiders were burning all the stores they could not carry away. The
division encountered by Hooker had been interested only in checking
any possible interference with the work of destruction.

This engagement near Bristoe Station enhanced the reputation of
Hooker and his men in the eyes of the Commanding General. Years later
Pope wrote:

"As I saw him [Hooker] that afternoon on his white horse riding in rear of his line of battle, and close up to it, with the excitement of battle in his eyes, and that gallant and chivalric appearance which he always presented under fire, I was struck with admiration. As a corps commander, with his whole force operating under his own eye, it is much to be doubted whether Hooker had a superior in the army."[13]

It began to look as though Hooker's men could not be kept from fighting: only three days off the boat and they had struck the first counterblow to Lee's campaign![14]

The division remained in camp at Broad Run that night. At eight the next morning their fighting companions of the Peninsula, Kearny's division, marched up the railroad in pursuit of Jackson. Pope had decided to throw more strength toward Manassas Junction, and Kearny and Reno had been redirected there. In the early afternoon Hooker's men proceeded on up the railroad, passing scenes of destruction visited on the Federal service of supply the day before. Jackson had retired northward that morning and was steadily withdrawing from Pope's trap. The vicinity of the old battlefield of Bull Run was reached before dark and debris remaining from that engagement reminded three of Hooker's veteran regiments of the old days when the war would be "over in a few weeks."[15] They bivouacked near Blackburn's Ford but the rumble of artillery from the west indicated that their rest might be short. Part of the force closing in on Jackson from Gainesville had encountered the Stonewall north of the Warrenton Pike at Groveton. One of the most stubborn fights of the war had occurred with neither side gaining an advantage.

Hooker received orders on the morning of the twenty-ninth to support General Kearny who was advancing on Jackson from the east. A march of ten miles through Centreville, speeded by the sound of constant firing, brought the division to the battlefield by noon. Here Hooker found Kearny's division on the right of a Federal line with Sigel's corps in the center and Reynolds' division of Pennsylvania Reserves on the left. Reno was coming up, but the remaining two corps of the Army of Virginia and Porter's corps of the Army of the Potomac were not in evidence. John Pope was not on hand, either. In his anxiety to trap Jackson and in his fear that the foe would try to get away without fighting, Pope had so scattered his forces that now, with the enemy at bay, he was busy hurrying up enough men to insure success. Jackson was posted along an unfinished railroad cut north of Groveton where he had spent the morning skir-

GENERAL
DARIUS N. COUCH

GENERAL
JOHN SEDGWICK

GENERAL
OLIVER O. HOWARD

GENERAL
HENRY W. SLOCUM

GENERAL DANIEL BUTTERFIELD

GENERAL
DANIEL SICKLES

GENERAL
ALFRED PLEASONTON

mishing with Sigel while awaiting the arrival of Lee and the rest of the army.

Hooker's 1st Brigade was temporarily placed under the orders of General Sigel by Pope's direction, when he finally arrived, and they marched down the Warrenton Turnpike almost to Groveton where they filed into a field north of the road. The 1st Massachusetts was soon sent up to support the front line.[16] Carr's brigade was stationed in support of a battery in Sigel's rear. Shortly the call came for two regiments and up went the 6th and 7th New Jersey. The Excelsiors were a little late in arriving and remained in reserve. By two in the afternoon Carr had advanced the rest of his brigade to the front line and was severely engaged for two hours when General Hooker directed the Excelsiors to relieve him.[17]

Meanwhile, the 1st Brigade had made one of the finest bayonet charges of the war on Jackson's strong position. Grover's men broke the Confederate line and swept across the railroad just to the right of the Groveton-Sudley Spring Road. Enemy reserves drove them back after a terrific hand-to-hand combat. In twenty minutes the 1st Brigade suffered 486 casualties out of approximately 1,500 men.[18] It had been a desperate venture and probably a foolish one. It is said that Hooker protested the order for the charge.[19] He later referred to it as "a useless slaughter of my men to attempt to win a position which was of no military value when it was gained."[20]

The 1st Brigade reorganized in support of Sigel's batteries but they were through for the day. Shortly after relieving Carr the Excelsiors advanced but the stampede of a regiment on the left gave the enemy an opening, through which they counterattacked, breaking up Colonel Taylor's line and forcing the Excelsiors to retreat. General Hooker directed them to an open field a half-mile to the rear where the 3rd Brigade had gone into camp and where the battered 1st Brigade followed.[21]

When the shooting ended that night nothing had been accomplished for the Union cause. Bungling management, misdirected marches and piecemeal attacks had been the order of the day. After the repulse of Hooker's men Kearny had made one of his driving attacks on Jackson's left and had temporarily broken through, but his force was not quite large enough to hold the advantage.[22] On the other end of the Federal line McDowell had arrived at sunset and sent a division against the Confederate right only to find that Lee's "old war horse," James E. Longstreet, and his fresh troops had joined Jackson and were spoiling for a fight.

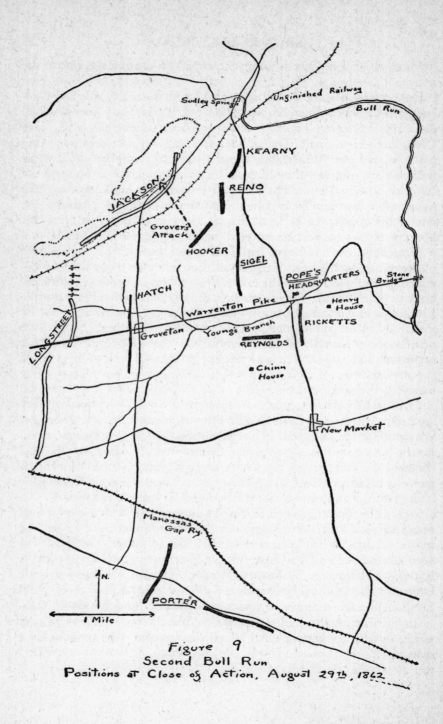

Figure 9
Second Bull Run
Positions at Close of Action, August 29th, 1842

The day's action had been unsatisfactory for Hooker. His division had been split and sent in by brigades, some not even under his direction. They had suffered heavily and nothing had been gained; only Grover's charge was as distinguished a performance as the Hooker division could have been expected to give.

As usual, a good part of the Federal Army had not been engaged. General Pope, of course, believed that the reason for this had been lack of co-operation by certain subordinates rather than his faulty dispositions. Porter's corps had not participated in the fighting, and Pope was to accuse the General of purposely withholding his support. This charge culminated in court-martial proceedings and the cashiering of a worthy officer.[23] Bank's corps had not been engaged, for it had been stationed at Warrenton Junction to guard and repair the railway.

Erroneous information to the effect that the enemy was retreating[24] and that there was a possibility of reinforcement from the balance of the Army of the Potomac encouraged Pope to hold his ground. This proved a mistake. His effective force, which had once totaled 63,000, was in great part exhausted and hungry. Many units were so shattered they were useless as a striking force. Pope didn't realize that the balance of Lee's army had arrived and was then being formed for an attack on the Federal left.[25]

On the thirtieth Pope planned to drive in Jackson by a forceful move but when he struck just after noon Longstreet's artillery was ready and the Federal lines were chewed up by an enfilading fire from south of the Warrenton Pike. Next came a powerful sweep by Lee's strong right wing and by dusk Pope's scattered army was driven from the field. General Hooker took little part in the action until the late afternoon. His division was held in reserve, being shifted from the center to the right and back to the left, but by six o'clock it was on its way to Centreville with the rest of the defeated army.[26] Hooker, however, remained on the field where he made himself extremely useful in extricating the battered Union forces. He took over the direction of King's division which had that day been attached to Porter's corps. King had taken sick and his successor, Hatch, was wounded. With this force and Hazlett's battery of the 5th United States Artillery, Hooker retired at dark to Centreville.[27] Here he rejoined his own division which had dwindled away to 2,400 men.[28]

On the thirty-first the army rested in the old entrenchments at Centreville. Only the enemy's cavalry put in an appearance. At eleven the next morning Hooker was sent for by General Pope. He was informed that the enemy was rapidly advancing down the Little River turnpike to the north of Centreville and would cut the army off at Germantown unless checked. He was called on to do the checking. This was a job to his liking and with genuine regret he told Pope his brigade commanders had just informed him their men were in no condition to meet the enemy. Their morale had been shattered by the severe losses in battle—1,209 were lost while serving under Pope.[29]

This situation did not make Pope less anxious to have Hooker at the danger point. He was told to hasten there anyway, making use of any troops he might find along the way. He ran his horse nearly to Germantown before he found the 1st Rhode Island Cavalry of Bayard's brigade attached to McDowell's corps. He started them at a trot up the Little River turnpike, instructing them to push on until they met the head of the Confederate column and to hold the advance until further orders.[30] Next he found Ricketts' division of McDowell's corps and led them up the road past Difficult Run where the 1st Rhode Island was engaged. Here Ricketts' infantry and artillery effectively barred the way.[31] In the late afternoon Colonel A. T. A. Torbert reported to Hooker with a brigade of Franklin's corps.[32]

As dark clouds let forth a tropical downpour accompanied by terrific bolts of thunder, Stonewall Jackson brought his heavy column down the Little River Road. A few miles past Chantilly the column veered south of the road, thus avoiding Hooker's conglomerate force but striking full upon the balance of Pope's army which extended from Hooker's left. Reno's corps first received the blow and the severe engagement known as Chantilly or Ox Hill (September 1, 1862) commenced in the midst of the storm. It was broken off at nightfall indecisively, but the Confederate pursuit had been checked. Of greater concern to the Federal cause was the loss of that promising fighter, Phil Kearny. A break in the Federal line had prompted him to reconnoiter and in the darkness he rode too far forward. Almost surrounded, he refused to surrender and was shot off his horse as he tried to gallop away. The next day his body was sent under a flag of truce to the Federal lines commanded by Hooker. The General was greatly affected at sight of the body and often thereafter reverted with feeling to this sorrowful episode of the war.[33]

Kearny would undoubtedly have been given command of a corps in the reorganization of the Army of the Potomac which was about to take place. There is some evidence to indicate that he might possibly have been considered as its commander.[34] He ranked Hooker and probably would have delayed his promotion to corps command; he most certainly

would have postponed Hooker's appointment to the command of the
army, for it would have been very difficult to promote anyone over the
head of General Philip Kearny! In a letter written the day before his
death, he expressed his appreciation of his fighting comrade, saying in regard to Second Bull Run, "The Army ran like sheep all but General
Hooker. . . ."[35]

Although the impromptu force collected under Hooker did not take
part in the Chantilly engagement, it securely held the Little River turnpike approach to the Federal line of retreat. The next morning cavalry
reinforcements joined him,[36] not to hold the position but to serve as rear
guard. General Pope had recommended to his superiors that all troops be
withdrawn into the defenses of Washington.[37] At noon, September
second, the order came to fall back toward Alexandria.

The next morning Fighting Joe reported that the return was without
incident and he awaited orders for the direction of the five brigades of
infantry and one of cavalry which had accompanied him.[38] It was not to
Pope he reported, however, for George B. McClellan was again back in
the saddle. In desperation Lincoln had given him command of the men
behind the fortifications of Washington and of all the troops called back
for the defense of the capital.[39] This had caused a stormy cabinet meeting. Secretary of the Treasury Chase direly predicted a national calam-
ity.[40] Stanton was beside himself with rage. According to Montgomery
Blair, the Postmaster General, Stanton and Chase "declared that they
would prefer the loss of the capital to the restoration of McClellan to
command."[41] This is undoubtedly an overstatement, but Lincoln's
action was a serious blow to their plan to humiliate and ditch McClellan
by taking his army out from under him and giving it to Pope. The President had read the picture correctly: Little Mac was needed for reorganizing the army and he and his generals possessed more of a hold than
the administration upon a considerable portion of the Army of the Potomac.[42] Shrewd Secretary of the Navy Welles thought that "to have
placed any other general than McClellan, or one of his circle, in command would be to risk disaster."[43]

Pope's failure had renewed the much debated question of what was
wrong with the leadership of this army and who could give it the strong
direction it needed. McClellan had satisfied the majority of the war administration and all the radicals in Congress that he was not the man.
He had not been removed from the command of the Army of the
Potomac, but the army had been removed from him. This anomalous

position had been unofficially changed when the troops streamed back from Centreville and his role as commander of all the troops for the defense of the capital gave him control not only of his Army of the Potomac but also the three corps of the Army of Virginia. The opposition to McClellan was such, however, that his chances of long retaining the command were slim.

No outstanding candidate among the corps commanders in the east was available as a successor. Sumner and Porter had distinguished themselves on the Peninsula, but one was too old and the other was about to be shelved for his alleged lack of support at Second Bull Run. In the Army of Virginia McDowell had already suffered a signal failure; Banks had done no better, and Sigel was handicapped by foreign birth and questionable ability. Burnside, recently returned from operations along the coast of North Carolina, had a good record but had missed the big battles of the year.

Of the division commanders none was more outstanding than Joseph Hooker. The press was aware of this[44] and, even more important, so were several members of the Cabinet. Shortly after the Second Bull Run disaster Lincoln asked Secretary of the Navy Gideon Welles whom he would suggest to take command of the Army of the Potomac. Without much consideration Welles named Hooker. Nodding approvingly, Lincoln responded, "I think as much as you or any other man of Hooker, but—I fear he gets excited." Postmaster General Blair, who was present, then put in a damper, saying, "He is too great a friend of John Barleycorn." Welles replied, "If his habits are bad, if he ever permits himself to get intoxicated, he ought not to be trusted with such a command."[45] In the stormy meeting of September second Secretary of the Treasury Chase had suggested Hooker, Sumner or Burnside to replace McClellan.[46]

Hooker had no expectation of receiving the chief command but was eager to take over a corps, an honor which he had earned. The impending removal of several high officers and the death or disablement of others opened up many opportunities for advancement. The generals of the eastern armies were fully aware of this situation, and a state of anxiety prevailed. As the New York *Tribune* said, "One of the most discouraging as well as disgusting features of the present condition of things is the bitter jealousies existing between many of the leading Generals. It is next to impossible to hear one General speak well of another."[47] Secretary Welles added that the generals "are now more ready to fight each other than the enemy."[48]

While Hooker confidently awaited an assignment to a larger command he rejoined his division which General Grover had taken into camp near Fort Lyon, just outside of Alexandria. Finding that Heintzelman was away visiting Washington he temporarily took command of the entire Third Corps.

McClellan had been directed, despite his restrictive position, to organize immediately a movable army to meet the enemy in the field, as it was feared that Lee intended a raid into Maryland or Pennsylvania.[49] He visited Hooker in his camp and discussed the condition of the Third Corps. Hooker had to admit that the regiments were in no shape to march or to engage the enemy. The material that had not been lost on the James River had been destroyed in what he called "our late detour into the country." In addition, the batteries of his division had all been ordered elsewhere.[50]

This was to be Hooker's last plea for his old division. Their steady fighting had reduced them to the status of reserve troops. It was time for them to recruit and recover strength, but their leader's rising fame would not permit his services to be shelved temporarily with them. General Pope, on September third, had made up a preliminary report on Second Bull Run in which he mentioned Hooker with special gratitude for hearty, cordial and untiring zeal and energy.[51] Even General Halleck found himself almost praising Hooker, referring to his troops as "this gallant division."[52] In the press Hooker was spoken of as well-tried, veteran and able, with the daring and judgment of a brave man.[53] At Second Bull Run a high-ranking officer of German descent had asked, "Who ish dat general mit a white horse and red face? He cares nothing for bullets."[54] Abraham Lincoln always admired the fighter generals and at all times was familiar with the shifting personnel of the buffeted Army of the Potomac. Joseph Hooker need have no fear for the immediate future!

## CHAPTER IX

# THE ANTIETAM CAMPAIGN

CHANGES in the high command could not long be delayed for Lee had already headed north toward Maryland. On September 5, 1862, Hooker's immediate ambition was realized when President Lincoln assigned him to the command of the Fifth Army Corps to replace Fitz-John Porter, who was to be relieved until Pope's charges against him could be investigated. By the same order and on the same grounds General William Franklin was to be relieved of the command of the Sixth Corps. No one was appointed to succeed Franklin; his troops were temporarily attached to the Third Corps. On the same day General Pope was instructed to report to the Secretary of War.[1] He soon left the Eastern armies for all time, loudly blaming his misfortunes on lack of support from the McClellan clique in the Army of the Potomac. McDowell's work during the recent battle had also been ineffective; General Reno who had performed creditably at Second Bull Run replaced him as head of the Third Corps of the Army of Virginia.[2]

This drastic reorganization was not to last. McClellan immediately took up the cudgels for his two chief supporters, Franklin and Porter. He asked that the reorganization order be suspended until he could deal with Lee's invasion. He recommended also that if Porter were retained Hooker be assigned to McDowell's corps in place of Reno, thus assuring Fighting Joe the promotion he deserved. These sensible suggestions were agreed to by the administration. Porter and Franklin were retained, and Hooker's command of the Fifth Corps lasted only one day.

On the sixth the General joined his new command, the Third Corps of the Army of Virginia, as it passed through Washington on its way north.[3] His new subordinates were as follows:

1st Division:  Brigadier General Rufus King of New York; a West Pointer and successful newspaper editor in Milwaukee where he had organized the famous Wisconsin "Iron Brigade." He was a victim of epilepsy and undependable in the trying conditions of battle.[4]

2nd Division:  Brigadier General James B. Ricketts, another New Yorker who was with Hooker in the 1st Artillery dur-

130

ing the northeastern boundary dispute. He had been
a good artillerist but was as yet to prove himself with
an infantry command.[5]

3rd Division:  Brigadier General John F. Reynolds of Pennsylvania;
a courageous, self-reliant, professional soldier; West
Point, 1841. His military ability was widely respected
by his fellow officers. He had recently returned from
Richmond where he had been a guest at Libby Prison
for six weeks after his capture at the battle of
Gaines's Mill.[6]

Prominent among Hooker's brigade commanders were John P. Hatch
and Abner Doubleday of New York, John Gibbon of North Carolina,
George G. Meade of Pennsylvania and Truman Seymour of Vermont.

A cavalry brigade of five skeleton regiments under Brigadier General
George D. Bayard was attached to the corps as were ten batteries. This
was the biggest force Hooker had commanded as yet—since the last battle it had been strengthened to 15,290 men not counting the cavalry[7]—
and it was a good one. McDowell had marched the corps all over the field
at Second Bull Run but it still had found time to get in enough fighting to suffer 5,443 casualties, highest loss of any corps involved.[8] Of the
forty-three regiments of infantry all were volunteers except one, the 2nd
U. S. Sharpshooters. Eighteen regiments were from Pennsylvania, including the Pennsylvania Reserves who, under McCall, had fought
desperately at Glendale. Sixteen were from New York, most of whom
had held their own against Jackson at Groveton on the evening of August
twenty-eighth. There were the Iron Brigade from Wisconsin and a
regiment from Indiana. Only three regiments came from New England.[9]

Hooker's General Order No. 1 assumed command of his corps and
announced his staff appointments. Major Joseph Dickinson, his assistant
adjutant general, and two of his aides, Captain William H. Lawrence and
Captain William L. Candler, had been with him since his first battle;
his other aide, Captain Alexander Moore, had been added to his official
family the day after the engagement of Bristoe Station.[10]

There was no time for Hooker to reorganize leisurely or to become
acquainted with his command. General Lee was hastening the march of
his triumphant legions. On the fifth General Alfred Pleasonton, in
charge of all McClellan's cavalry, had reported that Lee's vanguard was
already across the Potomac.[11] His destination could only be surmised,
and this added considerably to the alarm of the civil and military

authorities in Baltimore, Philadelphia and Harrisburg. To frustrate any startling success by this great raid, McClellan moved all the forces he could release from the defense of Washington. General Banks was left in charge of the city and General Heintzelman was put over all troops in the vicinity south of the Potomac.

The army advanced in three columns. Farthest west was the Sixth Corps (Army of the Potomac) under Franklin and Couch's division of the Fourth Corps (Army of the Potomac). In the center was the Second Corps (Army of the Potomac) and the Second Corps (Army of Virginia), all under Sumner. The right wing, composed of the Ninth Corps (Army of the Potomac), recently assigned to Reno, and the Third Corps (Army of Virginia) under Hooker, was commanded by Burnside. Fighting Joe advanced his troops due north out of Washington to Poplar Springs, Maryland, where Burnside ordered him to turn west on the old National Road running from Baltimore. Here he heard through a worthy Maryland unionist that Lee was well on his way to Harrisburg with 160,000 men.[12] He was not taken in by this "bear story," but he did pass the word on to the Commanding General—which was perhaps unfortunate since McClellan was always ready to believe the worst.

On the eleventh Hooker was ordered to continue westward on the National Road to support General Reno and the Ninth Corps.[13] Next day, by order of the President, the corps of the Army of Virginia were officially amalgamated with the Army of the Potomac. Hooker's new command became the First Corps, as it had been called originally before being detached from the Army of the Potomac for service with Pope. Sigel's and Banks's commands in the Army of Virginia became the Eleventh and Twelfth Corps of the Army of the Potomac.[14]

On the same day Porter's Fifth Corps left Washington to strengthen McClellan's command. Of even more value to the Commanding General was the discovery of a copy of Robert E. Lee's Special Order No. 191, now known as the famous "Lost Order." It was found near Frederick about noon on the thirteenth, wrapped around three cigars.[15] It disclosed Lee's position and told some of his plans, particularly the proposed capture of Harpers Ferry.[16] Thus General McClellan was able to concentrate his army with a speed hitherto unknown to him and to force battle before Lee was ready to receive it.

The threat of Lee's ragged and hungry army to prosperous Pennsylvania kept Governor Curtin of that state in constant communication with the President and the War Department. The Governor lost no opportunity to pour out his fears to all who would listen. His pleas for help—he wanted only 80,000 disciplined troops—were unheeded, but it was admitted that an experienced general officer should be sent him to organize the state's resources for defense. The best Pennsylvanian available was John Reynolds, commander of Hooker's 3rd Division.[17] The order sending him on this detached service brought an outraged cry from General Hooker. He dashed off one of his caustic masterpieces to McClellan.

". . . I request that the major general commanding will not heed this order; a scared Governor ought not to be permitted to destroy the usefulness of an entire division of the army, on the eve of important operations.

"General Reynolds commands a division of Pennsylvania troops of not the best character; is well known to them, and I have no officer to fill his place.

"It is satisfactory to my mind that the rebels have no more intention of going to Harrisburg than they have of going to heaven.

"It is only in the United States that atrocities like this are entertained."[18]

Nevertheless, the next day Reynolds was on his way. General George G. Meade was his not unworthy successor, but Hooker had a strong regard for Reynolds and felt done in. His bitter protest had the effect of antagonizing Meade who regarded it as a reflection on his ability.[19]

One other last-minute change was made in the division command within the corps. General King of the 1st Division was granted sick leave and General Hatch took his place.[20]

For three days the First Corps marched westward on the National Road, following General Reno who was hurrying on to force the gaps in South Mountain behind which was scattered a large part of the Confederate Army. At Middletown, Hooker's corps paused at noon on the fourteenth, and he was requested by McClellan to ride forward and examine the approaches to South Mountain.[21] A short ride brought him to the eastern slope which ran almost perpendicular to the main road. The ridge appeared to be precipitous, rugged, heavily-wooded and difficult to ascend.[22] Two gaps were in evidence: on the north Turner's Gap where the National Road cut through a deep depression; on the south Fox's Gap which, although not much of a cut, was approached by a good road. The enemy appeared to be in some force across Turner's Gap

and on the elevations dominating it. At Fox's Gap, Cox's division of
Reno's corps had already reached the crest pushing back a Confederate
brigade, and Reno's other three divisions were advancing toward the.
top.[23]

About two o'clock an order came from McClellan requesting a diversion in favor of General Reno. Hooker was to advance a full division
and the balance of the First Corps was to be held in readiness to support
the movement.[24] Two cavalry regiments were detached to serve with

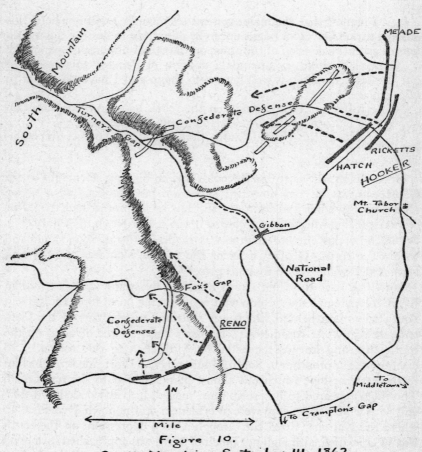

Figure 10.
South Mountain, September 14, 1862

Hooker: the 1st Massachusetts and the 3rd Indiana. The Indiana troopers were old friends—the "Horse Marines" of Hooker's lower Maryland command.[25]

While Hooker nervously awaited the arrival of his infantry he was joined by General Burnside. From headquarters established at Mount Tabor Church on a road running north from the National Road at the base of the mountain, enemy activity could be seen on a spur three-fourths of a mile east of Turner's Gap. The spur commanded any approach to the mountains on the north side of the main road and necessarily had to be reduced first.

It was nearly three when General Meade rode up ahead of his Pennsylvania Reserves. A short conference of the generals resulted in an order for Meade to move his division up the Mount Tabor Church road to a point due east of the mountain spur.[26] Here Hooker directed a battery to fire a few rounds while the infantry prepared for an attack. In a few minutes Meade was ready, and Hooker ordered his guns to cease firing while the First Pennsylvania Rifles, better known as the "Bucktails," went forward as skirmishers.[27] Their hot reception satisfied Hooker that the enemy held the spur in force, and Meade was told to try to outflank the position to the right. Seymour's brigade did it and the entire division moved forward with great vigor, pushing back the enemy at all points.[28]

Meanwhile, General Hatch had arrived with his division and Hooker started them up the mountainside on Meade's left. Unknown to Hooker, Hatch's largest brigade under General Gibbon had been detached by Burnside to form across the National Road. This depletion prevented the 1st Division from advancing as far or as gallantly as Meade's men. Its commander, General Hatch, was wounded and a call came back for reinforcements.[29]

Hooker's 2nd Division under General Ricketts arrived around 5:30 and a brigade was sent to support Doubleday who now commanded the 1st Division. Then came a report, which later proved false, that Meade was being outflanked on his right, and a reserve brigade was directed there. Finally the last of the reserves were sent in to fill the gap between the 1st and 3rd Divisions.[30] By dark the crest of the spur had been gained, but the main mountain ridge and the Gap were still Confederate. The troops were held in position; darkness and the difficult terrain made it unwise to think of further attack that night.

By morning the enemy had left the protecting mountain wall and the field of battle to the Federals. At Fox's Gap Reno's corps had succeeded about as well as Hooker, but the Confederate force had achieved its objective of holding off the Federals until Lee could concentrate his army.

General Hooker looked upon the battle of South Mountain as one of the most brilliant achievements of the army, claiming the principal glory for his First Corps.[31] Had the enemy possessed the "preponderating" numbers accredited to them in his report, plus the advantage of position which it undoubtedly had, the Federal attack would have been all Hooker claimed for it. The fact, however, was that eighteen Union brigades opposed only five Confederate brigades, under General Daniel H. Hill, for the best part of the day, though in late afternoon eight of Longstreet's brigades came to their rescue.[32]

The entire movement had proceeded cautiously on the Federal part considering that McClellan had in his possession unquestionable information about Lee's strung-out position. A similar move farther south at Crampton's Gap by General Franklin's wing of the army had met with more success, but in neither place was South Mountain forced early enough to enable McClellan to defeat Lee in detail or to drive him across the Potomac.

Once in action, General Hooker had maneuvered his corps well, working principally from his headquarters at Mount Tabor Church where General Marcy, McClellan's Chief of Staff, had been with him during much of the engagement.[33] McClellan indicated later that in his opinion Marcy deserved most of the credit for Hooker's success.[34] Burnside much later asserted that he had to order Hooker four times to move his command into action,[35] but this testimony came at a time when Burnside was feeling bitter toward the General. Shortly after the battle Burnside had reported that the country was indebted to the gallant Generals Hooker and Reno for the day's victory.[36]

Within his new command the General was much impressed with the intelligence and gallantry of General Meade, though he did not forget to commend the other division commanders. Hooker had received a pleasing reception from his troops despite the fact that his only previous fighting with them had occurred with the 1st Division in the retreat at Second Bull Run and with the Pennsylvania Reserves in their defeat at Glendale. When they had marched past him at Mount Tabor Church they manifested enthusiasm, evidently impressed with the belief that at last they had found a general able and willing to lead them forward to face the enemy.[37]

The casualty list would indicate that Gibbon, on the National Road away from the eye of Hooker, did the most severe fighting. He lost twenty to twenty-five percent of his brigade. His detached duty had placed him in an exposed position, and he tried to force the center of resistance. Toward the end of the encounter McClellan had asked Hooker what men were fighting on the pike and was informed that they were General Gibbon's brigade of western men. McClellan exclaimed, "They must be made of iron!" and Hooker replied, "By the Eternal, they are iron! If you had seen them at Bull Run as I did, you would know them to be iron."[38]

General Meade's division on the right lost around ten percent of its effectives. Hatch's attack is written up spectacularly in the *Official Records*, but his casualties numbered only 178 because his opposition was not so well placed as Meade's, since it had just arrived on the field. Ricketts' reserve division was hardly touched.[39] On the other side of the road the Union had lost a most promising officer in General Jesse L. Reno, mortally wounded on the mountaintop just at sunset.[40]

At daylight on the morning of September fifteenth Brigadier General Richardson reported to Hooker with his division of Sumner's corps. A heavy mist cleared sufficiently by seven o'clock to substantiate the belief that the enemy had gone, and Richardson was sent in pursuit. He was not to engage the enemy, if overtaken, until Hooker arrived. Meanwhile, the First Corps was to brew coffee and have breakfast.

General Hooker advanced through Turner's Gap in great good humor as soon as breakfast was over. He sent a message back to McClellan: "The enemy is making for Shepherdstown in a perfect panic; and General Lee last night stated publicly that he must admit they had been shockingly whipped." The information came from a "perfectly reliable" source.[41] By the time McClellan relayed this fable to Washington the story had grown to read that Lee was wounded, Hooker had over 1,000 prisoners, and Lee admitted his loss as 15,000![42]

The balance of the army advanced that morning into Pleasant Valley on the other side of South Mountain. Franklin, who had forced Crampton's Gap, midway between Turner's Gap and the Potomac, turned south to relieve the garrison at Harpers Ferry which had been beleaguered for twenty-four hours, but this gesture came too late. Jackson had forced its surrender early that morning while on his way up the west side of the Potomac to join Lee.

At ten o'clock Hooker got word that Richardson had found the enemy posted along the west bank of Antietam Creek in front of Sharpsburg.

Hooker rode on ahead of his men and found that Richardson had opened up on the enemy with a section of artillery. The Confederates seemed well posted to prevent a crossing of the stream, and Hooker estimated their number at 50,000—too many to attack even with the addition of his First Corps.[43] Major D. C. Houston of the Engineers was sent upstream to locate a practicable ford. A bridge was found and two fords were discovered which were satisfactory for both infantry and artillery.[44]

General McClellan arrived in the meantime and examined the enemy's position. The balance of his army, with the exception of Franklin's wing in the lower end of Pleasant Valley, was in easy marching distance of the Antietam. The weather was favorable and the roads were in good condition. A fast advance would take advantage of the scattered position of Lee's legions, but Little Mac concluded that it was too late for an attack that day.[45]

The delay was of value to Hooker, since in the interval McClellan suspended the order placing Burnside over the First Corps, and so left Hooker free to report directly to the Commanding General.[46] Burnside was convinced that his reduction to the command of just his own corps was due solely to Hooker's solicitation for independence of command.[47]

A slight change in the enemy's position discerned on the morning of the sixteenth necessitated another reconnaissance and a wait for the ammunition and supply trains stalled things until 2:00 P.M. Then General Hooker was ordered to move his corps against the enemy's left.[48] Meade's and Ricketts' divisions were sent across the bridge near Keedysville and Doubleday's division over the ford just below it. When the corps moved off, Hooker reported to McClellan and was told that he was at liberty to call for reinforcements when needed; they would be placed under his command.[49] Hooker then rejoined his troops and directed their march west of the river with two of Meade's regiments thrown forward as skirmishers. A half-mile past the river McClellan and his staff rode up to speed Hooker on and to guide his march. McClellan was not entirely satisfied that Fighting Joe was pushing the move hard enough, claiming that it was three-thirty or four o'clock before the First Corps got across.[50] In the conversation Hooker voiced his uneasiness by remarking to McClellan that the small First Corps of 12,000 to 13,000 men had been ordered to attack the whole Confederate Army. He believed that unless reinforcements were forwarded promptly or unless another attack were made on the enemy's right, he would be "eaten up." McClellan's reply is not recorded, but he had already ordered Mansfield's corps to cross the river that night in Hooker's footsteps.[51]

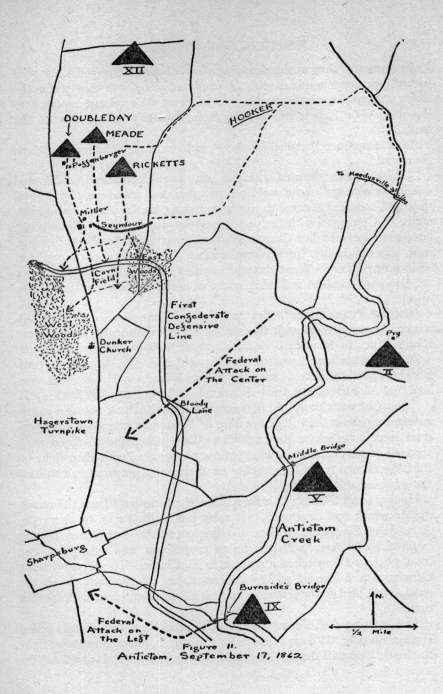

Figure 11.
Antietam, September 17, 1862

Progress was slow as the skirmishers soon became engaged. A special newspaper correspondent with Hooker's advance says that when the firing started the cavalry screen returned and their colonel reported to Hooker, "The Rebels are opening from a battery in the edge of the wood."

"Let them open," replied Hooker; "we have as many batteries as they. Forward!"

"Hooker's eyes gleamed with the fierce joy of battle and he disposed his forces with wonderful rapidity. Shot and shell fell about Hooker and his staff, covering them with dirt and making horses almost unmanageable."[52] Compared with the present style of war reporting, this account seems sophomoric, but George W. Smalley of the New York *Tribune*, who was responsible for the gem, was an accomplished correspondent. The noted Henry Villard thought Smalley's work with Hooker's corps at Antietam the best individual piece of correspondence for the whole war.[53]

The 1st Pennsylvania Rifles and the 3rd Pennsylvania Reserves advanced as skirmishers with the rest of Seymour's brigade in support.[54] The balance of Meade's division, along with Doubleday and Ricketts, kept farther north and avoided the skirmishing.[55] The Hagerstown turnpike was reached after a march of several miles, and Hooker was satisfied that his First Corps was well around on the enemy's left flank.

The night was cloudy and darkness came fast. After a personal reconnaissance Hooker laid his front line of Seymour's brigade a few hundred yards from where the enemy's vigilant picket line disclosed itself through constant firing. The rest of the corps rested with their right on the Hagerstown turnpike, sleeping on their arms, prepared to continue the advance at daybreak.

Hooker sought shelter in a barn along the turnpike[56] from the steady drizzle which had developed. He went out at 9:00 P.M. to check the alertness of Seymour's pickets. Finding everything satisfactory he was inspired, so he says, "with the fullest confidence" and returned to the barn where he dispatched a courier to McClellan. The Commanding General was informed of Hooker's position, assured that the battle would start at dawn and was requested to send reinforcements by that time.[57]

As the firing died down, a reporter for the New York *Times* heard Hooker remark: "We are through for tonight . . . but tomorrow we fight the battle that will decide the fate of the Republic."[58] He was not far from right. Many observers feel that the bloody battle of Antietam more truly represents the high-water mark of the Confederacy than Gettysburg.

Around one in the morning firing was resumed southeast of Hooker's barn, and the General arose and listened for a moment. He smiled grimly and said, "We have no troops there. The [enemy's] troops are shooting each other."[59]

He was up at break of day to take his first good look at the battlefield where he had prophesied the war would be settled. The morning was gray and misty, and visibility was poor. When the clouds lifted a bit Hooker could see to the south along the turnpike a rolling field, hemmed in by woods on the west side of the road. Four hundred yards to the east, where Seymour had skirmished the night before and was still in position, was another belt of timber. A farmhouse, with barn and outbuildings, a garden and an orchard, was less than a half-mile straight down the pike. Beyond was a large cornfield on slowly rising ground. At the top of a slight elevation a few hundred yards farther on down the west side of the road was a brick church. This building—the famous Dunker Church—appeared an excellent landmark upon which to guide the First Corps.[60]

Doubleday's 1st Division, posted along the east side of the road, was directed to advance toward the cornfield and the church. Ricketts, who was farther to the left, was to clear out the woods in front of Seymour's brigade and to continue on southward. Meade was to follow in reserve and to help wherever needed. Hooker was elated to find that Mansfield's Twelfth Corps had come up in the night and was now only a mile to the rear, ready to support him at any time.[61] A disappointment was the number of effectives in the First Corps; straggling on the march from South Mountain had reduced it to a little over 9,000 men.

The Confederate batteries did not wait long to open up on Hooker's massed infantry. The General was soon ready to answer this challenge and moved the leading units of his 1st and 2nd Divisions toward their objectives. As Doubleday's brigade, under Gibbon, pushed through the farmyard and orchard in front of them and Hartsuff's brigade of the 2nd Division headed for the east woods, Hooker noticed the flashing of enemy bayonets within the cornfield. The Confederate infantry appeared to be in strong force awaiting attack in the uncertain shelter of the tall corn. All the First Corps' spare batteries were assembled and fired their canister over the heads of the advancing Federal brigades. According to Hooker, "every stalk of corn . . . was cut as closely as could have been done with a knife, and the slain lay in rows precisely as they had stood in their ranks a few moments before. It was never my fortune to witness a more bloody, dismal battle field."[62] This description would seem quite overdone, but the terrible carnage is attested to by the survivors of the Confederate infantry. The foremost contemporary student of the Army of Northern Virginia states: "Never in all the Army's battles had so many high officers been put out of action so quickly."[63]

Two more brigades of the 1st Division were sent into the cornfield under Hooker's personal direction to follow up Gibbon's advantage, but strong resistance from the woods on the west side of the turnpike drew all three brigades over to their own right.[64] Meanwhile, the left wing under Ricketts was battling for the east wood and that part of the cornfield well east of the pike. The enemy rallied with the apparent intent of regaining the cornfield,[65] and Meade's division was moved to meet this threat. Word was then sent back to Mansfield to hurry forward his Twelfth Corps since all the First Corps reserves were engaged and hard-pressed.[66] General Alpheus S. Williams, second in command to Mansfield, rode forward to report to Hooker that the two divisions of the Twelfth Corps were ready to advance but their commander had been mortally wounded while deploying his troops. A few hurried directions were given Williams: one division was to go to the aid of Doubleday whose men were wavering in the woods along the turnpike; the other division was to move more to its left and head through the cornfield for the white church.[67]

While maneuvering a brigade of the Twelfth Corps into position in the west woods, Hooker's horse was hit by an enemy sharpshooter, but the General, ever at ease under fire, paid scant attention to this close call. He rode out in front of his farthest advanced troops to the south along the turnpike. It was now about nine o'clock. He had lingered for three hours in the hottest fire but was pressing his luck too far when he rode to the top of a slight elevation and made himself a perfect target. He dismounted and stepped forward a few paces to examine the ground and then remounted his wounded horse to return. The enemy fire increased suddenly and Hooker swayed unsteadily in the saddle. He rode back a short distance and was helped down. A surgeon on the spot found that a rifle ball had passed entirely through his foot but could not tell whether or not any bones were broken. Hooker was losing a good deal of blood and was definitely out of the fight. He was placed on a stretcher and, according to a reporter, gave his last command of the battle: "There is a regiment to the right. Order it forward! Crawford and Gordon are coming up. Tell them to carry the woods and hold them—and it is our fight!"[68]

On the way back to the rear Hooker met Sumner hurrying on with reinforcements—Sedgwick's division of the Second Corps. A few words were exchanged, but Fighting Joe was in a weakened condition, had fainted once and could not give Sumner much in the way of specific directions for placing his men.[69] Then he was carried across Antietam Creek to the large, square mansion of Mr. Pry where McClellan had established headquarters.

That afternoon Hooker was taken to Centreville, Maryland. Here he rallied sufficiently to send a dispatch to his brother-in-law in Watertown:

"A great battle has been fought, and we are victorious. I had the honor to open it yesterday afternoon, and it continued till 10 o'clock this morning, when I was wounded and compelled to quit the field.

"The battle was fought with great violence on both sides.

"The carnage has been awful.

"I only regret that I was not permitted to take part in the operations until they were concluded, for I had counted on either capturing their army or driving them into the Potomac.

"My wound has been painful, but it is not one that will be likely to lay me up. I was shot through the foot."[70]

This private dispatch turned out to be a good personal "plug" when it appeared in the New York papers two days later. The public accepted the view that if Hooker had not been wounded decisive victory would have resulted. Before the Committee on the Conduct of the War Hooker went even farther. He said that at the time he was wounded his "troops were in the finest spirits; they had whipped Jackson, and compelled the enemy to fly, throwing away their arms, their banners, and saving themselves as best they could . . . the troops almost rent the skies with their cheers; there was the greatest good feeling that I have ever witnessed on the field of battle."[71]

This picture was not that of the man in the ranks. The First Corps had taken a tremendous loss in numbers and several brigades were already dropping back when Hooker was wounded. The Twelfth Corps was arriving too late to exploit the break-through but did relieve the First Corps, which fell back to the camps of that morning, where General

Meade took over and tried to reorganize them. Two thousand five hundred and ninety casualties were finally counted within the corps,[72] two brigade commanders were wounded, and its effectiveness was ended for the day. The Twelfth Corps and Sedgwick's division of the Second Corps, which also fought over Hooker's ground, were repulsed in turn, both suffering a higher percentage lost than the First Corps. Sedgwick's three brigades alone lost 2,210 men.[73]

The fighting on the Federal right was over less than an hour after Hooker was wounded. It had been a series of unco-ordinated, sharp mass attacks, barely repulsed by Confederate reinforcements which arrived in the nick of time. The attacking force with which McClellan intended to open up the battle, supposedly consisting of three corps, operated never as a unit and never under one head. Both Mansfield and Sumner ranked Hooker, but he was given the responsibility of leading the attack. Sumner's corps had been left by the Commanding General on the other side of the Antietam until 7:30 A.M.[74] when Hooker was well under way. A combined attack at an early hour by all three corps in force would have crushed Jackson's outnumbered veterans on the Confederate left before any help could have come.

When the fighting on this part of the field ended, Sumner's divisions under French and Richardson attacked the Confederate center. When they had been finally stopped, after substantial gains, and quiet was restored, Burnside's Ninth Corps attacked with success on the left. The last enemy reserves arrived just in time to stop this attempt. Thus the Federals obligingly allowed Lee to shift his forces from one end of the battlefield to the other and to compensate for the great disparity in available numbers. The outcome was a drawn battle instead of a tremendous Federal victory. Nevertheless Antietam can be considered as possibly the most important battle in the East. Lee's invasion was checked, foreign intervention on behalf of the Confederacy was thoroughly discouraged, and Lincoln grasped the claim of victory as a foundation for issuing the Emancipation Proclamation—a document of slight immediate practical importance but of great moral significance, particularly abroad.

Hooker's work was once again spectacular; he had fought his men hard and achieved initial success. General McClellan sent him a friendly letter thanking him for what he had done and expressing regret for his wound. "Had you not been wounded when you were," he said, "I believe the result of the battle would have been the entire destruction of the rebel army, for I know that, with you at its head, your corps would have kept on until it gained the main road."[75] As an act of justice and fitting reward McClellan recommended Major General Joseph Hooker for an appointment as brigadier general in the regular army. He felt sure this appointment "would gratify the entire army."[76]

In the press Hooker was referred to as "fearless and indomitable," "sagacious and prompt in his movements." His "bravery and soldierly ability were to be admired." Most of these bouquets came from Smalley of the New York *Tribune,* who claimed never to have seen Hooker until the day before the battle and said he did not approve of his politics and opinions in general. Smalley was with Hooker constantly in the fight and even carried several orders for him. One of these instructed the Colonel of a wavering regiment to move his men to the front and keep them there. The Colonel refused to recognize the order, insisting that it should be presented to him by a staff officer or brigade commander. When Smalley said that he would report to General Hooker that the Colonel declined to obey, the latter replied, "Oh, for God's sake, don't do that. I had rather face the Rebels than Hooker." Just before Fighting Joe was wounded Smalley warned him that bullets were following him wherever he rode.[77] The New York *Times* regretted that the army would lose his services for a time, "though no one can regret his absence from any field of danger and of duty more keenly than Hooker himself."[78]

His California friends expressed their admiration in more tangible fashion. As a tribute to his gallantry the citizens of San Francisco undertook to raise the sum of $2,000 for a sword.[79] This project expanded in scope in true Western fashion; eventually the cost (at least as reported in the newspapers) was raised to $5,000.[80] The blade was forged in Philadelphia but the engraving and tooling on the finished product were the work of J. W. Tucker and Company, leading San Francisco jewelers. Just as the sword was finished it was learned that a commanding general could not accept so costly a gift from a group of individuals. It was then sent to Sacramento, the capital of California, where it was to be put on display until the state legislature passed a resolution to purchase it and present it to Hooker. The actual presentation did not take place until after the war. In addition, a huge white thoroughbred stallion was purchased in New Orleans and presented to the General as coming from the California boys in the army. To round out their good will his California admirers ordered a suit of horse trappings, at a cost of $500, made up for Fighting Joe.[81] The newspaper declaration that Hooker was as popular in California as he was with his forces on the battlefield seemed justified.[82]

## CHAPTER X

## SICK LEAVE AND FREDERICKSBURG

As soon as Hooker could be moved comfortably he was transferred to the capital. He was quartered in a room in the Washington Insane Asylum where he would be under the constant care of Dr. Nichols, the superintendent and an old friend. The wound was much less serious than at first believed; the rifle ball had passed through the bottom of his foot without injuring any of the bones.[1] It was of such a disabling nature, however, that the General was assured of a long rest. The newspapers kept the public informed of the invalid's condition and lionized him as the "hero of almost every battle fought in Virginia and Maryland."[2] Interest in the case was extensive. This story appeared on the front page of a Washington paper :

"A striking exemplification of the marvelous faculty of the electric telegraph has grown out of the accident to the above General. The news of the event has not only reached San Francisco, but a prescription has been received by the same medium for the wound. A lady of California deeply interested by the news, telegraphed back to apply lamp oil and cotton to the wound."[3]

Hooker's convalescence was cheered by news of his appointment as brigadier general in the regular army to date from September 20, 1862,[4] and by rumors in the press that he was being considered for a more important command.[5] Within a week many prominent visitors including the President and several members of the cabinet had consulted him on the conduct of the war.[6]

From the standpoint of Hooker's career the visits of the Secretary of the Treasury were perhaps more important than any other. Salmon P. Chase had high hopes of receiving the support of the radical faction of the Republican party for the Presidency in the next election. He possessed an all-powerful ambition which, it has been said, "always colored his career, diminished his usefulness, impaired his dignity, and blinded his judgment as to currents of public opinion."[7] He was tall, massive, handsome in feature and distinguished in bearing. A determined will and a self-righteous, opinionated approach to most problems made him difficult to work with.

At breakfast on the morning of September twenty-third he proposed to his equally ambitious, beautiful daughter, Kate, that they ride over to see General Hooker. With a large basket of peaches, grapes and other fruits they went off to the Insane Asylum. Mrs. Nichols ushered them into a cool and airy room where they found Fighting Joe lying on a couch. He was appreciative of their interest and talked freely—mostly about McClellan, reciting his errors as far back as the Peninsula campaign. Chase said, "General, if my advice had been followed, you would have commanded after the retreat to James River, if not before." Hooker hastened to reply, "If I had commanded, Richmond would have been ours." This was followed by a discussion of the battle of Antietam. The General believed that had he remained on the field three hours longer, the victory would have been complete, "for I had already gained enough and seen enough to make the route of the enemy sure."[8]

Chase recorded his impressions of the General in his diary that afternoon: "a frank, manly, brave and energetic soldier, of somewhat less breadth of intellect than I had expected, however, though not of less quickness, clearness and activity."[9] Chase was interested in Hooker. It was believed at this time that the general who succeeded in ending the rebellion would automatically become the outstanding candidate to succeed Lincoln. He would at least be able to name the next president.[10] Hooker might be the man and, providing he possessed no political ambitions of his own and if Chase could gain his support, an alliance might be formed which quite possibly would sway the election of 1864.

Mr. Chase returned the next day and the next. At one conference Hooker said that it was not true that the army or the officers were particularly attached to McClellan. Only two corps whose commanders were especial favorites and whose troops received indulgences were for him. "Other officers—he himself certainly—thought him not fit to lead a great army."[11] At subsequent meetings the General continued to harp on McClellan's timidity and hesitancy when decision was necessary. He added that there were many good officers among the Volunteer colonels but a new commander was needed to bring out their abilities.[12]

Hooker was visited also by a delegation from his old New Jersey Blues. They had come to urge him to recommend one of their colonels, whose name has not been recorded, for a commission as brigadier general. Hooker listened patiently, but wrathfully turned them down; the "Old

Pirate" wasn't fit to be trusted with the reputations of his officers.[13]

By the middle of October, Vice-President Hannibal Hamlin of Maine got around to calling on the General. He was accompanied by one of Hooker's chief supporters within the army, General Hiram G. Berry, also of Maine. They wanted to see him about a promotion for Berry. Fighting Joe greeted them heartily and promised to do all in his power to help. He immediately addressed a testimonial of Berry's service and ability to General Halleck. Then he got down to business and began to criticize McClellan's handling of the army at Antietam.[14]

The General resented his forced inactivity but made the most of his lot with several judicious releases to the press. He came out strongly in favor of the Emancipation Proclamation—a "must" for any ambitious officer. The New York *Tribune* reported:

"General Hooker declared with great freedom that the Proclamation was issued too late, rather than too early, that the time had fully arrived when it was impossible to prosecute the war vigorously and with a certainty of success without it."[15]

In another dispatch he hotly denied the spreading report that the First Corps had already been repulsed at Antietam when Sumner arrived, and made the following stirring declaration about his wound: "I would gladly have compromised with the enemy by receiving a mortal wound at night, could I have remained at my post until the day ended."[16]

October 1862 was an uneasy month for the war administration. The unwanted George McClellan had checked Lee's invasion, but his continuance as commander of the Army of the Potomac was not an encouraging outlook for the radical bloc in Congress. He was co-operating with his political foes by his hesitant pursuit of the enemy, a plausible foundation for their determined intention to sidetrack him. The political maneuvering which took place stirred up continuous rumors, and Hooker's name was seldom missing. In the press it was variously reported that he would soon be offered the command in the East, that he would be given an important position in the West, that he would be appointed McClellan's chief of staff.[17] It was a propitious time for an ambitious candidate to be in the center of the ferment.

It was generally conceded in the army that if McClellan were removed Hooker would succeed him.[18] He was undeniably popular with the public. It was said that photographers in New York City sold more portraits of Fighting Joe than of all other military chieftains put together.[19] Lincoln was more than friendly and Chase was showing great interest. The radical bloc, particularly Zach Chandler of the Committee on the Conduct of the War, was showing increasing awareness of his possibilities. An unanticipated boost came from General Pope, now in the Northwest, who sent his support in a lengthy letter to General Halleck. It was probably the most appreciative letter written during the war about Hooker's abilities and is quoted here only because of that; it carried little weight with Halleck.

"The pretorian faction in the Army of the Potomac is now seeking to remove every officer of distinction from that army who is not in their interests. Hooker, by his rising reputation and known hostility to them and their purposes, is becoming dangerous. He will be gotten rid of in some way. As it cannot now be done by detraction and slander, they will seek by affected commendation and applause to remove him to some other command. Do not allow such transparent intrigue to induce you to consent that Hooker should be separated from that army. You will find him a true man and one of incalculable use to you with that army. . . . Hooker is the only man I know available to succeed him [McClellan]."[20]

All this pointed to Hooker as the out-and-out favorite. Unfortunately, he had always been a stanch Democrat and disinterested in the abolition movement. General Meade, who knew his weaknesses well, expressed the opinion that this would present no obstacle, that he was open to temptation and easily seduced by flattery.[21] Many ranking soldiers had developed a leaning toward abolition when they saw how the wind was blowing. Ambitious as Hooker was to gain the command, he would need little rationalization to modify his political views if that would help him fulfill his early boast of climbing to the top of the army and taking Richmond.

The first step had been taken—his release to the press on the desirability of the Emancipation Proclamation—but this was not quite enough to satisfy the radicals. On October twentieth Mark Skinner, a Chicago radical, suggested to Stanton that since Hooker appeared to be the coming man he should declare himself to be antislavery and that this declaration be given wide publicity.[22]

By October second Hooker had recovered sufficiently to go by carriage across the Eastern Branch to the city.[23] As he gained strength in the injured foot his trips became more frequent. There were many talks with

Chase and several interviews with Stanton.[24] One trip came close to ending in tragedy. On the twenty-ninth at Willard's Hotel, in the room of Senator McDougall of California, an inventor was demonstrating an improved carbine to the General and the Senator. The two men were watching intently when the gun suddenly roared in an accidental discharge. As the smoke cleared they realized that the bullet had passed between them. According to a friendly newspaper account, they "pursued their conversation as if nothing had happened."[25]

The papers constantly kept the public informed of the General's progress and one offered up the prayer that "God in his goodness, will soon get fighting Joe Hooker well again."[26] They finally reported that he would be able to take to saddle by the first week in November.[27] This did not develop, however, for on November fifth when Chase, Stanton and Halleck dined with Hooker in his quarters in the Insane Asylum, he was still getting about with a crutch, but he promised that he would soon throw it away and take the field.[28]

By November second McClellan had taken all his men across the Potomac in pursuit of General Lee, whose troops were scattered from the Shenandoah Valley to Culpeper. Little Mac had, as usual, moved only when he was good and ready, but the fact that he marched with admirable celerity this time and was in a favorable position to fight the enemy in detail could not save his scalp. The radical members of the Joint Committee on the Conduct of the War were by now almost hysterical over his retention in command. The President had given up and was referring to the Army of the Potomac as "McClellan's bodyguard." He waited only until after the fall elections to swing the ax. His selection of the new commander, however, was a disappointment to almost everyone, including the appointee: General Ambrose E. Burnside, friend of McClellan. Thus Hooker's "Washington campaign" had come to naught for the present. But solid groundwork had been laid: there would be another battle and, unless the system were changed, another commander!

The possible reasons for Hooker's failure to receive the command at this time are worth conjecture. Perhaps it was because:

1. Lincoln hesitated to turn the direction of an army, preponderantly loyal to its commander, over to so violent an anti-McClellan man.
2. It would have been necessary to advance Hooker over his seniors in corps command—Burnside, Sumner and Franklin—a step for which Lincoln was not ready.

3. The President had a strong personal fondness for Ambrose E. Burnside.
4. Hooker's recovery had been slower than expected, and he was not in physical condition to take the field.
5. Hooker, by his many indiscretions during his prolonged stay in Washington, may have talked himself out of the position.[29] He was later to admit to General Meade that at one point during his convalescence he was confident of receiving the command.[30]
6. Edwin M. Stanton, Secretary of War, and Henry W. Halleck, General-in-Chief of all the armies, opposed him. Stanton, Lincoln's so-called "great" War Minister, did not appreciate Fighting Joe. Whereas he had carried on in a friendly manner with Hooker, that was his custom until he was ready to show his hand; then, if any underlying dissatisfaction existed, he expressed himself vituperatively, going to any end to thwart his victim's advancement. The astute Gideon Welles accredited Stanton with cunning and skill but considered him an intriguer, a hypocrite and a moral coward.[31] Halleck was mistakenly called "Old Brains." He was a military scholar but a great handicap to the Union cause as General-in-Chief. His dislike of Hooker dated back to California and, although they had had little contact to date during the war, this dislike had not abated. He probably influenced the Secretary of War in regard to Fighting Joe.

A soldier in the Army of the Potomac took over the role of prophet. "I suppose we shall have one more blunder, and then at last they will put 'Old Joe' in the right place."[32]

General Burnside was born in Indiana but was a Rhode Islander by adoption. After West Point and a short uneventful career in the Mexican War he had resigned from the army to manufacture a new breachloading rifle in Bristol, Rhode Island. Although this venture failed, his pleasing personality and genial manners contributed to other business successes. At the outbreak of the war he organized the 1st Rhode Island Volunteer Infantry. At Bull Run he led a brigade. In January 1862 he was detached for coastal operations in North Carolina where he captured several important fortified positions and received praise from the press. He had fought only one battle with the Army of the Potomac, the recent one at Antietam. His delay in attacking there had contributed as much as anything else to the indecisive character of the result. He had refused the command of the army at least once before, but his genuine doubts of his ability to command such a large body of men were interpreted as modesty. Lincoln this time issued a mandatory order for him to take command.[33] Burnside later told General Couch that he did so only to keep it from going to someone manifestly unfit for it—Couch assumed he meant Joseph Hooker.[34]

The command passed over to Burnside on November seventh while the army was on its way to Warrenton, Virginia. General Hooker joined him four days later as commander of the Fifth Corps, appointed by President Lincoln to relieve General Fitz-John Porter who was to stand trial for his alleged disobedience at Second Bull Run.[35] Hooker had not been told exactly what his "Washington campaign" had netted him until he applied to Halleck for instructions on the morning of the tenth. Not too pleased, he still promised to "obey fully all orders from all superiors whoever they may be."[36] He made the trip to Warrenton Junction by rail, passing General McClellan on his way back to Washington and military oblivion. The "Old Hooker Division," now under Sickles, was encountered at the Junction and the General received an enthusiastic greeting.[37] General Porter ordered his division commanders to join him at headquarters to be introduced to their new commander and sent the following curiously worded note to Hooker:

"In compliance with *what seems to be*[38] an order from the President of the United States, received from you this morning . . . I will be prepared to turn over the command of the Fifth Army Corps to you at 12 m to-day."

When it is recalled that Hooker had once before been given command of Porter's corps and that Porter had been reinstated a day later, it is not surprising that there was some hesitancy on Porter's part to accept this order at face value.

On the fourteenth Burnside announced a new scheme for the organization of the army. The corps were to be grouped into three grand divisions, as follows:[39]

| | |
|---|---|
| Left Grand Division: | First and Sixth Corps |
| | General William B. Franklin |
| Center Grand Division: | Third and Fifth Corps |
| | General Joseph Hooker |
| Right Grand Division: | Second and Ninth Corps |
| | General Edwin V. Sumner |

Seniority rather than the good will of Burnside dictated that Hooker should receive a Grand Division.

Fighting Joe assumed command of the Center Grand Division on the sixteenth. It totaled almost 40,000 men and was a much larger body than he had led before he was wounded. It was self-sufficient—an army in itself. An ambitious, aggressive general could expect to do much with such a force! The Third Corps was now commanded by General George Stoneman, an old California associate. Stoneman had been in charge of the cavalry in the Peninsula campaign and his troops had brought on Hooker's battle of Williamsburg. Recently he had succeeded General Heintzelman, the original leader of the corps. Heintzelman had been retained in Washington to command the defenses of that area. General Daniel Butterfield, the senior division commander, took over the Fifth Corps when Hooker stepped up.[40]

One would assume that the newly appointed Commanding General would be in perfect harmony with the war administration as to the immediate movements of the army, but this was not the case. Halleck visited Burnside to urge an advance via Culpeper and Gordonsville, but Burnside wanted to take the army to Fredericksburg. From there he planned to attack the enemy and march directly to Richmond along the shortest route.[41] This plan had been generally condemned but he adopted it when he understood that Lincoln finally approved. Hooker attended a meeting of Halleck and Burnside on the issue but his opinion was not asked. He afterward went on record as having been opposed.[42] On the march to Fredericksburg he was given the job of bringing up the rear and performed this duty so well that he received Burnside's written thanks.[43]

Apparently Fighting Joe was the first to realize that swiftness of movement was the only thing that could redeem the new plan of campaign. He proposed to Burnside that the men of the Center Grand Division be sent across the Rappahannock at once before the enemy could concentrate along the line of the river.[44] The suggestion was also transmitted to Secretary of War Stanton. "The rebels are as much in the dark with regard to our movements as we have heretofore been of theirs."[45] A bold move such as this did not correspond with Burnside's idea of "fair play" and Hooker was to be held on the north bank of the river until Lee set up his defenses along the south bank. The Commanding General shrugged off the suggestion by replying that the move seemed a little premature and that the lack of pontoons at Fredericksburg would keep the remainder of the army from crossing in conjunction with Hooker's force.[46]

In response to Burnside's wishes Hooker ordered his two corps to march the morning of the twenty-second for the Richmond, Fredericksburg and Potomac Railway crossing of Potomac Creek. Here on the south bank a permanent camp was established.[47] It was a position so well removed from the Rappahannock that there could be no danger of Hooker's bringing on a battle by some precipitate action.

While Burnside waited for his pontoon train and the enemy to concentrate on the other side of the river, Hooker reprovisioned his new command and prepared for action. He received a gratifying note from Senator Nesmith forwarding the appreciation of the Oregon legislature for the "daring deeds and heroic achievements which have so constantly marked the brilliant course of General Joseph Hooker, late a resident of this State." This welcome approbation did not long take his mind off what he considered Burnside's inability. His attitude was enhanced by the reflection that he, instead of the bungling Burnside, might now be directing the army. A letter bitterly criticizing the Commanding General was dispatched to Stanton.[48]

Henry Villard, the able correspondent, visited Hooker at his camp. He describes him as having the appearance of the ideal soldier and captain—six feet in height, fine proportions, erect carriage, handsome features, rosy complexion, an expressive mouth and large gray-blue eyes, with an abundance of blond hair. Villard had to add that he was even then notorious for his sharp tongue.[49] Hooker was in a bad humor. He was unsparing in his criticism of the conduct of the war in the East, of the government, of Halleck, McClellan, Pope and his new Commander.

When Burnside finally called a conference of his leading generals to discuss the place and method of crossing the Rappahannock, Hooker's humor had not improved. The Commanding General announced that he proposed to make the attempt at Skinker's Neck, fourteen miles below Fredericksburg, and asked for an expression of opinion. Sumner and Franklin said they were ready to do their best to carry out the plan but showed no real enthusiasm. Hooker was more outspoken; it was "preposterous to talk about our crossing the river in the face of Lee's army"; he "would like to be in command of fifty thousand men on the other side of the river, and have an enemy make the attempt."[50] He then suggested that the whole army should go across at United States Ford or Richards'

GENERAL JOSEPH HOOKER AND HIS STAFF IN THE SPRING OF 1863

### HOOKER'S HEADQUARTERS

The Chancellor Mansion, after Lee's artillery and fire had finished their work
of destruction on May 3, 1863.

Ford, about twelve miles above the town.[51] To this Burnside answered that his mind was made up.

Preparations were then made to carry out the plan, but the wary Lee was on the alert and a sufficient force had been sent down river to check it. Burnside then decided that he would "surprise" the enemy by crossing right at Fredericksburg.[52] Sumner's Grand Division was directed to prepare to cross opposite the town; Franklin's force was to do likewise two miles below; and Hooker was to advance to a position in the rear of Sumner ready to support whichever crossing showed more likelihood of success.[53] Sumner called a council of his generals to discuss what was to be done, and marked disapprobation was manifested. Burnside heard of the meeting and was irritated by the spirit of opposition but was determined to proceed.[54]

On December ninth Hooker, still incensed at Burnside's plan, ordered the commanders of his Third and Fifth Corps to provide their men with three days' cooked rations and sixty rounds of ammunition. Explicit instructions were given as to the manner in which the infantry and artillery would cross the river,[55] and Averell's cavalry brigade was ordered to follow the infantry to the new position opposite Fredericksburg.[56]

Fredericksburg was a historic Virginia town, the boyhood home of George Washington, and an important center of Revolutionary activity. In 1862 it had grown to 5,000 inhabitants and was the most important political and commercial town between Washington and Richmond. It was situated along the west bank of the Rappahannock at the base of a broken line of hills running parallel to the river. On these hills Lee had massed his veteran army in an admirable defensive position, particularly strong at Marye's Heights directly behind the town. On the Federal side were even more commanding hills, known as Stafford Heights, which furnished suitable artillery positions to protect a crossing. There was no doubt but that the Federal troops could be moved to the other side of the river; the question was how they would fare when they tried to go farther.

On the night of the tenth Burnside's Chief of Artillery, General H. J. Hunt, established an imposing array of batteries on Stafford Heights and at dawn the engineers began to set up their pontoon bridges. Resistance to the bridging in front of Fredericksburg was heavy and the attempt had to be abandoned. A concentration of artillery upon the sharpshooters in the town merely succeeded in setting fires. Only when a large force was sent across the river in boats were the Confederate skirmishers dispersed. The job was then completed, but by this time it was late afternoon.[57] The bridges below the town were not opposed so severely because of the lack of protective cover, and by 10:30 A.M. one was completed.

Part of Franklin's Grand Division went over that evening to establish a bridgehead, and Sumner's men occupied the town.[58] The entire next day was spent in crossing the remainder of the Right and Left Grand Divisions and in reconnoitering. Hooker, with the balance of the army, remained in reserve on the east bank. By now any surprise value of the move had been lost and Burnside was too committed to reconsider. That night two divisions of the Third Corps were detached to support General Franklin's crossing.[59] Unfortunately, they were Hooker's best— his old division and Kearny's late command. This was the first movement in a chain of circumstances which eventually reduced his command by two-thirds and his slight regard for Burnside by that much and more too.

There was a haze the following morning, not only in the sky but also in the Commanding General's mind. He had maintained sincerely that he was not the man to lead the army and he was now about to prove it. Though he had given his Grand Division Commanders reason to think that he contemplated an attack in force on the Confederate right,[60] his first orders on the morning of the thirteenth left them to wonder what the program really was. Franklin, who now had 60,000 men[61] on the plain across the river and at his bridges and who was in a position to deploy his large force for a grand attack, was ordered to send one division (5,000 men), or possibly two, to seize the heights on the enemy's right near Hamilton's Crossing on the railroad. The rest of his force was to be held in reserve for a rapid push down the old Stage Road to Richmond. Sumner also was ordered to make a partial attack: one division was to seize the heights in the rear of the town while another division was held in support. It was apparent that Burnside was going to conform to established Army of Potomac practice and fight his army in detail, thereby compensating the enemy for great disparity in numbers.

The sun chased away the fog before morning was half over and Hooker joined Burnside and Sumner on the roof of the Lacy House across from Fredericksburg. Before them were the veterans of the Second Corps occupying the town; to their left were the men of the Ninth Corps extending south, filling, in part, the gap between the Right and Left Grand Divisions. Three or four miles away in the same direction could be seen the massed array of blue coats commanded by Franklin. Even

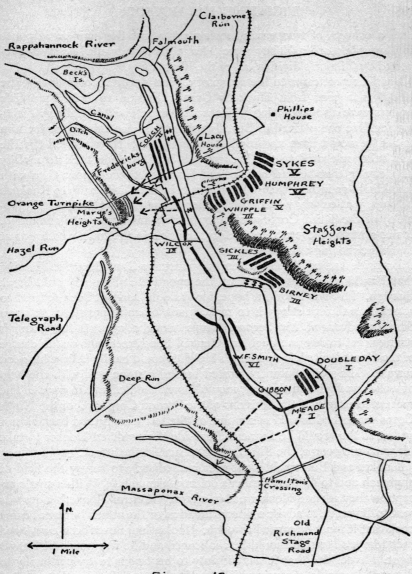

Figure 12.
Fredericksburg, December 13, 1863
☐ Confederate Defensive Position
█ Position of The Federal Troops
     at the Opening of the Action
⇌ Position of Federal Batteries

Rappahannock River
Claiborne Run
Falmouth
Beck's Is.
Phillips House
Canal
Ditch
COUCH II
Lacy House
Fredericksburg
SYKES V
HUMPHREY VI
Orange Turnpike
Marye's Heights
GRIFFIN V
WHIPPLE III
Stafford Heights
Hazel Run
WILCOX II
SICKLES III
BIRNEY III
Telegraph Road
W.F.SMITH VI
DOUBLEDAY I
Deep Run
GIBBON II
MEADE I
N.
1 Mile
Massaponax River
Hamilton's Crossing
Old Richmond Stage Road

then a column of troops was moving out across the plain in response to Burnside's order. They were Meade's Pennsylvania Reserves supported by Gibbon's division, all of the First Corps.[62]

Soon a report came to the group of officers on the Lacy roof that the 10,000 men sent from Hooker's Grand Division to hold Franklin's bridges were also advancing. This news was received bitterly by Fighting Joe. He complained to Burnside that when the time came for him to act he would have nothing left to fight with. He protested that he was being relegated to the background, but Burnside tried to mollify him, saying that he had not ordered Hooker's two divisions then with Franklin to go into battle.[63] This was true, but was little balm to Hooker's feelings, particularly when a little later the remaining division (Whipple's) of the Third Corps was removed from his immediate command. It was sent to relieve a Second Corps division in the town which was at that time moving out to the attack.

Burnside had held up his attempt against the Confederate left hoping that Franklin would so soften up the enemy that Sumner could break through. This was a forlorn hope, for Franklin had not been ordered to attack in sufficient strength to make much of an impression. At noon Sumner advanced his Second Corps straight against the enemy's strong point to certain slaughter. General Longstreet, who was in charge of the Confederate left on Marye's Heights, could hardly believe his good fortune. His steady infantry, posted behind a stone wall with the help of well-served guns in the rear, mowed down the Federals in waves. The successive attacks of the divisions of the Second Corps and of the Ninth Corps which had moved in support on the left were turned back almost as fast as they could be formed. Burnside then ordered Hooker to take his remaining corps, the Fifth, across to sustain the attack.

Hooker and Butterfield went over immediately to survey the field of approach and to talk to Sumner's defeated generals.[64] With a single exception they advised Hooker not to attack.[65] One of Hooker's aides was sent to Burnside to advise a discontinuation of the attack but word came back that it must be carried through. Hooker had never been convinced that Marye's Heights should be challenged and he was now sure he was right. He decided that it was his duty to his troops to try personally to dissuade Burnside. Spurring his horse back across the river he reported to the Commanding General that the whole army could not take the Confederate position.[66] His opinion was that of James E. Longstreet who told General Lee in the midst of the Federal attack: "General, if you put every man now on the other side of the Potomac on that field to approach me over the same line, and give me plenty of ammunition, I will kill them all before they reach my line."[67]

Hooker was calmly told that his orders remained unchanged.[68] He not only received this discouraging word but was also informed that Griffin's division of the Fifth Corps had meanwhile been detached to help out the Ninth Corps.[69] Now the leader of the Center Grand Division found his command whittled down to but two divisions (Humphreys' and Sykes'), less than 10,000 men. He remained with Burnside for some time but communicated his orders to his Fifth Corps commander, Butterfield, across the river. At 3:12 Humphreys' division was marching up through the town and thirty minutes later had advanced on the riflemen and batteries upon the hill. They charged no farther than had the Second Corps at an earlier hour and left twenty-five percent of the division sprawled on the bloody field.[70] Hooker returned to the battlefield in a violent temper. He massed all the available batteries and directed them at the stone wall. His remaining division under Sykes had already been ordered to the foot of the road leading up to the heights.[71] They were to be spared, however, for Hooker halted them. He testified later: "Finding that I had lost as many men as my orders required me to lose, I suspended the attack"[72]— a good reason, and a characteristic bit of phrasing.

The artillery continued firing briskly until sundown when preparations were made to bring in the wounded. The Second Corps was holding an advanced picket line which Hooker believed should be abandoned and he once more went across the river to army headquarters for orders, but Burnside was afraid such an abandonment would be an admission of defeat. Apparently the loss of over 7,000 soldiers at this one point was not sufficient evidence.[73] Hooker was ordered to relieve the advanced line with Sykes' Regulars, and 204 more men became casualties because of this needless exposure.[74]

That night Hooker was placed in command of the forces in the town, which then comprised the Fifth, Second and parts of the Third and Ninth Corps. Butterfield took charge of the north end of Fredericksburg and Couch of the Second Corps, the south end.[75] Hooker headquarters were set up near the Masonic Lodge which, on November 4, 1752, had initiated a neighboring farmer named George Washington.[76] It was a bitter night; the wounded were freezing on the slopes of Marye's Heights, and the troops crowded in the town were unnerved from the terrible drubbing. There was the constant fear that the enemy would shell the town or attempt an assault.[77] The officers knew they had been badly defeated and were free in admitting it, even though the Commanding General was not convinced. Franklin on the left had not lost so many men but had been equally unsuccessful in making an impression on the enemy's position. Hooker's two divisions on this flank had supported the advance and alone had suffered over 1,000 casualties.[78]

On Sunday December fourteenth, the men protected themselves as best they could with trenches around the buildings on the western edge of the town, and Burnside held a council of war. The completeness of the defeat had begun to sink in, and he wished to vindicate himself. He proposed a foolhardy attack on Marye's Heights with his old Ninth Corps, led by none other than himself. The other members of the council were successful in preventing this sacrifice.[79] In response to the question how the Confederate position could best be taken the answer of the majority was: Not at all! Hooker believed that the only possible chance was to form a heavy column of attack at night when the enemy could not see to use artillery.[80] It was finally decided that the army should fall back but hold Fredericksburg as a "symbol of achievement."

Hooker left the meeting to resume command of the town. During a conference with Couch it was agreed that 12,000 men of the Center Grand Division should be left to hold Fredericksburg.[81] Hooker soon concluded that even this number was unnecessarily large in view of the discomfort of the men and the possibility that the enemy might soon shell the crowded town. He asked Burnside to order all but two divisions back to their camps.[82]

Burnside came over on Monday to check Hooker's dispositions. Hooker's wish to send out a flag of truce for the purpose of burying the Federal dead was refused by Burnside, who looked upon it as an open admission of defeat.[83] He did, however, order most of the troops back across the river as Hooker desired.[84]

The town was held until early Tuesday morning when Burnside finally gave up.[85] The last troops crossed over to their own side of the river by eight o'clock under Hooker's supervision.[86] The strong Federal batteries on the east bank had discouraged a Confederate counterattack and had made it possible for the Army of the Potomac to depart in peace. Nothing had been gained and the services of 13,000 soldiers had been lost.[87] Confederate casualties totaled but 4,000.

The scattered divisions of Hooker's command were returned to the old camp on Potomac Creek where they were refitted and once more prepared for a renewal of action.[88] "Fighting Joe" was in a bad frame of mind. Burnside had robbed the army of a chance to accomplish something and had deprived him of an opportunity to show to advantage. His Grand Division, the largest body of men under his command to date, had been taken away from him and scattered up and down the Federal line at Fredericksburg. His division under Humphreys had made as spirited an attack as any during the war; Sykes' division had bravely clung to its advanced position the night after the battle; and the batteries under his immediate command had been served well. But this was little accomplishment for a general who had expected and deserved to be a kingpin in the battle.

In this bitter mood Hooker went up to Washington for his first appearance before the Joint Congressional Committee on the Conduct of the War. The public uproar over the disastrous defeat called for immediate investigation. Hooker was unsparing of Burnside. He stated that the strength of the Confederate position was well known beforehand and that there was no excuse for the attack. He added that Franklin did not do all that he could have done[89]—which statement was more to the Committee's taste. Franklin was a McClellan man and had already been settled on as the scapegoat for the disaster. Burnside was harmless and in spite of his defeat both Lincoln and the Committee wanted him to remain in command—this despite the fact that the Army of the Potomac had lost its morale for the first time. Even loyal General Sumner stated before the Committee:

"It is difficult to describe it [the condition of the army] any other way than by saying there is a great deal too much croaking—there is not sufficient confidence."[90]

Franklin stated in his own defense: "There was not a man in my command who did not believe that everything he [Burnside] would undertake would fail."[91]

Meanwhile as the men sulked in their camps desertion increased at a fearful rate. The Army of the Potomac was unquestionably demoralized. Honest Burnside muddled along for the balance of the month, absolving the President and the War Department of any blame, admitting that he had followed his own convictions. Four days after Christmas he was ready to put his head in the lion's mouth again. The infantry and artillery were ordered in readiness and the cavalry was already on its way when the President ordered that no general movement should be made without Burnside's first consulting him. Burnside countermanded his orders and went at once to Washington. There he was told that some of the officers under his command had informed the President the army was not in condition to move.[92]

Hooker's force remained in its old camp except for Averell's cavalry which scouted along the north bank of the Rappahannock as far as Warrenton Junction. A proposed raid around the Confederate Army by 1,000 cavalrymen under the eager General Averell, supported part way by four of Hooker's brigades, came to naught when the President issued his "no general movement" order.[93] Hooker had been strengthened by the transfer to his command of two good general officers. George Gordon Meade was put in charge of the Fifth Corps; he outranked Butterfield and had been a steady fighter with the Army of the Potomac since the Peninsula campaign.[94] Gershom Mott, who had been with the Jersey Blues on the Peninsula and at Second Bull Run, returned to Hooker as their commander.[95]

The new year of 1863 gave but slight promise of being a happy one for the Federals in the East. A correspondent of the New York *Times*, in a summary of conditions and prospects, reported Halleck as saying: "The Army of the Potomac has ceased to exist." Lincoln's war administration distrusted the army and the army distrusted the war administration. The situation was so bad that Halleck wished to dismember the army and get rid of Hooker by sending him to North Carolina.[96] The McClellan men were antagonized by the dismissal from the service of General Fitz-John Porter.[97] He had been found guilty, as planned. Perhaps he was, but the decision had been reached long before the evidence was presented.

The only bright spot was a letter from Burnside to Lincoln on New Year's Day in which he said it was his firm belief he ought to retire to private life. He added that neither Stanton nor Halleck had the confidence of the officers, the soldiers or the country, and he doubted that there was much confidence left in his own management of the army. The President was urged to rid himself of all three. It was the best advice Lincoln ever received on the conduct of the war. But he could not see that a clean sweep of this nature would better things and he even refused to keep his copy of the letter.[98]

Since he could not resign, the Commanding General had no alternative but to try to restore confidence in himself by some kind of military success. On January nineteenth Hooker's and Franklin's Grand Divisions were scheduled to go up the Rappahannock and turn the Confederate left flank while Sumner followed Franklin in reserve. The army had been increased by the addition of the Eleventh and Twelfth Corps under the command of General Franz Sigel. This Reserve Grand Division was to protect the army's communications.[99]

The movement did not get under way until noon of the twentieth and the place of crossing was changed at the last minute from United States Ford to Bank's Ford. The troops of the Center and Left Grand Divisions pressed toward the Ford but were bogged down by a driving storm of snow, sleet and rain which eliminated the roads and left only sticky mud for footing. The rain continued the following morning but the thicker the mud the more determined became Burnside. The pontoon wagons, the artillery and the ammunition trains were mired; even horses and mules needed assistance to extricate themselves.[100] It was impossible to lay the bridges for either of the Grand Divisions near the ford, and everyone except Burnside was ready to go home. It was obvious that the enemy was aware of the move and would have the entire day to mass defenses. The Confederate pickets even offered to come over and help build the bridges. As Burnside stewed over his misfortune the soldiers became more disheartened and his generals appealed to him for orders to move back to camp. Finally he saw the light and on the twenty-second gave the army permission to retrace its muddy steps. This completed what became known in the annals of the Army of the Potomac as the Mud March. Hooker had believed the chances against success were nineteen to one; Franklin corrected him saying the odds were twenty to zero![101] Again the army had been desperately humiliated.[102]

## CHAPTER XI

# APPOINTMENT TO THE COMMAND OF THE ARMY OF THE POTOMAC

PUBLIC opinion was now up in arms against the military policy of the administration. A successful end to the war seemed more remote than ever, and a spirit of defeatism was spreading. There was even talk of the government's falling and of a dictator's taking over to end the war. Hooker joined in, and possibly led, this kind of criticism within the army. Fighting Joe had never been one to refrain from speaking his mind, no matter how indiscreet his words might be. Now he talked to junior officers and news correspondents more freely than ever. One example of his indiscretion is a declaration made to Swinton of the New York *Times*. He said that the President and the government in Washington were "played out" and that nothing would go right until a dictator took over, the sooner the better.[1]

In the early part of January Hooker had been in Washington telling reporters what he could do with the army and, according to General Meade, investigating the possibilities of acquiring the command.[2] These possibilities looked bright: an alliance had been formed among those who sincerely believed in his military ability, those who hoped to prosper by his rise and, most important of all, the powerful group sponsoring Salmon P. Chase for President in 1864.[3] Chase had become convinced that Hooker entertained no political aspirations, and the ambitious Secretary of the Treasury had decided that Fighting Joe was just what he needed in the way of support from a popular military idol—a man who, he fondly thought, was certain to crush the rebellion. The radicals were looking upon Hooker with great favor. The Congressional Committee on the Conduct of the War had spent several days snooping around the camps after Fredericksburg and had agreed to the retention of Burnside only because he had seemed converted to their views. They feared that the army would force McClellan back into the command and would have liked Hooker to take over immediately.[4] All the papers except the more conservative ones were boosting Hooker's stock. The *Spirit of the Times* outdid the rest of the press with:

164

"We have in the Army of the Potomac, however, a General of the heroic stamp. A general who feels the enthusiasm of a soldier and who loves battle from an innate instinct for his business. The cry is universal, Hooker to the command."[5]

Ambrose E. Burnside was well aware of Hooker's attempt to replace him and had stood all he could. On the day after the Mud March was called off, he decided to bring the question of control to a head. He composed his General Order No. 8 which stated:

"General Joseph Hooker . . . having been guilty of unjust and unnecessary criticisms of the actions of his superior officers, and of the authorities, and having, by the general tone of his conversation, endeavored to create distrust in the minds of officers who have associated with him, and having, by omissions and otherwise, made reports and statements which were calculated to create incorrect impressions, and for habitually speaking in disparaging terms of other officers, is hereby dismissed from the service of the United States as a man unfit to hold an important commission, during a crisis like the present. . . ."

In addition, three brigadier generals were to be dismissed from the service for similar offenses, while Major Generals William Franklin and William Farrar Smith and two brigadiers were to be relieved from duty as no longer of service to the Army of the Potomac.[6]

Burnside told his Adjutant General to issue the order at once, but two personal friends persuaded him to show it to Abraham Lincoln first so as not to throw the President into an embarrassing position.[7] One of these friends, Henry J. Raymond of the New York *Times*, assured Burnside that he was on the right track but suggested the possibility that Hooker might attempt to raise a mutiny among his troops on the promulgation of the order. To this Burnside replied that in such event he would swing Hooker before sundown.[8] Strong words for Ambrose Burnside!

He then took the order, together with his resignation, to the President, making it clear that unless Lincoln approved the order he must accept the resignation. His demand staggered the beleaguered President and he turned the General away with the plea that he could do neither until he had consulted with his advisers.[9]

Henry Raymond took it upon himself to inform both Lincoln and Chase of Hooker's habitual indiscretions concerning the direction of the war. The way the two men responded to this taletelling is interesting. Lincoln replied, "That is all true—Hooker does talk badly; but the trouble is, he is stronger with the country today than any other man. Even if the country were told of Hooker's talk they would not believe it." Chase, on the other hand, professed great surprise, saying that he looked upon him as the man best fitted to command the Army of the Potomac— but that no man capable of so much selfish and unprincipled ambition was fit for so great a trust; that he would give up all thought of him henceforth.[10]  This was nonsense.  Chase had no thought of abandoning so promising an affiliation!

When Lincoln called together his advisers the consultation proceeded without any thought of retaining Burnside in command.  McClellan was straightway eliminated as a successor despite loud popular clamor for his return.  General William Starke Rosecrans, the recent victor in the battle of Stone's River, Tennessee, was then proposed as a repeatedly successful commander.  Unfortunately, Rosecrans was a Western man and affiliated with a Western army; the majority thought it unwise to place him over the Eastern-dominated Army of the Potomac.[11]

Within Burnside's army the top-ranking men were Generals Sumner, Franklin and Hooker.  Sumner was undoubtedly too old for the job, and Franklin was rapidly being made the scapegoat for Burnside's failure at Fredericksburg.  Thus, Hooker became the logical choice and undoubtedly would have been appointed without further discussion had it not been for the strenuous objections of Halleck and Stanton.  They said they knew his lack of qualifications too well and that he was not to be trusted with an independent command of such responsibility.  Halleck, particularly, contended that there were reasons of an imperative character why he thought Hooker should be passed by.

Despite Lincoln's apparent desire to have Hooker, the belligerency of Stanton and Halleck kept the issue open.  Two other candidates were suggested: General John F. Reynolds of the First Corps and General George G. Meade of the Fifth.  Reynolds was dropped; Halleck had already sounded him out on his availability and the straightforward Reynolds had been discouraging: his acceptance of the command would not be voluntary unless he were granted a liberty of action hitherto unknown to commanders of the Army of the Potomac.  The choice was then narrowed to Hooker and Meade, with Chase and the Committee on the Conduct of the War favoring Hooker, while Stanton and Halleck favored Meade.  Lincoln broke the deadlock by appointing Fighting Joe.[12]  Stanton wanted to resign in protest but persuaded himself that it was his duty to remain.

The news was conveyed to the army in War Department General Order No. 20 of January 25, 1863. Halleck wired Hooker that the President wished an interview with him immediately. The least surprised person in the army, when the news came out, was Hooker himself. He had never doubted but that sooner or later he would be called to the command. He also had never doubted his ability to command when his chance came. He disclaimed any use of improper influences to gain the position and of any previously expressed desire for it; it was conferred upon him, he said, "for his sword alone."[13] He ranked twenty-seventh in the *Official Army Register* at this time.[14] The men ahead of him were serving in the Western armies or had been either shunted to minor independent commands in the East or sidetracked permanently.

The new appointment was well received by the great majority of the rank and file who knew Hooker for the fighter he was. To them he was a soldier's general and they were genuinely fond of him. His bitter tongue might gall the officers but it was never directed at them. They were not concerned about his intemperance nor were they interested in evaluating his moral character. He shared the risks of battle and he took care of their bodily wants—attributes that loomed large in their eyes.

Many of the general officers and some of the field officers were not too well disposed toward him. Burnside could not be expected to work effectively or willingly under him and was given a thirty-day leave of absence. Edwin V. Sumner and William B. Franklin refused to serve under him.[15] The same War Department Order that promoted him banished these two veterans from the Army of the Potomac for good.[16]

Of the generals remaining, Darius N. Couch thought that Lincoln had committed a grave error.[17] William F. Smith, in the colloquialism of the day, remarked: "Hooker would start out to make a spoon and end by spoiling a horn."[18] Oliver Otis Howard had misgivings because of Hooker's personal conduct.[19] Carl Schurz said, "[Hooker] is a man with no firm moral force but he is a good soldier and in addition has the talent publicly to display his achievements in the most favorable light."[20] George Gordon Meade, who was one of the more intellectual men in the army and an honest critic, had known Hooker at West Point and in Mexico. In a letter to his son he wrote:

"Hooker is a very good soldier and a capital officer to command an army corps, but I should doubt his qualifications to command a large army. If fighting, however, is all that is necessary to make a general, he will certainly distinguish himself."[21]

Two of the lesser officers who were not enthusiastic about the new appointment were serving in the Massachusetts Cavalry and were worthy sons of honored Bay State families. They were Charles Russell Lowell and Charles Francis Adams, Jr. Lowell claimed to like Hooker very much personally but feared that he would do the army "a mischief" if he rose to the command, as he had his head in the clouds.[22] A more emphatically dissenting voice was that of young Adams. In a letter to his father, the United States Ambassador to England, on January 30, 1863, he said that only disgust was felt toward the government which had taken away McClellan, cashiered Porter, relieved Burnside, a good corps commander, lost Sumner, the best defensive fighter in the army, and Franklin, the ablest officer, "all this that Hooker may be placed in command, a man who has not the confidence of the army and who in private character is well known to be—I need not say what."[23]

To sum up these doubts of Hooker's ability to handle the oft-defeated Army of the Potomac, it is fair to say that no one questioned his fighting ability, but many wondered about his capacity to weld this demoralized body of men into a cohesive unit. Doubt was expressed not so much concerning his knowledge of the job, but the intangible attribute of moral character. Could he inspire the co-operation needed from his leading generals and put an end to the petty bickering among his officers? Could he curb his biting tongue and maintain what good will was proffered him? He was embarking on a hazardous path!

The Southern leaders were not impressed. Hooker's appointment came as a surprise to Robert E. Lee. He held no great respect for Fighting Joe's military ability in a position of such importance.[24] Pierre Beauregard defied him to handle successfully over 100,000 men and said, "If Hooker has two to one against Lee, then I pity the former."[25] General W. H. C. Whiting declared, "Hooker is a fool, and always was, and thats a comfort."[26]

The Northern press reacted generously. The radical papers announced that at last the right man had been found. The *Spirit of the Times*, as might be expected, was most enthusiastic:

"With Rosecrans in the West and Hooker in the East, there is not treason enough in the North, rebellion enough in the South, or imbecility or cross purposes sufficient in the Cabinet, to prevent the war for the Union from being brought to an early and satisfactory conclusion."[27]

The conservative editors, although disappointed with the selection, thought it wise to withhold their fire until Hooker was given a chance to prove himself. The New York *Herald* was not too well pleased. On January tenth it had sarcastically predicted Hooker's appointment on the ground that all indications pointed to the fact that he was not a desirable commander and that, therefore, the war administration would be sure to choose him![28] One of the leading California papers took a sensible view: "Whether he is competent for the chief command or not, time alone can develop"; it expressed the hope that the press would not "spoil" Hooker with flattery as it had preceding commanders.[29] The West Coast papers in general took a saner view of the military scene than those of the East—perhaps a case where distance lent enlightenment. The Richmond *Dispatch* was rather vicious and devoted itself to working over Hooker's unfortunate California days:

". . . He failed in this [farming] and applied himself most industriously to borrowing money of all who would lend it to him, and drinking whiskey whenever and wherever he could obtain it . . . he became a constant uninvited visitor to the Pacific Club of San Francisco to the annoyance of the members."[30]

The morning of January twenty-sixth, Hooker said in his General Orders No. 1:

"By direction of the President of the United States the undersigned assumes command of the Army of the Potomac. He enters upon the discharge of the duties imposed by this trust with a just appreciation of their responsibility. Since the formation of this army he has been identified with its history. He has shared with you its glories and reverses with no other desire than that these relations might remain unchanged until its destiny should be accomplished. In the record of your achievements there is much to be proud of, and, with the blessing of God, we will contribute something to the renown of our arms and the success of our cause. To secure these ends, your commander will require the cheerful and zealous co-operation of every officer and soldier in this army.

"In equipment, intelligence, and valor the enemy is our inferior; let us never hesitate to give him battle wherever we can find him. . . ."[31]

Hooker then left for Washington to meet with the President. During the ensuing conference he was asked whether he wished command of the Department of Washington and the Upper Potomac in addition to the main army. He declined on the ground that it would require all his time to place the Army of the Potomac in the field in good condition by spring. He then came out directly and asked the President to stand between him and Halleck. Halleck was extremely partial to the Western armies and neither the Army of the Potomac nor its officers expected justice from him. Hooker assured Lincoln that he was aware that Halleck had twice opposed his appointment to the command. In closing, he stated his apprehensions over morale, doubting that "it [the army] could be saved to the country."[32]

He left the President carrying the famous letter of appointment,[33] quoted in full in the foreword. His reaction to it is most thoroughly covered in Noah Brooks's account of Hooker's reading it to him in April 1863. When he reached the part where Lincoln accused him of thwarting Burnside, Hooker said: "The President is mistaken. I never thwarted Burnside in any way, shape or manner. Burnside was pre-eminently a man of deportment, and he took his deportment with him out of the Army of the Potomac, thank God!" This sounds like Hooker, but Brooks goes on to tell how, when the General had finished reading the letter, he had tears in his eyes. "That is just such a letter as a father might write to his son. It is a beautiful letter, and, although I think he was harder on me than I deserved, I will say that I love the man who wrote it."[34] This is strictly out of character and does not agree with other testimony to the effect that Hooker considered the letter a rebuke.[35] More than likely Fighting Joe's eyes flashed while he read and perhaps he concluded with, "By the Eternal! I will show him!"

## CHAPTER XII

## "ADMINISTRATIVE JOE"

ON THE evening of January 28, 1863, Hooker returned to army headquarters at Falmouth, a few miles north of Fredericksburg, to make his attempt to "save the Army of the Potomac for the country." He was in great spirits, telling Meade that he had been given everything he wanted![1]

At this time the army was organized into four grand divisions composed of eight corps of infantry with artillery and cavalry complements, plus a separate artillery reserve, a large provost guard and two battalions of engineers. The total number reported as present for duty, equipped, was 147,000[2]—a considerable exaggeration, but still the army was very respectable in size if not in tone. This great array was camped in the area opposite Fredericksburg between the Rappahannock and Potomac Rivers. Infantry and cavalry picket lines were duly extended and the camps were free from hostile threat. The base of supplies was located on the Potomac River at Aquia Landing, terminus of the Richmond, Fredericksburg and Potomac Railroad.

On the opposite side of the Rappahannock, stretched along from Bank's Ford through the old entrenchments at Fredericksburg and on to Skinker's Neck, the Army of Northern Virginia waited, 74,000 strong.[3] The Confederate infantry was protected by a continuous line of parapets with abatis and some swampland for further security, while the artillery was well situated on the hills to cover the river and the plain between. Cavalry outposts extended from Beverly Ford far down the Rappahannock.[4]

In addition to his two-to-one preponderance of numbers, Hooker had the satisfaction of knowing that Washington was protected by 45,000 men under Major General S. P. Heintzelman,[5] while Harpers Ferry and the upper Potomac were defended by 21,000 commanded by Major General R. C. Schenck.[6]

"Beware of rashness but with energy and sleepless vigilance go forward and give us victories" was the only instruction to Hooker from Lincoln in the letter of appointment. Halleck was more specific, referring him to the general instructions concerning the operation of the army issued to Burnside and approved by the President on January 7, 1863.[7] The main points were as follows:

1. The importance of covering Washington and Harpers Ferry was always to be kept in mind.
2. The first object was to defeat Lee, not to capture Richmond.
3. The move was to be made via the fords above Fredericksburg.
4. The cavalry and light artillery were to be used on the enemy's communications.
5. The enemy was to be kept from making large detachments or distant raids. This was to be accomplished by keeping him occupied with constant threats.

Lincoln from time to time added some of his homely witticisms, and Halleck made some slight suggestions, but the above points remained the general program.

Before attempting to activate it, the new Commander was compelled to turn his attention to the many pressing administrative problems inherited from Burnside. Of first importance was the selection of a general staff to aid him in handling them. This he did promptly. In General Order No. 2, issued January twenty-ninth, appointments were made for most phases of headquarters staffwork.[8]

Hooker's most important selection was that of Major General Daniel Butterfield as his alter ego, his Chief of Staff. "Little Dan" was frail of body, and in height came up only to Hooker's shoulders. Physically he was a sorry figure compared with the large, well-upholstered frame of Fighting Joe. He was not a West Pointer but a man of wide experience in business affairs with a genius for organization and the promotion of big enterprises.[9] He did not, however, have the detailed knowledge of military science so important to the work of Chief of Staff. At Fredericksburg he commanded the Fifth Corps but had since been superseded by Meade, who ranked him. Butterfield had been chagrined by this and believed that Stanton opposed him, possibly because of his personal friendship with Salmon P. Chase.[10] However, it is also possible that this friendship was responsible for his selection as Hooker's Chief of Staff. Chase may have urged it with the idea in mind of having in Butterfield a check on his investment in Fighting Joe.

Brigadier General Charles P. Stone had really been Hooker's first choice for Chief of Staff, but this capable soldier was still under a cloud because of the massacre of part of his division at Ball's Bluff in Octo-

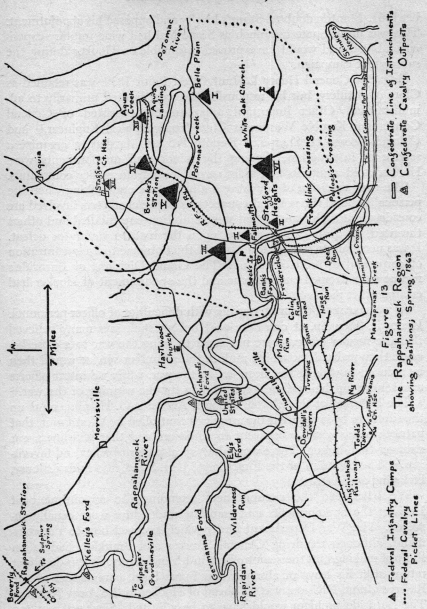

Figure 13

The Rappahannock Region
showing Positions; Spring, 1863

▲ Federal Infantry Camps
···· Federal Cavalry
      Picket Lines

□ Confederate Line of Intrenchments
◿ Confederate Cavalry Outposts

ber 1861. Stanton doubted Stone's loyalty and opposed his appointment. This was unfortunate inasmuch as Stone had had wide military experience abroad and would have proved invaluable to Hooker during the subsequent campaign.

Brigadier General Henry J. Hunt, West Point 1839, was retained as Chief of Artillery, but his responsibilities were limited primarily to administration. Other important appointments consisted of General Gouverneur Kemble Warren as Chief Topographical Engineer,[11] and Colonel George H. Sharpe as Deputy Provost Marshal to organize a service of information. Among the minor staff appointments were Hooker's old adjutants and aides carried over from earlier commands.

The reorganization of any army is a hazardous undertaking when the personalities and the political connections of the characters involved are considered; at such times, when some ambitions are fulfilled and others thwarted, an army can be started upon the road to victory or defeat. It was necessary to subject the Army of the Potomac to a reorganization of corps and division command. The Grand Divisions of Burnside's regime were deemed cumbersome and the appointment of Hooker had created other problems.

As we have seen, the army was rife with difficulties of officer personnel. Henry E. Tremain, at one time on Hooker's staff, says many believed that the regular officers were not eager to bring the war to a close because they realized their high rank in the volunteer service would then be reduced to what it had been before the war, while volunteer officers cared more for their political future than for the winning of the war.[12]

The historian of the Eleventh Corps, Augustus C. Hamlin, sums up the situation by saying that the army was controlled by West Point, that patriotism was often subservient to ambition, and that selfishness was stronger than honor. There were always jealousy, suspicion and favoritism.[13] The historian of the First Corps, J. H. Stine, also finds jealousy, bickering and distrust.[14]

We have seen the circumstances attending the appointment of Hooker; the appointments and transfers under him were equally involved. The War Department Order which assigned him to the command, although removing General Sumner and Franklin, had fallen short of making him the senior officer in his own army. Burnside might return after his leave of absence, and Franz Sigel, commander of the Reserve Grand Division, was far ahead of Hooker in the *Army Register*. The Burnside problem would have to be adjusted. Sigel was not too important; he had not been associated with the Army of the Potomac for long and might not be resentful of taking orders from Hooker. They had satisfactorily patched up a quarrel which had started when a report reached Sigel that Hooker had remarked to some officers: "He [Sigel] is a damned coward. He has an irresistible instinct to run, and manifests it on all occasions." Hooker denied this report: "No words of that character ever passed my lips."[15]

In General Order No. 6, issued February fifth, Hooker abandoned the Grand Divisions as impeding rather than facilitating the character of the movements planned.[16] It is interesting to note that Lee had but two main units of infantry at this time (Longstreet's and Jackson's corps); Hooker inherited four but deemed it necessary to increase the number. (When Grant took over the army the following spring he went back to a smaller number of units.)

The new organization set up the army as follows:

*First Corps:* Major General John F. Reynolds of Pennsylvania to be retained. Perhaps the best all-round soldier in the army, he had come close to receiving the position now held by Hooker. His division commanders were: James S. Wadsworth, lately military governor of Washington, a radical abolitionist and friend of Stanton; John C. Robinson, who had never completed his work at the Military Academy; and Abner Doubleday, a cool deliberate man of high intelligence and a West Pointer.

*Second Corps:* Major General Darius N. Couch of New York to be retained. He was frail and in bad health but was of strong, decisive character; a West Pointer of 1846 and a fighter in the Army of the Potomac since the Peninsula campaign. His division commanders were: Winfield S. Hancock, a real leader; John Gibbon of North Carolina; and William H. French. (Both Gibbon and French were artillery experts.) All were West Point graduates and had seen continuous service with the Army of the Potomac. This was a well-officered corps.

*Third Corps:* Brigadier General Daniel E. Sickles of New York to be appointed temporarily. He was the only non-West Point corps commander to last out Hooker's command. In lower Maryland his relations with Hooker had not been pleasant, but as he went through battle after battle with Hooker's old division a firm friendship had developed. Sickles now exerted considerable influence on him. The Third Corps and his old division would always be closest to Fighting Joe's heart. One of his first acts after receiving the command was to assign his friend, Hiram G. Berry, a Democratic state politician from Maine, to the "Hooker Division."[17] David Birney, a lawyer and son of the notorious abolitionist, commanded Kearny's old division. The third division was led by Amiel K. Whipple, the only West Pointer of the four leading officers of the Corps.

*Fifth Corps:* Major General George G. Meade of Pennsylvania to be retained. He was a West Point man of 1835, high-strung, a scholar of lofty character. He understood Hooker better than anyone else in the army. His division commanders were: Charles Griffin, a sound tactician; George Sykes, who led the regular army regiments; and Alexander Humphreys, a man of military brilliance who had been a member of McClellan's staff.

*Sixth Corps:* Major General John Sedgwick of Connecticut to be transferred from the Ninth Corps. He had been a classmate of Hooker's at West Point and was the oldest of the corps commanders. He had the reputation of a fighter, gained partly from the severe wounds he received while on the Peninsula and at Antietam. At the head of his divisions were: William Brooks, Albion Howe and John Newton—all from West Point.

*Eleventh Corps:* Major General Franz Sigel, a German revolutionary and military scholar, to be retained. He was a veteran of the war in the West, had faced Jackson in the Shenandoah Valley and had taken over part of Hooker's division at Second Bull Run. Experience had not taught him a great deal. Division commanders were Julius Stahel and the prominent German-American Generals Adolph von Steinwehr and Carl Schurz.

*Twelfth Corps:* Major General Henry W. Slocum of New York to be retained. Slocum was the youngest of the corps commanders, only eleven years out of West Point. He had been a fighter with the Army of the Potomac, however, since its first battle. There were only two divisions under his immediate command. They were led by Alpheus S. Williams and John Geary. Williams was a Yale graduate who had gone west where he acquired a controlling interest in the Detroit *Daily Advertiser.* He had been appointed a brigadier general of state troops in 1861 and had risen to command of a division at Antietam where he had brought his men to Hooker's relief.[18] Geary was 6 feet 5 inches tall. He had been a volunteer officer in the Mexican War, then became prominent in civil affairs as mayor of San Francisco and later as territorial governor of Kansas.

The same General Order provided that the army corps was to be considered a unit for the organization of the artillery. This reduced the power of the Chief of Artillery, General Hunt—and so created the probability of his becoming a critic of the new command. Of even more importance, it led to the crippling of a great arm of the service at a crucial hour. The artillery was not regrouped, despite uneven distribution. Only six field officers above the rank of captain were assigned to this branch of the service.[19] Despite his years in the 1st Artillery, Hooker was not showing an appreciation of the organization in the one field where the Federals had superiority.

The cavalry was to be consolidated into one corps instead of being distributed by regiments throughout the army. Brigadier General Stoneman of New York, who had recently commanded the Third Corps of infantry, was put in charge. He had had experience in this line previously: McClellan had taken him from his own staff to head the cavalry on the Peninsula. The Cavalry Corps was organized in four divisions under Alfred E. Pleasonton, W. W. Averell, David McMasters Gregg and John Buford.

The consolidation of the cavalry was a strong move. Up to this time it had been inferior in ability and spirit to the Confederate troopers under General Jeb Stuart. Hooker encouraged his horsemen to attack enemy pickets and outposts hoping that, stimulated by small successes, they would become instilled with a feeling of confidence.[20] Within four months the cavalry was holding its own in pitched battles with the foe. To quote a regular dragoon, "From the day of its reorganization under Hooker, the cavalry of the Army of the Potomac commenced a new life."[21] The remark "Who ever saw a dead cavalryman?" often accredited to Hooker, could no longer with justice be applied to the Federal troopers.

The Ninth Corps presented a problem: Burnside, its commander, would soon resume his leadership and this would create an impossible situation if it were to be retained as part of the Army of the Potomac. A very judicious decision was made: it was to be sent to Fortress Monroe to report to General Dix for further orders. Major General William F. Smith, late commander of the Sixth Corps, was sent along with it as temporary head, thus making way for Sedgwick to lead the Sixth Corps and, at the same time, removing a McClellan man from the scene.[22]

Halleck immediately approved Hooker's reorganization as a step in the right direction.[23] Within a week, however, a major change had to be made. Franz Sigel could not forget that he was the highest ranking general then in the army and petitioned to be relieved. His was the smallest corps in the army and he found this to be "exceedingly unpleasant and dispiriting."[24] Hooker could not assuage his feelings by breaking up other corps to give him men,[25] nor could Sigel increase his strength with replacements from Washington, since Halleck was notoriously antagonistic to foreigners in the army. Stanton could see no way to give him a better command.[26]

Oliver Otis Howard, as senior major general not in command of a corps, was eventually assigned to Sigel's place. This change was an important one in the light of future developments and it is worth-while to digress for a moment to discuss the Eleventh Corps. Along with the Twelfth Corps it was never accepted as a true part of the Army of the Potomac. The Eleventh was contemptuously referred to as the "foreign contingent." Hooker thought seriously of breaking it up, but the possibility of political repercussions probably prevented him. Actually the corps was only approximately two-fifths of foreign birth, but it had made the mistake of getting along with few West Pointers. The large number speaking only German were dissatisfied by Sigel's departure. They considered it a blow to their nationality and thought Howard was being advanced at Sigel's expense.

Howard was the great "Christian" among the Federal officers, but this carried little weight with the Germans. He had been born in Maine only thirty-three years before and had received his military training at West Point (1854). At Fair Oaks he had lost an arm but had rejoined the army in time to fight at Antietam. He had a novel distinction. Sherman once remarked to a group of general officers, "Let Howard alone! I want one officer who don't drink!"[27] Something had to be done for him since he ranked Sickles who had already been made a corps commander. Howard was greatly put out. He sent a written protest to Hooker that his claims had been overlooked. It would have seemed more natural to place at the head the senior division commander of the Eleventh Corps, Julius Stahel, or perhaps Schurz, who had been appointed temporarily after Sigel's resignation was accepted. Schurz believed that Howard was appointed only because Hooker wanted to get rid of him as a corps commander. Stahel was transferred out of the army within a month and was replaced by the popular General N. C. McLean.[28]

The greatest administrative problem had to do with morale. An inspiring force was greatly needed. Hooker was admirably fitted for this role, since he stood second only to McClellan in popularity with the soldiers when appointed to the command.

The men were disheartened, homesick, in poor health and without confidence in many of their officers.[29] Thousands had died in their quarters or in hospitals from want of proper care and necessary medicines, for which lack there was no excuse.[30] A majority of the officers and men were hostile to the government's policy set forth in the recently issued Emancipation Proclamation. Many said they would never have gone to war had they known that freeing the slaves was to be an objective of the conflict.[31]

Desertions were estimated at 200 per day, and Hooker reported to Washington that there were 85,000 officers and men absent from the army when he took command.[32] Many of these were, no doubt, on leave, hospitalized or on detached duty, but the majority were deserters. Probably the names of many long away without leave were still carried on the books. Civilian clothing was constantly being received through the mails by soldiers intent on deserting. Although Hooker wrote on February sixth that desertion was at an end, or nearly so, steps continued to be taken to prevent it as was brought out in later correspondence. Finally Lincoln was forced to issue a general proclamation of amnesty to all deserters who should rejoin their commands by April first.[33]

Many positive steps were taken to alleviate discontent and to improve morale. The troops were kept busy at drills, picket and fatigue duty, reviews and inspections,[34] at which Hooker often made it a point to appear personally. New hospitals were built and old ones renovated. Sanitary conditions were improved in the camps and more attention was given to the preparation of food. Brigade bakeries were established and more vegetables issued.[35] Hooker declared, "My men shall be fed before I am fed, and before any of my officers are fed."[36] This attitude and the improved rations did more than anything else to enhance his popularity.[37]

One of his first general orders systematized the granting of leaves of absence.[38] The Inspector General's staff was reorganized and more competent officers were appointed to it. In those regiments lacking discipline, inspection reports were used as a basis for canceling leaves and furloughs, while leaves were increased for those units earning high commendation.[39]

An old General Order of February 1862 had provided for inscription on regimental flags of the battles in which the regiment bore a meritorious part. Hooker was quick to see the value of this to morale and pushed the matter with the War Department.[40] In a circular of March twenty-first the army corps were given the distinctive badges which became so popular. Their use was continued throughout the war. The badges were roughly two inches square and were worn on the crown of the cap. They were varied in form, and the use of different colors to distinguish divisions made the wearers easily identifiable, thereby ending errors in reports of straggling and other misconduct.[41] The badge idea was an old favorite of Butterfield's. He had urged it on McClellan without success, but Kearny, it will be recalled, had adopted it for his division on the Peninsula.

Hooker enjoined strict compliance with the President's orders of November 15, 1862, in regard to observance of the Sabbath,[42] and steps were taken to reduce plundering and pillage.[43] The moral tone of some of the officers at Federal headquarters and of some of the men in the camps was not very high. Women and whisky followed the army as they always have. Lafayette Baker of the Secret Service was incensed over the "large number of obscene books and prints . . . constantly passing down through the post office . . . to the soldiers of the Army of the Potomac."[44]

On April fifteenth Adam Gurowski wrote to Hooker asking, for the sake of the country and his own good name, that he put an end to carousing in the camps and that he keep out all women.[45] Charles Francis Adams, Jr., says:

"During the winter (1862-63), when Hooker was in command . . . the headquarters of the Army of the Potomac was a place to which no self-respecting man liked to go, and no decent woman could go. It was a combination of bar-room and brothel."[46]

Stanton was to have some correspondence with Hooker on this subject, but the matter ended with Stanton's feeling that it was a hopeless job to keep women out of Hooker's camps if Fighting Joe's officers refused to co-operate.[47]

When Hooker took command the Army of the Potomac was dependent for information of Confederate movements on scouts, cavalry expeditions, observation balloons, loyal citizens and deserters. No co-ordinated bureau compiled this information and a Secret Service could hardly be said to exist. Hooker remedied this situation by establishing a Bureau of Military Information with Colonel George H. Sharpe in charge. From this time on the Federal Army was supplied with more accurate news of the enemy.

The Confederates were always well informed of Federal movements. Hooker took steps to keep citizens out of his lines by restricting permits to visitors and by clearing out proved rebel partisans.[48] It was even necessary to stop the citizens of Falmouth from fishing in the Rappahannock River when it was discovered that they were signaling to the Confederate pickets with their poles.[49] Hooker also found it expedient to ask Stanton to take action against certain Northern newspapers which were publishing revealing information about the army and offsetting his efforts to retain some secrecy.[50]

Halleck naturally resented the fact that Hooker dealt directly with Lincoln, but this method probably kept the two antagonists from having many serious conflicts during the early months of Hooker's command. The first bit of friction occurred when the Pennsylvania Reserves were sent to Heintzelman in an exchange. Hooker was deprived of several hundred men and was later refused a Massachusetts regiment of his old division which he particularly wanted. So, when Halleck suggested another exchange a few weeks later, he refused.[51]

A subsequent difficulty concerned authority to grant leaves of absence to officers. Hooker wished to detail this duty to corps commanders, but Halleck protested that not even Hooker had the authority and that leaves must be cleared through the Secretary of War.[52]

In the middle of March Hooker disagreed with Halleck on the advisability of sending relief to Harpers Ferry. He considered the Federal Commander there a "stampeder" and denied the possibility of any important threat against him. He then mistook a telegram from Halleck as a positive order to move to the relief of Harpers Ferry and went over Halleck's head to Stanton for an unconditional order. It was not forthcoming.[53]

Hooker successfully bridled his sharp tongue during this period, and antagonized only one of his seven corps commanders. Darius N. Couch had sent him a report concerning careless picketing within his Second Corps, adding: "Higher officers spend their time in reading newspapers or books, playing cards or the politician, drinking whiskey and grumbling." These remarks incensed Hooker and he replied with an unnecessarily abrupt note accusing Couch of expecting the Commanding General to discipline the officers of the Second Corps.[54]

The early months of 1863 which Hooker spent in tuning up his army were a period of comparative repose for the rank and file but not for the colonels and brigadier generals. A great struggle was going on in the

Senate over confirmation of nominations for brigadiers and major generals. Many a higher officer was using his leave of absence to make a trip to Washington and push his promotion with the President or influential members of the Cabinet and Congress. Between the demands of political intruders and the just claims of deserving officers the pressure was so great that Congress authorized the number of major generals increased to 70 and brigadiers to 275. The scramble of patronage-hungry Congressmen in making up the list was a disgrace.[55] Hooker took time to help the cases of several of his favorites, but was not uniformly successful. In correspondence with Stanton he showed much dissatisfaction that the names of David Birney and Gordon Granger had been dropped from the promotion role.[56]

On March eleventh he appeared before the Joint Committee on the Conduct of the War, at that time busy discrediting McClellan for the Peninsula campaign. His testimony was appreciated when he stated at once that the failure was "to be attributed to the want of generalship on the part of our commander."[57] As a matter of fact, it was so satisfactory that Ben Wade used it in his speech "Facts for the People" which represented his best effort against McClellan in the presidential campaign of 1864.[58] While in Washington Hooker talked also with Lincoln and Halleck. Whatever was discussed, at least his ardor was not dampened, for shortly after his return, while reviewing the Twelfth Corps, he remarked to its officers, "If the enemy does not run, God help them."[59]

In early April the President announced his intention to visit the army. Hooker immediately wired his welcome: "I only regret that your party is not as large as our hospitality."[60] He then sent to Washington for a new uniform coat.[61] Mrs. Lincoln, Tad Lincoln, Attorney General Bates, various foreign ministers, their military attachés, and guests were in the party. They arrived in a violent snowstorm and were met at Falmouth by Butterfield, two ambulances and an escort of cavalry. They were provided with three hospital tents adjoining Hooker's headquarters. The President was welcomed with flags, flowers and arches of evergreen in the fashion of the day. Nearly all of the open field in the rear of Falmouth was used for a parade ground. Ditches had been filled, stumps removed and quagmires drained.

On Monday April sixth the party reviewed Stoneman's cavalry, Hooker declaring it to be the biggest army of men and horses ever seen in the world. The next day many of the camps were inspected. On Wednesday and Thursday all of the infantry corps were reviewed. In the evenings jolly gatherings were held at headquarters, but the President seemed to enjoy more than anything else the many hours he spent wandering alone through the camps. Some members of the party were impressed with the easy confidence and nonchalance of Hooker and his favorite expression, "When I get to Richmond." Lincoln started a sentence with "If you get to Richmond, General——" when Hooker interrupted with "Excuse me, Mr. President, but there is no if in the case. I am going straight to Richmond if I live."[62]

Lincoln left delighted with the improved morale of the army but referred to Hooker's overconfidence as "about the worst thing I have seen since I have been down here."[63] Illustrations of Hooker's rosy view of the situation are numerous. In an interview with Alexander K. McClure he called his troops "the finest army on the planet"; he could "march it to New Orleans," and could "cross the Rapidan without losing a man, and then take the rebs where the hair is short."[64] In a conversation with James R. Gilmore of the New York *Tribune* he hedged a bit, referring to his army as only the "finest on this continent."[65]

One administrative worry concerned the 27,000 two-year and nine-month men whose enlistments were to run out early in May.[66] There was the probability that only a small percentage would re-enlist. Most of those who planned to continue in service would first go home and collect a bounty as a conscript substitute.[67] On April nineteenth Lincoln and Halleck came down to Aquia Creek to consult with Hooker on this question and to give talks to the soldiers who were dissatisfied with the government's interpretation of when their enlistment periods should end.[68] An interesting incident occurred during this visit. General Couch entered a tent where only Lincoln and Hooker were present and found them conversing in a grave manner. After discussing the rumor that Charleston had been taken,[69] Lincoln got up to leave. As Hooker arose from his chair, the President turned to the two men who ranked at the top of the Army of the Potomac and said, "I want to impress upon you two gentlemen in your next fight, put in all of your men."[70] This was sound advice, but little heeded!

Hooker's administration of the army had so far proved extremely successful. Many have attributed to Butterfield the reforms of February, March and April 1863. There is good ground for this point of view: Hooker lavishly praised his Chief of Staff for his accomplishments at this time. Nevertheless, Hooker himself must be given credit for effecting the reforms regardless of who suggested them. He devoted many hours to riding about his camps to see that the changes were being carried out.[71]

Hooker evinced more talent for organization than had ever been accredited to him. Indeed, he had made a contribution to the Army of the Potomac more important than any of the fighting he had engaged in as division and corps commander. Francis A. Walker, Assistant Adjutant General of the Second Corps, who was not particularly friendly with him, says: "The Army of the Potomac never spent three months to better advantage."[72]

In summing up his entire command of the army one writer went so far as to declare that Hooker should have been called "Administrative Joe" instead of "Fighting Joe."[73]

## CHAPTER XIII

# PRELIMINARIES OF THE SPRING CAMPAIGN

THE first three months of Hooker's command produced few engagements of consequence. The previous year McClellan had refused to move in the mud of an early Virginia spring, and Hooker wisely followed this same policy. As the winter developed it had become increasingly bleak with continuous snow and rain. Lee had been forced to remain on the defensive. His army suffered from scanty rations, insufficient shelter and clothing and a shortage of horses. He was also facing overwhelming odds and needed time to strengthen his ranks as much as possible.[1]

Hooker's most consistent operation was to run out his guns on Stafford Heights, move detachments of his men up and down the river and then return to his camps. Lee called this "playing the Chinese game, trying what frightening will do."[2] The Confederate pickets greeted the moves with wonderment and cheers. Small Federal cavalry raids were made and scouting parties sent out to bring in information and supplies from Fauquier, Stafford, King George, Richmond and Westmoreland Counties.

Federal infantry was dispatched to support a cavalry raid for the first time on February fifth, the purpose being to destroy the Orange and Alexandria Railroad bridge over the Rappahannock. Whereas General Meade, who directed the movement, claimed that the purpose of the expedition was accomplished despite a severe snowstorm, Wade Hampton, the Confederate cavalryman who countered it, reported that when the enemy was driven off at 2:00 A.M. on the seventh the bridge was still standing.[3]

On the twenty-fourth a good-sized skirmish was forced on Hooker when Fitzhugh Lee and 400 Confederate cavalrymen crossed the Rappahannock at Kelley's Ford on a reconnaissance. The next day they drove the Union cavalry back to their infantry picket lines and captured 150 men. This was done despite a swollen river, snow and mud. In his anxiety to cut off the party Hooker sent out three divisions of cavalry and a brigade of infantry. As an added incentive, he declared that a major general's commission was "staring somebody in the face." It was all in vain. Fitzhugh Lee recrossed the river on the twenty-sixth before

185

the Union forces could concentrate against him. The Federal generals, with the exception of Pleasonton, had moved with alacrity but not fast enough to win the proffered commission.[4]

Hooker overestimated the importance of this Confederate move. He was of the opinion that the enemy thought he was evacuating his base and was therefore raiding in force.[5] The truth, however, was that General Lee was seeking information only. He wrote Jefferson Davis that Hooker was apparently going to stay where he was for the rest of the winter.[6]

Fighting Joe was disgruntled that his reorganized cavalry should be surprised and outwitted as had happened so often in the past. To one of his cavalry brigadiers he let off steam:

"I know the South, and I know the North. In point of skill, of intelligence, and of pluck, the rebels will not compare with our men, if they are equally well led. Our soldiers are a better quality of men. They are better fed, better clothed, better armed, and infinitely better mounted; for the rebels are fully half mounted on mules, and their animals get but two rations of forage per week, while ours get seven. Now, with such soldiers, and such a cause as we have behind them—the best cause since the world began—we *ought* to be invincible, and by God, sir, we *shall* be! You have got to stop these disgraceful cavalry 'surprises.' I'll have no more of them. I give you full power over your officers, to arrest, cashier, shoot—whatever you will—only you must stop these 'surprises.' And by God, sir, if you don't do it, I give you fair notice, I will relieve the whole of you and take the command of the cavalry myself!"[7]

Meanwhile, a cavalry skirmish was going on in the Shenandoah Valley which even Milroy, the Federal commander there, admitted was a disaster for the Union forces involved.[8] This, along with the successful raids of Mosby, the Confederate Partisan Ranger, against Heintzelman's generals and other officers, left the Federals little to be happy about.[9]

In the middle of March Averell's cavalry division was sent out to punish Fitzhugh Lee.[10] With 2,100 men he forced the crossing of the Rappahannock at Kelley's Ford and a half mile west encountered 800 Confederates. The fighting lasted until 5:30 in the afternoon when Averell returned to his own side of the river alarmed by a Confederate ruse which led him to believe that infantry support had reached them. Both leaders claimed a victory. Fitzhugh Lee admitted more casualties, among them the brilliant John Pelham of the horse artillery.[11] Averell's elaborate report led Butterfield to call it the best cavalry fight of the war and Stanton to wire Hooker congratulations for drawing first blood.[12] This was more appreciation than the raid warranted. Hooker did not share the enthusiasm, feeling that Averell had shown a lack of ability.[13] Robert E. Lee considered the attack at Kelley's Ford as the possible opening of the Federal spring campaign, and he took steps to concentrate his army.[14] Hooker's interest in the raid was probably enhanced by the participation of his namesake, Joseph Hooker Wood. This boy was a son of Hooker's oldest sister, Nancy. He had just been commissioned a 2nd Lieutenant in the 6th U. S. Cavalry and had never before been under fire.[15]

By the end of March Halleck was becoming increasingly eager for a major move. He wrote to Hooker suggesting that, inasmuch as Lee's forces were considerably dispersed, it would seem practicable to strike a blow soon. He hinted that major conflicts, both in the South and West, would soon divert Confederate attention.[16] The War Department was well aware that Longstreet, Lee's Senior Corps Commander, had left with Hood's and Pickett's divisions in the early part of February for Suffolk, Virginia, there to face the Federals who were occupying the Virginia and North Carolina coastal region south of the James River. Major General Erasmus D. Keyes reported on April thirteenth from Suffolk that Confederate reinforcements were constantly arriving from Fredericksburg. His immediate request for two divisions from the Army of the Potomac acted as pressure on Hooker to move for Suffolk's relief or else see part of his army taken from his control for that purpose.

In the middle of April Fighting Joe at last felt that his army was ready and that conditions were right for the great adventure. On the eleventh he wrote Lincoln outlining his plan to turn Lee's left flank. He was apprehensive lest Lee retreat the minute the Federal infantry crossed the river but believed that his cavalry would hold the enemy up until the infantry could fall on his rear.[17] Butterfield was sent to deliver this letter to Lincoln in person. He was instructed to divulge the general plan only to the President to avoid leakage at the Washington end. Butterfield succeeded despite the ill-humored attempts of Sumner, Stanton and others to persuade him to confide in them also.[18] Lincoln returned the letter with the indorsement: "Our prime object is the enemy's army in front of us, and is not with or about Richmond at all, unless it be incidental to the main object."[19]

Hooker had given much thought to the problem of getting at Lee. It is probable that he at first favored a movement below Fredericksburg, but now he had concluded that a movement upriver was not only in line with his instructions but was the only possible solution. An approach might be made at Fredericksburg where Stafford Heights covered the river crossings, but Burnside had already paid dearly to discover that this was not feasible.

Moving toward Lee's right meant traversing the impossible roads on the ridge between the lower Rappahannock and the Potomac. These roads were cut by numerous streams and ravines. Below Lee's right, at Skinker's Neck, the river was too wide for the number of pontoons available.

On Lee's left above Beck's Island the river was bordered by bluffs 150 feet high which prohibited a crossing. The first possibility in this direction was at Bank's Ford, but here the Confederates had three strong defensive lines well manned. Next came United States Ford, but here entrenchments were laid out ready to be occupied if threatened. To cross the Rappahannock farther upstream meant crossing the Rapidan also—two rivers 200 to 300 feet wide. The roads to these upper crossings were bad in the springtime and not until the rivers were crossed and the Plank Road reached would sure footing be found. Despite these difficulties the move to Lee's left was well worth a try.[20]

Hooker's correspondence and orders show that he meant business. Hospitals were readied, arms and ammunition inspected and horses shod. Officers who permitted a lack of promptness in moving or who allowed straggling while on the march were to be court-martialed, as were those who reported false alarms from their pickets.[21] The Sanitary Commission was to be denied facilities for moving with the troops since all resources were to be used strictly by the army.[22]

A circular on Monday April thirteenth ordered all infantry commanders to see that their troops were ready by Wednesday with eight days' rations and 140 rounds of ammunition. Surplus clothing was to be stored, and every serviceable man was to march.[23] All the cavalry, except one brigade of Pleasonton's division, was to cross the Rappahannock at Sulphur Springs, Beverly Ford and the railroad bridge on Tuesday. They were to head for Culpeper Courthouse and Gordonsville, brushing away Fitzhugh Lee's cavalry on the way. There they were to cut southeast toward the Richmond to Fredericksburg Railroad, which was the line of Lee's supplies and his probable line of retreat. The orders were to "fight, fight, fight."[24]

On Tuesday Hooker ordered army mail held back for twenty-four hours[25] and tipped off Lincoln that Stoneman was on the move.[26] An infantry demonstration at Kelley's Ford was ordered for dawn on Wednesday.[27] Early that day Hooker wrote to the President in confidential vein detailing the cavalry's planned campaign and assuming that it was already across the river.[28] By evening he was forced to wire Washington that Stoneman was being held up by violent rains and that only one division had been able to cross.[29] Lincoln sensed another failure, and Hooker found it necessary to allay his anxiety. "No one, Mr. President, can be more anxious than myself to relieve your cares and anxieties, and you may be assured that I shall spare no labor and suffer no opportunity to pass unimproved for so doing." He defended Stoneman's work and maintained that there was no reason to suppose that the enemy had discovered the design of the movement.[30]

Hooker had made a worthy attempt to start his spring campaign and only the swollen river kept the two armies from a crucial meeting in mid-April.[31] It was a forceful move and he had shown every evidence that he meant to fight with his whole army. As Stoneman said, the elements had conspired against them and a postponement was in order.[32] The advanced cavalry division was withdrawn to the Federal side of the Rappahannock without too much difficulty and was posted along the Orange and Alexandria Railroad with the rest of the waiting troopers.[33] Mid-April would have been an inopportune time for Lee to fight a major battle; since early that month he had suffered a severe sickness and was still inactive at this time.

Hooker now became subjected to increasing pressure from Washington to take decisive action. On the eighteenth the Commanding General wrote Stoneman to prod him into resuming his forward movement,[34] and two days later the cavalry leader issued orders which encouraged Hooker to write Stanton that "General Stoneman is warming up to his position."[35] It rained again, however, on the night of the twentieth and all day of the twenty-first, so Hooker once again had to inform the President that Stoneman couldn't cross yet and that it would be a few days before he would be able to do so.[36]

The same day Hooker wrote to the Federal commander at Suffolk, "You must be patient with me. I must play with these devils before I can spring."[37] As a matter of fact, he had no desire to "play" at all; he was as eager as anyone to get started and he cursed the rains that held him back.

Finally there came a definite change in the weather. A bright sun gave promise of reasonable marching conditions. Hooker decided upon the early morning of the twenty-seventh as the zero hour for the all-important campaign. Fearing the discovery of his exact plans, he refused to divulge them over the telegraph, nor as late as the twenty-sixth would he tell them even to his corps commanders and staff.[38]

Stoneman's inability to cross the river combined with the desire to get under way as soon as possible, occasioned a change in the original intention of holding up the infantry until the cavalry was well in Lee's rear. Now three infantry corps—the Eleventh, Twelfth and Fifth—were scheduled to cross the upper Rappahannock at Kelley's Ford almost thirty miles above Fredericksburg. They were to cross at the same time as the cavalry farther upstream and so co-operate as a flanking force on Lee's left. Their instructions were to move quietly without alarming the enemy and to lay the pontoons at night. The corps commanders were instructed to leave as a rear guard any unreliable men whose term of service was about to expire.[39]

The Second Corps was to hold the center at Bank's Ford and at Falmouth. One division was to be left in camp near Falmouth where it was to display itself prominently, while the other two moved to Bank's Ford as secretly as possible.[40]

The rest of the infantry—the First, Third and Sixth Corps—all under Major General John Sedgwick, were to remain opposite the entrenched Confederates at Fredericksburg. They were to strike across the river on the afternoon of the twenty-ninth, the Sixth at Franklin's Crossing and the First at Pollock's Mill Creek. The Third Corps was to support them. The troops were to be concealed as much as possible until a demonstration was ordered against the Confederate defenses to secure the Telegraph Road south from Fredericksburg. If the Confederates retreated south, Sedgwick was to follow and attack continuously; if the enemy retreated west on the Plank Road, their works about the town were to be stormed.[41]

Thus, if Lee stayed and fought, he was to be caught between two forces of infantry, either of which was almost as large as his entire army. The Federal Eleventh, Twelfth and Fifth Corps numbered 42,000 and the Sixth, First and Third Corps 59,000, while Lee totaled 60,000 men.[42] (To indicate how well Hooker's new Bureau of Military Information was working, on April twenty-eighth an estimate was made of the strength of the Army of Northern Virginia which placed it at

61,800.)[43] In addition, Hooker had his center, composed of the Second Corps, 17,000 men, to throw in where it would be of the most service. If Lee retreated, the cavalry was to hold him up until the Federal infantry could fall upon him.

Lee had long studied the problem of how to confront a Federal move on his left and he had decided that he would attack if that were possible. On the twenty-seventh he had written Jefferson Davis that information recently received indicated a forward movement of the Federal Army.[44] On the twenty-eighth Stuart reported that a large Federal force was moving up the river.[45] Lee was, therefore, not unaware of what was going on, and, as he was predetermined to fight if success seemed possible, Hooker's plan was exposed to the dangers attendant upon launching an attack from widely separated wings against an opponent eager to seize the initiative. The Federal Commander would do well to shorten as swiftly as possible the long line of communications between his flanking column and his force at Fredericksburg. Only then would he be free to use to full advantage his preponderant numbers.

## CHAPTER XIV

# HOOKER LOSES CONFIDENCE IN HOOKER

THE oft-postponed campaign got under way, at last, at 5:30 A.M. on April 27, 1863, when the Eleventh Corps broke camp at Brooke's Station. The Twelfth Corps swung out behind, and the Fifth soon followed. A regiment of cavalry escorted the advance of each corps. The men moved full of anticipation for another test of strength with their determined foe. Marching was difficult inasmuch as the roads were still muddy, and a warm sun beat down on the heavily laden soldiers. The average weight carried by each man ranged from fifty-six to sixty pounds—far more than ever carried before.[1] Many abandoned their coats, blankets, rations and other articles.[2]

Hooker spent the morning entertaining Secretary of State Seward and other distinguished visitors by staging a review of the Third Corps and regaling them with remarks to the effect that he did not mean to drive the enemy but to bag him,[3] and that Lee's army was his "meat and drink."[4] In the late afternoon a telegram arrived from Lincoln asking, "How does it look now?"[5] Hooker cautiously replied: "We are busy."[6] This was no exaggeration. Orders streamed out of headquarters detailing the moves of the large army.

In the early evening he left his Falmouth headquarters to join the advance, passing through the temporary camps at Hartwood and on to Morrisville where he set up headquarters. On the way he stopped to goad Howard with, "General Meade has done better than you," referring to his order to keep down the number of wagons in the trains.[7] That night he at last confided the plan of campaign to Couch, his senior officer.[8] Hooker had perhaps gone too far in secretiveness but his every thought was to do all within his power to assure the success of this undertaking, the most important of his life. He even resolved to steer clear of intoxicating liquor while the campaign was going on.

On the morning of the twenty-eighth a steady rain began to fall. Professor T. S. C. Lowe, Hooker's balloonist acquaintance from the lower Maryland days, was again on hand.[9] He predicted a heavy storm. Because of this, Butterfield, who had been left at the old headquarters to act as co-ordinator between the right and left wings of the army, feared

192

a delay. At Falmouth it was too misty to see across the river, and the wind was blowing too hard for the observation balloons to ascend. Butterfield was able to report to Hooker, however, that information obtained from Confederate deserters indicated that the enemy had made no recent changes in position.[10]

The Eleventh and Twelfth Corps made an early start for Kelley's Ford, and about noon their foremost detachments passed Hooker at Morrisville. Here in the afternoon he conferred with Howard, Slocum, Stoneman and the division cavalry commanders. Stoneman was informed that he was expected to cross the river not later than eight o'clock the next morning to carry out his scheduled raid on the Confederate communications.[11] Slocum was put in temporary command of both the Eleventh and Twelfth Corps and ordered to push the Eleventh across the Rappahannock that night without waiting for the cavalry. From Kelley's Ford these two corps were to strike out for the Rapidan at Germanna Ford, nine miles away. They were to cross and proceed down the south bank of the river, progressively uncovering Ely's Ford (where the Fifth Corps was to cross the Rapidan) and then United States Ford which would give them a reasonably direct line of communication with Falmouth and the left wing of the army. They would then be in the vicinity of Chancellorsville. From this point on orders hinged on the Confederate reaction. If Lee did not come up from Fredericksburg, the column was to go up the Plank Road, uncovering Bank's Ford and so allowing the Second Corps to cross. This would insure an even shorter line of communication. If Lee reinforced his brigade at Bank's Ford, the Federals were to select a strong position and compel the Confederates to attack them on their own ground. Pleasonton's cavalry division was to operate with them.[12]

Hooker was somewhat uneasy about the progress of his flanking column,[13] fearing that it would not be far enough advanced when time came for Sedgwick to make his demonstration. A dispatch was sent to Butterfield ordering Sedgwick's crossing suspended until further notice.[14] Abraham Lincoln was also uneasy now that the campaign was under way; Fighting Joe was so sure of victory and his army seemed more than ready to meet the badly outnumbered foe, but those misgivings which the President had seen fit to include in the letter of appointment were giving him some bad moments. One thing was certain—the campaign would be either a startling success or a big failure! Hooker would win or lose—no drawn battles for him! The President sent a considerate telegram: "While I am anxious, please do not suppose I am impatient, or waste a moment's thought on me, to your own hindrance, or discomfort."[15]

In the early hours of the twenty-ninth the flanking column started across the Rappahannock on a canvas pontoon bridge. Fighting Joe was on hand at Kelley's Ford throughout the day, superintending the crossing and hurrying the men on to the Rapidan.[16] The men were lagging despite an overcast sky which made marching more pleasant, and orders had to be sent to both Slocum and Howard to close ranks.[17] Meade, however, was moving his Fifth Corps right along, and reached Ely's Ford at five in the afternoon. He straightway started across the swiftly flowing Rapidan.[18] At Germanna Ford the Eleventh and Twelfth Corps were not completely across until the following morning.[19]

As night came on Hooker returned to his Falmouth headquarters through another heavy rain. There he found reports stating that considerable enemy infantry was moving to his right, that their wagon trains were going to the rear, and that their line was thin in front of Sedgwick's prospective crossing below Fredericksburg.[20] He countered by directing the two divisions of the Second Corps at Bank's Ford to move on to United States Ford. General Couch was to get in communication with Meade and Slocum and tell them to push on with their infantry alone, if it were impracticable to move the artillery over the fords.[21] Hooker then ordered Sickles to have his Third Corps, in reserve on the left, ready to march at a moment's notice to reinforce the flanking column.[22]

Sedgwick's bridges had been laid that morning in a heavy fog—two at Franklin's Crossing and two at Pollock's Mill, after a four-hour delay due to the drunkenness of Hooker's old classmate, General Henry Benham of the Engineers' Brigade.[23] A force had been sent to cover the bridges and to man the rifle pits near by. Hooker was satisfied that Sedgwick had carried out his part of the plan well, and he sent a dispatch to Slocum telling him that the enemy anticipated the main attack at Fredericksburg; therefore, Slocum was to advance as far as Chancellorsville where he would be joined not only by the Fifth Corps but probably by the Second and Third as well.

A letter from Butterfield to Sedgwick, written after Hooker had retired for the night, shows that Hooker was favorably considering the possibility of taking a strong position near Chancellorsville and waiting for Lee to attack him on his chosen ground. Sedgwick was cautioned

GENERAL GEORGE H. ("PAP") THOMAS
Hooker's choice as the leading Federal general of the war.

Executive Mansion,

Washington, January 26, 1863.

Major General Hooker:

General.

I have placed you at the head of
the Army of the Potomac. Of course I have done this
upon what appear to me to be sufficient reasons. And
yet I think it best for you to know that there are
some things in regard to which, I am not quite satisfied with you. I believe you to be a brave and
a skilful soldier, which, of course, I like. I also believe you do not mix politics with your profession,
in which you are right. You have confidence in
yourself, which is a valuable, if not an indispensable quality. You are ambitious, which, within reasonable
bounds, does good rather than harm. But I think that
during Gen. Burnside's command of the Army, you have
taken counsel of your ambition, and thwarted him as much
as you could, in which you did a great wrong to the country, and to a most meritorious and honorable brother officer.
I have heard, in such way as to believe it, of your recent

ly saying that both the Army and the Government needed a Dictator. Of course it was not for this, but in spite of it, that I have given you the command. Only those generals who gain successes, can set up dictators. What I now ask of you is military success, and I will risk the dictatorship. The government will support you to the utmost of its ability, which is neither more nor less than it has done and will do for all commanders. I much fear that the spirit which you have aided to infuse into the Army, of criticising their Commander, and withholding confidence from him, will now turn upon you. I shall assist you as far as I can, to put it down. Neither you, nor Napoleon, if he were alive again, could get any good out of an army, while such a spirit prevails in it.

And now, beware of rashness—Beware of rashness, but with energy, and sleepless vigilance, go forward, and give us victories.

Yours very truly
A. Lincoln

TO-HOOKER LETTER

GENERAL ULYSSES SIMPSON GRANT     GENERAL WILLIAM TECUMSEH SHERMAN

not to upset the plan by allowing his demonstration to bring on a general engagement.[24] This was the first note of weakness to creep into the forceful moves of the last three days. An offensive campaign was supposedly being waged, but the General was now thinking of maneuvering in such manner as to permit him to fight a defensive battle. But what if Lee did not choose to fight on Hooker's chosen ground, was he to be allowed to retreat to a defense of Richmond? Was it possible that Hooker had already forgotten that his real purpose was to destroy the enemy and not just to maneuver Lee out of his defenses?

The last day of April dawned with every indication of favorable weather for the forward movement. Hooker believed the time had come for Sedgwick's postponed demonstration. It was ordered for one o'clock and was to be pointed at Hamilton's Crossing on the Richmond, Fredericksburg and Potomac Railroad for the purpose of discovering whether or not the Confederates were still in their fortifications. It was suggested that a full corps be used, but the men were to be cautioned not to attack heavily held positions. Sedgwick was given the power to call off the demonstration if he were sure the enemy stood in force before him.[25] Before noon, however, Hooker suspended the demonstration, offering no explanation. Possibly word from the Signal Corps that rebel troops were massing in their earthworks was the reason.[26]

He then occupied himself with reinforcing his flanking column. Orders were sent to Couch to have the bridge laid at United States Ford immediately and then to move his two divisions in support of Slocum and Meade. He was warned not to let a small force delay him.[27] Sickles' Third Corps was to follow and to be across the river not later than 7:30 the next morning.[28] Brigadier General Warren, who had charge of laying the bridge for Couch and Sickles, was to go to Chancellorsville when his work was completed, there to establish a defensive line or a line from which the offensive could be taken in the morning if it seemed desirable.[29] At 2:15 P.M. Hooker sent a message which was to play havoc with the Federal chance of success: Meade and then Couch were warned not to advance farther than Chancellorsville until the army was concentrated.[30]

In the late afternoon Hooker was informed by Reynolds that 3,000 to 5,000 Confederate reinforcements, probably from Richmond, were arriving in front of Sedgwick on the Federal left. He responded that he hoped they were from Richmond for then the greater would be his success.[31] This sounded well, perhaps, but did not make good sense and indicated that he was growing too well pleased with his prospects. In his General Order No. 47 he went out on a limb from which the ladder of victory was the only graceful escape:

"It is with heartfelt satisfaction the commanding general announces to the army that the operations of the last three days have determined that our enemy must either ingloriously fly, or come out from behind his defenses and give us battle on our own ground, where certain destruction awaits him. . . ."[32]

There are many personal narratives and regimental histories which indicate that the newcomers in the army were taken in by this congratulatory message, but not the veterans. Hooker was soon to add in conversation, in the presence of at least one newspaperman, "The rebel army . . . is now the legitimate property of the Army of the Potomac. They may as well pack up their haversacks and make for Richmond; and I shall be after them. . . ."[33]

About four Hooker, accompanied by most of his staff, left Falmouth headquarters for Chancellorsville to direct the main movement on the right. Butterfield was cautioned to keep him informed of every bit of news from the Fredericksburg front. Sedgwick was told that Hooker would advance up the Plank Road on the morrow and that he must be alert to press any advantage allowed by the enemy.[34] Hooker was optimistic; he said to Butterfield confidentially that, providing he met no opposition he would be on the heights west of Fredericksburg at noon the next day; if strongly opposed, he would be there by night.[35]

While Hooker lingered at United States Ford watching the Second Corps cross the Rappahannock, he learned that the enemy had subjected Reynolds to a shelling and that Sedgwick believed an attack likely.[36] It looked as though Lee were still concerned mostly with the threat on his front. A few miles beyond the Ford, Hooker passed behind the Fifth Corps posted north and east of Chancellorsville. At three o'clock Meade had sent a brigade to Bank's Ford as a result of a cavalry report that the Confederates there were leaving, but this was found untrue. When General Slocum arrived and took command of the entire flanking force, he ordered Meade's advanced brigade back to the Chancellorsville line.[37] This was in accordance with his instructions from Hooker and carried out over Meade's protests.[38] Slocum's men had been placed in a continuation of Meade's line parallel to, and south of, the

Plank Road for a mile and a half west of Chancellorsville. Howard's corps had followed the Twelfth and camped at Dowdall's Tavern. Slocum had then placed them in a line which continued his right.[39]

The army was now (the night of the thirtieth) in the midst of that region of Virginia known as the Wilderness.[40] It was an area of dense forests of oak and pine with here and there a clearing where attempts were made to farm the poor soil. The Plank Road and the macadam turnpike, running east and west, were excellent, but all other roads were plain Virginia mud. It was a difficult area in which to handle troops; artillery and cavalry were limited in their effectiveness, and high points for purposes of observation were lacking. Information concerning the progress of battle on a distant sector could be ascertained only by courier. The forest growth localized the sound of battle, and troops could move easily without being seen. Indeed, the Wilderness was a perfect setting for the natural camouflage of faded Confederate butternut uniforms. It was no place for Hooker to linger. An advance of little more than five miles toward Fredericksburg would be sufficient to extricate his army.

At Chancellorsville Hooker found a crossroads and a large brick mansion, the Chancellor House, with assorted outhouses. There was a clearing of fifty or more acres around the crossroads extending mainly to the south.[41] Headquarters were established in the mansion and callers began to drop in, the most talkative the cavalryman, Alfred Pleasonton. He was full of advice and supposedly brought to Hooker a captured Confederate diary and a dispatch, sent by Lee to one of his division commanders, which showed that although he had been surprised he had foreseen that the next battle was to be fought at Chancellorsville.[42] Pleasonton's advice was to move three or four miles toward Fredericksburg immediately, since he believed the army in an unfavorable position. Hooker would not advance that night, however, and Pleasonton (according to his own account) then advised him to form his line south from Chancellorsville to Spottsylvania Courthouse.[43] A cavalry scouting party was sent out toward Spottsylvania and fought a moonlight skirmish with some enemy troopers. It returned unable to give any information about the Confederate infantry in that direction.[44]

Hooker retired that night in great spirits, well satisfied with himself and his men.[45] The soldiers had greeted him exuberantly, appreciating his success in maneuvering them across the river without a fight.[46] His chief regret was his lack of data concerning the force facing him. Pleasonton's four regiments of cavalry had not been sufficient to give him this knowledge, for Stuart's troopers had successfully screened Lee's army instead of chasing off to confront Stoneman as Hooker had hoped.

That night Hooker had approximately 51,000 men massed behind Lee with about 22,000 more on the way. A retaining force of around 47,000 under Sedgwick remained on Lee's Fredericksburg front.[47] Yet the Commanding General retired too early; the objective of uncovering Bank's Ford had not been accomplished nor had arrangements been made for an early advance the next day.

April thirtieth had been designated by President Lincoln as a national day of fasting and humiliation. There was little of either around Chancellorsville that evening! A Philadelphia poet became so elated over the situation that he struck off several verses entitled "Hooker's Across."

On the early morning of May first a dense fog enveloped the army. The corps commanders were impatient to move, and several dropped in at headquarters, curious about the delay.[48] At 9:30 the weather had cleared and Hooker had a circular ready which ordered all corps commanders to be on the alert with pickets well placed for the safety of the army. No more wagons were to cross at United States Ford, and those already across were to be parked on the road between Chancellorsville and the river.[49] But still there was no order to start the army moving out of the forbidding Wilderness.

Within a half hour, however, oral directions were given and at eleven a second circular was issued outlining the program for the day. The Fifth Corps was to take the River Road toward Bank's Ford, the objective being a spot about midway between Mott's Run and Colin's Run, a half mile short of the Ford. The Twelfth Corps was to advance down the Plank Road to Tabernacle Church, arriving there by noon, while the Eleventh Corps was to come up a mile in the rear by two o'clock. One division of the Second Corps was to gain the crossroads at Todd's Tavern, eight miles south of Chancellorsville, starting immediately. The other division of the Second Corps, the Third Corps, which had arrived at nine, and the cavalry were to remain at Chancellorsville in reserve. Hooker's headquarters were to be located at Tabernacle Church.[50] Evidently Fighting Joe was so sure of reaching these advanced positions without hindrance that he did not consider it necessary to include instructions against whatever resistance might be encountered. The left wing under Sedgwick was ordered by telegraph to make a forceful demonstration at one o'clock and to continue it until further orders.[51]

By that hour Meade had advanced two divisions without opposition along the River Road to within view of Bank's Ford. His division of regulars under Sykes, advancing on the turnpike, had met and driven a number of enemy regiments to a point a little more than halfway to Tabernacle Church where resistance stiffened and Sykes found himself outflanked. This was reported to General Warren who rode back to headquarters with the information.

When Hooker got the news, he was in a state of hesitation. The immense responsibility of every decision from this point on was weighing heavily upon him. In the past, when he had been in command of a division or corps, there had always been someone else to make the chief decisions and someone for him to criticize later. Now it was all Hooker. The self-confidence fostered since boyhood was ebbing fast. Perhaps he missed the stimulant which he had resolved to deny himself. Fighting Joe had gained his reputation as a stand-up fighter, but he had hoped to prove by his direction of the army that this was not his only military accomplishment. He had started out to whip Lee by maneuver just as Lee had whipped the Army of the Potomac so many times before. Was he equal to this task? Then there was the matter of enemy reinforcements. Would Longstreet's two divisions, reported on the way from southern Virginia, arrive at the crucial moment? Lee's reserves had a habit of doing just this. Were they on hand already?

It all added up to an overwhelming mental struggle for Joseph Hooker and—as he later remarked to Abner Doubleday—"for once I lost confidence in Hooker."[52] His aggressiveness crumbled. From his Chancellorsville headquarters he ordered Sykes to retreat! This was the supreme decision in his military career. It climaxed the almost twenty years he had devoted to the profession of soldiering. The honors won in Mexico and in the last year of solid fighting would be forgotten by many in view of this fatal decision. When he called in his advance, the battle became Lee's, not his. He sacrificed freedom of offensive maneuver and the advantages of his successful tactics of the last few days. He was still commander of the Army of the Potomac, but Lee was commander of the field of battle!

Hancock's division of Couch's Second Corps was instructed to hold its advanced position only until Sykes had safely extricated his men.[53] Slocum, who had formed a line of battle along the Plank Road about two miles east of Chancellorsville, was ordered back to his position of the morning. Meade's divisions on the River Road were also recalled, as was French's division on its way to Todd's Tavern. Howard had hardly left his camp when his advance was countermanded.[54]

The orders were received with protest by Couch, Slocum, Meade, Hancock and Sykes. They believed that the ground just gained, being relatively high and open, should be held.[55] They were not yet out of the Wilderness but had reached a clearing within and wanted to try to hold on until the balance of the army could come to their support. Major Burt of Couch's staff came to Hooker for permission to stay; he was followed by Lieutenant Colonel Guindon of Slocum's staff. Both, however, were sent back with the imperative order to retreat.[56]

Too late Hooker, by now impressed with the unanimity of opinion, reversed his orders and told Couch he could hold on and that Slocum would do likewise. Couch replied with warmth: "Tell General Hooker he is too late, the enemy are already on my right and rear. I am in full retreat."[57] Slocum had already left, and Hancock was retreating under fire.

While riding back to Chancellorsville, Meade said to Couch, Sykes and Hancock: "My God, if we can't hold the top of a hill we certainly cannot hold the bottom of it."[58] When Couch reported to Hooker, who had been pacing to and fro on the Chancellor House porch while the advance was going on, Fighting Joe said confidently, "It is all right, Couch, I have got Lee just where I want him; he must fight me on my own ground."[59] But Couch left sensing that his commander was a whipped man.[60]

After Slocum returned with his troops, he went to headquarters and asked Hooker to reconsider. He urged an immediate attack with all available forces. He found the General irascible and wavering in his judgment, inclined to let conditions remain as they were. Slocum left deeply impressed that Hooker was not in fit condition to direct the army in the impending battle.[61] The testimony of Couch and Slocum should be viewed with some circumspection, for both became bitter enemies of Hooker before they recorded their thoughts. Generals Humphreys and Hancock, however, were also of the opinion that the army went out to fight on May first and should have done so.[62] The argument against the recall is upheld by the attitude of the men in the ranks who returned muttering, "On the retreat again!"[63]

The prize at stake was so great that it was well worth the risk of a

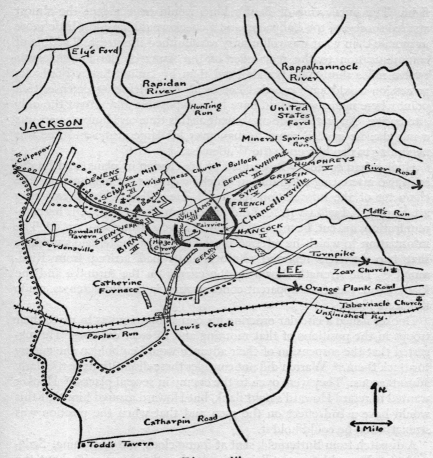

Figure 14.

Chancellorsville, May 1st and 2nd, 1863

↘ Limit of Federal Advance, May 1st

▬ Hooker's First Defensive Line

▨ Position of Federal Infantry in
    Sickles' Attack at 5:00 P.M., May 2nd

▭ Position of Confederate Forces
    at 5:00 P.M., May 2nd

○○○⟩ Route of Jackson's Flank Attack

fight. The uncovering of Bank's Ford would have meant the almost assured success of the campaign, and a check would have lost little more in morale than what was voluntarily relinquished in retreat. The line of communication to the remainder of the Army of the Potomac was twelve miles shorter by Bank's Ford than by United States Ford. Its possession would have crowded Lee in his Fredericksburg defenses to a point where maneuver would have been impossible and retreat the only alternative. Any retrograde movement at this time on Hooker's part was a mistake; he needed room to maneuver his large army, and Lee was beginning to pen him up in the Wilderness.

Hooker had to notify Butterfield of his change in plans, and he did so in two interesting telegrams, in which he gave as the main reason "the character of the information received." He added, "The enemy may attack me. . . . I will try it. . . . I did feel certain of success. . . . If his communications are cut, he must attack me. I have a strong position."[64] The information to which he referred must have been Butterfield's message that two deserters reported reinforcements had arrived from Richmond.[65] The strength shown by the enemy on the turnpike and the Plank Road, plus their apparent concentration in the old defenses, made this seem likely.

Hooker issued a circular ordering his corps commanders to place their troops in the positions of that morning and to erect defenses. He suggested that the suspension of their advance would embolden the enemy to attack them.[66] Warren did not consider these dispositions particularly advantageous. They were open to the enemy in several places.[67] Hooker wanted to retard Howard's right flank, but Howard assured him that this would have a bad effect on the men and that when the position was strengthened he could hold it.

A dispatch from Butterfield, sent at four o'clock, was disturbing. Sedgwick and Reynolds were still inactive, and nothing was said about the order for a demonstration at one o'clock. Indeed, the two Major Generals near Fredericksburg wanted Hooker to know that in their judgment an attack by them, before some success had been accomplished on the right, would possibly fail in view of the strong position and large numbers of the enemy. This would leave the Sixth and First Corps unserviceable when needed. Butterfield added that no other Confederate regiments appeared to be going toward Hooker and that he had not notified Washington of the impending battle.[68] At six o'clock Hooker issued another circular ordering all corps commanders to set their pioneers to work that night building abatis and making clearings for the artillery.[69]

The enemy was not inactive that late afternoon and evening. A Twelfth Corps brigade was driven in at Hazel Grove and Sykes was attacked in his camp, though not in force. A Confederate reconnaissance was made on Howard's front, and the Federal left was shelled from the rise of ground it had held earlier in the day.[70] These moves appeared to forecast a general attack the next day.

After supper Hooker discovered why Sedgwick's demonstration, ordered for one o'clock, had not been heard from. The telegraph line had broken down between Chancellorsville and Falmouth, and Butterfield had not received the order from the Commanding General until 4:55 P.M. The Chief of Staff had immediately sent it on to Sedgwick, and now all of the First Corps and a division of the Sixth Corps were advancing.[71] As there was no longer occasion for a supporting demonstration that evening, Hooker had Butterfield call it off at once.[72] Word came from the efficient Sharpe that Lee had no more than 59,000 infantry and artillery all told.[73]

The Chancellor House was converted into a hospital, and the yard was filled with wounded, but Hooker retained several rooms for his headquarters. Butterfield was ordered to telegraph Washington that reinforcements were arriving from Richmond. The Commanding General closed by plaintively saying, "I am all right"[74]—another indication that Hooker's self-assurance had departed.

According to Brigadier General Warren, an informal council of war was held that night, and two propositions were considered:

1. To choose a position and entrench.
2. To choose a point of attack and advance all five corps.

The first would save the men and would keep open the possibility of resuming the offensive in the event of an enemy repulse; the second would regain the initiative and improve the soldiers' morale. Hooker had already made up his mind to follow the first plan, and so it stood.[75] He now had with him approximately 73,000 men and 208 guns, but before retiring in the early hours he decided to strengthen his right wing even further. He ordered Reynolds to march his First Corps from Fredericksburg at once.

## CHAPTER XV

## ARMY WITHOUT A HEAD

Dawn of May second gave promise of a clear day for the anticipated encounter. Hooker's line was perhaps six miles long and somewhat irregular. The Eleventh Corps was on the extreme right, extending from a point almost a mile southwest of the sawmill on Hunting Run to just east of Dowdall's Tavern. One brigade, Barlow's, was in reserve. Next came Birney's division of the Third Corps connecting with the Eleventh and covering Hazel Grove, a bare eminence commanding Chancellorsville. Then came the Twelfth Corps, encircling the high ground at Fairview and reaching to the Plank Road below Chancellorsville. At this point the main line turned north, circling around and protecting the crossroads. The two divisions of the Second Corps were located here. The Fifth Corps connected with the left of the Second and extended to the northeast along the Mineral Springs Road. A reserve of two divisions of the Third Corps was camped in the field behind the Chancellor House.

At sunrise Hooker, Sickles, Colonel Comstock and a few staff officers rode out to inspect the lines.[1] When they arrived at Dowdall's Tavern they were joined by General Howard and several other officers of the Eleventh Corps. Comstock pointed out a number of weak spots and Hooker ordered them strengthened.[2] A circuit was made around the entire position of the army, and Hooker decided his defensive line was a good one considering the wooded country.[3] He was not satisfied, however, with the dispositions of either Howard or Slocum.

Shortly after nine o'clock in the morning Butterfield reported that the enemy was shelling Sedgwick, probably because of Reynolds' movement back across the river. Hooker said not to worry about the Sixth Corps since only one division confronted it. Sedgwick was to attack if a reasonable opportunity of success presented itself.[4] The enemy early resumed cannonading Hooker's center and occasionally there was a display of bayonets as though an attack were on the way.[5] According to one newspaper correspondent, Fighting Joe calmly stood on the lower veranda of the Chancellor House smoking a "segar" despite the fact that the Confederate fire was carrying to headquarters.[6]

In the middle of the morning an enemy column was reported moving across Birney's front to the southwest. A battery of the Third Corps opened against it, but the column of infantry, artillery, wagon trains and ambulances continued on its way. It was plain to General Sickles, from his point of observation, that the enemy was turning his back on the Army of the Potomac and appeared to be heading for the Gordonsville route to Richmond. According to J. Watts de Peyster, Hooker, with the aid of his field glasses, could also observe a part of this column from his headquarters. After studying his map, he remarked that it was not like Lee to retreat without a fight and that the Confederate Commander might be trying to flank him.[7] He sent a circular to Slocum and Howard pointing out that their dispositions were satisfactory for a frontal attack only and ordering them to examine the ground and decide what could be done in case of a flank attack on the right; heavy reserves should be kept ready for such a contingency. He said there was good reason to believe that the enemy was moving to the Federal right and, therefore, both generals should advance their pickets to gather information of an enemy approach.[8]

Clearly something had to be done about this column which was exposing itself to the whole Federal army. At noon Hooker told Sickles to harass it but to advance cautiously.[9] On Howard's front, infantry scouts and cavalry patrols all reported that the enemy appeared moving toward Culpeper.[10] At two o'clock Couch visited Hooker at headquarters and, as he related later, was told that Lee was in retreat and that Sickles had been sent to capture his artillery.[11]

Sickles carried out his instructions to annoy the Confederate movement by advancing Birney's division through the woods to the fork of the road at Catherine Furnace. Here he pushed back the skirmishers and reported to Hooker the approximate size of the column. Whipple's division was sent out from the reserve to support him. Sickles then sent word to Hooker that his men could reach the road by which the enemy was moving, but the Commanding General still urged caution. Sickles responded by placing Whipple in the large gap on Birney's left and then advancing to the road where he took many prisoners.[12]

At four, in response to a call from Sickles for more men, Hooker had his aides, Major Howard and Captain Moore, direct General Howard to send out a brigade.[13] Barlow's brigade, the only reserve of the Eleventh Corps, left its position accompanied by General Howard. Upon receiving a note from Sickles asking for his support, Slocum, with Hooker's consent, had allowed Williams' division to leave its entrenchments and to go to the left of the Third Corps.[14] Finally Hooker ordered three regiments of cavalry, under Pleasonton, to follow up what seemed a successful movement.

The afternoon news from Butterfield indicated that everything was quiet at Falmouth and Fredericksburg, but because of the heavy wind the balloons were unable to ascend for observation. Butterfield reminded the general that the supplies of the Fifth, Eleventh and Twelfth Corps would be exhausted by the morning of the fourth.[15]

Around four a number of messages came from the Chief of Staff telling of the withdrawal of considerable Confederate infantry and artillery from the Federal left, leaving few men before Sedgwick.[16] Hooker responded with an order for the Sixth Corps to cross as soon as indications permitted, to capture Fredericksburg and to pursue the enemy vigorously inasmuch as Lee was fleeing, trying to save his trains, and Sickles was upon him.[17] Although this dispatch would seem to indicate that Hooker unquestionably believed Lee was retreating, it is possible he was merely trying to encourage Sedgwick to make an immediate aggressive move. This at least was Hooker's story two years later.[18] The fact appears to be that the General was confused. If he was sure that a retreat was on he was extremely cautious about pursuing it.

The question of the enemy's intentions was settled definitely for him at about six-thirty. Captain Russell of his staff, hearing unusual noises from the right of the line, walked out in front of headquarters, looked down the Plank Road with his glass, and exclaimed: "My God, here they come!"[19] Hooker was sitting on the porch of the Chancellor House enjoying the spring evening, listening to the incessant cannonading against Hancock and Meade on the left, and no doubt wondering how Sickles was doing with his attack. Except for his morning circular to Slocum and Howard, and for the dispatch of his engineers, Warren and Comstock, to examine the line at five o'clock, he had paid little heed to the possibility of the "retreating" Confederates' falling upon his right flank. Although Jackson's entire corps—the "retreating" column—had furiously assaulted Howard's exposed men an hour and fifteen minutes before, no one had come to warn Hooker.[20] Peculiar atmospheric conditions and the dense woods had deadened the noise of battle. Lee had attacked on Hooker's chosen ground, all right, but had done so without announcing his intentions to the General.

Hooker, Russell and Captain Candler, another aide, mounted in haste and started down the road. They were met by stampeded pack mules, horses, camp followers and panic-stricken soldiers running for their lives. The Germans from the routed Eleventh Corps were crying, "Vere ist der pontoon?" Others, including many in the Third and Twelfth Corps, were just running. Hooker, his staff and some cavalrymen charged the fugitives, but could not stay them. It was apparent that nothing could be done with these demoralized men. The situation called for fresh troops and plenty of them. Hooker immediately thought of the First Corps, ordered early that morning to march for United States Ford. It should be close at hand by now. Candler was dispatched to hurry it on. A few minutes later its commander, John Reynolds, reported to Hooker in person. His order to move had not arrived promptly, due to a lost dispatch bearer and the faulty telegraph; therefore the First Corps was not yet across the Ford.

Fortunately, Hooker had refused Sickles his last division. It was only 6,000 strong but it was camped close at hand and it was a veteran outfit, none other than the "Old Hooker Division" organized by Hooker himself nineteen months earlier and now commanded by his good friend Hiram Berry. He rode up to Berry and shouted, "General . . . throw your men into the breach—receive the enemy on your bayonets—don't fire a shot—they can't see you."[21] For the first time since his letdown the day before Hooker seemed to come to life, rightful owner of the sobriquet "Fighting Joe."[22]

A defensive line had to be established. Howard had rallied a few batteries and some of his infantry under one of his brigadiers. With Berry's men a line was formed perpendicular to the Plank Road a half mile west of headquarters. Meanwhile, Schurz gathered such of his men as had remained steadfast—about a brigade—and went to Berry's right.[23] Williams' division of the Twelfth Corps was just then returning from its movement in support of Sickles and went in on Berry's left.[24] Hooker placed the Twelfth Corps' artillery behind the newly formed line, and soon a heavy fire was pouring over the Federal infantry at the enemy, still a half mile away.[25]

It was Hooker's good fortune that, by this time, the impetus of the Confederate attack was spent and Jackson was busy bringing a fresh division up to the front. At 8:30 P.M. Schurz's few men were withdrawn, and in response to Berry's appeal for an extension of his line on the right,

Hooker sent him Hay's brigade of the Second Corps.[26] This was the only reinforcement ordered from the left; Lee was demonstrating there with such vigor that a full-fledged attack was anticipated.[27]

Word had been sent to Pleasonton and Sickles to return to Hazel Grove; the enemy had marched all around them while they were skirmishing with the rear guard.[28] Eighteen guns of the Third Corps artillery were already on hand at Hazel Grove, and Pleasonton, who arrived first, tried to find someone at whom to point them, but the Confederates were hidden by the woods. From time to time more guns were added at this position, and one of the cavalry regiments charged into an enemy brigade on the Plank Road—all by accident, without Pleasonton's order, and of no consequence.

Yet Pleasonton afterward boldly claimed that his artillery fire and cavalry charge stalled the Confederate attack. Hooker was taken in to the extent of introducing Pleasonton to Lincoln as "the man who saved the Army of the Potomac the other night."[29] But the enemy had merely stopped to re-form and never knew that Pleasonton was around! These fables have been repeated again and again despite evidence to the contrary by Colonel Huey who led the cavalry charge, and by Colonel Huntington who directed most of the guns. His "terrific" defense cost Pleasonton only six casualties in his artillery.[30] He had to share the privilege of claiming to be the savior of the army with General Sickles who arrived shortly after and took command of Hazel Grove. Sickles was equally voluble in his writing but he had no more sizable contact than Pleasonton with Jackson's attack on May second.

As night came on the new defensive line was formally established and Hooker issued a memorandum detailing it. Reynolds' corps, just arriving, was to defend Hunting Run from the Rapidan to the juncture of the Ely's Ford road with the United States Ford Road. Sykes's division, which Meade had directed to this important crossroad when he heard of the attack, was to stay there while the remainder of the Fifth Corps supported this whole line. The Twelfth, Third and Second Corps were to hold the positions then occupied, and the disorganized Eleventh Corps was to take over Meade's line along the Mineral Springs Road. The lines of the First, Fifth and Eleventh Corps were to be held at all hazards, the others until further notice.[31] Pleasonton was to withdraw his cavalry from Hazel Grove and go into camp across the river.

Hooker sent Butterfield an urgent request for all news of Sedgwick and the enemy force left at Fredericksburg.[32] The indications were that

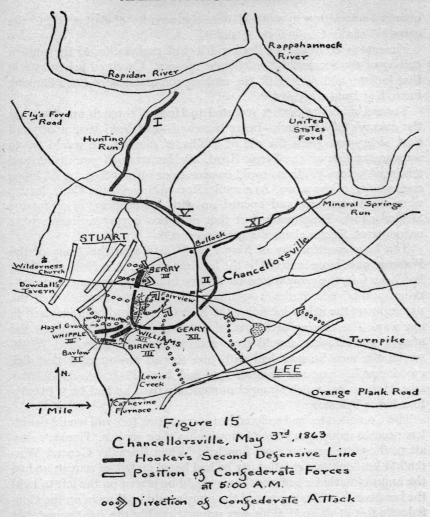

Figure 15
Chancellorsville, May 3rd, 1863
━━ Hooker's Second Defensive Line
▱ Position of Confederate Forces
at 5:00 A.M.
ooo⟫ Direction of Confederate Attack

the enemy had almost withdrawn from the town. Hooker ordered Sedgwick imperatively to advance up the Chancellorsville Road until he connected with the main part of the army; to attack and destroy all with which he came in contact. Hooker added that, between them, he expected to use up Lee.[33] This language was far more optimistic than the General honestly felt. At ten in the evening there was uncertainty around headquarters amounting to panic despite the security of darkness and the cessation of the Confederate attack.[34]

Pleasonton conveyed to Hooker a logical explanation of the sudden ending of the successful Confederate advance. Captured prisoners said that Jackson and A. P. Hill, the ranking commanders of Lee's flanking force, had been wounded.[35]

Toward midnight Sickles reported to Hooker, through an aide, that the enemy's night attack—never launched—had been beaten off, and that, if he were given the aid of Williams' division, he would try to recover the line of the Plank Road. Sickles received permission and advanced before Williams could co-operate or inform Slocum, his corps commander, of the move. As a result, Slocum thought the Confederates were again attacking and opened up with his artillery, disorganizing Sickles' effort. Despite the fact that only two enemy regiments were encountered Sickles claimed a great success.[36]

The long eventful day of May 2, 1863, had seen the Army of the Potomac once more buffeted by the fortunes of war. A defensive position had been lost, the army forced back three miles, and one entire corps—minus one brigade, Barlow's—routed. Yet only approximately half the men now on the field—including the First Corps—had been involved in any way. The coming of Reynolds' veterans did much to hearten the army,[37] and Hooker should have realized that the estimated 76,000 serviceable men he now had with him topped any number that Lee could possibly possess. Indeed, Lee had but 43,000. As Doubleday says, Hooker was much stronger numerically than he had been twenty-four hours before.[38]

The Confederates had suffered heavy casualties, too, and would doubtless need to reorganize before following up their success. Hooker's situation, therefore, was far from hopeless. When Brigadier General Warren left headquarters at ten-thirty he had heard no talk of retreat; he had the impression that a sufficient force would be placed on the left to hold the breastworks while the rest of the army would be thrown on the Confederate left at dawn.[39] This was unquestionably the right move, but Hooker failed to make any arrangements for it. After the brief excitement of organizing the defense based on his old division, he had lapsed back into melancholia. The realization that he was the hare and not the hound began to sink in. Where would the next blow fall?

At about three Sunday morning, May third, came the news that

Hooker was so eager to hear: Sedgwick was attacking in Fredericksburg.[40] Half an hour later Butterfield wired that the enemy was holding up the Sixth Corps and that, though Sedgwick was doing well, he could not join Hooker by daylight.[41] Hooker replied impatiently with a dispatch to Sedgwick, via Butterfield, that only a small force could be left in front of the Sixth Corps and that his advance must not be checked.[42]

At dawn the Commanding General and a few attendants went out to meet Sickles in the gully alongside Hazel Grove. Hooker was despondent. He believed that the predicament of the two divisions of the Third Corps and Barlow's brigade of the Eleventh was desperate. They held the high ground at Hazel Grove and menaced the right flank of the Confederate flanking column, but at any time Lee might close in from the south. Sickles wanted to hold on. Military critics now agree that he could have done so though he would have been in a hot spot. Hooker, however, was thinking primarily of saving his own army rather than of destroying Lee's. He ordered Sickles to withdraw to less exposed entrenchments at Fairview. This was done but with great difficulty, a brigade very nearly falling into the enemy's hands.[43]

The Confederate infantry did not wait long before falling upon Berry and Williams on either side of the Plank Road. It was now under the intrepid cavalryman, General "Jeb" Stuart, who had succeeded Jackson and who rode along his lines encouraging them with a special song for the occasion: "Old Joe Hooker, won't you come out of the Wilderness?"

Action close at hand once more revived "Old Joe's" spirits. He ordered two brigades of the Second Corps to help Berry attack the enemy and drive him through the woods.[44] Then he rode up and down inspecting his lines and directing the stalwart defense. The odds were even along the Plank Road that early Sunday morning. The battle was hotly contested and the struggle surged back and forth. But Hooker was hemmed into too small a position for strictly defensive tactics. The square mile left to him around the Chancellorsville crossroads was covered by Confederate artillery fire on the east, south and west. He held onto it, he says, only because Sedgwick was to make a juncture with him at the crossroads and he momentarily expected to hear the Sixth Corps' guns.[45] If, however, he had not been so "defense-conscious" and had thrown the fresh First and Fifth Corps on the flank of Stuart's approximately 23,000 men, they would have been in an extremely awkward fix.

Shortly after 7:30 A.M. Hooker rode up to a group gathered about a prostrate form and asked, "Who have you there, gentlemen?" When told it was General Berry he sprang from his horse and with genuine emotion bent over the dead body. "My God, Berry, why was this to happen? Why was the man on whom I relied so much to be taken away in this manner?"[46] It was a real blow to Hooker and he again lapsed into despondency. When at eight o'clock Slocum let him know that the advanced line must be supplied with both infantry and artillery ammunition or be relieved, he gave the unsatisfactory reply that he could not make soldiers or ammunition[47]—this despite the fact that the Fifth and First Corps were only a short distance from the hottest part of the fighting. Yet no word went out to Meade or Reynolds to pitch in. Meade was even censured for permitting one brigade to get involved in the fray.[48] A brigade of Birney's Third Corps division was indeed ordered up, but no ammunition was forthcoming.

Hooker went over to see how the Second Corps was doing on the east side of his square mile. A brisk demonstration by Lee's men had failed to move these veterans and they were in good shape.

During his absence General Revere, one of Berry's brigadiers, hearing that his general had been killed and his fellow brigadier, Gershom Mott, wounded, decided that he was now senior officer of the Old Hooker Division and took it upon himself to lead his brigade and other units off the field. This was done without the knowledge of Sickles, his corps commander, and against the soldiers' protests.[49] Soon the two brigades of the Second Corps in the front line were driven in. A heavy enfilading fire from the abandoned position of Hazel Grove caused Williams' division to withdraw and Geary would have followed had not Hooker ordered him to stick.[50] The advanced line retired to the rear of Fairview,[51] further contracting the fighting room.

Meanwhile, Hooker had received messages at half-hour intervals from Butterfield, all telling that Sedgwick was meeting hot resistance and was not too hopeful of results.[52] By 6:45 A.M. he had not been able to fight his way out of Fredericksburg. When no more promising news had come by 9:15, Hooker wired Sedgwick that the enemy's exposed flank now rested near the Plank Road at Chancellorsville. "You will attack at once, by command of Major General Hooker."[53] This was unreasonable and is further evidence that the Commander was losing his grip. Sedgwick was twelve miles away and had his hands full; he had the reputation of being a fighting general and was well aware of what was expected of him.

Shortly after sending this ill-considered message, the careworn and anxious General walked out to the porch on the south side of his head-quarters. Major Tremain, of Sickles' staff, came toward him with a report, and Hooker leaned over the rail to receive it. Just then Jackson's artillery at Hazel Grove succeeded in placing a twelve-pound solid shot squarely into a pillar of the Chancellor House just where the Commanding General was standing. The pillar was split in two and part of it thrown against his side and head. He was knocked down and stunned. When carried into the house he was thought to be dying, and the rumor spread that he was killed.[54]

This blow, together with the worry and fatigue of the past six days, probably left him unfit for immediate active command. Within five minutes, however, he was able to mount his horse and leave for the less-exposed Bullock House half a mile to the rear. On the way the pain became so intense that he felt as if he might fall, and he was aided to dismount. He was placed on a blanket and given some brandy—the only stimulant that we positively know he took during the campaign. It revived him and once more he mounted—and in good time; a few seconds later another solid shot, bearing the compliments of Jackson's artillery, destroyed the blanket upon which he had been lying.

He was taken to a tent near the Bullock House. General Meade came over immediately and advised Hooker that the First and Fifth Corps should move at once on the enemy's left flank. He would not give this common-sense order, however, and Meade was afraid to take the initiative, fearing that if things went wrong the blame for the loss of the campaign would be placed on him.[55] Forty-five minutes after his accident Hooker called Major General Couch to his tent and said, "Couch, I turn the command of the army over to you. You will withdraw it and place it in the position designated on this map."[56] This order really made Couch only the temporary executive officer of the army, not its commander, since he was not permitted full discretion to handle it as he saw fit.

The position designated was from Hunting Run down the Ely's Ford Road to Bullock's House, and up the Mineral Springs Road. As the First and Fifth Corps were already established on this line on the right, and the Eleventh Corps was entrenched on the left, the problem was to contract the center to a point from a half mile to a mile in the rear. There was barely time to do so, for Lee was continuing his tactic of pinching off the Chancellorsville crossroads. Geary's division, holding the south side of the square, was badly exposed. Hancock on the east was almost overwhelmed. In the face of a steady fire from the Confederate artillery, now advanced to Fairview, Couch accomplished the retirement, unassisted by Hooker, who rode on the scene later.[57] The Chancellor House and the forest around it were ablaze. Hancock did yeoman service in withdrawing the troops, and Couch was twice slightly wounded.[58] Meade assisted by advancing one brigade and giving good protection with his guns.[59] The Third Corps was placed on Meade's left; then came the Second and Twelfth Corps adjoining Howard. All were in position by noon.

By this time Hooker had received the happy news from Butterfield that Sedgwick had broken the opposition and that the enemy was retreating in great disorder.[60] This was fine, but Hooker had just lost the vital connecting link with Fredericksburg—the Plank Road.

At 1:15 P.M. he had recovered sufficiently to send a dispatch to Lincoln—his first report since the beginning of the battle. Although his natural exuberance was missing, he claimed that he still did not despair of success. He candidly admitted the loss of two defensive positions and indicated that Sedgwick's inability to get up was responsible. He did, however, speak well of the valor of his men.[61]

By two o'clock word had come that at last the enemy was leaving Bank's Ford—because of Sedgwick's advance—and that bridges could be laid there to insure direct communication between the two wings of the army.[62] Butterfield appealed to be allowed to advance with Sedgwick. Every man had been put in, and the Chief of Staff wanted "to share the fate and fortune of this army and my general."[63]

In mid-afternoon came the first details of Sedgwick's success. Marye's Heights and the heights south of Deep Run had been carried by eleven o'clock. The Sixth Corps had reached Guest's House on the Plank Road, four and a half miles west of Fredericksburg, two hours later. At two in the afternoon Sedgwick was still advancing, but General Warren, who was generally right, thought the enemy was planning to make a stand soon. The losses were heavier than the first reports indicated.[64]

Work at Bank's Ford had gone well: the bridge was almost down, the telegraph wires were across and Hunt had sent for the reserve artillery ammunition.[65] The same was true at Fredericksburg. Gibbon's division of the Second Corps had crossed the river into the town at sunrise and was ordered to stay there until further notice.[66]

During the late afternoon Butterfield kept Hooker constantly posted on the progress of the Sixth Corps. At four Sedgwick had advanced to the toll house and had opened up communications with Bank's Ford. At five signal officers reported that a Confederate column at Tabernacle

Church was advancing on Sedgwick.[67]  Butterfield then stirred up
Hooker's fear of Lee's being reinforced.  A captured Confederate captain
had told him that Hood and Picket were expected from Suffolk and that
Lee had telegraphed his right wing it would be reinforced that night.[68]
About eight came the news that Hooker's afternoon of inactivity had
made inevitable—Sedgwick was engaged in a bitter fight with the enemy
at Salem Church, six and a half miles from Chancellorsville.

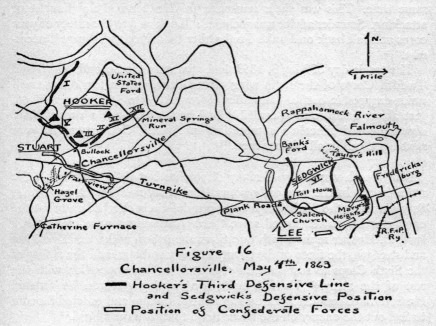

Figure 16
Chancellorsville, May 4th, 1863
━━━ Hooker's Third Defensive Line
        and Sedgwick's Defensive Position
▭ Position of Confederate Forces

The main body of the army had spent the Sunday afternoon and evening quietly.  The First Corps strengthened its position and cleared
ground for artillery.[69]  Meade did likewise, while Sickles threw up works
on his front where General Whipple was mortally wounded by a Confederate sharpshooter.[70]  A little skirmishing went on in front of Howard
and at nine in the evening the Twelfth Corps was moved to the extreme
left of the line.[71]  Hooker inspected his lines on horseback at least once
during the afternoon and though obviously suffering from pain seemed
his normal self.[72]

At eleven P.M. the capable General Warren rejoined Hooker behind

Chancellorsville. He found the Commander asleep, though still suffering from his injury. After learning Hooker's ideas, Warren sent a dispatch to Sedgwick. This note did not reach him until 6:30 the next morning and seems to be the only message he had received directly from Hooker's headquarters up to that time. Warren said that everything was going well on the right and that Hooker hoped the enemy would attack the next day. Sedgwick was not to attack unless Hooker did so at the same time. This was sheer nonsense, for Hooker had no thought of attacking. Sounder advice was included: "Look well to the safety of your corps and fall back on Bank's Ford rather than Fredericksburg, if necessary."[73]

The tragic day of May 3, 1863, had seen only the Second, Third and Twelfth Corps of the main wing of the army, with a few other small units, engaged in battle. Casualties of from 4,000 to 5,000 were suffered. Just about half the men available had been used—not a very faithful observance of Lincoln's admonition in April: "Gentlemen, in your next fight, put in all of your men."[74]

May fourth was a day of many dispatches but little fighting on the main front. In the very early hours Hooker received direct word from Sedgwick that the Sixth Corps had been definitely checked and that the enemy had been reinforced since then. Instructions were requested.[75] Instead, Hooker replied with questions about Sedgwick's exact position and strength, the force of the enemy in front and rear, and the ability of the Sixth Corps to sustain itself separately or in co-operation with the rest of the army.[76] He did make two helping gestures: he ordered Pleasonton to send Sedgwick a regiment of cavalry and ordered Slocum to feel out the enemy on the River Road toward Bank's Ford.[77]

He had no serious intention, however, of relieving Sedgwick, for he had told Butterfield that information obtained to date showed the enemy would try to pierce his center; consequently, he wanted Sedgwick to place two brigades in a position where they would be available for support of the main army![78] This clearly shows how ill-informed he was. His 74,000 men were confronting less than half their number while Sedgwick was about equally matched. Although the odds were shifting more and more against Sedgwick—Lee was soon to send another division to face him—Hooker was calling on him for help. Couch points out that there is something pathetic in this picture of Hooker, with roughly 80,000 men, waiting for Sedgwick with about 22,000 to come to his relief, while he retired to a safe position and left Sedgwick to shift for himself![79]

At eight Butterfield sent word that Gibbon was engaged in Fredericksburg and that, according to a "deserter," Longstreet's divisions were almost upon them.[80] Shortly after nine Sedgwick wired that he had beaten off an attack at Bank's Ford, that his communications were now secure with that place, but he would like instructions.[81] He followed this with a detailed statement answering Hooker's earlier questions: Losses of 5,000 men were admitted which reduced the Sixth Corps to 17,000 effectives; the cavalry was of no use to him; he could do no more than sustain himself and that only depending upon the condition and position of the main army.[82]

At 9:45 Sedgwick let the Commanding General know that he was being pressed and was taking position to cross the Rappahannock if necessary.[83] Hooker responded with several orders to reserve, if practicable, a position on the south side of the river which could be securely held until the following afternoon.[84] Sedgwick continued to report his difficulties, and an aide of Hooker's replied with the vague reassurance that Hooker wanted the Sixth Corps on the south side of the river: "If the necessary information shall be obtained today, and if it shall be of the character he anticipates, it is the intention of the general to advance tomorrow."[85] By mid-afternoon Sedgwick wired that he was facing 40,000 men and he was retiring to a position nearer Bank's Ford.[86] Hooker still urged him to stick it out.

On Hooker's front no action took place except the dispatch of several strong reconnaissance movements. The Confederates seemed in great force.[87] The General later testified that he would have attacked but he was fully convinced of the futility of trying to force fortified positions which could be approached only by slender columns, and he tried to induce the Confederates to attack but Lee would not accept the "challenge." At three in the afternoon President Lincoln, hearing that the enemy had reoccupied the heights at Fredericksburg, wired for confirmation or denial, since it looked suspiciously as though the Rebels were between the Army of the Potomac and Washington.[88] Hooker answered that this news was probably true but that he attached no importance to it.[89] Slight satisfaction to the worried President!

Between 10:30 and 11:00 that night the word came that Sedgwick was a half mile south of Bank's Ford and the Federal pontoon bridges were being shelled.[90]

At midnight Hooker called in his corps commanders for a council of war. All were present except Slocum, who did not arrive until the meeting was over, and Sedgwick who had his hands more than full elsewhere. Generals Warren and Butterfield also attended. Hooker first cited his general instructions to cover Washington and not to jeopardize the army. He set forth the condition of affairs, expressing apprehension over the possible unsteadiness of some of the troops. Then, with Butterfield, he withdrew, leaving the others to discuss whether to advance or retire.[91]

Reynolds and Howard were unqualifiedly in favor of fighting. Meade agreed, feeling that the guns could not be withdrawn, but he was later to waver in his judgment. Couch was for an advance, providing he could designate the point of attack. Sickles, Hooker's spokesman, admitted that he was not a professional soldier and because of this perhaps his opinion was entitled to little consideration; he believed, however, that a retreat would not be too hard on the morale of the country, that a victory was very doubtful and that a defeat would endanger Washington.[92] At this point Warren withdrew because, as he said, of his confidential relations with the Commanding General.

After further discussion of the possibilities of withdrawing the army, they were rejoined by Hooker. Whether or not a direct vote was taken on the question is doubtful. Couch says yes and gives the vote as three for advance (Meade, Reynolds and Howard) and two for retreat (Sickles and Couch). Sickles says that no written propositions were submitted for a vote of yea or nay, and no one else mentions a vote. More likely, the various opinions were given to Hooker who then expressed his clear conviction that the army should withdraw, saying that he would take the responsibility. Meade apparently withdrew his objections; Howard said nothing. Couch and Reynolds considered it laughable that they had been called together at all when Hooker had already decided to retreat regardless of their opinion.[93]

As the meeting was breaking up just after midnight, Hooker received a plea from Sedgwick to allow him to withdraw his corps unless the operations of the main army required the continued jeopardy of the Sixth Corps.[94] Brigadier General Tyler, commanding the artillery at Bank's Ford, reported at about the same time that Sedgwick's command was in great danger.[95] With this Hooker gave up his idea of keeping Sedgwick on the south side of the river and had Butterfield order him to retire.[96] Sedgwick immediately grasped the opportunity and hurried his corps across the river by 5:30 A.M.[97]

The fog was heavy on the morning of the fifth as the Army of the Potomac began its withdrawal. Under this cover all batteries not in line and all unnecessary equipment were removed. The engineers were ordered to United States Ford to speed the arrangements, while the soldiers pitched in to open roads to the ford and to build bridges over the small streams in that direction. Warren and Comstock laid out a supplementary defensive line in the rear to protect the retreat. An enemy attempt to get in behind them was feared and Reynolds was ordered to send a regiment and a battery to Richards' Ford where, with a brigade of Pleasonton's cavalry, they were to guard this approach. They were instructed to fight to the death in case the enemy came on.[98]

Hooker was downcast; he realized that the campaign was over and that nothing had been accomplished. He had so fully expected to be on his way to Richmond by now and instead here he was headed back to his old camps with harrowing thoughts of what might have been. Would he be given another chance or would he be cast aside like his predecessors?

Late in the morning Butterfield undertook the painful task of telling President Lincoln the state of affairs; Hooker said he entrusted this to another because of his pressing duties. Butterfield reported that the cavalry, as far as was known, had failed to execute orders. This supposition was based on the fact that the Richmond newspaper had come through the lines on Sunday as usual, indicating that communications had not been cut.[99] Butterfield added that Sedgwick had failed also; that the present position of the army was secure but circumstances made it expedient, in Hooker's judgment, to retire; that most of these circumstances would be fully explained in time.[100]

When Lincoln received this message he was a picture of despair. He walked up and down crying, "My God! My God! What will the country say!"[101] Horace Greeley exclaimed, "My God! It is horrible—horrible; and to think of it, 130,000 magnificent soldiers so cut to pieces by less than 60,000 half-starved ragamuffins!"[102] Rumors spread in the capital that Hooker would be placed under arrest and that Stanton had resigned.

At 4:30 P.M. a heavy spring storm broke, and by nightfall the Rappahannock was out of its banks. The wooden pontoon bridges at United States Ford could not be used by midnight. The bridge that had been

laid on the previous morning had to be taken up and used to piece the
two original bridges.

Hooker had crossed before then after giving his corps commanders
their marching orders. When the bridges became unserviceable communication was broken and the army was again removed from Hooker's
immediate command. General Couch once more was theoretically at
the head, and when Hunt told him the bridges might be lost entirely he
ordered preparations made to fight it out where they were.[103]

Meade tried to signal across the river their desire to stay and fight,
but if the signals were received they were not answered.[104] Meade then
sent an aide across to locate Hooker and get orders. He found Hooker
in a little house high up on the river's bank. The front rooms were filled
with wounded; on the back porch sat the despondent General nodding
in his chair alongside his Chief of Staff.[105] The faithful Butterfield would
not allow him to be disturbed and gave the aide an imperative order for
Meade to continue the retreat. General Hunt also sought out Hooker
and suggested a postponement of the withdrawal, since he feared that
only the artillery could get across by daylight, but this, too, was to no
avail.[106]

Two hours after midnight came what Couch termed a sharp message
from Hooker ordering the movement to go on.[107] All during the night
and the early morning of the sixth the Union troops took up the march
over the shaky bridges which were covered with pine boughs to deaden
the sound of retreat. General Meade, assigned to rear-guard duty, reported all across at nine without any trouble from the enemy.[108] Hooker
was fortunate: a well-directed Confederate battery could have ruined the
Army of the Potomac had it found the crowded approach to the
bridges.[109]

Hooker issued a circular on this dark and gloomy morning announcing
that headquarters would be established that night at the old location
near Falmouth.[110] In mid-afternoon two messages, which had been written at noon, were received from Lincoln. In one he quoted a Richmond
paper concerning the Confederate victory and the success of Stoneman's
raid in reaching almost to the Confederate capital. In the other message
he suggested that the heavy rain of the night before would secure
Hooker's flank and might lead him to think better of recrossing the
river.[111]

Hooker, of course, had to wire in reply that the army was already
across; he believed this action had been advisable on the score that none

of their trains or supplies were with them. He said, "I saw no way of giving the enemy a general battle with the prospect of success which I desire."[112] Toward evening he was informed by Stanton that Lincoln and Halleck were on their way to see him, having left before his letter of explanation arrived.[113]

All except the First and Sixth Corps were back that night in their old camps where many of the huts had been destroyed by the soldiers as they had never expected to use them again.[114] The corps commanders were in possession of a circular from Hooker directing them to have their commands well in hand, arms inspected, ammunition dry, and everything ready for action by the following afternoon. This could have been only a defensive gesture, for the return to the old camps had effectively ended the campaign and every man knew it only too well.

Hooker's General Order issued the same evening showed a return to his old form: The army was to be congratulated on its achievements; more had not been accomplished because of circumstances that could not have been "foreseen or prevented by human sagacity or resource"; the withdrawal of the army before delivering a general battle was evidence of its confidence, its consciousness of strength and its knowledge that fighting at a disadvantage would be recreant to its trust. He dwelt at length on the speed and secrecy of the army's movements, the long successful marches and the "surprise" of the enemy. An especially interesting contribution was: ". . . whenever we have fought [we] have inflicted heavier blows than we have received." Other claims were that 5,000 prisoners and seven pieces of artillery had been captured, 18,000 of the Confederacy's chosen troops rendered *hors de combat*, depots and communications destroyed and the South filled with fear and consternation.[115] This Order would seem to raise the question, where had Hooker been the last few days!

## CHAPTER XVI

# AFTERMATH OF THE CAMPAIGN

IT IS regrettable that Joseph Hooker's military career will always be remembered primarily in terms of his direction of the Army of the Potomac at Chancellorsville.[1] This was his big chance and he unquestionably fumbled. But he was never to repeat his error; always afterward when assigned to the offensive he pushed it aggressively.

The story of the campaign should rightfully be related from the Confederate standpoint since Chancellorsville was the supreme achievement of Robert E. Lee, Stonewall Jackson and the Army of Northern Virginia. In four days of fighting, though outnumbered two to one, they completely defeated their foe through offensive maneuver. Yet the benefits of their victory were few, and the costs were high; with many such victories as Chancellorsville the "Cause" soon would be lost. The battle was a sad preliminary to Lee's anticipated invasion of the Northern States.[2] Thirteen thousand men had been casualties, few of whom could be replaced, and corps organization was upset with the mortal wounding of Jackson. Confidence—probably overconfidence—was gained, but the enemy escaped destruction. The recuperative power of the North made a gradual wearing down of its armies an impossibility. The foreign intervention movement, upon which the South based so much hope, was not reawakened.[3] Hooker and the Army of the Potomac had lost prestige, over 17,000 casualties and fourteen guns, but all of these could be replaced.[4] Although civilian morale in the North was shaken, the general collapse predicted by many did not follow.

From the Union point of view the campaign had been a tragedy of errors and misfortunes. Of primary importance had been the breakdown of Fighting Joe's moral stamina when serious resistance was encountered on May first. This collapse dislocated his plan and caused him to abandon his true tactics—offensive battle!

The plan itself has been generally praised. Its main weakness was the dispatch of all the cavalry, with the exception of four regiments, on a raid which left an insufficient force to guard the flanks and bring in information. Perhaps it was too involved for Hooker. Neither the General nor his staff showed the ability necessary to co-ordinate an attack from widely separated wings. Confusion existed in the artillery. It had been removed as a unit in battle from the command of its chief, Henry J. Hunt. Hooker had told Hunt just to be "about" and to give orders in his name. This Hunt refused to do unless the orders were specifically authorized. No one except Hooker really assumed responsibility for all the artillery until the afternoon of the third when Hunt's rightful duties were returned to him.[5]

The campaign as conducted was marked by many mistakes: the failure to reach Bank's Ford on April thirtieth,[6] the refusal to fight it out in the advanced position of May first,[7] the lack of concern with defenses on the right flank during the afternoon of the second,[8] the withdrawal from Hazel Grove on the early morning of the third,[9] the failure to advance the First and Fifth Corps later that morning,[10] Hooker's retention of command when incapacitated at a critical moment, the failure to make an offensive move on the fourth while Sedgwick fought alone,[11] and the decision to retreat from a strong position when the army still had plenty of fight left.[12]

According to Hooker's partisans and some analysts of the campaign, the General wished to fight on the defensive until Sedgwick and Stoneman were successful; he then meant to throw in his huge reserve as soon as the enemy was exhausted and sweep the field.[13] He affirmed this to some extent in his testimony before the Joint Committee on the Conduct of the War. He maintained that as soon as Sedgwick was successful, Lee would have been forced to retreat toward Gordonsville, leaving the most direct road to Richmond open. He claimed that he had one and a half million rations ready to place on the direct road for his advance.[14]

The Joint Congressional Committee on the Conduct of the War did not get around to a hearing on Chancellorsville until February 25, 1864. It continued to take testimony for the next fourteen months, the final report appearing in May 1865.[15] The purpose of the hearing was to divest the Committee's favorite son of any responsibility for the loss of the battle. According to its report, the failure was due to:

1. The stampede of the Eleventh Corps.
2. Hooker's injury.
3. Sedgwick's failure.
4. Stoneman's failure.[16]

These conclusions were formulated well in advance of the hearing and the only questions asked were posed to substantiate them. The more intelligent generals realized that it was a farce and were careful not to speak unguardedly.[17]

The first point, the rout of the Eleventh Corps, was the obvious excuse for the failure of the campaign but was not as disastrous as it was made to appear. Jackson's attack was unquestionably a surprise to Howard, Sickles[18] and many of the higher officers of the corps. It should not have been! Many of Howard's men thought an attack was imminent and repeated warnings came in from the picket line.[19] The corps was unquestionably routed, but what body of 10,000 poorly posted men, overlapped on both flanks, could stand up to 25,000 of the best infantry of the time! They did delay Jackson until dusk and so gave Hooker the cover of darkness to organize a new defensive line.

It is difficult to estimate the immediate seriousness of Hooker's injury. Newspapermen at headquarters reported it as not serious; he was stunned but otherwise unhurt.[20] General Ingalls, Chief Quartermaster, wired Butterfield that Hooker had been slightly hurt but not at all severely.[21] Warren testified that Hooker's reaction to his wound was primarily one of weariness.[22] Pleasonton said Hooker's mind was not clear, and Birney claimed that he was insensible for two hours.[23] Surgeon Jonathan Letterman, Medical Director of the army, reports that Hooker's right side was partially paralyzed and livid for weeks afterward.[24] Surgeon General Hammond certified in 1867 that the Chancellorsville injury was the cause of Hooker's subsequent paralysis.[25] He said himself that he felt severe paroxysms of pain but was senseless for only a few moments.[26] There is no reason why his injury should have numbed the whole army. Had Butterfield been on hand this probably would not have happened, for Hooker would not have been fearful of turning full authority over to his faithful Chief of Staff.

The question of Sedgwick's co-operation has been argued at great length. Hooker claimed, and the Committee concluded, that the dilatory tactics of the Commander of the Sixth Corps was a major reason for the loss of the campaign. Hooker himself did so little that it was unjust of him to criticize Sedgwick who at least captured Marye's Heights. Butterfield, Birney, Warren and Howe, a Sixth Corps division commander, all testified that Sedgwick moved more slowly than was necessary.[27] Hooker stated that Sedgwick disobeyed the spirit of his order; he would have been justified in sacrificing every man in his command, if necessary, to comply with it. Sedgwick defended himself on the ground that ordering him to be at Chancellorsville the morning of May third was ridiculous. Gibbon confirmed this.[28]

The truth seems to be that Sedgwick was slow in getting ready to

## LOOKOUT MOUNTAIN

The peak of Lookout Mountain where Hooker's men raised the Stars and Stripes after the battle above the Clouds.

POSITION OF THE CONFEDERATES AT NEW HOPE CHURCH

The Confederate position at New Hope, Georgia, against which Hooker threw his hard-fighting corps.

attack the Confederate defenses behind Fredericksburg and delayed marching after his success there. It would have been impossible, however, for him to join Hooker at the appointed hour. Sedgwick was known to be slow and methodical. Hooker should have taken this into consideration when he left him in charge of the left wing.[29] After Sedgwick's death he testified that Reynolds would have been successful had he been in command on the left.[30] It would appear that Hooker and Sedgwick were each waiting for the other to do something.[31]

The failure of Stoneman was not so important as his absence. The army was defeated before the cavalry cut Lee's line of communications—it was broken for only three days. Hooker was very much dissatisfied with Stoneman, claiming that he could not have read his instructions and must have followed his own inclinations.[32]

There was one question the Committee saw fit to ask each witness: Did Hooker show any sign of intoxication during the battle? It was asked, of course, not to prove that he was drunk but that he was sober. As his reputation was that of a drinking man, it was natural that gossip would have him drunk during the battle. The Reverend Henry Ward Beecher stirred up the controversy by stating confidentially at a breakfast of temperance men that, although Hooker had abstained until he was wounded, whisky was prescribed medicinally for him then and he had made a good thing of his doctor's prescription.[33] Drunkenness as the explanation of his lethargy had gained widespread belief, even invading the Cabinet. Welles, for one, believed that liquor was the principal cause of Hooker's defeat.[34] Butterfield, Meade, Sickles, Pleasonton and Birney all absolved him on this issue.[35] Colonel Sharpe of the Secret Service grew vehement about it; he thundered, "Whoever says that General Hooker was drunk at the battle of Chancellorsville, lies in his throat."[36] The opposite contention—that his troubles came from his being sober—has more support. Couch and Schurz both felt that he would have been better off had he continued his usual habits.[37]

Certainly his confidence needed bolstering from the hour of the retreat on May first until the end of the campaign.

Both Generals Meade and Stoneman had known Hooker for many years. Stoneman told the newspaperman A. K. McClure shortly after the battle: "He [Hooker] could play the best game of poker I ever saw until it came to the point when he should go a thousand better, and then he would flunk." Stoneman also said that Hooker "was the most brilliant of all the generals up to a certain point, but when his limitation was reached he was utterly helpless."[38] Meade sized things up well when he remarked that the sense of responsibility overcame Hooker and modified his character.[39]

Regardless of the causes, Fighting Joe lost his nerve at the supreme test and history accords him the major blame for the disaster. The Army of the Potomac had fought bravely, as always, but to no avail. Lee had taken full advantage of his interior lines, his faithful lieutenant and that incomparable infantry which Hooker admitted had "acquired a character for steadiness and efficiency unsurpassed . . . in ancient or modern times."[40]

Lincoln and Halleck arrived at Falmouth on the morning of the seventh. They discussed with Hooker the campaign and the number and condition of the Federal armies in the Washington area. Fighting Joe had regained much of his self-confidence. He disclaimed the need of more troops; despite the losses in battle and those due to expiring enlistments, he still had about 100,000 men—all he could employ to advantage.[41] Lincoln blamed no one for the defeat but told General Meade he thought it would prove more serious and injurious than any other development of the war.[42] In a letter to Hooker, written on the way back to Washington, he declared that the movement had ended without effecting its object and that an early stroke would be desirable to overcome the bad moral effect. It was not, however, to be made in desperation or rashness. If Hooker had a plan he was to proceed without interference from the President; but if he did not, Lincoln would try to assist him to form one.[43]

Hooker immediately replied with a letter in which he again excused his failure on the ground of unforeseen circumstances; he must now learn the feeling of his troops before choosing a time to advance; a plan had already been formulated for the next move and "It has this to recommend it: it will be one in which the operations of all the corps . . . will be within my personal supervision."[44]

Halleck had remained in camp to find out the whole truth. When he returned to Washington he reported to Lincoln and Stanton that both the defeat and the retreat were inexcusable.[45] He brought an interesting message from Hooker: since he had never sought the command, he could resign without any embarrassment and he only hoped he might retain command of his old division and stay in active service.

In the meantime, Stanton had put on a show of going all out to Hooker's support, probably at the bidding of the radicals. On the seventh he had sent a dispatch to all independent army commanders and state governors minimizing the defeat and declaring that the Army of the Potomac would resume the offensive immediately.[46] That night he wired Hooker that public confidence and the gold market had not suffered. The next day he said that the state governors and Hooker's fellow officers were unshaken in their confidence in the Commander and the army.[47] Lincoln sent the cheering news to Hooker that a captured dispatch of Lee's indicated the Confederate losses were fearful. He added that Stoneman "could have gone in [to Richmond] and burned everything and brought in Jeff Davis."[48]

The Cabinet was divided on the question whether or not Hooker should be entrusted with the conduct of another battle. Despite Stanton's assurances to him one competent witness claims the Secretary of War agreed with Halleck that Hooker must go.[49] Secretary of State Seward wrote in his diary on May nineteenth that there was no intelligent agreement upon the causes of the failure.[50] It seems, however, that, along with Blair and Welles, he was opposed to giving Hooker another chance. Chase, of course, rallied to the support of "his man" and, with his Wall Street backing, blocked Hooker's ignominious removal at once. The President agreed, at least temporarily, to "give to Hooker one chance more,"[51] although he said, "If Hooker had been killed by the shot which knocked over the pillar that stunned him, we should have been successful."[52] The Committee on the Conduct of the War was still all for him.[53]

The weight of testimony indicates that the rank and file of the Army of the Potomac had lost confidence in its Commander. A veteran said, "Uncle Joe has bit off more than he could chew, and in attempting to swallow it has got choked."[54] Charles Francis Adams, Jr., in a letter of May twenty-fourth, writes:

"Hooker stands low in the estimation of the army as the truth about Chancellorsville comes out. Sickles, Butterfield and Hooker are the disgrace and bane of the army; they are our thrice humbugs, intriguers and demagogues."[55]

Unquestionably several of the corps commanders did not have faith in Hooker after the defeat. This was forcibly brought to his attention in an interview with the President in Washington on May thirteenth. Lincoln said to him: "I have some painful intimations that some of your corps and division commanders are not giving you their entire confidence."[56] It is not recorded whether the President saw fit to remind him of the words of his letter of appointment: "I much fear that the spirit which you have aided to infuse into the Army, of criticizing their Commander, and withholding confidence from him, will now turn upon you." At any rate Hooker asked Lincoln to name the dissatisfied generals. Lincoln apparently did not do so but disclosed his source of information—Governor Curtin of Pennsylvania. Hooker maintained that he could suspect no one and that none had frankly expressed distrust. He suggested that leaves be granted to all his generals so that they might visit Washington and Lincoln could ascertain their feelings himself.[57]

When he got back to camp the next day Hooker called on General Meade. He said that Governor Curtin was telling people he had lost the confidence of the army, particularly the confidence of Meade and Reynolds.[58] Meade reminded Hooker that they had differed in judgment on the withdrawal the night of May fourth, but said this was the extent of his criticism. Hooker was not satisfied, and on the nineteenth he accused Meade of having influenced him to withdraw across the river and of now denying it. Meade claimed that he had voted to stay, and he subsequently sent letters to those present at the council of war on the fourth to substantiate his point. The only thing accomplished by this interchange was the creation of an enduring coolness between Meade and Hooker.[59]

Hooker pursued the matter with Governor Curtin, questioning him about his alleged representation of disaffection. The Governor assured him that no general had spoken unkindly of him personally, but refused to pass on the criticism of his military movements.[60]

While the Commanding General was in Washington the Congressional Committee on the Conduct of the War visited the camps to learn of this dissension at first hand. They interviewed Hooker's friends but avoided most of the conservatives who, led by Couch and Slocum, were organizing a move to oust him.[61] They sounded out many of the division and corps commanders as to a possible successor and came to the conclusion that Meade would be the choice.[62] They left, however, with their own faith undiminished. Zach Chandler, in a letter to his wife immediately after his trip, absolved Hooker of any blame for the defeat and said, "I believe he can & will whip the Rebels in the next fight."[63] With Chase and Ben Wade, Chandler called on Stanton and insisted that great credit was due their hero for the courage, ability and prudence he displayed.[64]

Chase then took time to reassure his somewhat tarnished standard-bearer of the support he might expect from Washington and to suggest that he call for reinforcements at once and then move with his army according to his best judgment and with the utmost possible speed and decision. Chase added some sage observations:

"There must indeed be no disaffection. Better far make new generals of the best captains or lieutenants. I fear it is a mistake to have the Chiefs of Corps come up here to tell their several stories, though it may be for the best. We all like to be heroes and everybody knows so well what he himself has done, and how much better everything else would have been done, if his counsel or his ideas had been followed."[65]

Most of the corps commanders did visit the President, and it is certain that at least two—Couch and Reynolds—advocated Hooker's removal. General Couch, next in rank, said he would not take the command because he had no desire for it and because his health would not permit it. He recommended Meade.[66] When Hooker was retained, Couch, feeling that he was the leader of the opposition, asked to be relieved from service with the Army of the Potomac, June 10, 1863. Reynolds talked a whole evening and late into the night at the White House in early June. He still insisted on absolute control if he were to take charge of the army.[67] The President then said he would keep Hooker for he was not disposed to throw away a gun because it missed fire once.[68] Slocum had openly expressed dissatisfaction and Meade was not friendly. There is no reason to believe that Sedgwick, Howard or Stoneman, upon whom Hooker was trying to place the blame, spoke up for their commander. Hooker and Sedgwick had had a stormy scene in which the commander of the Sixth Corps hotly denied that he or his men had been in any way to blame.[69] That left Hooker with the support of only his close associates, Sickles, Pleasonton and Butterfield.

By the middle of May public reaction to the campaign was beginning to crystallize as the facts became known. The newspapers at first had published the customary optimistic reports, but now they were viewing the results more objectively. In the capital the Washington *Daily Morning Chronicle* was Hooker's strongest supporter, while the staid old *National Intelligencer* became a bitter foe.

The *Chronicle* on May seventh and eighth viewed the retirements as designed to accomplish some secret purpose; it cheerfully added that the soldiers themselves knew they had won. Within two days it had to recognize public disappointment and began making excuses for Hooker. The main alibi was Lee's preponderance of numbers after Longstreet joined him. This fell flat when it became known that Longstreet did not arrive until four days after the last shot had been fired. By the eleventh the *Chronicle* was on the defensive against those papers which, "for selfish and partisan purposes," were condemning Hooker as incompetent, slandering his character and creating disaffection in the army. The *Chronicle* said defensively that at least he had done better than anyone else.[70]

The *Intelligencer* began to assume a critical position by the ninth and within two weeks came to the point where it considered Hooker's disaster as the most signal which had yet overtaken the Army of the Potomac. It refrained from printing authentic intelligence to back up its assertion out of deference to the government's wish to give him another try. It suggested, however, that in the next campaign less should be said about what the General was going to do and more about what he did.[71]

In New York Horace Greeley's *Tribune* strongly supported him. On the fifth it had the "enemies of human liberty in retreat." Next day it hedged a bit; whereas the news was not so favorable as might have been expected, it still was very good. By the tenth it was forced to admit that the recrossing of the river was a disagreeable shock, but only a Copperhead could call the campaign disastrous.[72]

The New York *Herald*, a conservative paper, recognized the campaign as a failure by the eighth but, opposing Stanton and Halleck more than Hooker, placed the blame on "the pair at the head of the War Department." On the fifteenth it concluded that Fighting Joe's capacities were not equal to the management of so large an army and that there was no necessity for the retreat.[73]

The New York *Times* devoted itself to berating those who cried for the return of McClellan and to defending Hooker on the editorial page.[74] Its war correspondent, William Swinton, differed with the editors, and his article summarizing the action at Chancellorsville was suppressed, it is said, by request of Abraham Lincoln.[75]

The California papers were enthusiastic about their adopted son when the first news of Chancellorsville came in,[76] but as early as the eighth the *Alta California* said, "Hooker's sun, as the leader of a great army, has set." Doubts were expressed as to his ability to fill the station to which he had been elevated.[77]

A new drink was concocted after Chancellorsville, which became very popular in the bars of Washington and New York. It was known as "Hooker's Retreat."[78]

## CHAPTER XVII

## REMOVAL FROM THE COMMAND

CAMP life was back to normal by May tenth,[1] and for the next two weeks the soldiers enjoyed dry weather. The heat became oppressive, and as a sanitary precaution the old camping grounds were abandoned in favor of new sites in the same vicinity. The troops were well sheltered, clothed and fed. Drill was held early and late to avoid the midday sun.

The cavalry had finally returned, reporting that its raid[2] had been successful. General Hooker remained dubious and finally wired Stanton that it had amounted to little and that Stoneman had disregarded instructions.[3] On the twelfth he asked the cavalry commander for a full report of his operations and of the condition of his command. Stoneman saw the approaching storm and applied for sick leave.[4] Hooker endorsed the request, suggesting that the leave should not only be granted but granted for an indefinite period.[5]

There was some talk of breaking up the Eleventh Corps, but Hooker did not want this.[6] Schurz thought it should have a new commander to restore morale.[7] Chase recommended Sigel.[8] The corps had been dealt with severely by most newspapers and by the rest of the army after its rout on the second. Almost everyone accepted the story that the men failed to fight at all and just ran away in terror. Hooker, Sickles and Warren were foremost in this assertion. The officers of the corps could do little to offset the adverse publicity since the government refused to publish their reports until after the Commanding General had made his.[9]

A court-martial was convened at Third Corps headquarters on the twelfth to try Brigadier General J. W. Revere on charges of "Misbehavior before the Enemy and Neglect of Duty." A distinguished court was assembled with Winfield S. Hancock as president and Generals Newton, Wadsworth, Brooks, Humphreys, Gibbon and Barlow among the members. General Birney acted as Revere's counsel. It was a big show! Sickles, Revere's corps commander, testified bitterly against the man who marched the "Old Hooker Division" off the field without orders. After three days of testimony he was found guilty of "Conduct to the Prejudice of Good Order and Military Discipline" and was sentenced to be dismissed from the service. Hooker immediately approved the verdict—the more scapegoats the better![10]

Much correspondence passed between Hooker and Lee over the care of the Federal wounded and the recovery of the dead within the Confederate lines.[11] The scouts reported the enemy back in camp around Fredericksburg, and on the thirteenth the inevitable "deserter" said that Pickett and Hood had arrived at last.[12]

Many petty complaints arose over the wearing of the corps badges; Hooker had to issue strict orders that they be worn at all times and replaced immediately if lost. Flags were designed to identify brigade, division and corps headquarters.[13] The artillery was consolidated and the number of batteries attached to each corps reduced, so increasing the artillery reserve.[14]

Hooker wrote the President on the thirteenth that the advance he had in mind had been delayed because of the expiration of so many enlistments and because the cavalry would not be ready for a day or two; also, that there were but 80,000 infantry ready to march and, since double the necessary amount of artillery was on hand, half would be left in depot. He suggested, inasmuch as Longstreet could not be held in the vicinity of Richmond, that the Army of the Potomac should receive 25,000 reinforcements. He planned tentatively to move by the fourteenth. After asking Lincoln what he thought of the congratulatory orders issued at the close of the Chancellorsville campaign, he felt compelled to add a final, characteristic line: "Jackson is dead, and Lee beats McClellan in his untruthful bulletins."[15]

Lincoln replied by asking Hooker to come to Washington that evening. He told the General at this meeting that, considering the present situation, probably nothing could be gained by an early move. He proposed, instead, that the cavalry be sent out to raid while the army was put in condition. Hooker must not feel restrained, however, if an immediate attack gave promise of success.[16]

General Alfred Pleasonton, the "romancer of Chancellorsville," was put in charge of all the cavalry on the twenty-second.[17] His glowing tribute to his own work had resulted in a large amount of publicity and subsequent advancement. He was undeniably one of the few on the "inside" at headquarters, but his reputation was a "newspaper humbug."[18]

By the end of May the War Department had received warnings from many loyal citizens that Lee was planning an invasion aimed at either

Baltimore or Washington.[19] Hooker was told by Sharpe, his Provost Marshal General, that the Confederate Army had received marching orders recently and all rumors indicated the enemy was making important changes.[20] Unguarded statements in the Richmond press added color to this possibility. Hooker mentioned in a dispatch to Stanton that the move would most likely be up the Shenandoah Valley.[21] Information was still so uncertain that he was afraid to do much more than try to hold the crossings of the Rappahannock and push his cavalry out toward the valley to pick up information.

He was sensitive about an aggressive move by Lee because 16,000 more Federal enlistments were to run out within a month.[22] Hooker and Butterfield went up to Washington on the twenty-fifth to investigate the chances of acquiring reinforcements from the troops defending the capital and to talk to their friend Secretary Chase. Halleck had recently compiled a detailed report on the strength and location of the Washington forces concluding that not a man could be spared. There is no evidence that his mind was changed by "Fighting Joe."[23]

On the morning of June fourth word was received of the withdrawal of part of the enemy's force opposite the Federal left.[24] General Benham was ordered to throw a bridge across the Rappahannock at Franklin's Crossing to enable Sedgwick to make a reconnaissance on the Confederate side. The whole Sixth Corps was to cross the river, if necessary.[25] Sedgwick sent his skirmishers across the night of the fifth but the next day advised that he could not safely go over with his whole corps.[26]

The rest of the army was ordered to be ready to move on short notice. Buford's cavalry brigade was to shut off all communication across the Rappahannock as far up as Sulphur Springs.[27] He promptly sent back the alarming news that Stuart was preparing to make a raid with 20,000 men.[28] General Meade had to admit that Bank's Ford could be forced if the Confederates tried hard enough.[29]

Hooker reported the situation to Lincoln in a long letter on the fifth. He declared that Lee had been greatly reinforced and intended either to cross the upper Potomac and invade Maryland or to throw his army between the Army of the Potomac and Washington. In either case the Confederate column would be spread out from Fredericksburg northwest to Culpeper. If this occurred, the Commanding General believed it his duty to strike the rear of the column. The question was, would the administration consider such a move within the spirit of previous instructions to cover Washington and Harpers Ferry? Hooker then made the wise declaration that one commander was needed for all Federal troops whose operations might have a direct influence on the invasion. He meant by this the troops in the Valley, at Harpers Ferry, on the Potomac, at Washington, on the Peninsula and at Suffolk, as well as the Army of the Potomac. "I trust that I may not be considered in the way to this arrangement, as it is a position I do not desire. . . ."[30]

This letter does Hooker proud. It indicates that despite his bold talk after his failure at Chancellorsville his experience had left him chastened in spirit. He sensed that he would never receive the co-operation from Halleck necessary to meet a determined invasion, and he made an honest offer to withdraw, for the good of the country, in favor of anyone who would be given full confidence.

Lincoln turned the letter over to Halleck, for he believed it should be answered by someone with professional military skill. He did, however, advise against attacking at Fredericksburg and suggested that Hooker stay on the north side of the Rappahannock to do the fighting.[31] Lincoln used the homely expression:

"I would not take any risk of being entangled up on the river like an ox jumped half over the fence and liable to be torn by dogs front and rear, without a fair chance to gore one way or kick the other."

Halleck's reply assured Hooker that any ideas he might have for the movement of other Federal commands would be ordered, if deemed practicable, but avoided the matter of consolidating the command in any one person. Halleck disapproved of an attack at Fredericksburg. He preferred an attempt to cut Lee's moving column while still covering Harpers Ferry and Washington.[32]

Military authorities now agree that Hooker was right. An attack on the rear of Lee's column would almost surely have stopped the invasion far short of its eventual terminus, for Lee was always sensitive about his line of communications. Even Sedgwick's demonstration had the effect of stopping the Confederate move momentarily, but when Lee became satisfied that the Federals did not mean business he continued to advance toward the Shenandoah Valley.

Hooker then asked Halleck for the use of some of Stahel's cavalry from the Washington defenses to aid in an attempt to break up the heavy enemy cavalry force at Culpeper which he believed meant trouble.[33] This attempt was to be made on the ninth by Pleasonton, supported by

3,000 infantry.[34] The requested help was granted and Stahel rode to hold the fords at Beverly and Sulphur Springs.[35]

On the morning of the day set Pleasanton advanced in two columns across the Rappahannock—Buford at Beverly Ford and Gregg at Kelley's Ford.[36] They met Stuart's cavalry near Brandy Station and, with varying success, fought until mid-afternoon. The Federal losses were almost double those of the Confederates, but the Federal cavalry at last held its own. From this time on the cavalry skirmishes in the East were evenly contested. At noon Pleasonton reported his sharp fight and asked that 1,000 additional infantry be sent toward Brandy Station.[37] Hooker told him if he could not make headway to return to his own side of the river but to use his best judgment.[38] That night Pleasonton sent word he had recrossed the river. Characteristically he boasted of having crippled superior forces. He also claimed the capture of important papers which indicated that Stuart had planned to start a raid into Maryland the following day.[39]

By the tenth the War Department was convinced that steps must be taken to meet a possible Confederate raid into Pennsylvania. Brigadier General Brooks and Captain Comstock of the Army of the Potomac were ordered to prepare defenses for Pittsburgh. A departmental army corps of volunteers, to be known as the Army Corps of the Monongahela, was to be formed to take over the defense at that point.[40] Major General Couch was assigned to the command of the Department of the Susquehanna with headquarters at Chambersburg, Pennsylvania. He was to defend the line of the Susquehanna River, primarily Harrisburg.[41]

Hooker was not as yet convinced that Lee intended a raid with his whole army but believed he was shifting toward the upper Rappahannock. Colonel Sharpe had advised the day before[42] that the Army of Northern Virginia was now organized into three corps. Jackson's death from the wound received at Chancellorsville had obliged a Confederate reorganization. Lee's chief lieutenants were now James Longstreet, Richard S. Ewell and Ambrose Powell Hill.

Hooker sent another long telegram to Lincoln that afternoon. He gave it as his opinion that the best present means of striking a mortal blow would be to cross at Fredericksburg and march on Richmond in conjunction with the Federal troops on the Peninsula. Richmond, he alleged, was defended by only 1,500 men and could be easily captured and held while the body of the Army of the Potomac returned to meet Lee. Meanwhile, the defenders of Washington would be enough to protect

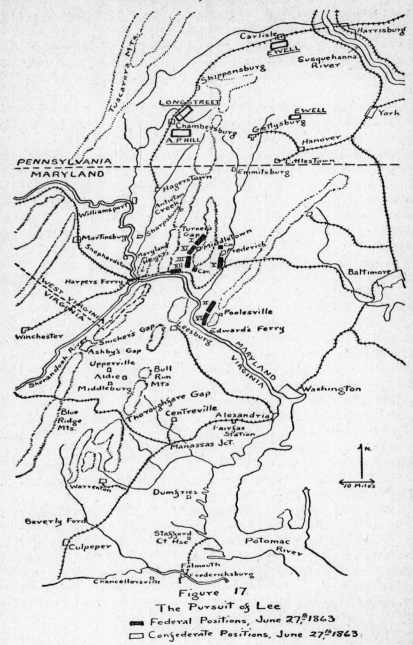

Figure 17

The Pursuit of Lee

◼ Federal Positions, June 27th 1863
☐ Confederate Positions, June 27th 1863

the capital temporarily.[43] Lincoln and Halleck very quickly let Hooker know that he was not to go south of the Rappahannock and was to consider Lee's army his objective—not Richmond. The President did not believe he could take Richmond in less than twenty days of siege operations, during which interval his communications with Washington would be cut.[44]

All information received the next day seemed to corroborate the picture of a heavy Confederate concentration at Culpeper, and three corps (First, Third and Eleventh) were sent in this direction to back up the cavalry at Beverly Ford.[45] As the purpose of the enemy was not yet certain, Hooker believed that his presence was required at the Falmouth Central Headquarters rather than at the apparently threatened point. General John Reynolds was ordered to take charge of the three corps on the upper Rappahannock. He was urged not to let the enemy cross the river and to attack if circumstance permitted.[46] Pleasonton was ordered to be on the alert and send in news. Instead of information Pleasonton came back with the ridiculous notion of buying off Mosby, the Confederate Partisan Ranger.[47]

By the afternoon of the thirteenth loyal citizens of Culpeper had given positive information that both Ewell's and Longstreet's corps had gone on toward the Shenandoah Valley.[48] Hooker could no longer wait beside the Rappahannock for developments. A hurried march and rapid concentration were in order lest Lee break past his right flank and cut him off from Washington or raid at will in Maryland and Pennsylvania. A circular was issued directing the transfer of the army to the line of the Orange and Alexandria Railroad at Manassas Junction and Centreville. The depots at Aquia Creek and at Potomac Creek were to be evacuated; the supplies and the 11,000 sick and wounded were to be removed on transports to Alexandria. The Engineer Brigade and a portion of the cavalry were to cover the withdrawal.[49] Reynolds, with the advance of the army, was cautioned against allowing Lee to fall on his line of retreat or to interpose between him and Washington.[50]

Next morning Hooker left his old headquarters at Falmouth for the last time. He was concerned over the loss of property inevitable in a retrograde movement, and issued stringent orders for the protection of his wagon trains.[51] He was not alone in his worries. The President and Secretary Stanton wired that the Confederates had surrounded the Federal troops at Winchester and Martinsburg. Lincoln asked whether or not Hooker could help them. "If the head of Lee's army is at Martinsburg and the tail of it on the Plank Road between Fredericksburg and Chancellorsville, the animal must be very slim somewhere. Could you not break him?"[52]

Hooker, who estimated the strength of the enemy at 100,000 men, replied that according to Hancock there were still 30,000 at Fredericksburg, probably A. P. Hill's corps, and it looked as though they might try to force the river the next morning. Hooker did not want to direct his army to Winchester unless the enemy was unquestionably there.[53] Pleasonton and Reynolds assured him by evening that Lee was headed for Harpers Ferry.[54]

Conflicting reports came in all day long on the fifteenth concerning the purpose and position of the Confederate Army. At night a telegram from the President removed any lingering doubt that invasion was Lee's intent. Winchester and Martinsburg had been lost and what was left of their garrisons concentrated at Harpers Ferry. It was thought that Lee's van was now crossing the Potomac at Williamsport.[55]

Hooker answered that it was not in his power to prevent the invasion; all he hoped to do was to check it. He believed Lee most likely to go north and incline to the west—an act of desperation but one certain to kill "Copperheadism" in the North. If he moved at once Hooker thought he could cut off A. P. Hill's corps before it crossed the Potomac and so force Lee to halt. But he would rather engage the enemy in Maryland than try to make a running fight in Virginia.[56]

From his new headquarters at Fairfax Station Hooker wired Lincoln at midnight the position of his army. The troops were all near expect the Second and Sixth Corps, and they were on the way.[57] The march northward had been one of the most grueling yet due to 100° temperature, thirst and clouds of dust.[58] A. P. Hill's corps had not crossed the Rappahannock after the Federal withdrawal but had followed Lee.

Early on the morning of the sixteenth Hooker suggested to the President that, as General Couch reported the enemy advancing only nine miles south of Chambersburg, it would seem wise to send Pleasonton's cavalry across the Potomac immediately.[59] Were this done, he recommended that Stahel's cavalry from the Washington defenses guard the flanks of the Army of the Potomac.[60] If Lee got any large body of infantry across the Potomac, Hooker wanted to do likewise.

Lincoln referred these proposals to Halleck but voted against shifting the cavalry across the river; this action would preclude the possibility of striking the enemy's moving column.[61] Halleck's reaction was in like vein: the cavalry should be kept with the main body of the army to aid in locating the enemy's strength, and most of the infantry should be moved to Leesburg.[62]

Fighting Joe was left in a bad state of mind. Every plan he offered had been overruled. When General Haupt asked where he intended to move he replied that he would move nowhere unless he got orders to do so; then he would obey them literally and let the responsibility rest where it belonged. If the powers in Washington would not permit him to carry out his own plans, they must give the orders.[63]

In a letter to the President sent at 11:00 A.M. Hooker expressed doubt of a successful attack against Lee's column and asked for a definite order if Lincoln wished him to attempt it. He went on:

"You have long been aware, Mr. President, that I have not enjoyed the confidence of the major-general commanding the army [Halleck], and I can assure you so long as this continues we may look in vain for success, especially as future operations will require our relations to be more dependent upon each other than heretofore."[64]

About four in the afternoon Halleck advised that Harpers Ferry was surrounded; could Hooker do something for its relief? Fighting Joe wired back for more information.[65] Before getting an answer he decided he was expected to march to the aid of Harpers Ferry and issued two circulars on the subject. The first stressed the importance of rapidity of movement and the need for reducing the wagon trains. The second directed the infantry corps to head for Leesburg. The advance was to break camp at three next morning. In the event of a fight, all corps were to march toward the sound of the heaviest firing.[66]

He wired Halleck that in compliance with his instructions the army would march in the morning for Harpers Ferry and should arrive there in two days.[67] This brought a denial from Halleck that he had given Hooker any directions to go to Harpers Ferry; he wanted him to go only as far as Leesburg. From there he was to move wherever circumstances indicated, depending upon the information brought in by the cavalry.[68]

Meanwhile, Lincoln had informed Hooker in order to avoid any misunderstanding that he was to consider himself in the accepted strict military relationship of a commanding general to his general-in-chief—Halleck was to give orders and Hooker was to obey them.[69] He tempered this official order by a friendly letter in which he tried to smooth out the feud; the General-in-Chief's only dissatisfaction with Hooker related to his method of reporting.[70] Hooker knew this to be but a small part of the long-standing quarrel.

Thus ended the five-month-old arrangement whereby he enjoyed the President's tacit consent to go around the General-in-Chief. He must have realized that his days as Commander of the Army of the Potomac were numbered.

When news came early the next morning that the Harpers Ferry garrison had been removed to Maryland Heights, orders went out to the corps commanders that the hurried march would not be necessary, and new objective points for the day were stated. Pleasonton was to move to Aldie and from there to reconnoiter toward Winchester and Harpers Ferry.[71] In the evening a message from Pleasonton said he had engaged and driven off at least a brigade of Confederate cavalry at Aldie. Hooker told him to push the enemy hard and find out what was behind the cavalry.[72]

Lee's invasion had created such panic in the North that the actual position of his forces could not be determined. Butterfield addressed a fervent plea to General Ingalls, in Washington, to stir up private sources of information in Pennsylvania. Official reports to headquarters placed the enemy in great force, at one time or another, at all points in West Virginia, Maryland and Pennsylvania.[73] On the eighteeth Hooker decided that no further moves would be ordered until it was clearer what Lee intended to do, except that headquarters were to be switched to Fairfax Courthouse that night.

In a confidential letter to the editors of the newspapers throughout the country, Hooker aired an old grievance. He asked them not to publish the location of headquarters or of any unit of the army; not to publish official reports without the sanction of the War Department; to have reporters sign all published letters. "These rules being observed, every facility possible will be given to reporters and newspapers in this army, including the license to abuse or criticize me to their hearts' content."[74]

Disagreement with Halleck continued as might have been expected. Hooker asked for information as to the whereabouts of Lee's army and Halleck implied that since Hooker was nearer to it he ought logically to have less trouble locating it; but Hooker might call upon Generals Schenck and Heintzelman for help from any of their forces within the sphere of operations of the Army of the Potomac.[75]

Hooker still believed on the nineteenth that reports of the enemy's infantry being in Pennsylvania were unreliable. He was misled, perhaps, by Pleasonton's notion that Lee was massing his forces at Upperville to break through Thoroughfare Gap that night.[76] On the morning of the twentieth in order to gain intelligence on which he could depend Hooker wired John Babcock of Frederick, Maryland—one of Sharpe's men—asking that he employ people not easily frightened by the presence of armed men to scout in the valley behind South Mountain and try to determine the number of the enemy north of the Potomac.[77]

Pleasonton reported at noon that Longstreet was so covering the gaps of the Blue Ridge, with Stuart out in front, that it was impossible to force them. He was ordered to move his whole corps against the enemy's cavalry the next day to determine where the main body of Confederate infantry was located, particularly A. P. Hill's corps. Two brigades of the Fifth Corps were ordered to assist the cavalry.[78]

By five o'clock Hooker had word from Babcock that no more than 5,000 Confederate infantry were over the river, about 1,200 cavalry but no artillery. Two hours later he wired that the enemy was just entering Frederick.[79] That evening Slocum was ordered to lay a bridge at Edward's Ferry.[80] It looked as though the Army of the Potomac would soon return to Northern soil.

Shortly after this Hooker had an encouraging letter from Secretary Chase, who had just returned to Washington from a visit with him at his Fairfax Courthouse headquarters. Chase had called on Lincoln and Stanton; they were for him and all admired the speed of his movements. Apparently Hooker had unburdened himself to Chase in regard to Halleck, for the Secretary assured the General that he was mistaken in thinking Halleck opposed him; Halleck would co-operate fully.[81]

Chase grossly misinterpreted the attitude of President and Cabinet. In his diary Secretary Welles tells of Chase's glowing account of his visit, the condition and spirit of the army, Hooker's control of the situation. Welles thought the public had lost confidence in Hooker but the President still clung to him.[82] Stanton is quoted as telling Lincoln: "I have no confidence in General Hooker, though his personal courage I do not question."[83] Senator Sumner of the radicals also had lost faith, looking on Hooker as a "blasphemous wretch." This stricture was based on the story that before the battle of Chancellorsville Fighting Joe had said: "The enemy is in my power, and God Almighty cannot deprive me of them."[84]

The cavalry fought a fierce engagement on June twenty-first near Upperville while trying to penetrate Lee's cavalry screen.[85] It was the fourteenth day of constant, wearing duty for Pleasonton's men in their attempt to push the opposing horsemen back through the Blue Ridge. Reinforcements in men and horses were asked for.[86] On the twenty-second Halleck placed the troops in the eastern half of General Schenck's department directly under Hooker's orders, but his use of Heintzelman's men would require Halleck's approval.[87]

The next day General Joe met in secret session at the War Department with Lincoln, Stanton and Halleck. Secretary Chase was not aware of the visit until it was mentioned at a Cabinet meeting later in the day. He went out abruptly, probably to see Hooker before he left town.[88]

Evidently the importance of holding Harpers Ferry was stressed at the war meeting, for upon Hooker's return to Fairfax Courthouse the Eleventh Corps and a force belonging to Heintzelman at Poolesville were ordered to proceed to Harpers Ferry at daylight.[89] Howard's orders were canceled, however, and the colonel in command at Poolesville refused to march without Heintzelman's direct approval. Hooker decided he would at least send Stahel's cavalry.[90]

It was about this time that Hooker told Butterfield the government was criticizing him for letting Lee cross the Potomac when, if he had his way, he would lay the bridges and help the Rebels over. Once the Confederates were across, he said, he would conform to Lee's line of march and fight him at Gettysburg with every available man on the field. He added: "If Lee escapes with his army the country are entitled to and should have my head for a football."[91]

Hooker addressed a long letter to Halleck. Present information indicated little change from the day before; since only Ewell's corps seemed to be across the Potomac, he would try to send a corps or two over the river to cut off the Confederate van from the balance of the army. He asked to have Schenck and Heintzelman told that they must obey his orders promptly since delays would most certainly cause reverses. Butterfield had left for Washington and Baltimore to gather a column of 15,000 men from the defenses of the two cities and to start them on the road to Frederick, Maryland. He was also to get a statement as to the number and position of the troops in both Heintzelman's and Schenck's departments. Hooker ended this letter with a request for definite orders, "for outside of the Army of the Potomac I don't know whether I am standing on my head or feet."[92]

At noon on the twenty-fourth another bridge was ordered for Edward's Ferry, and Heintzelman was advised to retire within his exterior lines around Alexandria if the Army of the Potomac crossed the river.[93] General Abercrombie's division from the defenses of Washington had been granted Hooker as a reinforcement and these three brigades were directed to join the Army of the Potomac promptly.[94]

Butterfield had to report from Washington in the early afternoon that he was getting nowhere with either Halleck or Lincoln. Their interpretation of the orders was that Hooker had no control over the troops within the defenses of Washington and Baltimore.[95] At four o'clock that day Babcock advised that the main body of Lee's army was then crossing the Potomac at Shepherdstown.[96] General William H. French, of Schenck's Department, who had recently been given the command at Harpers Ferry, was instructed to guard Maryland Heights which overlooked the town, and to observe the enemy.[97]

Another message came from Butterfield at three the next morning. He had succeeded in getting a brigade from Schenck at Baltimore, and it was to march the day following. Based on the figures he had computed, Butterfield thought Schenck could release 11,000 men (including the Harpers Ferry garrison of 8,500) and Heintzelman about 16,000 (most of whom had already been sent to Hooker).[98]

Hooker had now decided to conform to Lee's move and cross the Potomac also. This decision may have been inspired by a scholarly paper General Warren had submitted to him stressing the desirability of moving the Army of the Potomac to the vicinity of Harpers Ferry. Warren's main thought was that such an action would paralyze Lee's movement by threatening it on both flank and rear, and gain time for the arrival of reinforcements.[99]

Promptly that morning the army was set in motion for Edward's Ferry. Reynolds was put in command of the troops that were to cross on the twenty-fifth and move toward Middletown, about twenty-five miles north. This force was composed of the Eleventh, Third and First Corps. Stahel's cavalry was to protect them and seize Crampton's and Turner's Gaps in South Mountain.[100] The Second Corps and the Reserve Artillery were started on the march, and the Twelfth Corps and Pleasonton's cavalry were told to prepare for a quick move.[101]

A division of Pennsylvania Reserves under General Crawford, which had been put under Hooker's orders from the defenses of Washington, was also directed to Edward's Ferry.[102] At noon Reynolds reported that Howard and Stahel were across but urged Hooker to come up to Edward's Ferry and spur on the others.[103]

That evening marching orders were issued at headquarters for the next day. The Twelfth Corps and Pleasonton's cavalry were to cross the Potomac and proceed to Middletown. The Fifth Corps and the Second Corps were to go toward Frederick after they made the crossing. The Sixth Corps was to cover the removal of the bridges and to follow the Fifth and Second Corps. Fourteen batteries were to be sent back to Washington because there was not enough infantry to protect them.[104]

Hooker transferred his headquarters to Poolesville, Maryland, early on the twenty-sixth. He had had news from Pleasonton that Longstreet was still guarding the gaps in the Blue Ridge; it did not look as though Lee meant business, after all.[105] Then shortly after noon Butterfield got back from his fruitless errand. Halleck was afraid to strip Washington of its soldiery lest the secessionist element in the city be aroused.[106]

In the evening reports came in on the progress of the advance corps, and information that Lee had 60,000 to 70,000 men across the Potomac.[107] Hooker wired Halleck at seven o'clock asking if there were any reason why Maryland Heights should not be abandoned after all public property had been removed.[108]

On the morning of the twenty-seventh he left Poolesville for Harpers Ferry. On the way he ordered Butterfield to direct the cavalry toward Emmitsburg and Gettysburg to see what was up.[109] He examined Maryland Heights and Harpers Ferry, becoming even more convinced that there was no point in holding them, but Halleck's answer to his wire of the previous evening refused the evacuation unless absolutely necessary.[110] Hooker wired back in anger:

"I have received your telegram in regard to Harpers Ferry. I find 10,000 men here, in condition to take the field. Here they are of no earthly account. They cannot defend a ford of the river, and, as far as Harpers Ferry is concerned, there is nothing of it. As for the fortifications, the work of the troops, they remain when the troops are withdrawn. No enemy will ever take possession of them for them. This is my opinion. All the public property could have been secured to-night, and the troops marched to where they could have been of some service. Now they are but a bait for the rebels, should they return.

"I beg that this may be presented to the Secretary of War and His Excellency the President."[111]

So strongly did Hooker believe it now absolutely necessary to abandon the position that he wrote out an order. This conflicted with General

French's specific instructions from Halleck and with Hooker's knowledge he wired the General-in-Chief for confirmation. Hooker waited at his old classmate's headquarters for Halleck's reply. It was: "Pay no attention to General Hooker's orders." The contemptuous wording humiliated him. He was mounting his horse to leave when Andrew T. Reynolds, French's cavalry commander, an old friend, stepped up to him and remarked that a battle seemed imminent. "Yes," Hooker replied, "but I shall not fight the battle. Halleck's dispatch severs my connection with the Army of the Potomac."[112] His implacable foe had finally made it impossible for him to retain the command. A man on the inside in the War Department later remarked, "Severe measures had to be resorted to in order to wring from him that tender of resignation deemed to be necessary to enable his supporters at Washington to keep on outward terms with the Administration."[113]

At one o'clock Fighting Joe earnestly requested that he be relieved from the command at once.[114]

Halleck calmly replied that, inasmuch as Hooker had been appointed by the President, the question must be settled by executive action.[115] Hooker went over to Frederick that evening and told Butterfield he had asked to be relieved. He said that Halleck had not given him the needed co-operation; if every available man were not used against Lee there would be a disaster; he was forced to step aside for the good of the country.[116]

Hooker's request to be removed met with immediate action from the War Department and the President. The question was not brought before the Cabinet in a body, until many hours after he had been released. Possibly Stanton and Seward were the only Cabinet members originally consulted.[117] It cannot be denied that this was a particularly inopportune time to appoint a new commander, no matter how much the War Department wanted one. For once there was only one logical successor— General Meade—and he happened to be favored by both Stanton and Halleck. Lincoln gave his consent; he said to Stanton, "[Meade] will fight well on his own dunghill," referring to the fact that the General was a Pennsylvanian and the battle would probably be fought there.[118]

The only fear seems to have been that the transfer could not be effected quickly enough. Both Lincoln and Stanton were so concerned that elaborate steps were taken to insure the change at once. General James Hardie, Chief of Staff of the Secretary of War, was given duplicate copies of the removal order and sent immediately, in great secrecy, to

Meade and Hooker.[119] After an all-night trip he arrived at Meade's tent in the early morning of June twenty-eighth. Meade protested the change vigorously and wanted Reynolds named in his place,[120] but Hardie told him that there was no option. Together they went to Hooker's headquarters. When Fighting Joe saw them coming he knew that he was through. With much effort he tried to hide his feelings[121] and by extreme courtesy to relieve the situation of embarrassment.[122] Butterfield was called in and the position of the army discussed. When in the afternoon the consultation was over, orders were drawn up formally announcing the change of command. In his General Order No. 66 Hooker praised his successor and asked the army to extend to Meade the hearty support it had given him. He added:

"Impressed with the belief that my usefulness as the commander of the Army of the Potomac is impaired I part from it; yet not without the deepest emotion.

"The sorrow of parting with the comrades of so many battles is relieved by the conviction that the courage and devotion of this army will never cease nor fail. . . ."[123]

In the evening he said good-by to his friends about headquarters and, after a few final words with General Meade, left in a spring wagon for the railroad at Frederick.[124]

## CHAPTER XVIII

# HOOKER GOES WEST

A VERY bitter General arrived in Baltimore on June twenty-ninth. He had just resigned his hard-won command and he now faced the military oblivion thrust upon past commanders of the Army of the Potomac. By all precedent his number was up and he might just as well resign before he was banished to some insignificant department away from the scene of action. Yet his exuberance was such that he could not believe he merited such a fate!

He had been instructed to report to the Adjutant General's office at Baltimore and await orders. An anxious week of inactivity passed while the army he looked upon as his own engaged in a desperate struggle with the Army of Northern Virginia at a little town just over the Pennsylvania line. The strain was too much for him. No orders were forthcoming, so he left for Washington to see whether he could be of some immediate use. Conflicting reports were still arriving from the direction of Gettysburg and the war administration was in a nervous state. Halleck, ever suspicious of Hooker's actions, expressed his uneasiness by ordering him arrested for visiting the capital without a pass.[1] He immediately sent Lincoln a letter by messenger protesting the arrest; he had visited Washington many times before without a pass and never been bothered. He asked for a half hour of the President's time.[2] Lincoln must have come to his friend's aid, for the War Department made no attempt to prosecute him and let him stay in Washington. He resumed his old quarters at the Insane Asylum.

The indignity of the arrest hurt his pride and sharpened his fierce dislike of Halleck. His hatred and contempt knew no bounds. Before the Congressional Committee on the Conduct of the War he was to state that had Halleck been Commander in Chief of the Confederate Army he could not have done more to embarrass him.[3] To Noah Brooks, Washington correspondent of the Sacramento *Union*, Hooker alleged that Halleck, and to some extent Stanton, were responsible for all his misfortunes. He was naturally solicitous to know how Lincoln now regarded him. Brooks, choosing an unfortunate analogy, said the President looked on him very much as a father might look on a son who was lame or handicapped by some incurable infirmity! Hooker was angry. With tears of frustration in his eyes he replied: "Well, the President may regard me as a cripple; but if he will give me a chance I will yet show him that I know how to fight."[4]

Public reaction to his removal and Meade's succession was crowded from the papers by the stirring news from Gettysburg. General Meade, with the aid of Daniel Butterfield, whom he kept on as Chief of Staff, and with the hearty co-operation of all the generals under him, held the army together through three days of fierce fighting. On July first and second the army was pushed back on both flanks until the ranks were almost shattered, but they hung on. The next day Lee attacked the center with Pickett's fresh division and other units of Longstreet's corps but was disastrously beaten off. The invasion was checked and there was nothing left for Lee to do but go home.

The army had been surprised at Hooker's removal and, while the majority of the corps commanders looked on the change as definitely for the better, a large part of the rank and file regretted the loss of Fighting Joe. He had not brought them success in battle but he had taken care of their bodily wants and had returned to them the *esprit de corps* lost during Burnside's administration. Critics have not had much to say in his favor about Chancellorsville, but all have praised his work in trying to defend against Lee's invasion. Getting little assistance from his government and suspecting that he commanded on "borrowed time," he displayed "all the intelligence, energy and composure required of a commander at a critical period."[5]

Although Hooker had been relegated to that select group of major generals who had failed to lead the Army of the Potomac to victory, Lincoln was not inclined to discard him. Fighters were scarce and must be put to use. The President asked Meade if he would consider having Hooker under him as a corps commander; "I have not thrown General Hooker away," he said.[6] Meade resorted to the expedient of not actually asking for Hooker but of not objecting if the General were ordered to serve under him. Lincoln misconstrued this to mean that Meade really wanted him. When Lincoln asked if Hooker should be sent at once, Meade set the record straight by replying that he had never expressed or entertained any such desire.[7] In a letter home he stated his true feelings: "It would be very difficult for Hooker to be quiet under me or anyone else, and I sincerely trust some independent command will be found for him."[8] Hooker had known of the proposal to return him to his old corps and naturally resented the turn things took.

Meanwhile, it had been rumored that he would be appointed to have charge at Fortress Monroe[9] or in the Department of Missouri.[10] Chase was pushing him for the command of a demonstration to be made on Richmond via the James River, but Lincoln did not fall in with the idea.[11]

The General chafed at his inactivity and issued a press release that he would take any position in the field but would retire from the service if not assigned to active duty.[12] He made regular trips to town to worry Lincoln into a new appointment.[13] On one of these trips Hooker and Butterfield, who had left Meade's staff immediately after the battle of Gettysburg, dined with John Hay, the President's secretary, and others. General Joe drank little but, as Hay noted, he grew flushed, his eyes brightened, and he produced a fine flow of conversation. He said that he had been forced to resign the command of the Army of the Potomac because of repeated attacks which proved to him that he was not to be allowed to manage the army as he thought best; instead it was to be maneuvered from Washington.[14] He still believed the Army of the Potomac the finest army on the planet, which would be proved if it were sent against foreigners; it was superior even to the Southern armies in everything except vigor of attack. This weakness was due to McClellan: the army early "fell into evil hands—the hands of a baby, who knew something of drill, little of organization, and nothing of [its] morale. . . . It was fashioned by the congenial spirit of this man into a mass of languid inertness, destitute of either dash or cohesion."[15] Hooker was equally harsh with Stoneman, who, he said, had been "spoiled by McClellan and the piles."[16] Hay gathered that he was eager to raise an army on the Pacific Coast for a fight with some foreign nation[17]—probably France which had just captured the capital of Mexico.

At another dinner with the same people, this time at Willard's, Hooker turned his critical talents on the man who had recently whipped him though outnumbered roughly two to one. Lee was never much respected in the old army, and in Mexico he was surpassed by all his lieutenants; the strength of the Army of Northern Virginia rested on the broad shoulders of James E. Longstreet whom Lee consulted before each battle. "He [Lee] is a weak man and little of a soldier."[18] The party then turned to the more rational and favorite subject of the times—"pulling the Lion's tail." They discussed England's insults and injuries to the United States, the chances of Canada's falling and the possibility of the United States' taking Bermuda and near-by islands by force.[19] Hooker injected this prophecy:

"We will be the greatest military power on earth, greatest in numbers, in capability, in dash, in spirit, in intelligence of the soldiery. These fine fellows who have gotten a taste of campaigning in the last three years will not go back to plowing and spinning and trading, and hewing wood and drawing water. They are spoiled for that and shaped for better work. If they can find no war to their hand they will filibuster."[20]

These "brilliant" dinners occurred in September 1863, a month of sparse encouragement to the Federal cause. Meade's work after Gettysburg had been disappointing. He had let the enemy cross the Potomac almost unchallenged and he was now maneuvering to avoid fighting Lee until he could gain the better position—an almost hopeless aspiration. Lincoln was dissatisfied and rumor had it that he was considering the return of Hooker to the command.

In late September, however, affairs in the West became so critical that the President's attention was focused there. On the nineteenth and twentieth General Rosecrans and the Army of the Cumberland were soundly whipped at Chickamauga and driven back into the strategic point of Chattanooga, Tennessee. Here the army was still threatened by a dangerous force under General Braxton Bragg, which included several of Longstreet's divisions recently transferred from the East. Rosecrans was in bad straits. His direct line of supply, the railroad from Nashville, unfortunately ran through Bragg's outposts just before it reached Chattanooga. The Tennessee River was under the Confederate guns and the only Federal supply line left was a tortuous road over Walden's Ridge, sixty-two miles to the line of the railway beyond the point of enemy penetration. Rosecrans had advanced so rapidly just before the battle of Chickamauga that the railway had been barely repaired and no supplies accumulated.[21] The Union Army faced starvation or surrender.

Stanton got a telegram from Assistant Secretary of War Dana, making Rosecrans' dire position emphatically clear, on the night of the twenty-third. He immediately called Lincoln, Seward, Chase and Halleck into conference at the War Department. Part of the forces of General Ulysses S. Grant, who had opened up the Mississippi River by the capture of Vicksburg, had already been ordered to Rosecrans' relief, but no word had come that his men had started. Stanton proposed that help be sent from the Army of the Potomac; the transfer could be made in five days. The "profound" Halleck protested that it would take forty days and the President agreed with him, but finally Stanton won out when General

McCallum, director of Military Railways, said it could be done in a week.[22]

The Eleventh and Twelfth Corps were the most feasible units to detach from the Army of the Potomac since they had been a part of it for only a short time. The most likely commander for them was *not* Joseph Hooker, but he was available. It was hardly a position commensurate with his expectations but one he was glad to accept, all the same. Unfortunately his appointment was not welcomed by the corps commanders. Oliver Otis Howard had resented his attempt to pin his failure at Chancellorsville on the rout of the Eleventh Corps, and Henry Warner Slocum was so disgusted he offered his resignation as soon as the appointment was announced. In a letter to Lincoln on the twenty-fifth he said:

"I have just been informed that I have been placed under command of Major General Joseph Hooker. My opinion of General Hooker both as an officer and a gentleman is too well known to make it necessary for me to refer to it in this communication. The public service cannot be promoted by placing under his command an officer who has so little confidence in his ability as I have. Our relations are such that it would be degrading in me to accept any position under him. I have therefore to respectfully tender the resignation of my commission...."[23]

Lincoln refused Slocum's resignation and mollified him by promising a complete separation from Hooker as soon as possible, wiring Rosecrans to effect it.[24]

The Eleventh Corps now consisted of two divisions under Schurz and Steinwehr, while the Twelfth Corps was made up of two under A. S. Williams and Geary. They totaled only about 15,000 men[25]—the smallest command Hooker had had since Second Bull Run. The leading regiments boarded the cars on the twenty-fifth and within two weeks all the equipment of the two corps had left the Washington area, including over 700 wagons and almost 5,000 horses.[26] The trip took six days, covered 1,192 miles and involved several changes of cars because of varying rail gauges and lack of bridges over the Ohio River.[27] The route was via the Baltimore & Ohio Railroad to Benwood on the Ohio River, then on west through Columbus, Dayton and Indianapolis. Here it turned south to Louisville, Nashville and Stevenson, Alabama. This was the most successful movement of so large a body of troops by rail during the entire war.

Hooker did not have much to do with arranging the transfer. The War Department and the railway executives were primarily responsible, although by order of the President he was authorized to take military possession of all necessary railroads and equipment and all railway employees were instructed to obey his commands.[28] He did not follow his troops out of Washington until the morning of the twenty-eighth. On the evening before, he rode out with John Hay to the Soldiers' Home, Lincoln's summer abode, to say good-by. The President was always glad to talk with his favorite generals—this one in particular. Hooker came near to being the perfect soldier—was so convincing and so charming a companion; why could he not control his tongue? As the evening progressed Hooker worked around to his pet subject—criticism of other officers. He did not think too highly of the campaigns in the West since the Federal generals there always seemed to let the enemy choose the battleground.[29] When the visitors rose to go, the President charged Hooker to write to him and, according to some, begged him to avoid "Bourbon" County on his way through Kentucky.

The night of the twenty-ninth he spent in Cincinnati and part of the next day in Louisville.[30] At Nashville he stayed for two days until the greater part of his command could catch up with him.[31] In response to an order from Rosecrans he pushed his vanguard on toward Chattanooga.[32] On October second he arrived at Stevenson, fifty miles down the Tennessee River from Chattanooga. He was in high spirits at the prospect of immediate fighting and new distinction, and was greatly disappointed when he learned that he was only to guard Rosecrans' railway line of communications.[33]

Headquarters were no sooner established at Stevenson by Dan Butterfield, who was again with "his general" as Chief of Staff, than word came that the Confederate cavalry was loose on a raid behind Rosecrans' lines. The Federal cavalry had been unable to find subsistence near Chattanooga and was scattered along the meandering Tennessee in both directions from the town. It was a simple matter for the dashing Joe Wheeler's Confederate troopers to cross the river undetected. This time they had caught a Federal wagon train, had burned 500 wagons and were now headed for the railway. Hooker was ordered to see to the safety of the Stevenson and Bridgeport depots and to hold his army on the railway until danger from the raid had passed.[34] From Bridgeport on the Tennessee to Nashville the line to be protected was 125 miles long, of which he assumed responsibility for the lower seventy miles,[35] and General

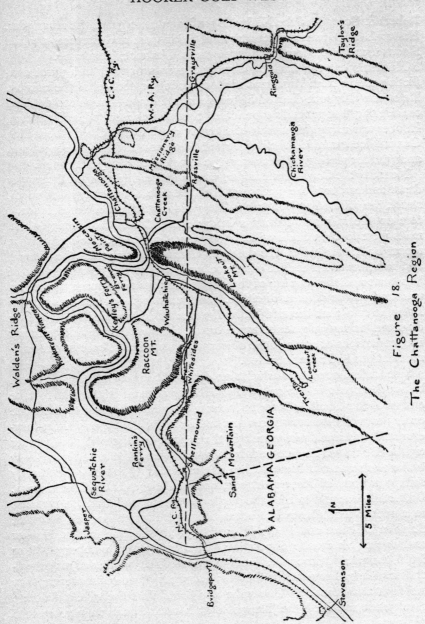

Figure 18.
The Chattanooga Region

Robert S. Granger of the Nashville garrison was to guard the remainder. Howard's corps was centered around Bridgeport and Stevenson while Slocum's men were located as far north as Wartrace, Tennessee.

Hooker spent the first few days at Stevenson straightening out conflicting orders from Rosecrans and organizing protection of the railway. He continually sent detailed instructions to Slocum—much too detailed considering that general's experience. Slocum was insulted, and believed Hooker was using this means of showing displeasure. On October fifth General Joe examined the defenses at Stevenson and at Bridgeport and arranged for placing bridges across the Tennessee at the latter point.[36]

Next day the Confederate raiders who had already destroyed the supply depot and captured the garrison at McMinnville, about sixty miles north, struck the railroad at Wartrace. They drove off the Federal defenders, tore up the rails and burned a bridge there. Then they went on ten miles west to burn Shelbyville. Hooker was outraged. He replied to a report by Butterfield on the damage: "I can scarcely retain the chagrin and mortification I feel at what you write me of the abandonment of Wartrace and the burning of the bridge. It does not appear that a gun was fired in the defense of either. Women would not act so badly."[37] Later he said that the raid broke the line of communications for four days and "in my judgment a much longer time will be required to repair the reputations of some of the officers to whom the defense of our communications had been intrusted."[38]

Slocum had gone to Nashville on duty and was cut off from his men below the break in the railway, so Hooker ordered Butterfield to take charge of the Twelfth Corps in the area of the trouble and to chase the enemy away.[39] Rosecrans' cavalry had been rallied by this time, however, and was already in pursuit of the raiders. By the night of October eighth the telegraph line had been repaired and the next day railway traffic was resumed. Nevertheless, the raid sharply reduced the already skimpy rations of Rosecrans' command beleaguered at Chattanooga. Butterfield was told to keep the cavalry on the enemy's trail. In response to a report that Generals Nathan Bedford Forrest, Joseph Wheeler, Stephen Dill Lee and Philip D. Roddey were with the raiders, Hooker sent one of his caustic dispatches: "The enemy may number 4,000 or 5,000, those half-starved and badly wounded. The number of major generals and brigadier generals they have along is of no consequence; they are flesh and blood."[40] The same day the main force of Confederate cavalrymen recrossed the Tennessee at Muscle Shoals in northeastern Alabama.

The railway continued to be interrupted by occasional raids and by guerrilla forces but not for any length of time. Orders had been sent out to hold the bridges and to keep the line intact at the cost of every man, if necessary. There was to be no surrender and no abandonment of the line.[41] All residents within twenty miles of the railway were warned that they would be held responsible for any damage done by guerrillas in their neighborhood on penalty of having their homes destroyed and their property confiscated[42]—a rather severe interpretation of the rules of "civilized warfare" as fought at that time. Hooker was never completely satisfied with the operation of the railway, and complained that there were too many accidents and too much irregularity. He said, "I have been furnished with a time table, but the running of the trains no more conforms to it than they do to the blowing of the winds."[43] When not guarding the railway Hooker's men were out on corn-gathering expeditions, a necessary though increasingly difficult method of adding to the rations that went from Nashville to Rosecrans' men. Working parties were detailed to improve the wagon road from Bridgeport through Jasper to Chattanooga over which the teamsters of the Army of the Cumberland struggled to keep their comrades in Chattanooga alive.

Hooker was well pleased with his efforts and reported ingratiatingly to Stanton how his prompt movement had saved Rosecrans' line of communications. He passed the palm to the Secretary of War with "If you projected the late movement of the Eleventh and Twelfth Corps you may justly claim the merit of having saved Chattanooga to us."[44] The next day he sent Abraham Lincoln a letter which he hoped would enable him to clean house. He suggested that since Rosecrans could find no other command for Slocum, the War Department should find something for him to do in Missouri—or elsewhere. He promised to act very deliberately with Slocum despite dissatisfaction with his services and mentioned how desirable it would be to give the Twelfth Corps to his old friend Butterfield.[45] His dissatisfaction was based more on personal dislike than on anything Slocum had done in Tennessee. Slocum had very intentionally avoided dealing with his commander as much as possible. It was an unsatisfactory situation but not the only unfortunate impasse in this theater of war.

Rosecrans was discouraged. His army was disintegrating from hunger, and retreat seemed his only alternative. The addition of Hooker's force had been of value to him, but when, on the twelfth, he asked Hooker to advance a division across the river and up the railway halfway to Chattanooga to extend Federal control of the direct line of communications,

Hooker replied that he would rather not move until his artillery arrived from Nashville.[46] Without baggage and transport, left behind when they hurried west and still on the way, the Eleventh and Twelfth Corps were not of much value as an attacking force. If the enemy chose to give up the siege of Chattanooga and cross the river above the town for an invasion of East Tennessee, neither Rosecrans or Hooker could do much to prevent it. Ambrose E. Burnside, who also had been sent west after his failure at the head of the Army of the Potomac, was at Knoxville, over a hundred miles northeast, with 12,000 men[47]—an easy plum for the Confederates to pick if they advanced that way. Unless earnest steps were taken, the Southern armies would soon surge up to the banks of the Ohio.

Mr. Dana, the Assistant Secretary of War, had been in Chattanooga for some time reporting on the condition of the army. Because of his pessimistic dispatches and disheartening messages from Rosecrans, Washington decided to make General Grant, victor at Fort Donelson, Shiloh and Vicksburg, head of a new military division which would embrace Rosecrans' department. If Grant thought it desirable, Rosecrans was to be replaced.[48] Stanton went west to meet Grant and confer the new responsibility upon him. While they were in Louisville a telegram came from Dana indicating that unless Rosecrans were prevented he would retreat. Grant immediately telegraphed Rosecrans that Major General George H. Thomas, "the Rock of Chickamauga," had superseded him. Thomas was ordered to hold Chattanooga at all hazards.[49]

Thomas was the foremost Southern soldier to remain with the Union when the war broke out. A man of impressive physique, with a determined mind and great dignity, he moved deliberately and with conviction. On defense he was without equal in the Federal army. To his soldiers there was no greater man than "Pap" Thomas. Without delay he adopted a plan which some say Rosecrans originated, others General William F. (Baldy) Smith,[50] Chief Engineer of the Army of the Cumberland, to open up the river line of communications. Orders had already been issued to Hooker to hold his command in readiness to move at short notice,[51] and part of Slocum's corps had been drawn down the railway as far as Stevenson.[52] On October twenty-fourth Hooker was informed that his part of the plan was to march for Brown's Ferry, five miles from Chattanooga on the river, with the Eleventh Corps and one division of the Twelfth, to gain and hold the railway and wagon road to that point if possible.[53] At the same time a division of the Fourth Corps was to march along the north side of the Tennessee to Rankin's Ferry, there to cross over and support Hooker as needed. In conjunction two brigades of the Fourth Corps were to seize a bridgehead at Brown's Ferry by sunrise and lay a bridge to connect the Chattanooga troops with Hooker's line of advance.

In the meantime the silent General Grant had come down from Louisville and had taken charge personally of the besieged force at Chattanooga. When he was to pass through Stevenson, General Hooker made preparations to receive at his quarters his new commander and old companion of Mexican War days. He sent a staff officer to the depot with a spring wagon to bring Grant back but did not see fit to go himself. General Howard who had run into Grant on his way to Bridgeport was with him when the staff officer met them. Grant chose to look upon Hooker's failure to appear as a violation of military etiquette and bade the officer tell his chief: "If General Hooker wishes to see me he will find me on this train." The aide soon returned with General Joe but Grant was not restored to good humor. Perhaps a recent crippling fall from his horse in New Orleans was responsible, or perhaps he wanted to make it clear to Hooker just who was Commander in Chief. At any rate, he took the opportunity to assert himself and, as Howard reports, to gain the proper ascendancy. It must have been an interesting meeting. At the time Grant was thin in flesh and pale in complexion—he was always self-contained and retiring—while Hooker was robust in health and bursting with enthusiasm. The invitation to headquarters was not accepted and Grant went on with Howard to Bridgeport where they shared a tent.

That night Grant remarked that he had no sympathy with grumbling officers of rank dissatisfied with the size of their commands or with those officers who were selfishly ambitious.[54] His path had not crossed Hooker's before during this war. It is quite likely that his opinion was colored by that of his trusted friend, William Tecumseh Sherman, who had written home two weeks before Chancellorsville:

"I know Hooker well and tremble to think of his handling 100,000 men in the presence of Lee. I don't think Lee will attack Hooker in position because he will doubt if it will pay, but let Hooker once advance or move laterally and I fear for the result. . . ."[55]

With Grant on hand and Sherman soon to join up, Hooker could look forward to rough treatment!

He did not enter too wholeheartedly into the plan for the relief of Chattanooga, for he feared the enemy would sweep down on him from Lookout Mountain while he was marching up the valley below. He told Howard: "It is a very hazardous operation, and almost certain to procure us a defeat."[56] His fears were delivered by telegram to Thomas but no change was made in the plans. While concentrating his forces Hooker continued his wrangling with Slocum, but as the latter was to be left to guard the railway there was little danger of the friction interfering with the impending advance. On October twenty-sixth Thomas decided to take no chances and removed Slocum from Hooker's command.[57]

The same day Dana, called by some Stanton's spy,[58] went over to Bridgeport to check up on Hooker. He found him "in an unfortunate state of mind . . . fault finding, criticising, dissatisfied . . . he is quite as truculent toward the plan he is now to execute as toward the impotence and confusion of the old regime."[59]

The plan to open up the river line of communications was to be put in effect as soon as Hooker was ready to move.[60] Geary's division of the Twelfth Corps could not be on hand until the twenty-sixth and so the morning of the twenty-seventh was set for both the surprise attack on Brown's Ferry and for Hooker's advance. At sunrise the Eleventh Corps, preceded by two loyalist companies of cavalry known as the 1st Tennessee and the 1st Alabama, took up the march along the railway. The country was rugged and the road rough, but the air was balmy and the men were glad to be on the move again.[61] Seven regiments and one battery of the Twelfth Corps were all that could be gathered at Bridgeport in time, and they followed Howard's men through the narrow defiles of Raccoon Mountain. The enemy's pickets fell back as Hooker went forward but the General prudently detached several regiments to guard the route. That night the advance stopped at Whitesides, fifteen miles closer to Chattanooga.

The march was resumed at daybreak on the twenty-eighth down into Lookout Valley where the railroad turned north to Wauhatchie. Here on the right flank loomed the forbidding heights of Lookout Mountain where the enemy lurked in unknown numbers. Confederate signal flags could be seen busily sending messages and, no doubt, enemy officers were sizing up Hooker's column from this excellent observation post. Perhaps he had been right in protesting against the move: at any moment the enemy might sweep out from the foothills and cut off his small force of 6,000 to 7,000 men. When the advance reached Wauhatchie the Confederates started a brisk rifle fire from the mountain spurs and soon added a shelling from the summit.[62] Fighting Joe went on with Howard's men to the junction of the Chattanooga and Brown's Ferry roads, the most exposed point on the route, and there sat his horse quietly, assuring his men that they were in no danger[63] and hoping he was right.

It was a tense situation—a setback now would undoubtedly end his military career. He gazed back at his long column so vulnerable to attack and measured the distance up the Brown's Ferry road where he was scheduled to make contact with W. F. Smith's surprise party. Howard's men were hastened on and in mid-afternoon were rewarded by the greetings of their comrades of the Army of the Cumberland who had been successful in securing their bridgehead the day before. Amid cries of "Hurrah! Hurrah! you have opened up our breadline!"[64] Hooker's confidence, never long submerged, returned in full vigor.

Geary's small force halted just north of Wauhatchie to guard the road from that point to Kelly's Ferry, and Howard camped three miles north near Brown's Ferry. Pickets were thrown out at both camps but no attempt was made to establish communication between them.[65] This was foolhardy inasmuch as Geary was still under the brow of Lookout Mountain. General Hazen from the Army of the Cumberland tried to persuade Hooker to bring his forces together and make a more compact defensive line across the valley, but he was now confident that he would not be disturbed.[66]

Shortly after midnight the roar of cannon and rattle of musketry brought Hooker out of his tent half a mile south of Brown's Ferry. The enemy had obviously fallen in some strength on his detached force to the south. He sent word to Howard to hurry to Geary's relief and he himself climbed into the saddle to direct the rescue.[67] The Eleventh Corps turned out smartly and began to retrace its steps to Wauhatchie. Within a mile they were subjected to a strong fire from the foothills along the river north of the railway. Hooker ordered two brigades detached to clean out the enemy but, unfortunately, the rest of the column was halted through mistaken directions. They finally pushed on but did not reach Geary until five o'clock, long after he had successfully beaten off the attack.[68]

Geary's men had fought desperately throughout the bright moonlight night but if the Confederate attack had been well organized it is doubtful that they could have saved either themselves or their train.[69] One account has it that only the stampeding of their mules, mistaken by the enemy for a cavalry charge, saved them from defeat.[70] Twelfth Corps casualties were 216, among them General Geary's son. Howard lost 204 men in his skirmishing among the foothills.[71]

Hooker had remained with Howard's men and contributed little toward beating off the attack. In his report he wrote up the engagement as a stirring victory and bestowed praise lavishly on all except General Schurz, whose two brigades directed to Geary's relief failed to arrive until the fight was over. Schurz asked for a Court of Inquiry to review Hooker's reflections on his and his subordinates' conduct. This added considerably to the lack of harmony in the new command.[72] General Thomas was hearty in his congratulations,[73] and Hooker gained a new nickname, "Hardtack Joe," in honor of the opening of the new line of supplies.[74]

Grant and Thomas went out to the scene of the battle of Wauhatchie the morning of the twenty-ninth. The Commanding General was not impressed. Dana that afternoon reported to Stanton that Grant would like to have both Hooker and Slocum removed and the Eleventh and Twelfth Corps consolidated under Howard; Grant would order them away himself except that he preferred to have so serious a move come from above. "Grant feels that their presence here is replete with both trouble and danger."[75]

## CHAPTER XIX

# THE BATTLE ABOVE THE CLOUDS

Now THAT supplies could reach Chattanooga with reasonable safety and in sufficient quantities to satisfy the Army of the Cumberland, General Grant could turn to the next problem—succoring Burnside at Knoxville. Half rations had left Thomas' command in poor condition as a striking force, and it was decided that nothing could be done to help Burnside until Sherman arrived with troops from the Mississippi. Then an attempt could be made to drive the enemy from Chattanooga which, if success-ful, would relieve the threat to East Tennessee. Fortunately for Burn-side he was not in too severe straits; on the day Hooker opened up the "cracker-line" Sherman was still 200 miles away.[1]

While waiting for reinforcements the Army of the Cumberland im-proved the fortifications around Chattanooga. Hooker was ordered to take up and strengthen a line running across Lookout Valley from the base of Raccoon Mountain to the Tennessee River and to protect the supply road from Kelly's Ferry to Brown's Ferry.[2] The division of the Fourth Corps which had been sent to protect his rear on the march to Wauhatchie had advanced as far as Whitesides. General Charles Cruft, who now commanded this division and who was reporting to Hooker, was ordered to halt here and hold the gap through which the railway ran.[3]

On November second Hooker fully expected an attack in strength against the new line he was fortifying, and he urged Howard and Geary to be alert.[4] He asked for authority over Hazen's brigade at Brown's Ferry should he become involved.[5] But the days passed quietly and work on his defenses was uninterrupted. Dana, the hard taskmaster, did not think well of these defenses. He wired Stanton on the sixth: "Hooker seems to pay little attention to his duties." Apparently Lincoln stood stanchly behind General Joe for neither Dana's critical dispatches nor Grant's lack of regard resulted in his removal from command.

He was gravely concerned over the enemy's activity on Lookout Moun-tain and wrote Thomas that he would like the remaining division of the Twelfth Corps to join him. He believed he should be strengthened since he feared the Confederates might pass a large force into the valley at night and overwhelm him before help could arrive.[6]

Meanwhile, the government was plaguing Grant with pleas to save Burnside and East Tennessee from Longstreet who had left Bragg in early November and was now on his way to besiege Knoxville. The stolid Grant could do little except perfect his plan for driving Bragg away, urge Sherman on and encourage Burnside to hold out.[7]

On the fourteenth a straight, grizzly-bearded, hawk-eyed old soldier strode into the headquarters of the Commander of the Division of the Mississippi, and the team of Grant and Sherman was ready to resume work together. Grant's plan to push Bragg from Tennessee featured his faithful lieutenant in the star role. The army, still on the march, with which both had won their reputations was to overwhelm Bragg's right on Missionary Ridge; Thomas was to advance on the center while the enemy was engaged with Sherman, and Hooker would have the negative task of holding Lookout Valley with Geary's and Cruft's divisions. His Eleventh Corps was to cross the river and serve as a reserve for the attack on Bragg's right.

The movement was first intended for the twenty-first, but heavy rains so bogged down Sherman's march that his foremost troops had got only as far as Brown's Ferry by that date and a postponement was necessary. Two more days elapsed before all of this force had reached Hooker's lines. While passing through a camp of the Twelfth Corps, one of Sherman's boys, who had never before seen a corps badge, noted the star worn by all of Geary's men. Natural curiosity prompted him to ask if they were all brigadier generals—a fair question considering the turn-over of generals within the Army of the Potomac! After explanations were made, Sherman's hardy campaigner was asked what his corps badge was. The quick-witted boy replied, "Forty rounds in the cartridge box and twenty in the pocket." Soon after, the Fifteenth Corps to which he belonged adopted the cartridge box and forty rounds as the corps insignia.[8]

On November twenty-second Howard took his corps, which was the largest unit under Hooker's command, over to Chattanooga according to Grant's plan. Realizing that a spectator's seat was being arranged for him, Fighting Joe, never one to be shoved into the background when a battle was impending, asked Thomas to let him accompany that part of his command which was going into action. The reasonable Thomas said yes but next day asked Hooker to remain in the valley and make a demonstration as early as possible on the morning of the twenty-fourth directed at the northern point of Lookout Mountain.[9] He meant this as a diversion primarily, but authorized Hooker to take Geary's and Cruft's divisions. At the last minute Osterhaus' division of Sherman's troops was added.[10] This division had been the last element in Sherman's march and had been cut off from the others at Brown's Ferry. The bridge had washed out before Osterhaus arrived and, since haste was necessary, Sherman proceeded without him. The unplanned addition to Hooker's command was indeed vexing to those directing the campaign. It began to look as though he could not be kept in the background—even the elements had intervened in his behalf!

Reports that Bragg was withdrawing led Grant to send out two corps on the twenty-third to drive back the enemy's skirmish line in front of Chattanooga and learn Confederate intentions. The affair was conducted handsomely: a strong position was gained, based on Orchard Knob halfway between the town and Missionary Ridge, and it was determined that the Confederates were still on hand and eager to fight. As Sherman was now ready to advance on the Federal left, a definite decision between Grant and Bragg would soon be reached.

At daylight on the twenty-fourth Hooker's conglomerate force, made up of three divisions from three different armies, was ready for the diversion on the mist-enshrouded mountaintop looming above them. He had been authorized to make a full-scale attack if the demonstration seemed to warrant it. It does not appear that he ever intended to make anything else despite the ruggedness of the field of operations and the fact that he had but 10,000 men, no two divisions of whom had ever worked together before.[11]

Geary's division and one of Cruft's brigades were sent up the valley to Wauhatchie where they crossed Lookout Creek at 8:30. They then turned north and marched along the western slope of the mountain protected by fog and rolling mists. In time they uncovered the fords farther down the valley where the rest of the force was waiting to cross the creek.[12] The General observed Geary's advance from the top of a low hill near his headquarters along the Tennessee. Satisfied that he was off to a good start, he ordered the three brigades still on the west side of the creek to join onto Geary's left and to sweep around the point of the mountain.[13]

This was no mean undertaking even if unopposed. They would have to get over or around ravines, ledges and boulders on a precipitous slope, as well as overcome the artificial defenses erected on the mountain during the enemy's two months' stay. On the northern slope a plateau 1,000 feet below the top was defended by earthworks and rifle pits planted at intervals. On the crest the Confederate guns were ready. Poor visibility would prevent Hooker's men from seeing exactly where they were going—though, to be sure, this would handicap the enemy at the same time.

Before noon Geary, up on the slope, had pushed the enemy around the corner of the mountain within range of the Union batteries on Moccasin Point. The Confederate batteries on the crest tried to retaliate but the guns could not be depressed sufficiently and the artillerists resorted to lighting the fuses of their shells and hurling them over the palisade.[14] Meanwhile Hooker, with Osterhaus' division, advanced along the Chattanooga Road at the base of the mountain where they cleared away the Confederate pickets and prolonged Geary's line on the lower slope. By 12:30 P.M. two brigades of the enemy, numbering some 2,500 men, had been driven away from the bench of land on the northern side. Hooker said the Confederates "were hurled in great numbers over the rocks and precipices into the valley."[15] Geary was ordered to halt his advance and strengthen his position.[16]

A continuous line was organized from just below the palisade at the point of the mountain down to the source of Chattanooga Creek. Enemy reinforcements arrived and skirmishing continued up and down the mountainside for the rest of the day. General Hooker struggled up the precipitous incline to inspect his lines and at four notified Thomas that his position was impregnable.[17] Ammunition was running short, however, and Chattanooga Valley was obscured by the darkness of an approaching storm. He judged it would be unwise to descend into this unknown area until the next day. Carlin's brigade of the Army of the Cumberland was sent to him directly from Chattanooga with extra ammunition and the front line was reorganized, bringing welcome relief to Geary's tired command.

It was a miserable night on the mountain slopes. The men were wet from the evening's storm and the wind was intensely cold. Bivouac fires burning brightly revealed to the rest of the army the extent of Hooker's progress on Lookout.[18]

Sherman had spent the day capturing a group of hills which he mistook for the northern end of Bragg's line, and at dusk the Confederate position in front of him remained firm. Thomas' men satisfied themselves with heavy skirmishing in the center. Thus the unwelcome Joseph Hooker carried off the honors—honors Grant was loath to bestow. He

GENERAL
ROBERT E. LEE

GENERAL
THOMAS J. JACKSON

GENERAL
JAMES LONGSTREET

GENERAL JOSEPH
EGGLESTON JOHNSTON

SKETCH OF FIGHTING JOE HOOKER
Drawn in 1879 by J. E. Kelly

says: "The battle of Lookout Mountain is one of the romances of the war. There was no such battle and no action even worthy to be called a battle on Lookout Mountain. It is all poetry."[19] This could hardly be reckoned generous from one who could well afford to share some glory. Confederate resistance to Hooker, though inadequate, had been enough to inflict 362 casualties. The South had lost 1,250 men—almost 1,000 by capture—out of the three and a half brigades involved on the mountainside.[20] During most of the day the odds had been four to one in Hooker's favor, and never less than two to one, but the enemy had the advantage of superior and prepared positions. The positive gains of the battle were important: navigation of the river and control of the railway to Chattanooga were assured, much equipment was captured, the enemy's defenses across Chattanooga Valley were flanked, and the morale of the army was given a big boost. A soldier on Orchard Knob, watching the advance on Lookout Mountain through an occasional break in the weather, had remarked: "Look at old Hooker. Don't he fight for keeps?"[21] Even the Confederates admitted that his men had battled with daring and desperation.

Anticipating that the enemy would be gone by morning, Hooker was at the front early. He sent details to scale the summit. They found it deserted and flung the Union flag at the peak. There was a heavy mist below but it lifted by ten and then they could see that the valley too had been deserted.[22] Thomas was well pleased with Hooker's success and ordered him on to Missionary Ridge via the Rossville Road.[23] At Chattanooga Creek the bridge had been destroyed and the march was delayed nearly three hours. When it reached Rossville the column turned north up Missionary Ridge. There it encountered resistance and the divisions spread out, one on the eastern slope, one on the ridge and one in the valley to the west. They rolled up the enemy line with little loss and took many prisoners. It was a new experience for the men of the Twelfth Corps to find their opposition so ready to quit. At sunset the fun was over and the troops went into camp.[24]

The leading role on that November day, however, did not belong to Hooker but to Thomas' men in the center. By mid-afternoon Sherman had been unable to break the Confederate grip on the north end of Missionary Ridge and Grant ordered Thomas to advance his men to the base of the ridge. They had been waiting for two months to get even for the thrashing they had taken at Chickamauga and refused to halt at the base. They went right on up to the top! Bragg's center fell into a panic and made the poorest showing of Southern arms during the whole war, retreating in disorder, abandoning equipment and almost losing their general as prisoner. Thomas' men camped that night on the ridge just north of Hooker's bivouac.

Scouts were sent out the next morning to locate the defeated enemy. From the information they brought in Hooker concluded that the Confederates were in full retirement. He applied to General Thomas for permission to follow on the Graysville Road via Rossville.[25] Thomas assented and added Palmer's corps to the column, showing that his confidence in Hooker was still unshaken by Grant's obvious distrust. The march was delayed because of the destruction of the bridge over the west branch of the Chickamauga, but by nightfall Palmer had reached Graysville, and Hooker, with his original force, was within five miles of Ringgold.[26]

They resumed the pursuit at daylight on the twenty-seventh and took many more prisoners. At the east branch of Chickamauga Creek they encountered Confederate cavalry and pursued it into Ringgold. There was every indication that the enemy's rear guard was holding a gap in Taylor's Ridge, directly behind the town. Through this gap ran the creek, the Western and Atlantic Railway and the road to Dalton, Georgia. To Hooker's thinking, when one follows a retreating army the thing to do is to hit hard and try to delay the retreat until support arrives. Osterhaus advanced a brigade on the gap but met firm opposition and lost heavily. Another brigade of his division was then sent to clear the ridge on the Federal left while Geary moved for the same purpose several hundred yards farther north. Both columns were repulsed and Hooker decided to wait for his artillery before throwing in the rest of his force. The guns came at 12:30 and were set to work softening up the foe in the gap and on the ridge. In the midst of this shelling General Grant rode up and ordered Hooker to discontinue the pursuit despite the fact that the enemy was then leaving the ridge.[27]

This ended the battle of Ringgold—more bloody than the much-publicized "Battle above the Clouds" but less successful because of sterner resistance. The hard fight did not elevate Hooker in the estimation of the Grant and Sherman team. Grant believed the whole affair unfortunate[28] and gave Hooker positive instructions which permitted him to advance only when he could do so without fighting a battle.[29] Hooker said, "This puts me in the condition of the boy who was permitted to learn to swim provided he would not go near the water."[30] On hearing that a stiff struggle was going on at Ringgold, Sherman remarked, "If Hooker would only keep quiet a little longer the enemy will run away, or else be captured by my force which are getting in their rear."[31] The snooping Dana was on hand the day after the engagement and wired Stanton, "The first great fault in this admirable campaign occurred at this place." Common sense should have told Hooker not to attack the pass in front but he did so with "the loss of 500 killed and wounded, where there was no necessity of losing 50."[32]

It was evident that, with the exception of Thomas, Hooker could do nothing to the satisfaction of his superiors. When he submitted his report on the campaign Grant indorsed it to the effect that the number of prisoners and small arms Hooker said his command had captured exceeded the number actually taken by the whole army.[33] Despite the belittling of Hooker's work from headquarters he came off with columns of highly favorable publicity. In their memoirs both Grant and Sherman try to perpetuate the tale that the great victory on Missionary Ridge resulted from a carefully prepared plan. The battle was fought strictly *not* according to plan! Hooker upset the general scheme with his unexpected success on Lookout Mountain and his advance up Missionary Ridge from Rossville. This threat on the enemy's flank contributed to the demoralization which Thomas soon found in his attack on the center. A very competent authority, William F. Smith, Chief Engineer of the Army of the Cumberland, believed that Hooker's movements won the Battle of Chattanooga.[34] When Thomas launched his attack and his men had victoriously exceeded their instructions, Grant asked angrily who gave the order and remarked that somebody would suffer if it did not turn out well.[35] His lack of confidence in the movement up the ridge was reported in the press within a week and has since been substantiated.[36] He was unhappy that Sherman had not played a bigger part in the show.

On the twenty-eighth, twenty-ninth and thirtieth Hooker remained at Ringgold according to instructions to protect the rear of General Sherman's column which had marched off to relieve Knoxville. The Confederates had halted ten miles away but Grant's orders prevented Hooker from molesting them. While at Ringgold Hooker destroyed the bridges and railroad track near by, the local tannery and the county jail.[37]

In obedience to orders from Thomas, Hooker's command started back at daybreak on December first for the old camps around Chattanooga.[38] In the middle of the month Howard's Eleventh Corps returned from the

Knoxville expedition. Upon Sherman's approach the Confederates had withdrawn from their siege and retreated farther into East Tennessee.

So operations concluded in this area for the year 1863, and the men settled down to a milder winter in camp. The quarters were not so comfortable as those of the year before but the weather was an improvement. Baseball furnished diversion from drill and picket duty. Hooker's staff and bodyguard made up a team but the General had given up the sport.[39] He held daily court in his pleasant headquarters on a hillside near the river. Officers of every rank were cordially received; past battles and campaigns were reviewed and new ones projected.[40] "Wooden hoop" beer was very popular that winter.[41] In January many regiments went home on furlough. Howard absented himself and Schurz was given temporary command of the Eleventh Corps.

Hooker's forces stretched from Wartrace on the Nashville and Chattanooga Railway to Lookout Valley. The troops were cautioned to hold their depots and bridges along the railway at all hazards—no surrender or abandonment in any circumstances.[42] Guerrillas increased their depredations and expeditions were continually sent out to capture them. Supplies did not come in as regularly as needed since the railway could not completely serve the four corps attached to the Army of the Cumberland.[43] Hooker suggested that more use be made of the Tennessee River as a supplementary line of communication.[44] Grant had removed his headquarters to Nashville, and Sherman had taken his troops west, camping along the Memphis and Charleston and the Nashville to Decatur Railways.

Hooker took time out from his supervisory work to write an extremely long letter to his supporter, Secretary of the Treasury Salmon P. Chase, in which he explained how Grant and Sherman had meant to leave him out of the recent campaign and how well he had done in spite of their machinations. Ever aggressive, he proposed that the army should take Montgomery and Mobile instead of going into winter quarters. He feared the country was too elated over the recent victories, thinking the war nearly over, and so might see no cause for further exertion. The incautious critic then blasted Meade: "He is a small craft, and carries no ballast." As for Grant's report on the campaign, "[it] reads well, and, *if true*, would be a good one."[45]

In a letter to Stanton, Hooker let his highly developed critical talent run riot. He started out by complaining about a newspaper article which gave him little credit for opening up the "cracker-line" and went on to declare that Grant was simple-minded—a foolish declaration to make to a man unscrupulous in using any weapon at hand if it served his purpose, and also a very foolish declaration to make about one who was to come to the supreme command of all Federal armies within two weeks! He told Stanton: "The point of . . . [Grant's plan] was to shut me out of the fight, Grant's object being to give the éclat to his old army. . . ."[46]

As soon as active campaigning was over, the question of his command of two corps was revived. This situation prevented Howard and Slocum, who was again under his jurisdiction, from reporting directly to the Commanding General of the Army of the Cumberland, an irregularity which Slocum could not tolerate. He protested to Thomas against the continuation of an anomalous position.[47] Thomas thought the solution was to transfer Hooker to the command of his Fourteenth Corps.[48] Grant suggested that he be given the military department covering the states of Ohio, Indiana and Illinois. This, of course, would be a nonactive command and would conform to the accepted method of putting "out-of-favor" generals on the shelf. Grant continued to fire at him. "The position occupied by General Hooker is embarrassing to the service, and I think injurious."[49] Grant claimed that Hooker's report on Lookout Mountain had appeared in the press before being submitted to him,[50] a breach of military etiquette that nettled him considerably.

How best to dispose of Hooker was complicated by dissatisfaction with Meade's handling of the Army of the Potomac. His maneuvering against Lee in the five months after Gettysburg had brought nothing resembling a victory and the wheels of removal were beginning to turn. He wrote his wife on December eleventh that his supersedure had already been decided on; Lincoln and Chase were very anxious to have Hooker, but Halleck and Stanton opposed.[51] A campaign to return Hooker to the command was gaining momentum. George Wilkes, editor of the New York *Spirit of the Times*, kept his work before the public with constant references to his clever handling of the army before Gettysburg, and claims that Fighting Joe and Butterfield should receive full credit for the success of the battle.[52] Senator Wilson of Massachusetts pushed the following resolution through Congress:

"Resolved by the Senate and House of Representatives of the United States of America in Congress assembled, that the gratitude of the American people, and the thanks of their Representatives in Congress are due, and are hereby tendered to Major General Joseph Hooker, and the officers and soldiers of the Army of the Potomac for the skill, energy, and endurance which first covered Washington and Baltimore from the meditated blow of the advancing and powerful army of rebels led by General Robert E. Lee. . . ."

The resolution eventually got around to thanking Meade and Howard for holding Lee back at Gettysburg, but it was a handsome tribute to a man who wasn't even there.[53]

The Committee on the Conduct of the War then did its part by encouraging testimony critical of Meade's work at Gettysburg in the hearing on that campaign. Zach Chandler, radical senator from Michigan, still an ardent booster of Hooker, said that it had been a mistake to remove him; he firmly believed in his courage, patriotism and ability and counted him a victim of circumstances.[54] On March 4, 1864, Chandler and his colleague, Ben Wade, said to Lincoln that the army and the country demanded Meade's removal; and that it would be satisfactory if Hooker were given command again.[55]

Meade summed up the agitation as follows:

"My enemies consist of certain politicians who wish me removed to restore Hooker; then of certain subordinates, whose military reputations are involved in the destruction of mine; finally, a class of vultures who in Hooker's day preyed upon the army, and who sigh for a return of these glorious days."[56]

The campaign was brought to naught by the appointment on March 9, 1864, of Ulysses S. Grant as Lieutenant General and Commander of All the Armies. On the following day Grant decided that his place was with the Army of the Potomac.[57] This ended any chance of Hooker's being brought east to serve with that army in any capacity.

## CHAPTER XX

# THE ATLANTA CAMPAIGN

THE appointment of Grant to the supreme command elevated William Tecumseh Sherman to the head of the Division of the Mississippi. With these two men directing the main armies, east and west, chances brightened for an early ending of the war. Simultaneous blows at the Confederate Army of Northern Virginia and the Army of Tennessee were agreed on. Grant traveled east to take over the Army of the Potomac and Sherman went to Nashville to administer his military division.

The Army of the Cumberland was in need of reorganization—particularly with regard to the high command. Thomas was eminently satisfactory as its leader, but among his corps commanders General Gordon Granger of the Fourth was dissatisfied and wanted a leave of absence, Palmer was unsatisfactory as the head of the Fourteenth, and Hooker was still in the peculiar position of having two corps reporting to him. On April second Sherman submitted his solution for Grant's approval. He recommended that General Howard replace Granger, that Palmer be relieved, that the Eleventh and Twelfth Corps be consolidated and given to Hooker, and that Slocum be given a small command on the Mississippi or transferred to the East.[1] Sherman must have become convinced that as long as Lincoln continued to support Hooker he was stuck with him and might as well make the best of it. Grant agreed to the reorganization immediately, but Palmer was not relieved until August sixth. Hooker's new command was christened the Twentieth Corps.[2]

The reorganization within this corps was another problem. There were to be three divisions and Hooker wanted Butterfield to have one of them. He looked with favor also on Geary, but wished to be rid of Williams, Schurz and Steinwehr, the division commanders remaining from the old Eleventh and Twelfth Corps. Thomas wired Sherman that Schurz's removal would meet with his approval, since he did not consider him of much worth; as for Steinwehr, it would be better if a place could be found for him elsewhere.[3] These two men were sent away, but Williams was retained.

Hooker was well pleased with his new command. His aggregate present for duty was just over 20,000. In deference to the pride and wishes of the men, he would have preferred to call the new corps the Twelfth rather

271

than the Twentieth, but the administration would not agree. When finally set up the Twentieth was organized as follows:

| | | |
|---|---|---|
| *1st Division:* | Alpheus S. Williams | |
| | Brigade Commanders: | Joseph F. Knipe |
| | | Thomas H. Ruger |
| | | Hector Tyndal |
| *2nd Division:* | John W. Geary | |
| | Brigade Commanders: | Charles Candy |
| | | Adolphus Bushbeck |
| | | David Ireland |
| *3rd Division:* | Daniel Butterfield | |
| | Brigade Commanders: | William T. Ward |
| | | Samuel Ross |
| | | James Wood, Jr.[4] |

By mid-April Sherman had arranged his plans for concentrating as many men as could be spared from the departments under his command to attack the Confederate Army under Joseph E. Johnston at Dalton, Georgia. From John M. Schofield's Army of the Ohio, approximately 14,000 men and 28 guns were available; James B. McPherson's Army of the Tennessee would contribute 24,000 men and 96 guns; while George H. Thomas would bring onto the field 61,000 men and 130 guns.[5] This mobile force of nearly 100,000 men and 254 guns should be sufficient to deal with Joe Johnston and still leave an adequate number for garrison work along the lines of communication. A separate cavalry division of about 10,000 men was in process of being organized to join up as soon as possible. The three armies were composed almost entirely of regiments from the Mississippi Valley.[6] Almost all of those from the East were in Hooker's corps.

On April twenty-fourth Hooker was directed to call in his forces from their task of guarding the railway and concentrate them in Lookout Valley.[7] He looked forward with pleasure to the coming campaign, even though Sherman was to direct it. Dan Sickles, who had lost a leg at Gettysburg and was at this time visiting him, asked what he considered the highest form of human enjoyment. Fighting Joe replied, "Campaigning in an enemy's country."[8] Hooker and Joe Johnston were old friends; they had fought side by side in Mexico and had entered Chapultepec together.[9] Hooker thought highly of Johnston's war record and realized that from now on he would be confronting an extremely capable foe.

Despite his anticipation of active fighting, he wrote to Senator Zach Chandler: "I am utterly disgusted and would resign today were it admissable to think of self at such times." This alleged despondency was due to his belief that Grant and Sherman were out to "get" him. He criticized recent promotions of Generals Schofield and William F. Smith and could not resist a jibe at his old foe, Halleck. He remarked that although Halleck was really the Chief of Staff in Washington, Grant would have nothing to do with him. Hooker called this "very much like a fellow marrying a woman with the understanding that he should not sleep with her."[10]

By May fourth all three divisions of the Twentieth Corps had passed by Hooker's winter headquarters and were on their way toward the Confederate defensive position at Rocky Face Ridge in front of Dalton. In concert with Hooker moved the other two corps of the Army of the Cumberland, supported by the Army of the Ohio, coming down from the North, and the Army of the Tennessee, hurrying into Chattanooga from the West.

The Federal forces in the West were going off to do battle through co-ordinated movements under the guidance of a dominating personality who intended to make his numbers count! At the same time in the East Grant was launching the Army of the Potomac across the Rapidan at the same fords Hooker had used in May 1863, and another force advancing up the James River was closing in on Richmond from the East.

Hooker's men took the old route to Rossville, then turned south through the Chickamauga battlefield and crossed the creek at Lee and Gordon's Mills. From here the way was across Chickamauga Valley to Taylor's Ridge which they traversed at Nickajack Pass and Gordon's Gap. The roads were fair, the gaps passable, and, though there was no forage in the countryside, grazing land was plentiful.[11]

On the seventh headquarters were set up at Trickum Post Office, five miles from the frowning palisades of Rocky Face Ridge. To the north was Tunnel Hill, the position held by the enemy when Hooker's pursuit ended at Ringgold. A force could now be seen on the hill. Hooker and Butterfield could not agree as to its identity and a friendly argument ensued which Hooker finally won when it proved a Federal detachment. Butterfield did the gentlemanly honors and offered to "pay a bottle or two."[12]

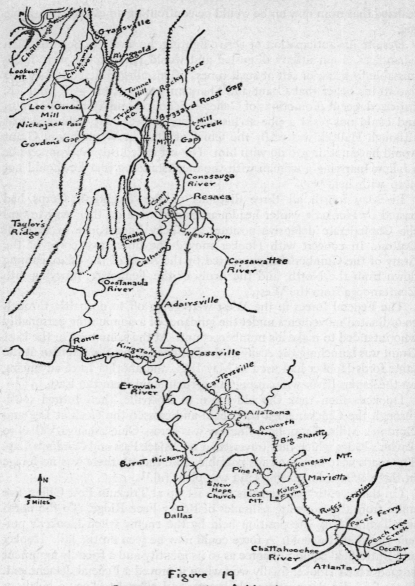

Figure 19
Chattanooga To Atlanta
→ Route of the Twentieth Corps

Thomas visited Hooker's headquarters on the morning of the eighth. The other two corps of the Army of the Cumberland, he said, were posted on Hooker's left near Tunnel Hill and were about to seize the northern end of Rocky Face Ridge.[13] He asked the co-operation of Butterfield's division to test the enemy's strength at Buzzard Roost Gap while Geary's division went for Mill Gap. At Buzzard's Roost the Confederates were found in impregnable strength. After close personal inspection Hooker agreed that this position would be difficult to force.[14] Geary's definite orders were to seize Mill Gap. At 3:00 P.M. he advanced two brigades and two batteries across sluggish, muddy Mill Creek, through marshy thickets and on up the steep slope. He drove the enemy skirmishers to the base of the palisades and then his men began to climb to the crest. It was a stiflingly hot afternoon; the ascent was difficult and the defense furious. Five different assaults were made and losses were heavy—357 men.[15] By 9:40 P.M. Hooker had to report that Geary could not reach the top.[16]

Although the attack was a failure it had helped keep the enemy busy while McPherson took his Army of the Tennessee farther south through Snake Creek Gap in an attempt to outflank the Confederate defenses before Dalton. Hooker and the rest of the army, with the exception of Howard's corps, followed McPherson,[17] and on the twelfth the Twentieth Corps was massed at the lower end of Snake Creek Gap. Meanwhile Joe Johnston had effected the first of his strategic withdrawals and fallen back to Resaca. Here he occupied a strong position with his left on Camp Creek and his right four miles above the town on the Conasauga River.

McPherson had moved too hesitantly to cut Johnston's railway line of supplies. He had run into unexpected resistance and had fallen back without forcing a battle. Sherman was furious. "Such an opportunity does not occur twice in a single life."[18] His anger soon cooled. He favored McPherson and perhaps he now realized that he had not worded his orders so decisively as he should have.

On the fourteenth of May Sherman began to press the enemy around Resaca.[19] In mid-afternoon he ordered Hooker well over to the Federal left where General Howard was hard-pressed. Fighting Joe, eager for battle, double-quicked his 1st Division to the threatened point just in time to repel a fierce attack.[20] The whole corps fell to erecting breastworks of rails and logs preparatory to resuming the battle at daybreak.

The next morning Howard, to show deference to Hooker's seniority, reported at his headquarters where they organized their joint attack.[21] When Howard left, Generals Sherman, Thomas and Schofield, with their staffs, came along and with Hooker climbed up a bald hill in the forward line to survey the enemy's works. So large a party attracted attention and a Confederate battery on the next ridge was quick to try its marksmanship. It proved good, and the Federal officers scattered—all except Sherman and Hooker. Both drew themselves to full height, summoned all their dignity, and with apparent indifference strode around in complete silence, each waiting for the other to seek cover first. Finally by some mysterious impulse—certainly not by any oral agreement—they simultaneously marched to the rear.[22] This schoolboy performance was quite humorous to their associates, but the bitter gulf between Sherman and Hooker made it deadly serious to them.

The entire Twentieth Corps attacked a series of irregular hills on the enemy's right flank at eleven o'clock. The hills were steep, rough and thickly wooded, with strong entrenchments and with batteries protected by earthworks. The cross fire was galling, but Hooker's men gallantly plowed ahead in column by brigades. Several hills were taken and a battery captured but before it could be withdrawn the Federals had to rush for cover. A Southern counterattack was repulsed and the abandoned battery remained between the lines as night came on. A Federal detail went out, skillfully removed the breastworks around the four guns and dragged them in while the enemy furiously attacked again.[23] It had been a day of hard fighting: 600 fewer men answered roll call in Hooker's corps alone.

Sherman had the foresight to send a force across the Oostenaula River around Johnston's left to threaten his line of supplies at Calhoun. Once more Johnston found it necessary to withdraw and in the early morning after the battle of Resaca he disappeared. His retirement was so complete, so well organized, and accomplished in such a short time that it was extremely discouraging to the Federal Army.[24] This new antagonist would not be easily overcome!

The Federals pursued immediately. Hooker had trouble crossing the Coosawattee River but by the seventeenth all three of his divisions had arrived at a crossroads four miles east of Calhoun. The next day his 3rd Division caught up with the enemy on the gravelly plateau north of Cassville. Skirmishing continued until ten the following night when his men occupied the town.[25] The main Confederate line was located on a ridge about a mile east of Cassville. According to Joe Johnston it was the most advantageous position he occupied during the course of the war.[26] His lieutenants did not agree and influenced him to retreat again down the Western and Atlantic Railway.

At Cassville Hooker's corps received a hard-earned rest while supplies were brought down. Joe Johnston's troops had destroyed the railroad as they retreated but it had been repaired just as quickly by Sherman's engineers. Since Sherman knew that a strong defensive position existed for Johnston on the ridge in front of Allatoona, little more than ten miles southeast, he decided to maneuver his way straight south to avoid the obstacle. This meant leaving the railway for some time.

By the twenty-third, twenty days' supplies had been accumulated. The army moved off over poor roads through rugged, densely wooded country.[27] The Twentieth Corps crossed the Etowah River on a pontoon bridge and continued on southward along the Burnt Hickory route to Dallas which was slated as the next concentration point.

The twenty-fifth was a bright, cloudless day; a fiercely hot sun beat down, and the dust was choking. At Pumpkin Vine Creek the enemy's cavalry was found in the act of burning the bridge. The crossing was secured, however, and two miles farther on infantry was encountered in considerable force.

Hooker and Thomas had accompanied Geary's division in the vanguard which was six or seven miles in front of the nearest support. The generals grew very anxious. Strong Confederate opposition was developing, but they agreed to put on as bold a front as possible.[28] They halted the troops along a ridge where defenses were thrown up until the rest of the army could be concentrated.

This movement had drawn Hooker northeast of Dallas on a road to New Hope Church, an important road junction. Appreciating its value Sherman ordered the Twentieth Corps to push on and seize it if possible.[29] By five in the afternoon Hooker was ready and he advanced with Williams' leading brigade through murderous volleys of canister to the foot of the slope upon which the enemy was entrenched.[30] Resistance stiffened here and the remainder of the Twentieth Corps joined in a sharp battle in the dense woods. Darkness and a severe thunderstorm ended the fight with Hooker still short of the junction, but his command had behaved creditably. According to one of Thomas' staff officers, "No more gallant struggle was made during the war."[31] Losses had been high, totaling 1,389 men.[32] Breastworks were thrown up as fast as possible with the idea of attacking again the next day.[33]

The morning of the twenty-sixth found the enemy once more thoroughly entrenched and inviting attack. McPherson's army was now posted on Hooker's right at Dallas, and Thomas' other two corps and Schofield went in on the left as soon as they came up. The difficult nature of the ground delayed the immediate general attack which Sherman proposed. Before all deployments could be completed he decided it would be wiser to try another flanking move, this time to his left, in an attempt to cut Johnston off from his railway. The five remaining days in the month of May were spent in trying to shunt the entire army to the northeast, in skirmishing all along the line and in repelling a Confederate counterattack at Dallas.[34]

Hooker's command remained in front of New Hope, which the soldiers had rechristened Hell Hole, until June first when they pulled out of line to join the movement to the left. Heavy rains made the going slow and the creeks almost impassable. Skirmishing continued as the army sloughed its way over. The wily Johnston had no notion of being cut off from his railroad, and on the night of the fourth retreated to a carefully prepared position defending his line of supplies.

Fighting Joe was getting tired of all this maneuvering. McClellan also had maneuvered well but had ended by losing the campaign. Sherman did not seem to want to fight. He had the men and the guns but so far no general battle had been projected to decide the issue. Hooker was restless. True to form, his corps had done more than its share of the fighting and recognition had not been forthcoming. His relations with the individual army commanders had been correct and pleasant on the whole, but he could not refrain from letting his staff officers and particular friends know that Sherman was doing a bad job. This weakness finally led Butterfield to write "his general," as friend to friend, cautioning him to be more circumspect in speaking his views; his subordinates, impressed, passed them on as "Hooker's opinions," and so he would be suspected of trying to get Sherman's place—the offense of which he had previously been accused with both McClellan and Burnside. "You never were, nor never will be a politic man—of that I am well aware—but you must be guarded."[35]

On the maneuver toward Johnston's railway friction arose with "Old Pap" Thomas. Hooker began it by writing: "Hereafter I request that it [the Twentieth Corps] may be kept together. I have been supporting everybody and everything."[36] He followed this by a complaint of the length of line assigned to him and the incorrect information and errors in the maps he received.[37] Thomas stood his ground and made it clear that these complaints were unjustified.[38] Irritation never again rose between the two. After the war Hooker declared Thomas to have been by far the Union's most outstanding leader.

Johnston's new position was a good one. His line was twelve miles long covering the railroad and the town of Marietta and making full use of Kennesaw, Pine and Lost Mountains.[39] By the eleventh Sherman had moved his three armies up to close contact and was ready to probe for a weak spot. Pine Mountain was found to be a detached bastion in front of the main defensive line, and the Army of the Cumberland was assigned the job of isolating it. This was done on the fourteenth by Palmer's and Howard's corps and during the night the enemy evacuated. On the morrow Federal troops took possession of the crest and Sherman, Thomas, Hooker, Howard and Geary gathered at this excellent vantage point to observe the enemy's main line of fortifications on a ridge running between Lost and Kennesaw Mountains.

Only the day before, a group of Confederate officers had gathered near this exposed spot and Bishop-General Leonidas Polk had been killed by Federal artillery fire. Polk was a Lieutenant General in the Confederacy and the first Protestant Episcopal Bishop of Louisiana. General Geary claimed the credit of Polk's death for Captain McGill's battery of three-inch rifled guns,[40] but Captain Hubert Dilger's Ohio light battery has also received the dubious credit, as has Simonson's 5th Indiana battery. It seemed that whenever a general officer was killed nearly everyone near the scene who had a firearm asserted responsibility for the lucky shot!

The Army of the Cumberland was ordered to develop the enemy's main line of fortifications in the direction of Lost Mountain. At 2:15 Hooker sent Geary's hard-fighting division and one brigade of Butterfield's command out over the rough ground. The Confederates were forced across two timbered ridges right up to their main works. Heavy fighting continued until dark and Geary lost 519 men, Butterfield 114.[41] The attack had not been well supported on either right or left. Schofield, who was supposed to be on the right, laconically remarked that Hooker's men "just happened" to strike that point of the line which was the strongest.[42]

The next night Johnston contracted his lines, giving up Lost Mountain, and Sherman's right wing swung around to the southeast. Hooker was ordered to push forward vigorously.[43] He did so through extremely dense woods in the midst of very bad weather, over swollen creeks, skirmishing as he went. On the twenty-second of June the weather cleared and the Twentieth Corps and a division of Schofield's army made a determined effort against the enemy's left flank. They gained a commanding ridge only five miles from Marietta, and under Hooker's personal direction the men began to dig in. The outlook was not too bright: numerous prisoners testified that the whole Confederate Army of Tennessee was in the neighborhood marching on this new position.[44]

The General asked for relief throughout the afternoon,[45] but before Thomas could respond the "Rebel yell" rang out in the woods and heavy columns of infantry advanced on the run. Williams' division and the corps' artillery were heavily engaged, yet stood their ground. Hooker was uneasy. He signaled to Sherman, "We have repulsed two heavy attacks and feel confident, our only apprehension being from our extreme right flank. Three entire corps are in front of us."[46] This was an unfortunate message, for it gave Sherman the excuse he had been seeking.

To show how badly he attempted to make Hooker appear, it is necessary to view the matter in some detail.

(1) Sherman accused Hooker of lack of propriety in directing his message to the Commanding General instead of to Thomas.[47] Yet Hooker was merely answering Sherman's own question, signaled directly to him, asking how he was making out.

(2) Sherman assumed that Hooker's "apprehension" was for his own right flank, which Schofield was supposed to protect, when the message could just as clearly and much more logically be interpreted to mean the right flank of the whole army. Sherman considered it a dastardly slander of Schofield and spoke of the bitter words it caused between Schofield and Hooker. Yet Schofield, in his *Memoirs*, does not interpret the message in this light and denies having been angry about it. He was with Hooker both before and after the battle and says that no sharp words passed between them—only Sherman was angry.[48]

(3) Sherman made much of the sentence, "Three entire corps are in front of us." There were only three corps in all Johnston's army; before he got the message Sherman had just ridden along the line to find the enemy confronting him at all points. Not entire corps but only units from three corps were before Hooker. The excitement of battle may very understandably exaggerate opposing strength, and it would seem that this slip did not deserve censure.

The fact remains that Hooker had been attacked in great force and in this engagement, known as Kulp's Farm,[49] he had punished the enemy sharply. The Confederates were compelled to retire under cover of darkness. The following day Sherman rode over to the battlefield and met Hooker.[50] It started to rain and the two sought shelter in a little church near by, where Hooker received a stern lecture from his superior concerning the sending of false dispatches. He was told that "such a thing must not occur again."[51] Sherman later remarked, "I reproved him more gently than the occasion demanded."[52] This was sorry treatment of the man who so far had carried the brunt of Sherman's fighting. The incident threw the Hooker-Sherman feud into the open[53] and, since Sherman held the reins, presaged a quick end for Fighting Joe.

The enemy still maintained a strong position around Marietta. According to his report General Sherman, believing that everyone in both armies counted on him to use nothing but flanking tactics, decided this time to order a frontal assault[54]—an imprudent change and a step which some ascribe to a desire to show the country that he could hit as hard as Grant. In the East, Grant had hurled his large army at Lee in two titanic battles, first west and then south of Chancellorsville, but no matter how hard he struck or how skillfully he maneuvered, he could not break the Army of Northern Virginia. He had capped his overland campaign with a hopeless attack at Cold Harbor, just to the northeast of Richmond, and had reeled back amid great slaughter. On June fourteenth he gave up his overland approach, crossed to the other side of the James River and laid siege to Petersburg, the back door of Richmond.

For his frontal attack Sherman selected two spots on Kennesaw Mountain, both thoroughly fortified and held in strength. On the hottest day in June, the twenty-seventh, under a blazing sun, McPherson's men and part of the Army of the Cumberland attacked up the steep rocky slope. Approximately 2,600 were sacrificed to find out what many had already suspected—that the heights were impregnable. For the first time in the campaign Hooker had a subsidiary part in the action and his decimated corps was spared the butchering Sherman suffered. Only Geary's division got into the battle and then only in a supporting role.

His lesson learned, Sherman immediately went back to his regular flanking program. He sent McPherson around the Confederate left to gain the Chattahoochee River crossings. On the same night Johnston retreated down the railway to Ruff's Station.[55]

Sherman believed that this was his best chance to fight Johnston to advantage, hoping to get at him when he crossed the Chattahoochee. He issued orders for "most intense energy of attack . . . to press with vehemence at any cost of life and material."[56] These directions were of no avail. As soon as Johnston discovered that the Federals were again bypassing him, he retired to prearranged fortifications along the river, and on the night of July ninth quietly crossed his entire army unhampered.[57] Hooker had followed over irregular roads down the west side of the railway, skirmishing as he went until the enemy's river fortifications brought him to a halt. From their camps the men could see the steeples and chimneys of Atlanta—the rail junction and industrial prize they had spent two months in approaching.[58] Sherman decided that a rest was in order for his worn-out soldiers, but on the seventeenth the advance began again. Hooker's men crossed the river at Pace's Ferry and went forward with Palmer's corps, now on the right wing of the army, since Schofield and McPherson had passed over to the left in the direction of Decatur.

They reached Peach Tree Creek, a deep, muddy stream with marshy banks and hills on either side, on the nineteenth. Under Hooker's supervision a footbridge was constructed and a brigade went over to establish a *tête-de-pont*. Over bridges for artillery and wagons built during the night the Twentieth Corps advanced to within four miles of Atlanta. Prisoners now gave the startling news that Joe Johnston had been replaced by John Bell Hood.[59] Here was an opponent of an entirely different nature. There would be no more tactically perfect retreats; from now on it would be plain stand-up fighting. In aggressiveness Hood was the Joe Hooker of the Confederate Army. His hard-fighting Texans had early in the war created a name for him as a driving brigade commander. His progress upward as a division leader under Lee and a corps commander in the West had resulted from fighting—stern, personal fighting—which had cost him an arm at Gettysburg and a leg at Chickamauga. McPherson and Schofield knew him well; they had been classmates at West Point, 1853—McPherson No. 1, Schofield No. 7, Hood No. 44—a fair evaluation of their ability to direct an army.

At 4:00 P.M. on the twentieth, as Hooker's men were carefully advancing from ridge to ridge in the heavy timber south of Peach Tree Creek, Confederate infantry in strong force rapidly and fiercely burst upon his corps and the supporting divisions of the Army of the Cumberland on either flank. For three hours the attack continued with unabated fury.[60] Hooker was up front as usual, encouraging his faltering line, shaming the fainthearted into standing firm, and successfully holding his ground.

Colonel Benjamin Harrison, later to become the twenty-third President of the United States, contributed considerably to the result by seizing an outlying hill with his brigade of the Twentieth Corps. As night fell Hood had to call back his inaugural attempt to fight his way out of Sherman's closing trap. Hooker had received the main force of the blow and his casualties of 1,607[61] reduced his corps to 13,000 men. He had lost 7,000 by stiff fighting during the two and a half months since they left Chattanooga—a greater number than any other corps.

The next morning Sherman and Thomas visited Twentieth Corps headquarters and Fighting Joe spoke with pardonable pride of what his men had done, mentioning his heavy losses. To this Sherman flippantly snapped: "Oh, most of 'em will be back in a day or two." Hooker's reaction to this unwarranted implication of desertion is not recorded, but it so infuriated Lieutenant Colonel C. H. Asmussen, the Assistant Inspector General of the corps, that he begged a fellow officer for a pistol that he might shoot the "God-damned son of a bitch" who cast such a slur upon brave men.[62] Asmussen was cooled off and Sherman was spared "to break the back of the rebellion."

Constant pressure revealed that the enemy held formidable works two miles and a half from the city's limits. On the twenty-second this line was found abandoned, and word came from headquarters that Atlanta had been evacuated.[63] As Hooker's men skirmished ahead this report proved untrue but the General was of the opinion that only a strong rear guard confronted them and that the city would be abandoned that night. He ordered his men to be constantly on the alert and ever ready to take advantage of a general withdrawal. "It will be a great compliment to the Twentieth Corps to have it said that it was the first to enter Atlanta."[64] The strenuous campaign had not dulled Hooker's flare for publicity.

The slander that John Bell Hood would give up without a fight the city he had been appointed to defend was refuted that afternoon when the Confederates again suddenly sallied forth, this time on the Federal left where McPherson's Army of the Tennessee had been placed in a compromised position east of Atlanta. It was a flank attack in the best tradition of Stonewall Jackson but was not supported as planned, and the Federals fought stubbornly until the Confederates retired to their Atlanta fortifications.

This battle ended the career of one of the most notable of all Federal commanders, James Birdseye McPherson, the man on whom both Grant and Sherman looked as their likely successor if they should be incapacitated. He was only thirty-five years old. Erect, tall, of striking personal appearance, he had risen to command of an army on merit alone without benefit of any sudden, brilliant success or political preferment.[65] His death was a great tragedy to the Union. It not only deprived the army of the leadership of this outstanding soldier but, as it turned out, caused the loss of one of its foremost fighters—Joseph Hooker!

McPherson's death left open the command of the Army of the Tennessee. On military grounds Hooker, as senior corps commander in the three army groups on hand and as the leader of the "fightingest" corps in the army, seemed the logical choice for the promotion. Aside from the disaster of Chancellorsville his war record had been good. He had fought hard and well. His successes, however, had been marred by constant quarreling with his superiors and fellow officers and criticism of them. Now when harmony among its leaders was about all that was needed to bring victory to the Union, could a chance be taken on a possible troublemaker in so important a position? Since William Tecumseh Sherman was the one who would choose the new commander, there was little likelihood that Hooker's shortcomings would be glossed over at this critical time. The origin of Sherman's extreme dislike for him has been commented on in an earlier chapter. Whatever the reason, it was enduring and had been well nurtured in a nervously active mind. Perhaps the two generals were too much alike in temperament to get along together. Sherman believed that Hooker's publicity for the "Battle above the Clouds" had turned his head and that he was jealous of McPherson and Schofield. He was their senior in rank, experience and age,[66] yet he was but a corps commander and they each had charge of an army. According to one of Thomas' staff officers, during the entire campaign Sherman "had shown unrelenting prejudice against him [Hooker], had listened to all gossip about him, had spoken slightingly and sneeringly of his work and done what he could to belittle his service."[67] On the other hand, Hooker had been unguarded in criticism of Sherman and his plans, particularly after Dan Butterfield's restraining influence was withdrawn. Butterfield had had to leave the army on June twenty-ninth because of a bad case of diarrhea.

Four days after McPherson's death Sherman brought the "pot to a boil" by announcing that General Howard had been appointed to command the Army of the Tennessee by the direction of the President.[68] "By direction of the President" was just a military form. The appointment had been made on recommendation of General Sherman after several consultations with General Thomas who also favored Howard. On hearing the news Hooker took the same step he had taken thirteen months earlier when General Halleck had refused him the Harpers Ferry garrison: he submitted his resignation. To Thomas he wrote:

"I have just learned that Major General Howard my junior, has been assigned to the command of the Army of the Tennessee. If this is the case I request that I may be relieved from duty with this army. Justice and self-respect alike require my removal from an army in which rank and service are ignored."[69]

He wrote to General John A. Logan who, after McPherson's death, had temporarily held command of the Army of the Tennessee and had as much cause as he to feel bitter about Howard's sudden promotion: "Had you retained the Command I could have remained on duty without the sacrifice of honor or of principle. . . . I am ordered to report to the Adj't Gen-l—the hopper into which all of us have to go now-a-days."[70]

Perhaps he hoped that Logan would follow his example and he would benefit by the public indignation over the resignation of two such popular leaders. Logan was quite like Hooker in many ways. General Cox says: "[Logan] could see fifty reasons why a different order should have been issued; but when once in battle his conduct was brilliant as well as judicious and his personal gallantry was proverbial."[71] But Logan had a promising political career to consider and refrained from so bold a step. The reasons for ignoring him were much the same as for by-passing Hooker, only in this instance it was Thomas who expressed dislike: he offered to resign if Logan received the command.

The correspondence on the Hooker case in the *Official Records* is marred by obvious gaps. A much repeated story indicates that Abraham Lincoln, who had befriended General Joe consistently throughout the war, stuck with him to the last. It is said that after McPherson's death he telegraphed Sherman to give the Army of the Tennessee to Hooker, but that Sherman replied he wanted Howard. Lincoln again urged Hooker's appointment, whereupon Sherman wired that his resignation was at the service of the President.[72] Lincoln was not prepared to go that far. He knew Sherman meant just what he said.

In his correspondence during the rest of the summer Sherman pointedly tried to justify his course. On the day Hooker asked to be relieved Sherman wrote Halleck:

"All are well pleased with General Howard's appointment but Generals Logan and Hooker. . . .General Hooker is offended because he thinks he is entitled to the command. I must be honest and say he is not qualified or suited to it. He talks of quitting. . . . I shall not object. He is not indispensable to our success. He is welcome to my place if the President awards it, but I cannot name him to so important a command as the Army of the Tennessee."[73]

Two days later he wrote home that he did not regret Hooker's leaving. ". . . he is envious, imperious and braggert. Self prevailed with him and knowing him intimately I honestly preferred Howard."[74] On August sixteenth he defended his choice as in good military practice: "No indignity was offered nor intended, and I must say that General Hooker was not justified in retiring." In a pacifying tone he added that if General Hooker had appealed to him "Every explanation and concession he could have expected would have been made."[75] It is difficult to picture Hooker appealing to Sherman or Sherman making explanations and concessions to Hooker. By September fourth Sherman had written the whole thing off to his satisfaction by telling Halleck: "Hooker was a fool. Had he staid a couple of weeks he could have marched into Atlanta and claimed all the honors."[76]

Both Grant and Sherman make a great point in their memoirs of Hooker's propensity for getting out from under rank. Grant says:

"I . . . regarded him as a dangerous man. He was not subordinate to his superiors. He was ambitious to the extent of caring nothing for the rights of others. His disposition was, when engaged in battle, to get detached from the main body of the army and exercise a separate command, gathering to his standard all he could of his juniors."[77]

This, perhaps, could have been charged to Hooker in the East when he was on the way up but cannot be said of his operations in the West. Though Sherman alleges that both Schofield and McPherson appealed to him for protection against Hooker's attempts to assert his seniority over them,[78] Schofield says Hooker never tried to give him an order.[79] McPherson did not live to contribute to the war's literature. Schofield's only complaint was that Hooker had a habit of pre-empting the roads assigned to him but attributed this conduct to Fighting Joe's desire to advance as quickly as possible.[80]

However strong the part that ambition had always played in Hooker's life, he was not at this time so much concerned with the future. His correspondence shows that he realized his sun had set; as Grant and Sherman loomed larger on the horizon, it would be unlikely he would ever again receive an independent command. His thoughts had to do with the past. He must account to the country for his only failure— Chancellorsville—and he was encouraging his friends on the Joint Congressional Committee to give him this opportunity.[81]

Just before he took leave of the army Hooker invited his foremost officers to headquarters and explained that he had resigned because he had been subjected to unbearable insults and indignities. The corps' performance had been underrated and disparaged and his reputation as a soldier and his honor as a man would not admit of his remaining.[82] He had never become so attached to a body of men as he had to the Twentieth Corps. The number of its casualties was a true measure of the service it had rendered.[83]

Then he rode along his lines, "erect and soldierly, a tinge of sadness on his ruddy face."[84] The soldiers cheered and waved good-by to their leader. They had great confidence in him and deeply regretted his going.[85] Many of their comrades had given their lives behind him and he had shared their risks. What was more important to the living, he had always kept his commissary efficient. It was a common saying throughout the army that "Joe Hooker fed his men the best and fought them the best, of any of the corps commanders."[86] A soldier in the 33rd Massachusetts wrote the *Christian Register* on August third a handsome and deserved tribute:

"What the 20th Corps has accomplished under Hooker's command, and how much the success of the campaign is due to him, the public will never learn from Western correspondents or official dispatches . . . no General was more careful of the comfort and welfare of his men. When other corps were hungry, we always had rations; when other corps were ragged, we had clothes."[87]

On the very hot day of July 29, 1864, the General and his staff went to the rear on a "dinky." Fighting Joe had departed for good from the way to glory and fame!

## CHAPTER XXI

## LATER LIFE

ONCE more Hooker returned to Washington bereft of a command. Two months passed before a position could be found for this warrior who was no longer wanted on the fighting front. On September 28, 1864, Lincoln assigned him to the command of the Northern Department which em braced the states of Michigan, Ohio, Indiana and Illinois.[1]

The General had spent his two months' vacation in Niagara Falls, Watertown and New York City. At Watertown he had visited his sisters and their families and been royally serenaded by the townspeople. He delivered a stirring war speech:

"This Union, gentlemen, cannot be dissolved as long as the army have guns to fight with. . . . I believe in treating the rebellion as Gen. Jackson treated Indians—whip them first and treat with them afterwards."[2]

In Brooklyn he appeared at the Academy of Music where a "highly intelligent" audience gathered to do him honor. Senator Wilson of Massachusetts spoke first and then Hooker added a few remarks: "There are no Copperheads in the army. The troops will fight well, and they will vote well"[3]—referring to the support they would give Abraham Lincoln in his contest with George B. McClellan, the Democratic nominee, in the Presidential election.

At a reception in the Union League Club of New York he was more voluble. He predicted that the fighting was nearly over.

"The people have been ahead of the government in promoting the war but the administration has come along, and on the whole, done tolerably well. . . . We have fought England as well as the South. She has furnished the rebels with all their arms and clothing, and for these she holds a mortgage on the whole South. I don't think she will undertake to foreclose it."[4]

While in Washington he could not resist telling all who would listen that Sherman would fail, that his army was discouraged and dissatisfied.[5] His friend George Wilkes tried to stir up public support for him in the

*Spirit of the Times.* "The malice of that cool calculating owl [Halleck], who broods in the shadows of the War Department, distilling evil upon every noble character which rubs his envy, has again triumphed over General Hooker."[6] Response was not forthcoming; Grant and Sherman were firmly in the saddle. Day by day Grant was extending his ring around Petersburg, and on September second Atlanta surrendered to Sherman.

On the twenty-ninth of that month Hooker was on his way to take over the new command. He was charged to look to the security of prisoners of war in the camps within his department, to guard the northern frontier along the lakes, to protect the line of the Ohio River and to exercise inspection and supervision over the draft—anemic duties for a man who for three years had been foremost in the fight! Two days later he arrived at departmental headquarters in Columbus, Ohio. On assuming command he made it clear that he would require "energy, earnestness and fidelity in the performance of duty on the part of every officer and soldier in the department." He added the platitude, "No one will consider the day as ended until the duties it brings have been discharged."[7]

On October sixth he moved headquarters to Cincinnati, a more central and convenient location for the dispatch of departmental business. Sensational reports were pouring in about draft resistance, uprisings of Southern sympathizers, alleged attempts to release Confederate prisoners, smuggling of arms across the Canadian border. He referred to most of these reports with his favorite term—"stuff"—and refused to get excited. A more bothersome problem concerned the guerrilla raids into Indiana of Southern sympathizers who crossed the Ohio River from the Kentucky shore. He discouraged them by sending more troops into the disturbed area.

The "Sons of Liberty," a Copperhead organization, was responsible for much of the draft resistance and was behind many of the half-baked plans for the release of prisoners. These plots were aimed primarily at Camp Johnson on an island off Sandusky, Ohio, and at Camp Douglas in Chicago. In November Hooker was told that General Nathan Bedford Forrest, the famous Confederate cavalry leader, had traveled to Chicago in disguise. With 14,000 draft dodgers he was to seize the rail and telegraph lines, to release the prisoners, arm them and sack the city.[8] This wild story was revived three months later, only now the leader was to be General Simon Bolivar Buckner.[9] Hooker was not impressed. But the President of the Chicago Board of Trade was convinced and as head of the local Committee of Public Safety he urged the General to come and take charge.[10] All that ensued was the arrest of several Sons of Liberty.

Reports came in from the Canadian border that the Suspension Bridge at Niagara was to be blown up;[11] that "Greek fire" was being prepared in Windsor, Ontario, to burn Buffalo, Cleveland and Detroit, and armed efforts were to be made to rob and plunder the lake cities.[12] Hooker remained skeptical but told Governor Brough of Ohio:

". . . if anything of this sort is attempted I intend that somebody shall be hurt before it is over, if I have to go into Canada to do it. If the Canadian authorities allow our enemies to enter the territory to organize for hostile purposes, I shall exercise the same right, and if exception is taken it can be arranged afterward by negotiation."[13]

Hooker traveled throughout his department visiting the large towns, prison camps and hospitals. He was often called on to talk. In October he made a fighting speech before the Chicago Board of Trade:

"I have never failed to attack the conspirators of my country wherever found or with whatever odds. If I cannot fight them South, I'll meet them here. I expect to see the Union restored, and I am ready to take any responsibilities to effect that object. I am in this business earnestly."[14]

Before the lady managers of the Chicago Fair for the Benefit of the of the Sanitary Commission Soldiers' Aid Society, he struck a softer note. "While Europe during the Crimean War produced but one Florence Nightingale, we of the Young Republic have such a goddess enshrined in almost every household."[15]

At Toledo, two days after the presidential election in November, he made an impromptu speech at the Board of Trade in which he termed Lincoln's election the greatest victory of the war.[16]

A misunderstanding arose with Stanton in late November over a rumor that the headquarters of the Northern Department would be moved back to Columbus. Hooker was indignant.

"I can only conclude that I am to be made use of in my official character to subserve some private interests. Some railroad, some proprietor of a public house and other buildings are to be propitiated at the expense of the public good. . . . If I have forfeited it [confidence], as now appears;

I shall make no complaint to the assignment of the command of one who is more fortunate. I have no wish to exercise an office in which I cannot receive the courtesy and consideration which belongs to it."[17]

This was an unnecessary flare-up and, as it was based entirely upon rumor, called for a sharper reply than Hooker got. Stanton denied any change contemplated. "Newspapers are not very good authority for the action of this Department."[18] Hooker was quick to apologize and to explain that he had no intention of resigning.[19]

Besides Cincinnati's central location within the department, there was another reason why he preferred to keep his headquarters there. The General, at the age of fifty, had at last come to the point of paying serious courtship! His lady was Miss Olivia Groesbeck, daughter of John H. Groesbeck and sister of William S. Groesbeck, an Ohio State Senator. The family was a leading one in Cincinnati, both in social position and wealth. The General became a steady caller.

During the winter Hooker corresponded at length with his friends, Senators Wade, Wilson and Chandler. His letters were twofold in purpose.

He protested the advancement of Sherman, Sheridan and Meade to the rank of major general in the regular army. "Would it not be far better to put military commissions in the market and dispose of them at public auction as any other commodity?"[20] His anger was directed primarily at Sherman whom he called "crazy" and who, he said, possessed "no more judgment than a child. . . . a studied effort has been made by Generals Grant and Sherman to keep me in the background . . . it would have given me the greatest satisfaction to have broken my sabre over the head of Sherman."[21]

His other major complaint had to do with the fact that he had not been given opportunity to vindicate his actions as commander of the Army of the Potomac. He believed that Halleck was trying to prevent his appearance before the Congressional Committee on the Conduct of the War and he insisted on being summoned.

"I am, and have been, censured for that which I consider as the most meritorious of my military service. . . . if my services have not been such as to merit reward, they should shield me from punishment. It has been my wish to continue in service until the rebellion is dead and buried but unless I can be protected from indignity, the sooner I quit the better."[22]

The request for a hearing was granted and toward the end of February 1865 he went to Washington. On March fourth he attended Abraham Lincoln's Second Inaugural Ball in the large hall of the Department of the Interior,[23] and one week later he began his testimony. When the Committee's final report appeared in May, he was greatly pleased. One section of Volume I, *Report*, 1865, was devoted to a eulogy of his command of the Army of the Potomac, and sixty-seven pages were filled with his testimony. The Committee concluded that he was blameless for the Chancellorsville disaster. This was the exoneration he had been working for, the past year. Now he was content.

When he returned to Cincinnati he got the news of the fall of Richmond and of Petersburg and was ordered to fire a salute of 100 guns in celebration. On the day Lee surrendered to Grant—April 9, 1865—he wrote his old friend Senator Nesmith, bemoaning his absence from the army at this time.[24] He realized that his contribution to winning the war would be shoved into the background in favor of those who were in at the finish.

Within a week came the sorrowful news of the assassination of Abraham Lincoln. To Hooker this was a personal bereavement. Lincoln had been a stanch friend for the last four years and had supported him in the face of adversity. The President was to be buried in Springfield, Illinois, which was within the Northern Department. Hooker was ordered to meet the funeral party on its entrance into his department, to escort the body to Springfield and to take charge of the funeral cortege there.[25] The body did not reach Springfield until May third. The next morning a procession led by Hooker and a Guard of Honor, composed of high-ranking military officers, escorted the remains to Oak Ridge Cemetery. There the Second Inaugural Address was read and Bishop Simpson delivered an oration; the infantry stood at attention and General Hooker sat stiffly in his saddle as the closing prayer was offered.[26]

At the end of May he traveled east again, this time to receive the sword subscribed to by the citizens of San Francisco two years and a half before. At a gathering of notables in the hall of the Union League Club in New York, Senator Connes of California made the presentation.[27] It was a magnificent dress sword. A piece of native gold quartz and over 400 diamonds had been set amid numerous inscriptions on hilt and shaft. A massive, heavy gold chain reached from figurehead to guard.[28] California had done well by her adopted son. Besides the sword she had voiced her official appreciation in a Senate Concurrent Resolution, adopted by the legislature after his appointment to the command of the Army of the Potomac.[29]

When Hooker returned to headquarters he devoted much of his time to arranging for the discharge of the troops in his department. Only two volunteer regiments and the Veteran Reserve Corps were to be retained.[30] He was made Honorary President of the Sanitary Fair at Chicago and in this capacity presided in the latter part of June at a meeting of 10,000 people who had come to hear and see General Ulysses S. Grant—the man who had won the laurels Fighting Joe expected to be his. This first meeting since Chattanooga days went well. Hooker escorted Grant up to the platform and applauded his few remarks politely.[31]

Now that the war was over the army had to be returned to a peacetime footing. In the reorganization of June 27, 1865, Joseph Hooker was placed in charge of the Department of the East, comprising New England, New York and New Jersey, within the Military Division of the Atlantic which was commanded by General Meade.[32] One of the seven generals assigned to his department was his old friend Daniel Sickles.

He took over his new command on July eighth. His headquarters were in New York City and he stayed at the Astor House. Many New York and New England regiments were passing through the city on their way home and several of those who had been with him in the West stopped to salute their old general. He responded with words of Godspeed and heartfelt appreciation.[33] This reminder that the boys in the ranks had not forgotten him was followed by the official recognition he coveted: in August he was brevetted major general in the regular army—a distinction he had long since earned.

His suit for the hand of Miss Groesbeck had progressed favorably and in late September he returned to Cincinnati for the wedding. They were married at the residence of the bride on October 3, 1865, by the Reverend Dr. Henry Smith, assisted by Hooker's brother-in-law, the Reverend M. L. P. Thompson.[34] The union was not to be blessed with the continued good health of either. First the General was stricken with paralysis and then Mrs. Hooker began to fail. His stroke occurred in New York City in November 1865 at a reception for General Grant. He was carried to his residence in a helpless state and for some time lost the complete use of his right side, leg and arm. He lost weight and only slowly regained partial use of his limbs; he required the constant attention of a valet.[35] He could sign his name only by guiding the pen with both hands.[36]

Nevertheless, he clung to his command and by the summer of 1866 had recovered sufficiently to take a new post. He was transferred to the Department of the Lakes with headquarters in Detroit.[37] In early 1867 he suffered another stroke and had to apply for leave of absence. He left for Europe with his wife, hoping that both might recover there. But Mrs. Hooker did not improve and on July 15, 1868, shortly after their return, she died at the home of the General's sister Mary in Watertown, New York. Three months later he retired from the army.

His last years were spent in comfort. His wife had left considerable property, mostly Cincinnati real estate, and he now enjoyed the earned rest of an old soldier. He was prominent at the many reunions of the Grand Army of the Republic, the Army of the Cumberland, the Third Corps of the Army of the Potomac, etc. At the dedication of Boston's Army and Navy Monument he was escorted by 600 survivors of three regiments from his old brigade.[38]

On these occasions Hooker was no more guarded in his remarks than he had been during the war. He had praise only for Thomas. Sherman, he still insisted, was "crazy." Grant, he said, had "no more moral sense than a dog," and Howard "would command a prayer meeting with a good deal more ability than he would an army."[39]

He was greatly interested in the mass of writing which gushed forth after the war but he thought the aim of most of the writers appeared to be to deceive rather than to enlighten the public mind.[40] He highly approved Van Horne's biography of Thomas but was "revolted" by General Sherman's *Memoirs*: ". . . if I consider it to be my duty to go for him again I will not leave a grease spot of him. His ravings have become intolerable."[41]

Hooker busied himself sorting out his own war papers. He completed his report on the Battle of Antietam but did nothing with the important campaigns on which he had neglected to report. He complied with the Adjutant General's request for many papers in his possession which would be of value to the *Official Records*, lending his copies of many battle reports.[42] He commissioned a well-known artist, James Walker, to do a mammoth painting of the Battle of Lookout Mountain. It was completed and put on exhibition in a New York gallery in the fall of 1874. The painter had been on hand during the battle and knew his subject well but was thought by some to have indulged in undue artistic license. The General was well pleased and valued the painting at $25,000.

He was an inveterate traveler and he wanted once more to see his old haunts around Sonoma, California. In the summer of 1872, crippled though he was, the trip was made—probably by way of the three-year-old Union Pacific-Central Pacific transcontinental railway route. At Vallejo, California, the Society of California Pioneers, the Grand Army of the Republic and the veterans of the Mexican War staged an elaborate reception.[43] From here he went to Sonoma and spent many days looking over his old property. He left for home in time to cast his vote for Horace Greeley against Grant in the presidential election of 1872. As might be expected, he was strong for Greeley and even went so far as to predict a crushing defeat for Grant.[44]

After his wartime tie-up with the radicals, Hooker had reverted to his true political preferment. He early admitted, "I never was anything else than a Democrat."[45] During Reconstruction days he gloated over the slow but steady gains of the Democratic party and when it carried the Congressional elections of 1874 he wrote: "I should regard, were I a Republican, every message coming to the North from South as the tolling of the bell on the relinquishment of power (I hope) for ever."[46] Toward the defeated South he always spoke for peace and reconciliation, setting an example by lavishly entertaining his Southern friends, among whom was the indomitable fighter, General John B. Gordon of Georgia.[47]

After the death of his wife and his retirement from the army the General lived in Watertown, but in November 1874 took up residence in a hotel at Garden City, Long Island. He became extremely fond of this little village and thought that in all the country only Sonoma was a more healthful place to live. But he could not stay in one spot for long. He made many trips to the old battlefields, to his birthplace at Hadley and up to Watertown to visit.

He put on weight in the late 1870's but retained his military bearing. Though his hair grayed, he kept the rosy complexion of his youth to the end.[48]

The summer of 1879 he spent in New Hampshire where he went to enjoy the mountains. He attended a reunion of his old 2nd New Hampshire while there and promised laughingly to do more in the next war than he had done in the last. On his return to Garden City he seemed in the best of spirits and his usual health, but on the last day of October 1879 death came suddenly. His last thoughts were of the war. Ironically, after a lifetime habit of criticizing others, his parting message was one of praise. He had just penned a letter to the Reverend William Earnshaw of Cincinnati about a statue of General George H. Thomas:

"I assure you it is the only equestrian statue in Washington that will be likely to receive the admiration of all who gaze upon it; and in my judgment the representative of the most gifted soldier this country ever produced, and the best man in all respects it has ever been my fortune to know."[49]

Brief services were held in Garden City, and the body was then taken to New York where it lay in state in the City Hall. It was said that the turnout to see Fighting Joe in his casket was surpassed only by the numbers who paid tribute to Abraham Lincoln and Horace Greeley.[50] On the afternoon of November fifth a church ceremony was held and a military procession escorted the body to a special train for Cincinnati. Prominent in the imposing list of pallbearers were Generals Butterfield, Doubleday and Hancock, John Jacob Astor and Charles L. Tiffany. The cortege reached Cincinnati on the night of the sixth and on the next day another church service was held. A procession formed to accompany the remains to Spring Grove Cemetery where his wife was buried. The coffin was borne by a gun carriage followed by a riderless horse and a detail of veterans carrying furled and tattered battle flags bound with crepe. At sundown Fighting Joe was laid to rest.[51]

Joseph Hooker's military ability has been a controversial subject ever since his lapse at Chancellorsville. Most have maintained that he was admirably fitted to head a corps or a division but was not up to the command of an army. The evidence conclusively substantiates his power to lead men into battle and discloses undeniable administrative ability. It is unfortunate that he was to have but one independent command with which to try out his capacity for directing a general movement. He might have had another opportunity had it not been for his greatest fault—his propensity for criticizing superiors. Many have marveled at his vitriolic tongue and wondered why he did not try to bridle it in his own self-interest. The General's only recorded recognition of this failing occurred in a conversation with a Reverend Mr. Twichell of Hartford, Connecticut. After patiently listening to a remonstrance for an "unpleasant and unchristian habit," Fighting Joe replied, "That's right, Chaplain, that's all right . . . but don't you see that what I say about these gentlemen don't hurt them and it does me a heap of good?"[52]

ACKNOWLEDGMENTS, BIBLIOGRAPHY
AND NOTES

# ACKNOWLEDGMENTS

THE author is indebted to many people for material, encouragement and counsel. Mr. Joseph Hooker Wood of Lancaster, California, General Hooker's grand-nephew, was most generous in making available the "Hooker Papers" and other items of interest which proved invaluable. Mrs. George D. Huntington of Grosse Point, Michigan, one of the General's few living relatives, produced a voluminous clipping collection concerning his military career and his death. Dr. Milton H. Shutes of Oakland, California, was of great aid in pointing out newspaper source material concerning the period Hooker spent on the Pacific Coast. Dr. Otto Eisenschiml of Chicago proffered the use of his collection of Hooker letters, and Mr. Lloyd Lewis of Chicago went through his files for useful notes concerning the General. Of especial value were notes forwarded by Mr. T. Harry Williams of Louisiana State University from the Chandler and Stanton Manuscript Collections which have been evacuated from the Library of Congress for the duration of the war. Mr. Robert Bruce of New York gave of his time searching for information relating to the General's last days. Historical societies, particularly those in Oregon, New York and Massachusetts, produced material from their files. The Staff of the Library of Congress gave every aid toward the completion of research. I am indebted to the Meserve Collection for use of the portrait of General Hooker which appears on the jacket.

The Civil War Round Table of Chicago, a group of earnest men devoted to critical study of the personalities and events of the period, provided the encouragement necessary to undertake this book. Among this group, Mr. Ralph Newman of the Abraham Lincoln Bookshop and Mr. Alfred W. Stern were unflagging in their interest. Mr. Stern, as owner of the famous Lincoln-to-Hooker letter, graciously permitted reproduction of the letter in this volume.

Wise counsel was furnished by Mr. Monroe Cockrell of Chicago who devoted innumerable evenings to reading the entire manuscript. His carefully considered suggestions have been incorporated into each chapter. Professor William T. Hutchinson, Chairman of the Department of History at the University of Chicago, who guided the author's formal work in American History, edited in scholarly style those chapters which time permitted him to read.

Without the assistance of Mrs. Frank E. Dunn of Chicago this work could never have been started.

# BIBLIOGRAPHY

## Public Documents

*Official Army Register* for September, 1861. U. S. Adjutant General's Office. Washington: Government Printing Office, 1861.

*Official Army Register* for April, 1863. U. S. Adujtant General's Office. Washington: Government Printing Office, 1863.

U. S. Congress, *Executive Documents*. 2nd Sess., 25th Cong., Vol. IX, Doc. 299; 2nd Sess., 28th Cong., Vol. I, Doc. 2; 1st Sess., 29th Cong., Vol. I, Doc. 2; 2nd Sess., 29th Cong., Vol. I, Doc. 4; 1st Sess., 30th Cong., Vol. III, Doc. 17; 1st Sess., 30th Cong., Vol. II, Doc. 8; 2nd Sess., 30th Cong., Vol. I, Doc. 1.

U. S. Congress, *Senate Documents*. 2nd Sess., 25th Cong., Vol. I, Doc. 1; Vol. VI, Doc. 507; 3rd Sess., 25th Cong., Vol. I, Doc. 1; 2nd Sess., 26th Cong., Vol. I, Doc. 1; Vol. II, Doc. 17; 3rd Sess., 27th Cong., Vol. I, Doc. 1; 1st Sess., 28th Cong., Vol. I, Doc. 1; 1st Sess., 30th Cong., Vol. VIII, Doc. 65; 1st Sess., 30th Cong., Vol. I, Doc. 1; 1st Sess., 30th Cong., Vol. I, Doc. 1; 1st Sess., 31st Cong., Vol. I, Doc. 1; 2nd Sess., 31st Cong., Vol. I.

U. S. Congress, Senate. Joint Committee on the Conduct of the War. *Report*, Pt. I. 37th Cong., 3rd Sess. Washington: Government Printing Office, 1863.

U. S. Congress, Senate. Joint Committee on the Conduct of the War. *Report*, Vol. I. 38th Cong., 2nd Sess. Washington: Government Printing Office, 1865.

U. S. War Department, *Report of a Board of Army Officers upon the Claim of Maj. Gen. William Farrar Smith*. Washington: Government Printing Office, 1901.

U. S. War Department, *The War of the Rebellion—A Compilation of the Official Records of the Union and Confederate Armies*. Washington: Government Printing Office, 1889.

## Books and Articles

Adams, Charles F. *Charles Francis Adams, 1835-1916, an Autobiography*. Boston: Houghton Mifflin Co., 1916.

Allaban, Frank. *John Watts de Peyster*. Vol. II. New York: Frank Allaban Genealogical Co., 1908.

Angle, Paul M. *New Letters and Papers of Lincoln*. Boston: Houghton Mifflin Co., 1930.

*Annual Report of the American Historical Association for the Year 1902*. Vol. II. Washington: Government Printing Office, 1903. Article: "Diary of Salmon P. Chase."

Bache, Richard M. *Life of General George Gordon Meade*. Philadelphia: Henry T. Coates & Co., 1897.

Bacon, Georgeana Woolsey and Howland, Eliza Woolsey. *Letters of a Family during the War for the Union, 1861-1865* (1899). Vol. II.

300

Baker, Lafayette Charles. *History of the United States Secret Service.* Philadelphia: L. C. Baker, 1867.

Bancroft, Frederic (ed.). *Speeches, Correspondence and Political Papers of Carl Schurz.* Vol. I. New York: G. P. Putnam's Sons, 1913.

Bartlett, A. W. *History of the Twelfth Regiment, New Hampshire Volunteers.* Concord: Ira C. Evans, 1897.

Barton, William E. *President Lincoln.* Vol. II. Indianapolis: The Bobbs-Merrill Co., 1933.

Bates, Samuel P. *The Battle of Chancellorsville.* Meadville, Pa.: Edward T. Bates, 1882.

*Battles and Leaders of the Civil War.* 4 vols. New York: The Century Co., 1888.

Bigelow, John, Jr. *The Campaign of Chancellorsville.* New Haven: Yale University Press, 1910.

Blake, Henry N. *Three Years in the Army of the Potomac.* Boston: Lee and Shepard, 1865.

Boutwell, George S. "The Career of Abraham Lincoln," *The Magazine of History with Notes and Queries.* Extra Number, No. 196. Reprint, 1935.

Bradford, Gamaliel. *Union Portraits.* Boston: Houghton Mifflin Co., 1916.

Brooks, Noah. "Glimpses of Lincoln in War Time," *Century Magazine* (November 1894).

———. "Personal Reminiscences of Lincoln," *Scribner's Monthly,* XV (March 1878).

———. *Washington in Lincoln's Time.* New York: The Century Co., 1895.

Brown, Henry Le Fevre. *History of the Third Regiment Excelsior Brigade 72d New York Volunteer Infantry, 1861-1865.* Jamestown, N. Y.: Journal Printing Co., 1902.

Bullard, F. Lauriston. *Famous War Correspondents.* Boston: Little, Brown & Co., 1914.

Burns, James R. *Battle of Williamsburgh with Reminiscences of the Campaign, Vital Experiences, Debates, etc.* New York: James R. Burns, 1865.

Butterfield, Julia A. *A Biographical Memorial of General Daniel Butterfield.* New York: The Grafton Press, 1903.

Caughey, John Watton. *California.* New York: Prentice-Hall, Inc., 1940.

Chamberlain, Joshua L. *Antietam to Appomattox with 118th Penna. Vols., Corn Exchange Regiment.* Philadelphia: J. L. Smith, 1892.

Cox, Jacob D. *Atlanta,* Vol. IX of *Campaigns of the Civil War.* New York: Charles Scribner's Sons, 1882.

———. *Military Reminiscences of the Civil War.* 2 vols. New York: Charles Scribner's Sons, 1900.

———. *The Second Battle of Bull Run as Connected with the Fitz-John Porter Case.* Cincinnati: Peter G. Thomson, 1882.

Crotty, D. G. *Four Years Campaigning in the Army of the Potomac.* Grand Rapids, Mich.: Dygert•Bros. & Co., 1874.

Cudworth, Warren H. *History of the First Regiment Massachusetts Infantry.* Boston: Walker, Fuller & Co., 1866.

Cullum, George W. *Biographical Register of the Officers and Graduates of the United States Military Academy at West Point, New York, from its establishment March 16, 1802, to the Army Reorganization of 1866-1867.* Vol. I, 1802-1840. 3rd ed. New York: D. Van Nostrand, 1868.

Curtis, Newton M. *From Bull Run to Chancellorsville.* New York: G. P. Putnam's Sons, 1906.

Davis, Charles E., Jr. *Three Years in the Army.* Boston: Estes and Lauriat, 1894.

Dawson, George Francis. *Life and Services of Gen. John A. Logan as Soldier and Statesman.* Chicago: Belford, Clarke & Co., 1887.

Dennett, Tyler. *Lincoln and the Civil War in the Diaries and Letters of John Hay.* New York: Dodd, Mead & Co., 1939.

de Peyster, John Watts. *Personal and Military History of Philip Kearny.* New York: Rice and Gage, 1869.

de Trobriand, Regis. *Four Years with the Army of the Potomac.* Boston: Ticknor & Co., 1889.

Detroit *Post and Tribune. Zachariah Chandler, An Outline Sketch of His Life and Public Services.* Detroit: The Post and Tribune Co., 1880.

*The Dictionary of American Biography.* Edited by Dumas Malone. 21 vols. New York: Charles Scribner's Sons, 1936.

Dodge, Theodore A. *The Campaign of Chancellorsville.* Boston: Ticknor & Co., 1881.

Doubleday, Abner. *Chancellorsville and Gettysburg,* Vol. VI, *Campaigns of the Civil War.* New York: Charles Scribner's Sons, 1882.

Eldredge, Zoeth Skinner. *History of California.* Vol. III. New York: The Century History Co.

Emerson, Edward W. *The Life and Letters of Charles Russell Lowell.* Boston: Houghton Mifflin Co., 1907.

Flowers, Frank Abial. *Edwin McMasters Stanton, the Autocrat of Rebellion, Emancipation and Reconstruction.* Akron, Ohio: The Saalfield Publishing Co., 1905.

Ford, Worthington C. (ed.). *A Cycle of Adams Letters.* Vols. I, II. Boston: Houghton Mifflin Co., 1920.

Freeman, Douglas Southall. *Lee's Lieutenants, A Study in Command,* Vol. II, *Cedar Mountain to Chancellorsville.* New York: Charles Scribner's Sons, 1943.
———. *R. E. Lee.* 4 vols. New York: Charles Scribner's Sons, 1935.

Fuess, Claude M. *The Life of Caleb Cushing.* Vol. II. New York: Harcourt, Brace & Co., 1923.

Gibbon, John. *Personal Recollections of the Civil War.* New York: G. P. Putnam's Sons, 1928.

Gilmore, James R. *Personal Recollections of Abraham Lincoln and the Civil War.* Boston: L. C. Page & Co., 1898.

Gordon, John B. *Reminiscences of the Civil War.* New York: Charles Scribner's Sons, 1904.

Gorham, George C. *Life and Public Services of Edwin M. Stanton.* Vol. II. Boston: Houghton Mifflin Co., 1899.

Gorham, John B. *Reminiscences of the Civil War.* New York: Charles Scribner's Sons, 1904.

Goss, Warren Lee. *Recollections of a Private.* New York: Thomas Y. Crowell & Co., 1890.

Gould, Edward K. *Major General Hiram G. Berry.* Rockland, Me.: Press of the Courier Gazette, 1899.

Gragg, Isaac P. *Homes of the Massachusetts Ancestors of Major General Joseph Hooker.* Boston: Wallace Spooner, 1900.

Grant, Ulysses S. *Personal Memoirs of U. S. Grant.* 2 vols. New York: Charles L. Webster & Co., 1885.

Gregg, J. Chandler. *Life in the Army, in the Departments of Virginia, and the Gulf.* Philadelphia: Perkinpine & Higgins, 1866.

Gurowski, Adam. *Diary from November 18, 1862, to October 18, 1863.* Vol. II. New York: Carleton, Publisher, 1864.

Hamlin, Augustus Choate. *The Battle of Chancellorsville, Jackson's Flank Attack.* Bangor, Maine: 1896.

Haupt, Hermann. *Reminiscences of General Hermann Haupt.* New York: John R. Anderson Co., 1901.

Haydon, F. Stansbury. *Aeronautics in the Union and Confederate Armies.* Vol. I. Baltimore: Johns Hopkins Press, 1941.

Haynes, Martin A. *A History of the Second Regiment, New Hampshire Volunteer Infantry, in the War of the Rebellion.* Lakeport, New Hampshire: 1896.

Headley, Joel Tyler. *Grant and Sherman: Their Campaigns and Generals.* New York: E. B. Treat & Co., 1866.

————. *The Life and Travels of General Grant.* Philadelphia: Hubbard Bros., 1879.

Henry, W. S. *Campaign Sketches of the War with Mexico.* New York: Harper & Bros., 1847.

Hinkley, Julian Wisner. *A Narrative of Service with the Third Wisconsin Infantry.* Wisconsin Historical Commission, 1912.

Hittell, Theodore H. *History of California.* Vols. III, IV. San Francisco: N. J. Stone & Co., 1898.

Hotchkiss, Jed, and Allan, William. *The Battlefields of Virginia: Chancellorsville.* New York: D. Van Nostrand, 1867.

Howard, Oliver O. *Autobiography of Oliver Otis Howard.* Vol. I. New York: The Baker and Taylor Co., 1908.

————. "Grant at Chattanooga," *Personal Recollections of the War of the Rebellion.* New York: N. Y. Commandery of the Loyal Legion of the U. S., 1891.

Howe, M. A. De Wolfe (ed.). *Home Letters of General Sherman.* New York: Charles Scribner's Sons, 1909.

Hurtubis, Francis, Jr. (ed.). *The Equestrian Statue of Major General Joseph Hooker.* Boston: Wright and Potter Printing Co., 1903.

Hutchinson, Gustavus B. *A Narrative of the Formation and Services of the Eleventh Massachusetts Volunteers.* Boston: Alfred Mudge & Sons, 1893.

*Indiana at Antietam.* Report of the Indiana Antietam Monument Commission. Indianapolis: 1911.

Jenney, William Le Barron. "With Sherman and Grant from Memphis to Chattanooga. A Reminiscence," *Military Essays and Recollections, Military Order of the Loyal Legion of the United States, Illinois Commandery.* Vol. IV. Chicago: Cozzens & Beaton Co., 1907.

Johnston, Joseph E. *Narrative of Military Operations Directed, During the Late War Between the States.* New York: D. Appleton & Co., 1874.

Johnston, R. M. *Bull Run, Its Strategy and Tactics.* Boston: Houghton Mifflin Co., 1913.

Judd, Sylvester. *History of Hadley.* Springfield, Mass.: H. R. Huntington & Co., 1905.

Kearny, Thomas. *General Philip Kearny, Battle Soldier of Five Wars.* New York: G. P. Putnam's Sons, 1937.

Kelley, William D. *Lincoln and Stanton.* New York: G. P. Putnam's Sons, 1885.

Knowland, Joseph R. *California, A Landmark History.* Oakland: Tribune Press, 1941.

Lee, Robert E. *Recollections and Letters of General Robert E. Lee.* Garden City, New York: Garden City Publishing Co., 1924.

Letterman, Jonathan. *Medical Recollections of the Army of the Potomac.* New York: D. Appleton & Co., 1866.

Livermore, Thomas L. *Days and Events, 1860-1866.* Boston: Houghton Mifflin Co., 1920.

Long, A. L. *Memoirs of Robert E. Lee.* Richmond, Va.: B. F. Johnson and Co., 1886.

Marks, James J. *The Peninsula Campaign in Virginia.* Philadelphia: J. B. Lippincott & Co., 1864.

McClellan, George B. *McClellan's Own Story.* New York: Charles L. Webster & Co., 1887.

McClellan, H. B. *The Life and Campaigns of Major General J. E. B. Stuart.* Boston: Houghton Mifflin Co., 1886.

McClure, Alexander K. *Recollections of Half a Century.* Salem, Mass.: The Salem Press Co., 1902.

Meade, George G., Jr. *The Life and Letters of George Gordon Meade.* 2 vols. New York: Charles Scribner's Sons, 1913.

*Military Historical Society of Massachusetts, Papers of.* Vols. III, XIII. Boston: Military Historical Society of Massachusetts, 1913.

Mills, William Howard. "From Burnside to Hooker," *Magazine of American History with Notes and Queries,* XV (January-June, 1886).

————. "Army of the Potomac under Hooker," *Magazine of American History with Notes and Queries.* XV (January-June 1886).

Moore, Frank. *Anecdotes, Poetry and Incidents of the War: North and South 1860-1865.* New York: 1866.

————. *The Rebellion Record.* Vol. VI. New York: D. Van Nostrand, 1871.

Moore-Wilson, Minnie. *The Seminoles of Florida.* New York: Moffat, Yard and Co., 1916.

Neville, Amelia Ransome. *The Fantastic City, Memoirs of the Social and Romantic Life of Old San Francisco.* Boston: Houghton Mifflin Co., 1932.

Nicolay, John G., and Hay, John. *Abraham Lincoln, A History.* Vol. VII. New York: The Century Co., 1890.

———— (ed.). *Complete Works of Abraham Lincoln.* Vols. VI, VIII, IX. New York: The Tandy-Thomas Co., 1905.

Osborn, Hartwell. "Eleventh Corps in East Tennessee," *Military Essays and Recollections.* Vol. IV. Chicago: Cozzens & Beaton Co., 1907.

————. *Trials and Triumphs.* Chicago: A. C. McClurg & Co., 1904.

Parker, David B. *A Chautauqua Boy in '61 and Afterward.* Edited by Torrance Parker. Boston: Small, Maynard & Co., 1912.

Pearson, Henry Greenleaf. *James W. Wadsworth of Geneseo.* London: John Murray, 1913.

Pierce, Edward L. *Memoirs and Letters of Charles Sumner.* Vol. IV. 1860-1874. Boston: Roberts Brothers, 1894.

Pierson, William W., Jr. "The Committee on the Conduct of the War," *The American Historical Review.* XXIII (April 1918).

Poore, Ben Perley. *Perley's Reminiscences of Sixty Years in the National Metropolis.* Vol. II. Philadelphia: Hubbard Bros., 1886.

Randall, James G. "The Newspaper During the Civil War," *American Historical Review.* Vol. 23. January 1918.

Raymond, Henry W. "Extracts from the Journal of Henry J. Raymond," *Scribner's Monthly.* XIX (January 1880).

"The Record of Major General Joseph Hooker" as furnished by the War Department, appearing in Daniel Butterfield, *Address on General Hooker and His Command at Lookout Mountain and Chattanooga.* New York: Exchange Printing Co., 1896.

Rodenbaugh, Theo F. *From Everglade to Cañon with the Second Dragoons.* New York: D. Van Nostrand, 1875.

Rogers, Horatio. "Personal Experiences of the Chancellorsville Campaign," *Personal Narratives of Events in the War of the Rebellion.* Providence, R. I.: N. Bangs Williams Co., 1880.

Rusling, James F. *Men and Things I Saw in Civil War Days.* New York: Eaton and Mains, 1899.

Schell, Mary L. *The Love Life of Brig. Gen. Henry M. Naglee.* (No publisher) 1867.

Schofield, John M. *Forty-Six Years in the Army.* New York: The Century Co., 1897.

Schuckers, J. W. *The Life and Public Service of Salmon Portland Chase.* New York: D. Appleton and Co., 1874.

Schurz, Carl. *The Reminiscences of Carl Schurz.* Vol. II. New York: The McClure Co., 1907.

Seward, Frederick W. *Seward at Washington as Senator and Secretary of State.* Vol. III, 1861-1872. New York: Derby and Miller, 1891.

Shanks, William F. G. *Personal Recollections of Distinguished Generals.* New York: Harper & Brothers, 1866.

Sherman, William T. *Personal Memoirs of General W. T. Sherman.* 2 vols., 3rd ed. New York: Charles L. Webster Co., 1890.

Shutes, Milton H. "Fighting Joe Hooker," *California Historical Society Quarterly* (December 1937).

Sickles, Daniel Edgar. *Address delivered in Boston before the Hooker Association of Massachusetts.* Norwood, Mass.: Norwood Press, 1910.

Slocum, Charles E. *The Life and Services of Major General Henry Warner Slocum.* Toledo, Ohio: The Slocum Publishing Co., 1913.

Smith, James E. *A Famous Battery and its Campaigns, 1861-64.* Washington: W. H. Lowdermilk & Co., 1892.

Smith, Justin H. *The War with Mexico.* 2 vols. New York: The Macmillan Co., 1919.

Smith, William F. "An Historical Sketch of the Military Operations Around Chattanooga, Tennessee, September 22 to November 27, 1863," *Papers of the Military Historical Society of Massachusetts.* Vol. VIII.

*Society of the Army of the Cumberland, 12th Reunion, Sept. 1880.* Cincinnati: Robert Clark & Co., 1881.

*A Statement of the Case of Brigadier General Joseph W. Revere.* New York: C. A. Alvord, 1863.

Stevens, Hazard. *The Life of Isaac Ingalls Stevens.* 2 vols. Boston: Houghton Mifflin Co., 1901.

Stine, J. H. *History of the Army of the Potomac.* Philadelphia: J. B. Rodgers Co., 1892.

Stone, Henry. "The Atlanta Campaign," in *Papers of the Military Historical Society of Massachusetts.* Vol. VIII. Boston: The Military Historical Society of Massachusetts, 1910.

Swinton, William. *Campaigns of the Army of the Potomac.* New York: Charles Scribner's Sons, 1882.

Taylor, Benjamin F. *Mission Ridge and Lookout Mountain with Pictures of Life in Camp and Field.* New York: D. Appleton & Co., 1872.

Taylor, Emerson Gifford. *Gouverneur Kemble Warren, the Life and Letters of an American Soldier, 1830-1882.* Boston: Houghton Mifflin Co., 1932.

Teillard, Dorothy Lamon. *Recollections of Abraham Lincoln, 1847-1865, by Ward Hill Lamon.* Washington: Dorothy Lamon Teillard, 1911.

Thayer, George A. "A Railroad Feat of War," *Sketches of War History, 1861-1865.* Ed. by W. H. Chamberlin. Vol. IV. Cincinnati: The Robert Clarke Co., 1896.

Thayer, William Roscoe. "Lincoln and Some Union Generals from the Unpublished Diaries of John Hay," *Harper's Monthly Magazine,* CXXX (December 1914).

Tremain, Henry E. *Two Days of War.* New York: Bonnell, Silver and Bowers, 1905.

Underwood, Adam B. *The Three Years Service of the 3rd Massachusetts Infantry Regiment, 1862-1865.* Boston: A. Williams & Co., 1881.

Villard, Henry. *Memoirs of Henry Villard, Journalist and Financier, 1835-1900.* 2 vols. Boston: Houghton Mifflin Co., 1904.

Walker, Francis A. *History of the Second Corps in the Army of the Potomac.* New York: Charles Scribner's Sons, 1886.

Weld, Stephen M. *War Diary and Letters of Stephen Minot Weld.* Cambridge: The Riverside Press, 1912.

Welles, Gideon. *Diary of Gideon Welles.* Vol. I, 1861-March 30, 1864. Boston: Houghton Mifflin Co., 1911.

Williams, George H. "Political History of Oregon from 1853 to 1865," *The Quarterly of the Oregon Historical Society.* II. March-December 1901.

Williams, T. Harry. *Lincoln and the Radicals.* Madison: University of Wisconsin Press, 1941.

Young, Jesse Bowman. *What a Boy Saw in the Army.* New York: Hunt & Eaton, 1894.

Young, John Russell. *Around the World with General Grant.* Vol. II. New York: The American News Co., 1879.

### NEWSPAPERS

*Alta California.*
Boston *Daily Evening Transcript.*
Boston *Herald.*
Cincinnati *Daily Commercial.*
*The Confederate Veteran* (Nashville).
Grants Pass, Oregon, *Courier.*
*Hampshire Gazette.*
*Harpers Weekly.*
New York *Daily Tribune.*
New York *Herald.*
New York *Times.*
*Oregon Statesman.*
Philadelphia *Inquirer.*
Sacramento *Union.*
San Francisco *Chronicle.*
San Francisco *Evening Bulletin.*
San Francisco *Examiner.*
*Spirit of the Times.*
Springfield, Massachusetts, *Republican.*
*U. S. Army and Navy Journal.*
Washington *Daily Morning Chronicle.*
Washington *National Intelligencer.*
Watertown, N. Y., *Daily Times.*

### MANUSCRIPTS AND COLLECTIONS

Chandler Manuscripts in the Library of Congress.
Hooker Letters in the New York Historical Society.
Hooker Papers in the possession of Joseph Hooker Wood of Lancaster, California.
Huntington Collection.
Letter in the possession of Samuel L. Abbott, 135 King Street, San Francisco, California.
Letters in the possession of Dr. Otto Eisenschiml of Chicago, Illinois.
Nesmith Papers in the Oregon Historical Society.
Notes in the possession of Dr. George Hope Ryder of New York, N. Y.
Papers in the Massachusetts Historical Society.

# NOTES

## CHAPTER I

[1] Isaac P. Gragg, *Homes of the Massachusetts Ancestors of Major General Joseph Hooker* (Boston: Wallace Spooner, 1900), pp. 5-18.

[2] The affairs of the Hooker family in Hadley during Joseph's youth can be found in an article by Dr. Franklin Bonney, the local historian, in the Springfield [Mass.] *Republican* of May 8, 1895; also in two clippings (undated) from the Springfield [Mass.] *Republican* and the *Hampshire Gazette* in the Huntington Collection.

[3] Sylvester Judd, *History of Hadley* (Springfield, Mass.: H. R. Huntington & Co., 1905), p. 459.

[4] Springfield [Mass.] *Republican*, May 8, 1895.

[5] Eulogy of Hooker by Rev. Warren Cudworth, unidentified clipping among the Hooker Papers.

[6] Gragg, pp. 10-11, 14-16.

[7] Clipping (undated) from the *Hampshire Gazette* in the Huntington Collection.

[8] Springfield [Mass.] *Republican*, May 8, 1895.

[9] U. S. Congress, *Senate Documents*, 2nd Sess., 25th Cong., Vol. I, Doc. 1, pp. 409, 418.

[10] Gragg, p. 19.

[11] Eulogy by Cudworth, in the Hooker Papers.

[12] Springfield [Mass.] *Republican*, May 8, 1895.

[13] William F. G. Shanks, *Personal Recollections of Distinguished Generals.* (New York: Harper & Bros., 1866), p. 166.

[14] U. S. Congress, *S. Doc.*, 2nd Sess., 25th Cong., Vol. I, Doc. 1, p. 406.

[15] George W. Cullum, *Biographical Register of the Officers and Graduates of the U. S. Military Academy*, Vol. I, 1802-1840, 3rd ed. (New York: D. Van Nostrand, 1868), pp. 518-547.

[16] U. S. Congress, *S. Doc.*, 2nd Sess., 25th Cong., Vol. I, Doc. 1, p. 415.

[17] Minnie Moore-Wilson, *The Seminoles of Florida* (New York: Moffat, Yard and Co., 1916), pp. 15-20.

[18] U. S. Congress, *Executive Documents*, 2nd Sess., 25th Cong., Vol. IX, Doc. 299, pp. 4, 5.

[19] U. S. Congress, *S. Doc.*, 2nd Sess., 25th Cong., Vol. I, Doc. 1, pp. 226-227.

[20] It is said that Hooker was wounded in the arm, but verification is lacking. Boston *Herald*, March 19, 1896, address by Mr. Evans of Cambridge given in the State House.

[21] U. S. Congress, *S. Doc.*, 2nd Sess., 25th Cong., Vol. VI, Doc. 507, pp. 6, 10, 11.

[22] *Ibid.*, 3rd Sess., 25th Cong., Vol. I, Doc. 1, pp. 115-117; *Ibid.*, 2nd Sess., 26th Cong., Vol. II, Doc. 17, p. 54.

[23] *Ibid.*, 3rd Sess., 25th Cong., Vol. I, Doc. 1, pp. 117-119, 128.

[24] *Ibid.*, 2nd Sess., 26th Cong., Vol. I, Doc. 1, pp. 42-44.

[25] *Ibid.*, 3rd Sess., 27th Cong., Vol. I, Doc. 1, p. 210; *Ibid.*, 1st Sess., 28th Cong., Vol. I, Doc. 1, p. 67b; *Ibid., Ex. Doc.*, 2nd Sess., 28th Cong., Vol. I, Doc. 2, p. 132d.

[26] "Old Army Reminiscences," a manuscript written by Captain Richard Livingston Ogden in the possession of his grandson, Samuel L. Abbott of 135 King St., San Francisco, Cal.

[27] Hazard Stevens, *The Life of Isaac Ingalls Stevens* (Boston: Houghton Mifflin Co., 1901), II, 62.

[28] Springfield [Mass.] *Republican*, May 8, 1895.

[29] U. S. Congress, *Ex. Doc.*, 1st Sess., 29th Cong., Vol. I, Doc. 2, p. 220d.

[30] "The Record of Major General Joseph Hooker" as furnished by the War Department, appearing in Daniel Butterfield, *Address on General Hooker and His Command at Lookout Mountain and Chattanooga* (New York: Exchange Printing Co., 1896), p. 24. (Hereinafter referred to as "Hooker's Record.")

[31] Shanks, pp. 166-167.

[32] Francis Hurtubis, Jr. (ed.), *The Equestrian Statue of Major General Joseph Hooker* (Boston: Wright & Potter Printing Co., 1903), p. 196.

[33] *The Dictionary of American Biography*, Edited by Dumas Malone (New York: Charles Scribner's Sons, 1936), XVII, 331-332; Justin H. Smith, *The War with Mexico* (New York: The Macmillan Co., 1919), I, 337; II, 109.

[34] Smith, I, 481. Hamer had obtained an appointment to the Military Academy for U. S. Grant.

[35] *Ibid.*, p. 254.

[36] U. S. Congress, *Ex. Doc.*, 2nd Sess., 29th Cong., Vol. I, Doc. 4, p. 89.

[37] *Ibid.*, 1st Sess., 30th Cong., Vol. III, Doc. 17, p. 11.

[38] W. S. Henry, *Campaign Sketches of the War with Mexico* (New York: Harper & Bros., 1847), p. 252.

[39] *Dictionary of American Biography*, III, 371.

[40] Smith, II, 78.

[41] U. S. Congress, *Ex. Doc.*, 1st Sess., 30th Cong., Vol. II, Doc. 8, Appendix, pp. 18-20.

[42] Cullum, pp. 536-537.

[43] Smith, II, 71, 77-78.

[44] *Ibid.*, I, p. 367.

[45] *Dictionary of American Biography*, XIV, 603-604.

[46] Shanks, p. 167.

[47] Watertown [N. Y.] *Daily Times*, Nov. 1, 1879.

[48] Springfield [Mass.] *Republican*, May 8, 1895.

[49] Hooker's testimony in U. S. Congress, *S. Doc.*, 1st Sess., 30th Cong., Vol. VIII, Doc. 65, p. 162.

[50] *Ibid.*, p. 297.

[51] *Ibid.*, pp. 71, 140, 154, 155, 163.

[52] *Ibid.*, pp. 165-168.

[53] Smith, II, 109.

[54] U. S. Congress, *S. Doc.*, 1st Sess., 30th Cong., Vol. I, Doc. 1, p. 338.

[55] Shanks, p. 187.

[56] U. S. Congress, *S. Doc.*, 1st Sess., 30th Cong., Vol. VIII, Doc. 65, p. 169.

[57] Polk was eager to negotiate a peace before Scott won too much glory.

[58] U. S. Congress, *S. Doc.*, 1st Sess., 30th Cong., Vol. VIII, Doc. 65, p. 168.

[59] *Ibid.*, p. 169.

[60] Smith, II, 151-153.

[61] U. S. Congress, *S. Doc.*, 1st Sess., 30th Cong., Vol. VIII, Doc. 65, p. 169.

[62] Smith, II, 161-164.

[63] U. S. Congress, *S. Doc.*, 1st Sess., 30th Cong., Vol. I, Doc. 1, p. 380.

[64] *Ibid.*, p. 407.

[65] Shanks, p. 191.

[66] *Ibid.*, pp. 167-168, 188.

[67] See Constitution of the Aztec Club in the Hooker Papers.

[68] *Dictionary of American Biography*, IV, 623-630; Claude M. Fuess, *The Life of Caleb Cushing* (New York: Harcourt, Brace & Co., 1923), II, 60, 61, 75.

[69] U. S. Congress, *S. Doc.*, 1st Sess., 30th Cong., Vol. VIII, Doc. 65, for the full account of the court's proceedings.

[70] Springfield [Mass.] *Republican,* May 8, 1895.

[71] Shanks, p. 188.

[72] U. S. Congress, *Ex. Doc.*, 2nd Sess., 30th Cong., Vol. I, Doc. 1, pp. 179-184d.

## Chapter II

[1] Milton H. Shutes, "Fighting Joe Hooker," *California Historical Society Quarterly,* December 1937, pp. 304-305.

[2] *Alta California,* June 29, 1862.

[3] Zoeth Skinner Eldredge, *History of California* (New York: The Century History Co.), III, 210.

[4] Shutes, p. 318.

[5] William T. Sherman, *Personal Memoirs of General W. T. Sherman* (New York: Charles L. Webster Co., 1890), I, 101.

[6] Joseph R. Knowland, *California, A Landmark History* (Oakland: Tribune Press, 1941), pp. 162-167.

[7] U. S. Congress, *S. Doc.*, 1st Sess., 31st Cong., Vol. I, Doc. 1, pp. 182-188.

[8] Sherman, p. 105.

[9] U. S. Congress, *S. Doc.*, 2nd Sess., 31st Cong., Vol. I, Pt. II, pp. 75-77.

[10] Theodore H. Hittell, *History of California* (San Francisco: N. J. Stone & Co., 1898), III, 897.

[11] Sherman, pp. 95-106.

[12] Knowland, pp. 162-167.

[13] Gamaliel Bradford, *Union Portraits* (Boston: Houghton Mifflin Co., 1916), p. 41.

[14] Shanks, p. 169.

[15] San Francisco *Examiner,* June 24, 1921.

[16] Unidentified newspaper clipping in the Hooker Papers.

[17] Unidentified newspaper clipping in the Hooker Papers. Shutes, p. 306.

[18] San Francisco *Examiner*, June 24, 1921.

[19] Unidentified newspaper clipping in Hooker Papers.

[20] *Ibid.*

[21] San Francisco *Examiner*, June 24, 1921.

[22] *Ibid.*

[23] *Ibid.*

[24] Shutes, p. 306.

[25] San Francisco *Examiner*, June 24, 1921.

[26] Shanks, p. 169.

[27] Shutes, p. 306.

[28] Bradford, p. 42.

[29] Sherman, II, 117. Letter of Sept. 16, 1864.

[30] Shutes, p. 306.

[31] Amelia Ransome Neville, *The Fantastic City, Memoirs of the Social and Romantic Life of Old San Francisco* (Boston: Houghton Mifflin Co., 1932), pp. 116-117.

[32] John Watton Caughey, *California* (New York: Prentice-Hall Inc., 1940), pp. 334-336.

[33] *Oregon Statesman*, Oct. 12, 1858.

[34] Clipping from Grants Pass *Courier* (date unidentified) in possession of R. B. Carter of Carlton, Oregon.

[35] *Oregon Statesman*, Oct. 12, 1858.

[36] San Francisco *Bulletin*, Nov. 1, 1879.

[37] *Oregon Statesman*, Oct. 11, 1859.

[38] Letter, Hooker to J. W. Nesmith, Dec. 19, 1859, in possession of the Oregon Historical Society.

[39] George H. Williams, "Political History of Oregon from 1853 to 1865," *The Quarterly of the Oregon Historical Society*, Vol. II, Mar.-Dec., 1901, pp. 19-25.

[40] Letter, Hooker to J. W. Nesmith, Dec. 19, 1859, in possession of the Oregon Historical Society.

[41] *Ibid.*

[42] Cudworth Funeral Oration, unidentified clipping in the Hooker Papers.

[43] *Dictionary of American Biography*, I, 517-518.

[44] Letter, Hooker to Nesmith, Jan. 18, 1861, in possession of the Oregon Historical Society.

[45] Caughey, p. 338.

[46] This account of the manner in which Hooker received funds to go to Washington is taken from an unidentified magazine article in the Hooker Papers. Credence is given it in most part as the story has been generally accepted that Hooker received the money from one or more of his "blue chip" tavern friends. It seems unlikely, in view of other evidence, that Hooker took the particular boat to which Chapman referred, or else the article errs in the time of its sailing. Billy was killed a few months later by a drunken jockey.

[47] *Alta California*, May 21, 1861.

[48] *Ibid.*

[49] San Francisco *Evening Bulletin*, May 21, 1861.

CHAPTER III

[1] Letter, Hooker to Nesmith, June 14, 1861, in possession of the Oregon Historical Society.

[2] Letter, Baker to Lincoln, June 16, 1861, in possession of Dr. Otto Eisenschiml of Chicago.

[3] George S. Boutwell, "The Career of Abraham Lincoln," *The Magazine of History with Notes and Queries*, Extra Number, No. 196 (1935), Reprint, p. 10.

[4] *Papers of the Military Historical Society of Massachusetts* (Boston, 1913), XIII, 186.

[5] Letter, Lincoln to Mansfield, June 19, 1861, in the *Complete Works of Abraham Lincoln*, edited by John G. Nicolay and John Hay (New York: The Tandy-Thomas Co., 1905), VI, 293.

[6] Daniel E. Sickles, *Address delivered in Boston before the Hooker Association of Massachusetts* (Norwood, Mass.: Norwood Press, 1910), pp. 2-3.

[7] Unidentified clipping in the Hooker Papers. Repeated in many newspapers and all articles concerning Hooker.

[8] *Alta California,* Feb. 28, 1863.

[9] *Ibid.*

[10] New York *Daily Tribune,* Aug. 1, 1861.

[11] Hooker's Record, p. 11.

[12] *Official Army Register for September, 1861.* U. S. Adjutant General's Office (Washington: Government Printing Office, 1861).

[13] U. S. War Department, *The War of the Rebellion—A Compilation of the Official Records of the Union and Confederate Armies* (Washington: Government Printing Office, 1889), V, 15. (Hereinafter referred to as *O. R.*)

[14] George B. McClellan, *McClellan's Own Story* (New York: Charles L. Webster & Co., 1887), p. 87.

[15] Joseph E. Johnston, *Narrative of Military Operations Directed, During the Late War Between the States* (New York: D. Appleton & Co., 1874), p. 70.

[16] McClellan, p. 76.

[17] *Ibid.*, pp. 79-80.

[18] Warren H. Cudworth, *History of the First Regiment Massachusetts Infantry* (Boston: Walker, Fuller & Co., 1866), p. 66.

[19] R. M. Johnston, *Bull Run, Its Strategy and Tactics* (Boston: Houghton Mifflin Co., 1913), pp. 191, 215, 222, 258. For a more enthusiastic but partisan account of the work of the 11th Massachusetts at Bull Run see Gustavus B. Hutchinson, *A Narrative of the Formation and Services of the Eleventh Massachusetts Volunteers* (Boston: Alfred Mudge & Son, 1893).

[20] Martin A. Haynes, *A History of the Second Regiment, New Hampshire Volunteer Infantry, in the War of the Rebellion* (Lakeport, N. H.: 1896), p. 32.

[21] *Ibid.*, p. 42.

[22] "Stephen Decatur," *The Dictionary of American Biography*, V, 187-189.

[23] Hooker was a great believer in mastery of the bayonet as a builder of morale to imbue the soldier with a feeling of superiority. He admitted, however, that few battles were decided by the use of this weapon. *O. R., V,* 645-646.

[24] Cudworth, pp. 78-79.

[25] *Ibid.*, p. 80.

[26] Hooker's Record, p. 12.

[27] Haynes, p. 43.

[28] Cudworth, p. 85.

[29] *O. R.*, V, 602-606. Another regiment of infantry and a cavalry force were sent at the same time from other brigades to do similar duty.

[30] The Excelsiors had arrived at the capital the end of July and were then located at Camp Caldwell, four miles southeast of the city. Henry Le Fevre Brown, *History of the Third Regiment Excelsior Brigade 72nd New York Volunteer Infantry, 1861-1865* (Jamestown, N. Y.: Journal Printing Co., 1902), p. 9.

[31] *O. R.*, V, 17; McClellan, p. 81.

## Chapter IV

[1] Order, McClellan to Hooker, Oct. 23, 1861, in the Hooker Papers.

[2] McClellan, p. 161.

[3] *Ibid.*, p. 96.

[4] *Ibid.*, p. 77. Opposed were 44,000 Confederates.

[5] U. S. Congress, Senate, Joint Committee on the Conduct of the War, 37th Cong. 3rd Sess. (Washington: Government Printing Office, 1863), Part I, p. 66. (Hereinafter referred to as Jt. Comm. Conduct of the War, *Report*).

[6] William W. Pierson, Jr., "The Committee on the Conduct of the War," *The American Historical Review*, XXIII (April 1918), 559.

[7] Hooker's Record, p. 13.

[8] *O. R.*, V, 376.

[9] *Ibid.*, p. 384.

[10] *Ibid.*, p. 639.

[11] William Swinton, *Campaigns of the Army of the Potomac* (New York: Charles Scribner's Sons, 1882), p. 70.

[12] *O. R.*, V, 633-634.

[13] *Ibid.*, pp. 635-636.

[14] Letter, Sickles to Hooker, Nov. 5, 1861, in the Hooker Papers.

[15] *O. R.*, V, 638.

[16] *Ibid.*, p. 642.

[17] *Ibid.*, pp. 643, 646-647, 650.

[18] *O. R.*, V, 653.

[19] F. Stansbury Haydon, *Aeronautics in the Union and Confederate Armies* (Baltimore: Johns Hopkins Press, 1941), I, 349-356.

[20] Cudworth, p. 112.

[21] *O. R.*, V, 645-646.

[22] *Ibid.*, p. 410.

[23] *Ibid.*, pp. 407-408.

[24] Telegram to Hooker, Nov. 16, 1861, in the Hooker Papers. Graham was returned to duty when he proved that the houses he had burned were being used for military purposes by the Confederates. Jt. Comm. Conduct of the War, *Report* (1863), III, 638.

[25] James F. Rusling, *Men and Things I Saw in Civil War Days* (New York: Eaton and Mains, 1899), pp. 212-216.

[26] *Ibid.*, pp. 52, 207.

[27] Orders in the Hooker Papers.

[28] Cudworth, pp. 102-103.

[29] *Ibid.*

[30] McClellan, p. 147.

[31] *O. R.*, Series 2, Vol. I, p. 703. Hooker released Davis after being assured by him that he really intended to vote against the ordinance of secession if elected.

[32] *Ibid.*, V, 645.

[33] Lafayette Charles Baker, *History of the United States Secret Service* (Philadelphia: L. C. Baker, 1867), p. 118.

[34] Letter, Baker to Hooker, Nov. 25, 1861, in the Hooker Papers.

[35] Hutchinson, p. 27.

[36] Report of the Indiana Antietam Monument Commission, *Indiana at Antietam* (Indianapolis, 1911), pp. 141-143.

[37] This note may be found in the Hooker Papers.

[38] Miscellaneous letters and reports contained in the Hooker Papers.

[39] Haynes, pp. 47-48.

[40] *O. R.*, Series 2, Vol. II, pp. 1027-1030.

[41] *Ibid.*, I, 813-814.

[42] Jt. Comm. Conduct of the War, *Report* (1863), III, 640.

[43] Letter, Hooker to Nesmith, May 4, 1862, in possession of the Oregon Historical Society.

[44] Rusling, pp. 61-62.

[45] In the Hooker Papers there are numerous petitions, duly annotated, on this question.

[46] Letter, A. Porter (Provost Marshal of Washington) to Hooker, Jan. 31, 1862, in the Hooker Papers.

[47] Letter, Major De Venoge to Hooker, Mar. 6, 1862, in the Hooker Papers.

[48] Henry N. Blake, *Three Years in the Army of the Potomac* (Boston: Lee and Shepard, 1865), p. 314.

[49] *Ibid.*, p. 315.

[50] Baker, p. 154.

[51] Court-martial proceedings in the Hooker Papers.

[52] Letter, Sickles to Hooker, Mar. 8, 1862, in the Hooker Papers.

[53] See the Hooker Papers for testimony.

[54] *O. R.*, V, sec. 5, p. 637.

[55] Letter, Hooker to Nesmith, Dec. 26, 1861, in possession of the Oregon Historical Society.

[56] Mary L. Schell, *The Love Life of Brig. Gen. Henry M. Naglee* (1867), p. 135. Letter, Naglee to "My Dear Baby."

[57] Letter, Naglee to Dickinson, Feb. 24, 1862, in the Hooker Papers.

[58] Sickles, p. 2.

[59] Letters in the Hooker Papers.

[60] Letter, Adjutant General L. Thomas to Sickles, Mar. 20, 1862, in the Hooker Papers.

[61] Letter, Sickles to Hooker, April 6, in the Hooker Papers.

[62] *O. R.*, V, 697.

[63] Letter, McClellan to Hooker, Jan. 20, 1861, in the Hooker Papers.

[64] *O. R.*, V, 710.

[65] *Ibid.*, p. 41.

[66] *Ibid.*

[67] *Ibid.*, p. 725.

[68] Haynes, p. 53.

[69] *O. R.*, V, 721.

[70] *Ibid.*, Vol. LI, Part 1, p. 536.

[71] *Ibid.*, p. 543.

[72] *Ibid.*, p. 542.

[73] McClellan, p. 246.

[74] Ben Perley Poore, *Perley's Reminiscences of Sixty Years in the National Metropolis* (Philadelphia: Hubbard Bros., 1886), II, 118.

[75] Invitation in the Hooker Papers. Leading officers of the Army of the Potomac were invited to attend memorial ceremonies in the House of Representatives in honor of George Washington, whom both North and South rightfully claimed as the "Father of their Country."

[76] Haynes, pp. 127-128; Rusling, pp. 223-224. The same afternoon the *Monitor* forced the *Merrimac* to retire to Norfolk, and Manassas was evacuated by the Confederate Army under J. E. Johnston.

[77] *O. R.*, V, 524-525.

[78] Haynes, pp. 130-131.

[79] *O. R.*, V, 526.

[80] Telegram, McClellan to Hooker, Mar. 14, in the Hooker Papers.

[81] *Dictionary of American Biography*, VIII, 505-506.

[82] *O. R.*, V, 18.

[83] Pierson, p. 570.

[84] *O. R.*, V, 756, 761.

[85] *Ibid.*, XI, Part 3, p. 19.

[86] *Ibid.*, p. 16.

[87] *Ibid.*, pp. 19-20.

[88] *Ibid.*, V, 1100.

## CHAPTER V

[1] William D. Kelley, *Lincoln and Stanton* (New York: G. P. Putnam's Sons, 1885), pp. 32, 42, 43. When the vote was announced as eight to four for McClellan's plan, Stanton, in an aside to Lincoln, suggested that the vote was really four to one against, inasmuch as the eight generals on the affirmative were sycophants only faithfully speaking for "Little Mac." Lincoln refused to go along with this sophistry.

[2] Swinton, pp. 99, 100.

[3] Cudworth, p. 137; Haynes, p. 55.

[4] Rusling, p. 238.

[5] Haynes, p. 56.

6 *Ibid.*

7 Letters: Sickles to Hooker, April 5, 1862; Taylor to Hooker, April 7, 1862, in the Hooker Papers.

8 See list of vessels assigned to Hooker's division in the Hooker Papers.

9 Haynes, p. 56.

10 McClellan believed it would be too risky to use any of the divisions already available for such a turning movement. McClellan, p. 287.

11 This was an unfortunate choice, for an aggressive move at this time would probably have saved several weeks' delay and lessened the grumbling on the home front. Hooker was to testify a year later before the Congressional Committee on the Conduct of the War that the line at Yorktown could have been pierced by one corps without any considerable loss. This, however, is what the Committee wanted to hear, and the testimony should be viewed in that light. Jt. Comm. Conduct of the War, *Report* (1863), Part I, pp. 575-576.

12 Cudworth, p. 141.

13 Hooker to McClellan, Williams to Hooker in the Hooker Papers.

14 Haynes, p. 58.

15 *O. R.*, XI, Part III, 124.

16 From an unidentified clipping in the Huntington Collection.

17 Testimony of Colonel Taylor and Lieutenant William H. Lawrence, aide-de-camp to Hooker, April 18, 1862, in the Hooker Papers.

18 Seth Williams to Hooker, April 20, 1862, in the Hooker Papers.

19 Haynes, p. 62. Naglee had continued in his character as a martinet during the first weeks of the siege, reviewing his troops before sunrise each morning to make sure that they were ready. Hooker finally ordered this nonsense discontinued.

20 *Dictionary of American Biography*, VIII, 28.

21 Charges of May 1, 1862, in the Hooker Papers.

22 *O. R.*, XI, Part I, 133.

23 Patterson lived only seven months after joining Hooker, killing himself by the accidental discharge of his own pistol. *Dictionary of American Biography*, XIV, 307.

24 Wainwright to Hooker, April 23, 1862, in the Hooker Papers.

25 *O. R.*, XI, Part I, 382-383.

26 *Ibid.*, Part III, p. 131.

27 James E. Smith, *A Famous Battery and its Campaigns, 1861-64* (Washington: W. H. Lowdermilk & Co., 1892), p. 54.

28 Haynes, p. 63.

29 Letter, Hooker to Nesmith, May 4, 1862, in the possession of the Oregon Historical Society.

30 Haynes, p. 64. The use of subterranean mines was not approved by the Confederate command at this time. General Longstreet, writing to his brigadier in charge of the rear guard, said: "It is the desire of the major-general commanding that you put no shells or torpedoes behind you, as he does not recognize it as a proper or effective method of war." Secretary of War G. W. Randolph backed up Longstreet as follows: "It is not admissable in civilized warfare to take life with

no other object than the destruction of life." "Confederate Use of Subterranean Shells on the Peninsula," *Battles and Leaders of the Civil War* (New York: The Century Co., 1888), II, 201. We have made great strides in our views on civilized warfare in these past eighty years!

[31] Jt. Comm. Conduct of the War, *Report* (1863), Part I, p. 576.

[32] *O. R.*, XI, Part I, 464.

[33] *Ibid.*, p. 465.

[34] *Ibid.*

[35] *Ibid.*

[36] *Ibid.*, pp. 465-466.

[37] *Ibid.*, p. 466.

[38] *Ibid.*

[39] Henry E. Tremain, *Two Days of War* (New York: Bonnell, Silver and Bowers, 1905), pp. 306-309. The new type of guns did not show to advantage during the battle although they were used under Hooker's eyes. The heavy rain and continuous firing combined to make them temporarily useless. One carriage stalled in the mud and was left on the field after the gun was removed. The enemy didn't know what the strange carriage was for and did not bother to take it in. Disfavor of regular artillery officers and ordnance men caused these guns to be shelved for the balance of the war.

[40] *O. R.*, XI, Part I, 467.

[41] Haynes, p. 69.

[42] *O. R.*, XI, Part I, 462-463.

[43] *Ibid.*, p. 473.

[44] *Ibid.*, p. 466.

[45] *Ibid.*, p. 469.

[46] *Ibid.*

[47] James E. Smith, p. 59.

[48] *Ibid.*, p. 60.

[49] *O. R.*, XI, Part I, 467.

[50] In his Official Report, Hooker very generously accepted whatever dishonor, if any, could be attached to the loss of the guns, completely absolving his Chief of Artillery and the men. To attempt to bring them off would have been an unwarranted sacrifice on the part of his infantry command. *O. R.*, XI, Part I, 468.

[51] Hutchinson, p. 32.

[52] Cudworth, p. 168.

[53] Heintzelman had left Sumner's headquarters near the Yorktown Road at 11:00 A.M. but didn't get to Hooker until 1:45 P.M.—a lapse of three hours in the midst of his corps' first battle. A long time to ride a mile and one-half and eat lunch.

[54] *O. R.*, XI, Part I, 473.

[55] John Watts de Peyster, *Personal and Military History of Philip Kearny* (New York: Rice and Gage, 1869), p. 281.

[56] There is much question as to the actual time Kearny's men arrived to save the day. Hooker and his officers claim to have held out unassisted until 4:00-5:00 P.M. Kearney's adherents maintain that his division got into the fight as early as 2:00

P.M. One of Kearny's aides, expressly charged with noting the time they appeared, is authority for 3:00 P.M. De Peyster, p. 282.

[57] Kearny had replaced General Hamilton in charge of the 3rd Division of Heintzelman's Corps on May first.

[58] Jt. Comm. Conduct of the War, *Report* (1863), Part I, p. 577.

[59] *O. R.*, XI, Part I, 463.

[60] Kearny's division had lost 417 in its counterattack. *Ibid.*, p. 450.

[61] *Ibid.*, p. 455.

[62] De Peyster, pp. 283, 286.

[63] *O. R.*, XI, Part I, 468.

[64] *Ibid.*, p. 450.

[65] *Ibid.*, pp. 533-543.

[66] McClellan, p. 330.

[67] Jt. Comm. Conduct of the War, *Report* (1863), Part I, p. 577.

[68] De Peyster, p. 282.

[69] See letter to Stanton of May 11. *O. R.*, XI, Part III, 165.

[70] Rusling, p. 63.

[71] Undated letter, Hooker to Nesmith, in possession of the Oregon Historical Society.

[72] Letter, Hooker to Nesmith, May 13, 1862, in possession of the Oregon Historical Society.

[73] Jt. Comm. Conduct of the War, Report (1863), Part I, p. 577.

[74] Kearny, p. 244.

[75] New York *Herald*, May 9, 1862.

[76] The typesetter account appears in John Bigelow, Jr., *The Campaign of Chancellorsville* (New Haven: Yale University Press, 1910), p. 6. It is taken from a manuscript belonging to Sidney V. Lowell of Brooklyn, N. Y., and is quoted in full: "It was three o'clock in the morning. . . . McClellan had come to grips with the Confederate forces, and was pressing them back upon Richmond. Every two or three hours through the night had come from the Associated Press Reporters' Agency sheets of manifold, that is tissue paper upon which a dozen sheets (by the use of carbon sheets interleaved) could be written at once—one for each newspaper. These sheets told of desperate fighting all along McClellan's line. Among his Corps Commanders was General Hooker, whose command had been perhaps too gravely engaged.

"Just as the forms—indeed the last form, was being locked, that is, the type firmly held together in a great frame that the impression might be taken for printing, came another dispatch from the reporters with the Union army. It was a continuation of the report of the fighting in which General Hooker's Corps had been so gravely involved. At the top was written 'Fighting—Joe Hooker.' I knew that this was so written to indicate that it should be added to what we had had before. The compositor (typesetter) who had set it up had known nothing about the previous matter, however and had set it up as a heading 'Fighting Joe Hooker.'

"I rapidly considered what to do and decided it made a good heading and let it go, realizing that if other proof readers did likewise Hooker would always be 'Fighting Joe.' Some did and some didn't, but enough did to do the business."

Another account of the naming of "Fighting Joe" Hooker appears in *The Confederate Veteran*, XII, 523. It was probably written by S. A. Cunningham, editor of this periodical, and was based on hearsay testimony from General Dabney H. Maury of the Confederacy. This story has it that "Fighting Joe" was tacked onto Hooker at West Point in derision when he received a half-dozen kicks in the pants from Cadet Kirby Smith and failed to retaliate in any manner. The flaws in this account are obvious:

1. Maury, the alleged witness, was a cadet at West Point 1842-1846.

2. Kirby Smith, alleged attacker, was a cadet 1841-1845.

3. Hooker was a cadet 1833-1837 and Adjutant there July 1, 1841, to October 3, 1841.

4. It is very unlikely that a first-year man at West Point would kick the Adjutant in the seat of his pants, and certainly this act of daring could not have been witnessed by a man who was not there.

[77] *Harpers Weekly*, Feb. 7, 1863.

## Chapter VI

[1] Haynes, p. 83.

[2] Cudworth, p. 176.

[3] *Ibid.*, p. 175.

[4] *O. R.*, XI, Part I, 450.

[5] *Battles and Leaders*, II, 200.

[6] Orders, Hooker to Webber and Hooker to Bramhall, May 9, 1862, in the Hooker Papers.

[7] *O. R.*, XI, Part I, 464-469.

[8] *Ibid.*, Part III, 173.

[9] *Ibid.*, p. 166.

[10] McClellan, pp. 345, 346.

[11] Haynes, pp. 85-86.

[12] Order, McClellan to Hooker, May.19, 1862, in the Hooker Papers.

[13] *O. R.*, VI, Part III, 190-191.

[14] *O. R.*, XI, Part I, 818, 835.

[15] General Patterson was too ill to take the responsibility of active command.

[16] *O. R.*, XI, Part I, 835.

[17] Rusling, p. 258.

[18] Hooker had to order one of Kearny's regiments to cease firing as he feared that they were shooting down more of the Jersey Blues than the enemy. *O. R.*, XI, Part III, 860.

[19] *O. R.*, XI, Part I, 819.

[20] *Ibid.*, p. 988.

[21] *Battles and Leaders*, II, 219.

[22] Rusling, p. 27. The other arm had been lost in a cavalry charge at Churubusco.

[23] Jt. Comm. Conduct of the War, *Report* (1863), Part I, 578.

[24] *O. R.*, XI, Part III, 209-210.

[25] Jt. Comm. Conduct of the War, *Report* (1863), Part I, 578. The actual telegram which appears in the Hooker Papers is not worded as severely as the General testified, McClellan merely saying that he could not afford to have Hooker cut off.

[26] Haynes, p. 89.

[27] De Peyster, p. 322; Thomas Kearny, *General Philip Kearny, Battle Soldier of Five Wars* (New York: G. P. Putnam's Sons, 1937), p. 292.

[28] Haynes, p. 91.

[29] Hutchinson, p. 26.

[30] Cudworth, p. 197.

[31] De Peyster, p. 366.

[32] Abstract of Official Returns, June 20th. *O. R.*, XI, Part III, p. 238. Hooker now had 9,342 in his division.

[33] *O. R.*, XI, Part III, 249-251; McClellan, pp. 391-392.

[34] Note, Heintzelman to Hooker, June 24, 1862, in the Hooker Papers.

[35] Brigadier General Patterson was still ill.

[36] Haynes, p. 95.

[37] Telegram, Marcy to Heintzelman, June 25, in the Hooker Papers.

[38] New York *Times,* July 9, 1862.

[39] *O. R.*, XI, Part I, 109.

[40] Rusling, pp. 35-36.

[41] *O. R.*, XI, Part II, 807.

[42] *Ibid.*, pp. 108-110.

[43] *Ibid.*, Part III, 251-252.

[44] *Ibid.*, Part II, 97.

[45] 1,575 at Williamsburg, 153 at Fair Oaks, 313 at Oak Grove, plus an estimated 250 in front-line skirmishing. Kearny had lost about 1,900 men so far. Thus, almost 50 percent of the Federal casualties had occurred in the Third Corps.

## CHAPTER VII

[1] *O. R.*, XI, Part III, 259.

[2] Haynes, p. 103.

[3] *O. R.*, XI, Part III, 265-267.

[4] *Ibid.*

[5] Kearny, p. 294.

[6] Haynes, pp. 103-104.

[7] *O. R.*, XI, Part II, 98.

[8] *Ibid.*, pp. 99, 100, 111, 162, 389, 435.

[9] *Ibid.*, Part II, p. 111.

[10] *Ibid.*

[11] Colonel Wyman of the 16th Massachusetts lost his life in the process.

[12] *O. R.*, XI, Part II, 123.

[13] *Ibid.*, p. 138.

[14] *Ibid.*, p. 22.

[15] *Ibid.*, pp. 51, 101.

[16] *Ibid.*, p. 102.

[17] *Ibid.*, p. 116.

[18] Haynes, pp. 114-115.

[19] *O. R.*, XI, Part II, 116.

[20] Haynes, p. 115.

[21] *O. R.*, XI, Part II, 140-142.

[22] New York *Times*, July 8, 1862.

[23] New York *Weekly Tribune*, July 12, 1862.

[24] James G. Randall, "The Newspaper During the Civil War," *American Historical Review*, Vol. 23, Jan. 1918, p. 307.

[25] Hooker was to testify before the Committee on the Conduct of the War that McClellan could also have gone right into Richmond after Malvern Hill. Jt. Comm. Conduct of the War, *Report* (1863), Part I, p. 579. Kearny went even further, saying in the presence of many officers: "I, Philip Kearny, an old soldier, enter my solemn protest against this order for retreat,—we ought, instead of retreating, to follow up the enemy and take Richmond. And in full view of all the responsibility of such a declaration, I say to you all, such an order can only be prompted by cowardice or treason." James J. Marks, *The Peninsula Campaign in Virginia* (Philadelphia: J. B. Lippincott & Co., 1864).

[26] *O. R.*, Vol. I, Plate XIX.

[27] Cudworth, pp. 241, 242, 247, 248.

[28] *Ibid.*, p. 242.

[29] David B. Parker, *A Chautauqua Boy in '61 and Afterward*, edited by Torrance Parker (Boston: Small, Maynard & Co., 1912), pp. 21, 22. *Spirit of the Times*, July 19, 1862, and subsequent issues during the time McClellan was in the public eye.

[30] Hooker's original report on Glendale dated July 15, 1862, in the Hooker Papers. Only his toned-down second report appears in the *Official Records*.

[31] *O. R.*, XI, Part II, 113-114, 393-398.

[32] Letter, Hooker to Nesmith, July 11, 1862, in possession of the Oregon Historical Society.

[33] Hooker to Heintzelman, July 4, 1862, and Williams to Hooker, July 19, 1862, in the Hooker Papers.

[34] *O. R.*, XI, Part II, 153.

[35] Rusling, in *Men and Things I Saw in Civil War Days*.

[36] Letter, Fitz-John Porter to Hooker, July 12, 1862, in the Hooker Papers.

[37] Kearny, pp. 325-326.

[38] Hooker's Record, pp. 16, 17.

[39] New York *Times*, Aug. 9, 1862.

[40] McClellan, p. 491.

[41] *Ibid.*

[42] New York *Herald*, Aug. 8, 1862.

[43] *O. R.*, XI, Part II, 951-952.

[44] Haynes, p. 119.

[45] *O. R.*, XI, Part II, 952.

[46] Cudworth, p. 236.

[47] Sedgwick's Report in the Hooker Papers.

[48] New York *Herald,* Aug. 8, 1862.

[49] Telegram, Marcy to Hooker, in the Hooker Papers.

[50] This reconnaissance has been unexplainably ignored in most part by the *Official Records.* The facts stated herein are taken almost entirely from the full quota of reports in the Hooker Papers.

[51] Jt. Comm. Conduct of the War, *Report* (1863), Part I, p. 579. He told about the same story to Salmon P. Chase on September 3, 1862. "Diary of Salmon P. Chase," *Annual Report of the American Historical Association for the Year 1902,* Vol. II. (Washington: Government Printing Office, 1903), pp. 90-91. Hereinafter referred to as "Chase's Diary."

[52] *O. R.,* XII, Part II, 453; Cudworth, pp. 257-258; Haynes, pp. 121-122.

[53] New York *Times,* July 9, 1862.

[54] Rusling, p. 53.

[55] New York *Times,* Aug. 13, 1862.

[56] *Alta California,* June 29, 1862.

## Chapter VIII

[1] *O. R.,* XII, Part II, 443.

[2] *Ibid.,* Part III, 648.

[3] *Ibid.,* p. 650.

[4] *Ibid.,* p. 662.

[5] *Ibid.,* Part II, 438; Hermann Haupt, *Reminiscences of General Hermann Haupt* (New York: John R. Anderson Co., 1901), p. 93.

[6] Haynes, pp. 123-124.

[7] *The Dictionary of American Biography,* XV, 76, 77; Gideon Welles, *Diary of Gideon Welles,* Vol. I, 1861-March 30, 1864 (Boston: Houghton Mifflin Co., 1911), p. 221. Hereinafter referred to as Welles, *Diary.*

[8] *O. R.,* XII, Part II, 34-35.

[9] *Ibid.,* pp. 450-451.

[10] *Ibid.,* p. 423.

[11] *Ibid.,* pp. 437-438.

[12] *Ibid.,* pp. 423, 438, 443-444, 453-454, 459.

[13] John Pope, "The Second Battle of Bull Run," *Battles and Leaders,* II, 465.

[14] On the morning of August twenty-seventh a brigade of Franklin's division on the way from Alexandria had stumbled into Jackson's men at Bull Run bridge, but they were slaughtered. It was not a counterblow, merely a mistake. *O. R.,* XII, Part II, 539-543.

[15] Cudworth, pp. 270-271.

[16] *O. R.,* XII, Part II, 435-439.

[17] *Ibid.,* pp. 444-445, 455.

[18] *Ibid.,* p. 439.

[19] Swinton, p. 185.

[20] Blake, in *Three Years in the Army of the Potomac.*

[21] *O. R.,* XII, Part II, 445.

[22] *Ibid.,* p. 416.

[23] The proceedings are covered fully in *O. R.*, XII, Supplement; also see Jacob D. Cox, *The Second Battle of Bull Run as Connected with the Fitz-John Porter Case* (Cincinnati: Peter G. Thomson, 1882).

[24] Pope, *Battles and Leaders*, III, 485.

[25] *O. R.*, XII, Part II, 42.

[26] *Ibid.*, p. 413. The 6th New Jersey became separated and saw a bit of action while supporting a battery on the right. They rejoined their brigade the morning of September first. *Ibid*, pp. 459-460.

[27] *Ibid.*, pp. 370, 379, 469-470.

[28] *Ibid.*, p. 415.

[29] *Ibid.*, pp. 258, 437; Hooker's Record, p. 17.

[30] Hooker's Record, p. 18.

[31] *Ibid.*, p. 18; *O. R.*, XII, Part II, 344.

[32] *O. R.*, XII, Part II, 538.

[33] De Peyster, pp. 450-451.

[34] *Ibid.*, p. 448.

[35] Kearny, p. 362.

[36] *O. R.*, XII, Part II, 278.

[37] *Ibid.*, p. 46.

[38] *Ibid.*, p. 171.

[39] McClellan, p. 536.

[40] Welles, *Diary*, p. 106.

[41] McClellan, p. 545.

[42] Welles, *Diary*, I, p. 113.

[43] *Ibid.*, p. 115.

[44] New York *Times*, Sept. 6, 1862.

[45] Welles, *Diary*, I, 229-230.

[46] Chase's Diary, p. 65.

[47] New York *Tribune*, Sept. 3, 1862.

[48] Welles, *Diary*, I, p. 110.

[49] *O. R.*, XIX, Part II, 169.

[50] *Ibid.*, p. 184.

[51] *Ibid.*, XII, Part II, 17.

[52] *Ibid.*, p. 7.

[53] New York *Tribune*, Sept. 1, 1862; New York *Times*, Sept. 2, 1862.

[54] Blake, p. 136.

## CHAPTER IX

[1] *O. R.*, XIX, Part II, 188.

[2] *Ibid.*, p. 189.

[3] Hooker's Record, p. 18.

[4] "Rufus King," *Dictionary of American Biography*, X, 400.

[5] "James B. Ricketts," *Ibid.*, XV, 587.

[6] "John F. Reynolds," *Ibid.*, XV, 320-321.

[7] *O. R.*, XIX, Part I, 170-172; *Ibid.*, Part II, 196.

[8] "The Opposing Forces at the Second Bull Run," *Battles and Leaders*, II, 497-499.

[9] *O. R.*, XIX, Part I, 170-172.

[10] *Ibid.*, Part II, 202-203; Hooker's Record, p. 17.

[11] *O. R.*, XIX, Part II, 186.

[12] *Ibid.*, p. 257.

[13] *Ibid.*

[14] *Ibid.*, p. 279.

[15] Silas Colgrove, "The Finding of Lee's Lost Order," *Battles and Leaders*, II, 603.

[16] *O. R.*, XIX, Part II, 603-604.

[17] *Ibid.*, p. 269.

[18] *Ibid.*, pp. 273, 274.

[19] George G. Meade, Jr., *The Life and Letters of George Gordon Meade* (New York: Charles Scribner's Sons, 1913), I, 310.

[20] *O. R.*, XIX, I, 221.

[21] *Ibid.*, p. 214.

[22] *Ibid.*

[23] *Ibid.*, p. 459.

[24] *Ibid.*, p. 50.

[25] Ibid., p. 210.

[26] *Ibid.*, p. 267.

[27] *Ibid.*, pp. 267, 271.

[28] *Ibid.*, pp. 214-215, 267.

[29] *Ibid.*, pp. 215, 222, 241.

[30] *Ibid.*, p. 215.

[31] *Ibid.* General Jacob D. Cox of the Ninth Corps looked upon Hooker's report as one of his "characteristic efforts to grasp all the glory of the battle at the expense of truth and of honorable dealing with his commander and his comrades." Jacob Dolson Cox, *Military Reminiscences of the Civil War* (New York: Charles Scribner's Sons, 1900), I, 291.

[32] *O. R.*, XIX, Part I, 839.

[33] *Ibid.*, p. 216.

[34] McClellan, p. 583.

[35] *O. R.*, XIX, Part I, 422.

[36] *Ibid.*, p. 418.

[37] New York *Times*, Sept. 16, 1862.

[38] *Indiana at Antietam*, p. 111.

[39] *O. R.*, XIX, Part I, 184-186.

[40] Jacob Dolson Cox, "Forcing Fox's Gap and Turner's Gap," *Battles and Leaders*, II, 589.

[41] *O. R.*, XIX, Part II, 294.

[42] *Ibid.*, p. 295.

[43] Hooker's Report of July 5, 1877, in the Hooker Papers. The *Official Records* include an unfinished report by Hooker on Antietam under date of November 8, 1862, which differs with Hooker's later report only in a few spots. The *O. R.* Report has Hooker's estimate of the enemy as 30,000.

44 Hooker's Report on Antietam, Hooker Papers.

45 *O. R.*, XIX, Part I, 53-54.

46 *Ibid.*, Part II, 397.

47 Jacob Dolson Cox, "The Battle of Antietam," *Battles and Leaders*, II, 631.

48 *Ibid.*, p. 55.

49 *Ibid.*, p. 217.

50 McClellan, p. 590-591.

51 *O. R.*, XIX, Part I, 55.

52 New York *Tribune*, Sept. 20.

53 F. Lauriston Bullard, *Famous War Correspondents* (Boston: Little, Brown & Co., 1914), pp. 399-400.

54 *O. R.*, XIX, Part I, 268-269.

55 *Battles and Leaders*, II, 635.

56 Hooker's report says it was the barn of Mr. Miller, *O. R.*, XIX, Part I, 218; but General Cox in *Battles and Leaders*, II, 637, says it was in Poffenberger's.

57 *O. R.*, XIX, Part I, 218.

58 New York *Times*, Sept. 20, 1862.

59 *Ibid.*

60 *Battles and Leaders*, II, 637, 638.

61 *O. R.*, XIX, Part I, 218.

62 *Ibid.*

63 Douglas Southall Freeman, *Lee's Lieutenants, A Study in Command*, II, *Cedar Mountain to Chancellorsville* (New York: Charles Scribner's Sons, 1943), p. 207.

64 *O. R.*, XIX, Part I, 224.

65 *Ibid.*, pp. 269-270.

66 *Ibid.*, p. 475.

67 *Ibid.*, pp. 475-476.

68 New York *Times*, Sept. 20, 1862; Washington *National Intelligencer* (Tri-weekly), Sept. 23, 1862.

69 *Battles and Leaders*, II, 643.

70 New York *Herald*, Sept. 19, 1862; New York *Tribune*, Sept. 19, 1862; New York *Times*, Sept. 19, 1862.

71 Jt. Comm. Conduct of the War, *Report* (1863), I, 581.

72 *O. R.*, XIX, Part I, 191.

73 *Ibid.*, pp. 193, 199.

74 *Ibid.*, p. 275.

75 *Ibid.*, p. 219.

76 *Ibid.*, p. 182.

77 New York *Tribune*, Sept. 20, 1862. Hooker was so well pleased with Smalley's story on Antietam that he congratulated the correspondent by letter. See *The Spirit of the Times*, Feb. 7, 1863.

78 New York *Times*, Sept. 19, 1862.

79 New York *Herald*, Jan. 27, 1863.

80 New York *Times*, June 2, 1865.

81 *Alta California*, Jan. 26, 1863.

82 *Ibid.*, Sept. 21, 1862.

CHAPTER X

[1] New York *Herald,* Sept. 23, 1862.

[2] *Ibid.,* Sept. 22, 1862.

[3] Washington *National Intelligencer* (Triweekly), Sept. 23, 1862.

[4] Hooker told a reporter of the New York *Tribune* that he hesitated to accept this commission because he so far had been entirely identified with the volunteers, that he was proud of their magnificent fighting and did not want to seem to desert them. New York *Tribune,* Sept. 24, 1863.

[5] New York *Herald,* Sept. 22, 1862.

[6] New York *Tribune,* Sept. 24, 1862; Chase's *Diary,* pp. 90-97.

[7] "Salmon Portland Chase," *Dictionary of American Biography,* IV, 34.

[8] Chase's Diary, pp. 90-91.

[9] *Ibid.*

[10] Charles F. Benjamin, "Hooker's Appointment and Removal," *Battles and Leaders,* III, 240.

[11] Chase's Diary, p. 94.

[12] *Ibid.,* p. 101.

[13] Rusling, pp. 63-64.

[14] Edward K. Gould, *Major General Hiram G. Berry* (Rockland, Me.: Press of The Courier Gazette, 1899), p. 229.

[15] New York *Tribune,* Sept. 24, 1862.

[16] Sacramento *Union,* Jan. 27, 1862; New York *Herald,* Sept. 23, 1862.

[17] New York *Herald,* Sept. 22, 1862, and October 9 and Oct. 24, 1862. *Spirit of the Times,* Oct. 11, 1862.

[18] *Spirit of the Times,* Dec. 6, 1862.

[19] Meade, I, 318. Letter to his son, Oct. 11, 1862.

[20] *O. R.,* XII, Part III, 818.

[21] Meade, I, 318-319. Letter to his wife, Oct. 12, 1862.

[22] Mark Skinner to Stanton, Oct. 20, 1862, in Williams, p. 271.

[23] New York *Herald,* Oct. 3, 1862.

[24] *Ibid.,* Oct. 28 and Oct. 29, 1862.

[25] *Ibid.,* Oct. 30, 1862.

[26] *Spirit of the Times,* Sept. 27, 1862.

[27] New York *Herald,* Oct. 28, 1862.

[28] *Ibid.,* Nov. 6, 1862.

[29] Meade, I, 326.

[30] *Ibid.,* p. 332.

[31] Welles, *Diary,* I, 127-129.

[32] Rusling, p. 287.

[33] "Ambrose E. Burnside," *Dictionary of American Biography,* III, 309-311.

[34] Darius N. Couch, "Sumner's 'Right Grand Division,'" *Battles and Leaders,* p. 106.

[35] *O. R.,* XIX, Part II, 168, 545, 569.

[36] New York *Herald,* Nov. 11, 1862.

37 *O. R.*, XIX, Part II, 168.
38 The italics are the author's.
39 *O. R.*, XIX, Part II, p. 583. In addition there was to be a reserve force consisting of the Eleventh Corps under General Franz Sigel.
40 *O. R.*, XXI, 761-762.
41 *Ibid.*, pp. 99-101.
42 Jt. Comm. Conduct of the War, *Report* (1863), Part I, pp. 665-666.
43 *O. R.*, XXI, 773.
44 *Ibid.*, p. 355.
45 *Ibid.*, p. 774.
46 *Ibid.*, p. 104.
47 *Ibid.*, p. 786.
48 Hooker to Stanton, Dec. 4, 1862. T. Harry Williams, *Lincoln and the Radicals* (Madison: University of Wisconsin Press, 1941), p. 271.
49 Henry Villard, *Memoirs of Henry Villard, Journalist and Financier, 1835-1900* (Boston: Houghton Mifflin Co., 1904), I, 347-348.
50 "Franklin's 'Left Grand Division,'" by William Farrar Smith, *Battles and Leaders*, III, 129.
51 Jt. Comm. Conduct of the War, *Report* (1863), Part I, 666.
52 *O. R.*, XXI, 87.
53 *Ibid.*, pp. 88-89.
54 Couch, "Sumner's 'Left Grand Division,'" *Battles and Leaders*, III, 107-108.
55 *O. R.*, XXI, 845.
56 *Ibid.*, pp. 842, 845.
57 *Ibid.*, pp. 88-89.
58 *Ibid.*, p. 89.
59 *Ibid.*, p. 355.
60 Testimony of Hooker and Franklin in Jt. Comm. Conduct of the War, *Report* (1863), Part I, pp. 667, 708.
61 *O. R.*, XXI, 90.
62 *Ibid.*, pp. 91, 92.
63 Jt. Comm. Conduct of the War, *Report* (1863), Part I, p. 667.
64 Sumner did not cross the river during the fight. It is said that he had been ordered not to do so by Burnside, who thought him to be rash. *Battles and Leaders*, III, 110.
65 Jt. Comm. Conduct of the War, (1863), Part I, pp. 667-668.
66 *Ibid.*, p. 668.
67 *Battles and Leaders*, III, 81.
68 *O. R.*, XXI, 356.
69 *Ibid.*
70 *Ibid.*, pp. 72, 116.
71 *Ibid.*, p. 116.
72 Jt. Comm. Conduct of the War, *Report* (1863), Part I, p. 668.
73 *O. R.*, XXI, 129-136.
74 Jt. Comm. Conduct of the War, *Report* (1863), Part I, p. 669.
75 *Ibid.*

[76] *O. R.*, XXI, 115.

[77] Couch, "Sumner's 'Right Grand Division,' " *Battles and Leaders*, III, 117.

[78] *O. R.*, XXI, 134.

[79] *Ibid.*, p. 95; *Battles and Leaders*, III, 117.

[80] Jt. Comm. Conduct of the War, *Report* (1863), Part I, p. 669.

[81] *Battles and Leaders*, III, 118.

[82] *O. R.*, XXI, 121.

[83] *Ibid.*, p. 75.

[84] *Ibid.*, p. 76.

[85] *Battles and Leaders*, II, 118; Jt. Comm. Conduct of the War, *Report* (1863), Part I, p. 669.

[86] *O. R.*, XXI, 401.

[87] *Ibid.*, p. 142.

[88] *Ibid.*, pp. 859-860.

[89] Jt. Comm. Conduct of the War, *Report* (1863), Part I, p. 665.

[90] *Ibid.*, p. 660.

[91] *O. R.*, XXI, 1010.

[92] *Ibid.*, pp. 95-96. They were Generals Newton and Cochrane.

[93] *Ibid.*, pp. 895-897, 900-902.

[94] *Ibid.*, p. 879.

[95] *Ibid.*, p. 882.

[96] New York *Times*, Jan. 16, 1863.

[97] *Ibid.*, Jan. 22, 1863. The verdict was, of course, reversed after the war but deprived the Union of a capable general at a time when he was most needed.

[98] *O. R.*, XXI, 941, 944-945. Burnside again tried to resign four days later.

[99] *Ibid.*, pp. 77-79.

[100] Swinton, p. 260.

[101] Henry W. Raymond, "Extracts from the Journal of Henry J. Raymond," *Scribner's Monthly*, Jan., 1880, XIX, 422.

[102] William Howard Mills, "From Burnside to Hooker," *Magazine of American History with Notes and Queries*, XV (Jan.-June, 1886), 51.

CHAPTER XI

[1] Raymond, *Scribner's Monthly*, XIX (1880), 422. Report of a conversation between Hooker and Swinton of the New York *Times*. Also see Alexander K. McClure, *Recollections of Half a Century* (Salem, Mass.: The Salem Press Co., 1902), p. 347.

[2] Meade, I, 346.

[3] Benjamin, *Battles and Leaders*, III, 240; Dorothy Lamon Teillard, *Recollections of Abraham Lincoln, 1847-1865, by Ward Hill Lamon* (Washington: Dorothy Lamon Teillard, 1911), p. 193.

[4] Williams, *Lincoln and the Radicals*, pp. 201-204.

[5] *Spirit of the Times*, Jan. 17, 1863.

[6] *O. R.*, XXI, 998-999.

[7] Mills, *Magazine of American History*, XV (1886), 52.

[8] Raymond, *Scribner's Monthly*, XIX (1880), 704.

[9] Jt. Comm. Conduct of the War, *Report* (1863), Part I, p. 670. This order was suppressed for three months but finally appeared in the newspapers. Hooker wrote a letter of protest to Stanton: "I see that Burnside's stupid Order No. 8 has at last found its way into the newspapers. It causes me no regret, and would no one else if the character of the author was as well understood by them as by myself. His moral degradation is unfathomable. . . . It has, and still grieves me to reflect that my surroundings at this time are such that I cannot call him to account for his atrocities, swallow his words or face the music, before going into another fight. He must swallow his words as soon as I am in a condition to address him, or I will hunt him to the ends of the earth." *O. R.*, XXV, Part II, pp. 855-856.

[10] Raymond, *Scribner's Monthly*, XIX (1880), 704-705.

[11] Benjamin, *Battles and Leaders*, III, 240.

[12] *Ibid.*

[13] Jt. Comm. Conduct of the War, *Report* (1865), I, 111-112.

[14] *Official Army Register* for April 1863. U. S. Adjutant General's Office (Washington: Government Printing Office, 1863). On this Register he is No. 26 but on January 25 at least one other man, Sumner, not listed in April, was ahead of him.

[15] Adam Gurowski, *Diary from Nov. 18, 1862 to Oct. 18, 1863* (New York: Carleton, Publisher, 1864), II, 111.

[16] *O. R.*, XXV, Part II, 3.

[17] Darius N. Couch, "The Chancellorsville Campaign," *Battles and Leaders*, III, 154.

[18] William Howard Mills, "Army of the Potomac under Hooker," *Magazine of American History with Notes and Queries*, XV (Jan.-June, 1886), 197.

[19] Oliver O. Howard, *Autobiography of Oliver Otis Howard* (New York: The Baker and Taylor Co., 1908), I, 347.

[20] Frederic Bancroft (ed.), *Speeches, Correspondence and Political Papers of Carl Schurz* (New York: G. P. Putnam's Sons, 1913), I, 251.

[21] Meade, I, 318. Letter to his son, Oct. 11, 1862.

[22] Edward W. Emerson, *Life and Letters of Charles Russell Lowell* (Boston: Houghton Mifflin Co., 1907), p. 231. Letter to J. M. Forbes, Oct. 30, 1862.

[23] Worthington C. Ford (ed.), *A Cycle of Adams Letters* (Boston: Houghton Mifflin Co., 1920), I, 249-250.

[24] A. L. Long, *Memoirs of Robert E. Lee* (Richmond, Va.: B. F. Johnson and Co., 1886), p. 248.

[25] *O. R.*, LIII, 288.

[26] *Ibid.*, XXVII, Part III, 966.

[27] *Spirit of the Times*, Jan. 31, 1863.

[28] New York *Herald*, Jan. 10, 1863.

[29] *Alta California*, Jan. 27 and Feb. 24, 1863.

[30] Quoted *Ibid.*, Feb. 24, 1863.

[31] *O. R.*, XXV, Part II, 5.

[32] Jt. Comm. Conduct of the War, *Report* (1865), I, 112.

[33] The letter first appeared for public consumption in the Providence *Journal*, May 6, 1879.

[34] Noah Brooks, *Washington in Lincoln's Time* (New York: The Century Co., 1895), pp. 45-56.

[35] Teillard, p. 195.

## Chapter XII

[1] Meade, I, 352.

[2] *O. R.*, XXV, Part II, 15. Abstract of the Army of the Potomac Report for Jan. 31, 1863.

[3] *Ibid.*, p. 602; *Ibid.*, Part I, p. 194.

[4] Jed Hotchkiss and William Allan, *The Battlefields of Virginia: Chancellorsville* (New York: D. Van Nostrand, 1867), p. 7.

[5] *O. R.*, XXV, Part II, 29. Abstract of Defenses of Washington, Jan. 31, 1865.

[6] *Ibid.*, pp. 32-35. This command was called the Middle Department.

[7] *Ibid.*, p. 13.

[8] *Ibid.*, p. 6.

[9] "Daniel Butterfield," *The Dictionary of American Biography,* III, 372-374.

[10] Julia A. Butterfield, *A Biographical Memorial of General Daniel Butterfield* (New York: The Grafton Press, 1903), p. 111.

[11] Warren accepted this position with some reservation for he did not have full confidence in Hooker's ability and character. Emerson Gifford Taylor, *Gouverneur Kemble Warren, the Life and Letters of an American Soldier, 1830-1882* (Boston: Houghton Mifflin Co., 1932), pp. 105-106.

[12] Tremain, p. 319.

[13] Augustus Choate Hamlin, *The Battle of Chancellorsville, Jackson's Flank Attack* (Bangor, Maine: 1896), pp. 33-34.

[14] J. H. Stine, *History of the Army of the Potomac* (Philadelphia: J. B. Rodgers Co., 1892), p. 310.

[15] Letter, Hooker to Sigel, Dec. 7, 1862, in the possession of the New York Historical Society.

[16] *O. R.*, XXV, Part II, 51.

[17] Gould, p. 235.

[18] "Alpheus Starkey Williams," *Dictionary of American Biography,* XX, 247.

[19] Jt. Comm. Conduct of the War, *Report* (1865), I, 93-94.

[20] *O. R.*, XXV, Part II, 71, 72, 79.

[21] Theo F. Rodenbaugh, *From Everglade to Cañon with the Second Dragoons* (New York: D. Van Nostrand, 1875), p. 285.

[22] *O. R.*, XXV, Part II, 53.

[23] *Ibid.*, p. 61.

[24] *Ibid.*, p. 70.

[25] Letter, Hooker to Sigel, Feb. 8, 1863, in the possession of the New York Historical Society.

[26] *Ibid.*, p. 71; Hamlin, p. 24; Gurowski, II, 169.

[27] Howard, I, 537.

[28] Hamlin, pp. 27, 34-35; Howard, *Autobiography,* I, 347-349; Carl Schurz,

*The Reminiscences of Carl Schurz* (New York: The McClure Co., 1907), II, 404-405; Abner Doubleday, *Chancellorsville and Gettysburg*, Vol. VI of *Campaigns of the Civil War* (12 vols.; New York: Charles Scribner's Sons, 1882), p. 3; Hartwell Osborn, *Trials and Triumphs* (Chicago: A. C. McClurg & Co., 1904), p. 61.

29 Mills, *Magazine of American History*, XV (1886), 186.

30 A. W. Bartlett, *History of the Twelfth Regiment, New Hampshire Volunteers* (Concord: Ira C. Evans, 1897), p. 57.

31 Hooker's testimony in Jt. Comm. Conduct of the War, *Report* (1865), I, 112; Mills, *Magazine of American History*, XV (1886), 186.

32 *O. R.*, XXV, Part II, 78.

33 Mills, *Magazine of American History*, XV (1886), 193.

34 Howard, *Autobiography*, I, 347.

35 Mills, *Magazine of American History*, XV (1886), 189-190.

36 Jesse Bowman Young, *What a Boy Saw in the Army* (New York: Hunt and Eaton, 1894), p. 212.

37 Charles E. Davis, Jr., *Three Years in the Army* (Boston: Estes and Lauriat, 1894), p. 195.

38 General Order No. 3, *O. R.*, XXV, Part II, 11.

39 *Ibid.*, p. 120.

40 *Ibid.*, p. 38.

41 *Ibid.*, p. 152.

42 *Ibid.*, p. 89.

43 *Ibid.*, p. 55.

44 Baker, p. 383.

45 Gurowski, *Diary*, II, 199.

46 Charles F. Adams, *Charles Francis Adams, 1835-1916, an Autobiography* (Boston: Houghton Mifflin Co., 1916), p. 161.

47 *O. R.*, XXVII, Part III, 18.

48 *Ibid.*, XXV, Part II, 153-154.

49 Blake, p. 166.

50 *O.R.*, XXV, Part II, 239, for case of the Washington *Morning Chronicle;* pp. 269-270 for cases of the New York *Times* and the Philadelphia *Inquirer.*

51 *Ibid.*, pp. 53, 69, 83, 87, 89, 90; *Ibid.*, Series 2, V, 280.

52 *Ibid.*, XXV, Part II, 57, 119, 123.

53 *Ibid.*, pp. 127, 128, 132, 139-140.

54 *Ibid.*, pp. 93-94.

55 Regis de Trobriand, *Four Years with the Army of the Potomac* (Boston: Ticknor & Co., 1889), pp. 416-421; Cox, *Military Reminiscences of the Civil War*, I, 432-433.

56 Letter, Stanton to Hooker of March 22, 1863, in the possession of Dr. Otto Eisenschiml of Chicago; *Life of David Bell Birney, Major General United States Volunteers* (Philadelphia: King and Baird, 1867), p. 110.

57 Jt. Comm. Conduct of the War, *Report* (1863), Part I, p. 575.

58 Pierson, *The American Historical Review*, XXIII (April, 1918), 573.

59 New York *Tribune*, March 21.

[60] *O. R.*, LI, Part I, 1000.

[61] Parker, p. 77.

[62] Noah Brooks, "Personal Reminiscences of Lincoln," *Scribner's Monthly*, XV (March, 1878), 673.

[63] *Ibid.*, p. 674. The best accounts of this visit can be found in Noah Brooks, *Washington in Lincoln's Time*, pp. 45-56, and in Butterfield, pp. 159-161.

[64] McClure, p. 347.

[65] James R. Gilmore, *Personal Recollections of Abraham Lincoln and the Civil War* (Boston: L. C. Page & Co., 1898), 95-96.

[66] Theodore A. Dodge, *The Campaign of Chancellorsville* (Boston: Ticknor and Co., 1881), p. 24.

[67] *O. R.*, XXV, Part II, 243.

[68] At a recent conference in Washington the question of the exact end of these enlistment periods had been discussed. It was decided to judge them as having started when the soldiers entered the national service rather than the state service. This decision added several weeks to the enlistment period.

[69] This rumor was untrue.

[70] Couch, *Battles and Leaders*, III, 155. This incident possibly took place during Lincoln's earlier visit in April.

[71] Rusling, p. 57; Tremain, p. 318.

[72] Francis A. Walker, *History of the Second Corps in the Army of the Potomac* (New York: Charles Scribner's Sons, 1886), p. 202.

[73] *United States Army and Navy Journal*, Nov. 8, 1879.

## CHAPTER XIII

[1] Hotchkiss and Allan, p. 6.

[2] Robert E. Lee, *Recollections and Letters of General Robert E. Lee* (Garden City, New York: Garden City Publishing Co., 1924), p. 92.

[3] *O. R.*, XXV, Part I, 7-9; *Ibid.*, Part II, pp. 45-50, 54-55.

[4] *Ibid.*, Part I, pp. 21-26; *Ibid*, Part II, pp. 100-108.

[5] *Ibid*, Part II, p 99.

[6] *Ibid.*, p. 642.

[7] Frank Moore, *Anecdotes, Poetry and Incidents of the War: North and South 1860-1865* (New York: 1886), p. 305.

[8] *O. R.*, XXV, Part I, 30.

[9] Mosby, operating primarily in Fauquier County, captured Brigadier General Stoughton in bed at about 3:00 A.M. on March ninth. *Ibid.*, Part II, pp. 43-44.

[10] Averell and Fitzhugh Lee had been friends and classmates at West Point. Averell was eager to get back at Fitzhugh Lee for his recent raid and asked Hooker for permission to do so. Bigelow, p. 73.

[11] *O R.*, XXV, Part I, 47-64.

[12] *Ibid.*, Part II, pp. 147-148.

[13] *Ibid.*, Part I, pp. 1072-1073.

[14] *Ibid.*, Part II, p. 675.

[15] Military career of Joseph Hooker Wood in the Hooker Papers.

[16] *O. R.*, XXV, Part II, 158.

[17] *Ibid.*, p. 199.

[18] Butterfield, pp. 153-158.

[19] Nicolay and Hay, VIII, 243.

[20] The advantages and disadvantages of all crossings of the Rappahannock for 25 miles above and below Fredericksburg, as stated by the most prominent Federal officers, had been published in the reports of the Congressional Committee on the Conduct of the War. The Confederates had taken full advantage of these opinions. Jt. Comm. Conduct of the War, *Report* (1865), I, 115.

[21] *O. R.*, XXV, Part II, 197-198.

[22] *Ibid.*, p. 196.

[23] *Ibid.*, p. 203.

[24] *Ibid.*, p. 204.

[25] *Ibid.*, p. 209.

[26] *Ibid.*

[27] *Ibid.*, p. 212.

[28] *Ibid.*, p. 213.

[29] *Ibid.*, p. 214.

[30] *Ibid.*, p. 220.

[31] The most complete account of the cavalry crossing and its reception is found in H. B. McClellan, *The Life and Campaigns of Major General J. E. B. Stuart* (Boston: Houghton Mifflin Co., 1886), pp. 219-224.

[32] *O. R.*, XXV, Part II, 221.

[33] *Ibid.*, p. 242.

[34] *Ibid.*, p. 228.

[35] *Ibid.*, p. 232.

[36] *Ibid.*, pp. 227, 238. Hooker also stated his fear that the Confederates intended to fall on his base at Aquia if he moved to their left.

[37] *Ibid.*, p. 241.

[38] *Ibid.*, p. 256; Meade, I, 369. General Hermann Haupt, Chief of Railway Transportation, claims that Hooker divulged his plans to him before this date as he was responsible for the service of supply. Haupt, p. 193. General Howard claims that he was confidentially told in advance that his corps would move the morning of the twenty-seventh. It is probable that the plan was gradually revealed verbally to several of the corps commanders. Howard, *Autobiography*, I, 350-351.

[39] *O. R.*, XXV, Part II, 255-256, 262, 264.

[40] *Ibid.*, p. 266.

[41] *Ibid.*, p. 268.

[42] *Ibid.*, pp. 320, 696.

[43] Estimated strength of the Army of Northern Virginia, April 28, 1863, in the Hooker Papers.

[44] *Ibid.*, p. 752.

[45] *Ibid.*, Part I, p. 796.

CHAPTER XIV

[1] *O. R.*, XXV, Part II, 554.

[2] Osborn, p. 62; Adam B. Underwood, *The Three Years Service of the 33rd Massachusetts Infantry Regiment, 1862-1865* (Boston: A. Williams & Co., 1881), p. 21.

[3] Edward L. Pierce, *Memoirs and Letters of Charles Sumner*, Vol. IV, 1860-1874 (Boston: Roberts Brothers, 1894), p. 139.

[4] *United States Army and Navy Journal*, Nov. 8, 1879.

[5] *O. R.*, XXV, Part II, 263.

[6] *Ibid.*

[7] Howard, *Autobiography*, I, 353.

[8] Couch, *Battles and Leaders*, III, 157.

[9] See "Balloon Reports" of Chancellorsville Campaign in the Hooker Papers.

[10] *O. R.*, XXV, Part II, 276-277.

[11] *Ibid.*, Part I, p. 1065. According to Stoneman he did not receive these instructions until 5:45 P.M. This was unreasonably short notice for him to return to his camp, call in his pickets and scouting parties and make last-minute arrangements for an advance, especially considering the dense fog of that evening.

[12] *Ibid.*, Part II, 273-274.

[13] Even though Hooker was not too well pleased with the celerity of this flanking movement, all critics have praised him for it and his success in getting the army across the two rivers without a fight. Most critics have credited him with surprising Lee, yet the Confederate General knew about the Rapidan crossings within four hours. He was surprised only to the extent of thinking that Stoneman's cavalry was headed for the Shenandoah Valley. Hotchkiss and Allan, p. 28; *O. R.*, XXV, Part II, 749-750.

[14] *O. R.*, XXV, Part II, 278.

[15] Paul M. Angle, *New Letters and Papers of Lincoln* (Boston: Houghton Mifflin Co., 1930), p. 323.

[16] *O. R.*, XXV, Part II, 288-289.

[17] *Ibid.*, p. 289.

[18] *Ibid.*, Part I, pp. 505, 669.

[19] *Ibid.*, p. 627. Between the Rappahannock and the Rapidan the Eleventh Corps underwent a bit of shelling but Pleasonton's cavalry was out on their right flank and gave them fair protection. At this time the enemy had approximately 2,700 cavalry in the area but they limited themselves primarily to observation. Hotchkiss and Allan, p. 26.

[20] *O. R.*, XXV, Part II, 291, 293.

[21] *Ibid.*, p. 291.

[22] *Ibid.*, Part I, p. 213.

[23] Stephen M. Weld, *War Diary and Letters of Stephen Minot Weld* (Cambridge: The Riverside Press, 1912), p. 189.

[24] *O. R.*, XXV, Part II, 292.

[25] *Ibid.*, p. 306.

26 *Ibid.*, pp. 304, 307.
27 *Ibid.*, p. 305.
28 *Ibid.*, p. 314.
29 *Ibid.*, p. 305.
30 *Ibid.*, p. 304.
31 *Ibid.*, p. 309.
32 *Ibid.*, Part I, p. 171.
33 Swinton, p. 275.
34 *O. R.*, XXV, Part II, 306-307.
35 *Ibid.*, Part I, p. 198; *Ibid.*, Part II, p. 312.
36 *Ibid.*, Part II, pp. 302, 311.
37 Meade's advanced brigade had gone up the turnpike instead of the Bank's Ford Road.
38 *Ibid.*, Part I, pp. 505-507; Richard M. Bache, *Life of General George Gordon Meade* (Philadelphia: Henry T. Coates & Co., 1897), p. 260.
39 *O. R.*, XXV, Part I, 627-628.
40 Douglas Southall Freeman compares it to the Meuse-Argonne area of the First World War. Douglas Southall Freeman, *R. E. Lee* (New York: Charles Scribner's Sons, 1935), II, 518.
41 The mansion at Chancellorsville was built about 1812 by George Chancellor. Major Sanford Chancellor's widow and family were living there at this time. Bartlett, p. 105.
42 Alfred Pleasonton, *Battles and Leaders*, III, 174. These great finds were never located among the war records. Pleasonton contradicts himself so often in his several accounts of this incident that it is difficult to place much credence in them.
43 *Ibid.* This was sound advice in the light of what happened later, but Pleasonton is an unreliable witness, since he wrote after the errors of the campaign had been revealed. He did not remember his facts well and was too eager to point out his own contribution to the battle.
44 *Ibid.*, pp. 174-176.
45 Walker, p. 218.
46 Couch, *Battles and Leaders*, III, 157.
47 *O. R.*, XXV, Part II, 320.
48 Bigelow, p. 237.
49 *O. R.*, XXV, Part II, 323-324.
50 *Ibid.*, p. 324.
51 *Ibid.*, p. 338.
52 Bigelow, p. 478.
53 *Ibid.*, Part I, pp. 311, 507; Tremain, p. 430.
54 *Ibid.*, pp. 362, 507, 627, 669.
55 Newton M. Curtis, *From Bull Run to Chancellorsville* (New York: G. P. Putnam's Sons, 1906), pp. 236-237.
56 *Ibid.*, pp. 236-237.
57 Walker, p. 222; Couch, *Battles and Leaders*, III, 159.
58 Walker, p. 224.

[59] Couch, *Battles and Leaders*, III, 159.

[60] *Ibid.*, p. 161.

[61] Charles E. Slocum, *The Life and Services of Major General Henry Warner Slocum* (Toledo, Ohio: The Slocum Publishing Co., 1913), p. 77.

[62] Jt. Comm. Conduct of the War, *Report* (1865), 63-66.

[63] Washington *Daily Morning Chronicle*, May 1863.

[64] *O. R.*, XXV, Part II, 326, 328.

[65] *Ibid.*, p. 327.

[66] *Ibid.*, p. 328.

[67] *Ibid.*, p. 199.

[68] *Ibid.*, p. 326.

[69] *Ibid.*, p. 328.

[70] *Ibid.*, Part I, pp. 507, 627; Couch, *Battles and Leaders*, III, 161; Doubleday, p. 17.

[71] *O. R.*, XXV, Part II, 329, 442.

[72] *Ibid.*, p. 331.

[73] *Ibid.*, p. 329.

[74] *Ibid.*, p. 330.

[75] *Ibid.*, Part I, p. 199.

CHAPTER XV

[1] *O. R.*, XXV, Part I, 385, 650.

[2] *Ibid.*, p. 628.

[3] Bates, *Battles and Leaders*, III, 218.

[4] *O. R.*, XXV, Part II, 353, 362.

[5] Couch, *Battles and Leaders*, III, 162; O. R., XXV, Part I, 385-386; *Ibid.*, Part II, 360.

[6] New York *Herald*, May 5, 1863.

[7] Bigelow, p. 276.

[8] *O. R.*, XXV, Part II, 360-361. Howard claimed in later years that the circular addressed to Slocum and Howard never arrived. He said that his division commanders did what the circular called for, anyway. Slocum received his copy but of course did not forward it to Howard, there being no reason why he should do so. There is evidence that General Schurz received Howard's copy and read it to his corps commander. The dispatch was entered in Howard's order-book only after Hooker was relieved from the command. Howard, *Battles and Leaders*, III, 196; Hamlin, *The Battle of Chancellorsville*, p. 21; Schurz, *Reminiscences of Carl Schurz*, II, 417.

[9] *O. R.*, XXV, Part I, 386.

[10] *Ibid.*, p. 628.

[11] Couch, *Battles and Leaders*, III, 163.

[12] *O. R.*, XXV, Part I, 386-387; Doubleday, p. 23.

[13] *Ibid.*, pp. 386-387, 630, 670. Howard went along with Barlow's brigade to see what Sickles was up to. Doubleday, p. 32.

[14] *O. R.*, XXV, Part I, 670.

[15] *Ibid.*, Part II, 354.

[16] *Ibid.*, p. 355.

[17] *Ibid.*, p. 363.

[18] Jt. Comm. Conduct of the War, *Report* (1865), I, 147.

[19] Hamlin, p. 51.

[20] *Ibid.*, p. 52.

[21] New York *Times*, May 5, 1863.

[22] Frank Allaban, *John Watts de Peyster* (New York: Frank Allaban Genealogical Co., 1908), II, 127.

[23] *O. R.*, XXV, Part I, 646, 657.

[24] *Ibid.*, pp. 387, 670; Doubleday, p. 35.

[25] *O. R.*, XXV, Part I, 675. Jackson's men did not come within 700 yards of Berry's line the night of May second except in small parties of skirmishers.

[26] *Ibid.*, pp. 388, 657.

[27] *Ibid.*, p. 364.

[28] *Ibid.*, pp. 630-775.

[29] Pleasonton, "The Successes and Failures of Chancellorsville," *Battles and Leaders*, III, 180.

[30] For an accurate account of these incidents see Hamlin, pp. 90-103.

[31] *O. R.*, XXV, Part II, 359.

[32] *Ibid.*, p. 357.

[33] *Ibid.*, pp. 365-366.

[34] Hamlin, p. 115.

[35] Pleasonton, *Battles and Leaders*, III, 181. It had been Jackson's intention to advance along an undefended road leading behind the Federal army to the Bullock House. Here Jackson's corps would have been in the rear of the whole Chancellorsville position and might have cut Hooker off from United States Ford.

[36] *O. R.*, XXV, Part I, 389-390. This was Sickles' famous "midnight charge"—another fable. D. G. Crotty, Color Sergeant of the Third Michigan of Birney's division, says, "Whoever took part in the fizzle in the woods on the night of the 2nd of May, will remember it as long as they live." D. G. Crotty, *Four Years Campaigning in the Army of the Potomac* (Grand Rapids, Michigan: Dygert Bros. & Co., 1874), p. 84.

[37] Doubleday, p. 43. They had marched thirty miles in twenty-four hours. Davis, p. 204.

[38] Doubleday, p. 44.

[39] *O. R.*, XXV, Part I, 201.

[40] *Ibid.*, Part II, p. 383.

[41] *Ibid.*, p. 385.

[42] *Ibid.*

[43] *Ibid.*, Part I, p. 390.

[44] *Ibid.*, p. 363.

[45] Bates, "Hooker's Comments on Chancellorsville," *Battles and Leaders*, III, 223.

[46] Gould, p. 267.

[47] Swinton, p. 293.

[48] *O. R.*, XXV, Part I, 363.

[49] *Ibid.*, pp. 392, 445-446, 460, 462.

[50] *Ibid.*, p. 371.

[51] *Ibid.*, pp. 392, 671.

[52] *Ibid.*, Part II, p. 386.

[53] *Ibid.*, p. 387.

[54] Hooker's description of the incident is in Samuel P. Bates, "Hooker's Comments on Chancellorsville," *Battles and Leaders*, III, 220-221. Couch's description can be found in: Couch, *Battles and Leaders*, III, 167. Also see accounts in: Tremain, p. 328; Allaban, II, 133.

[55] Doubleday, p. 55.

[56] Couch, *Battles and Leaders*, III, 169.

[57] *Ibid.*, p. 170.

[58] Walker, p. 246.

[59] *O. R.*, XXV, Part I, 508, 512.

[60] *Ibid.*, Part II, pp. 390-391.

[61] *Ibid.*, p. 379.

[62] *Ibid.*, p. 392.

[63] *Ibid.*, pp. 377-378.

[64] *Ibid.*, p. 393.

[65] *Ibid.*, p. 381.

[66] *Ibid.*, p. 397.

[67] *Ibid.*, p. 394.

[68] *Ibid.*, p. 381.

[69] *Ibid.*, Part I, p. 254.

[70] *Ibid.*, p. 393.

[71] *Ibid.*, p. 671; *Ibid.*, Part II, pp. 383-384.

[72] Jt. Comm. Conduct of the War, *Report* (1865), I, 10, 73; Davis, p. 250; Thomas L. Livermore, *Days and Events, 1860-1866* (Boston: Houghton Mifflin Co., 1920), p. 209.

[73] *O. R.*, XXV, Part II, p. 396; *Ibid.*, Part I, p. 203.

[74] Couch, *Battles and Leaders*, III, 155.

[75] *O. R.*, XXV, Part II, 402.

[76] *Ibid.*, pp. 402-403.

[77] *Ibid.*, pp. 401, 403.

[78] *Ibid.*, p. 404.

[79] Couch, *Battles and Leaders*, III, 222.

[80] *O. R.*, XXV, Part II, 403-404.

[81] *Ibid.*, p. 405.

[82] *Ibid.*, p. 406.

[83] *Ibid.*, pp. 407.

[84] *Ibid.*, pp. 407-408.

[85] *Ibid.*

[86] *Ibid.*, p. 406.

[87] *Ibid.*, Part I, pp. 255, 506; *Ibid.*, Part II, 401, 413.

[88] *Ibid.*, Part II, p. 401.

[89] *Ibid.*

[90] *Ibid.*, p. 411.

[91] *Ibid.*, Part I, p. 512; Couch, *Battles and Leaders*, III, 171.

[92] Sickles was more interested in the political aspects of the problem than in the military. He feared that a disaster to the army would cause European governments to recognize the Confederacy.

[93] *O. R.*, XXV, Part I, 510-512; Couch, *Battles and Leaders*, III, 171.

[94] *O. R.*, XXV, Part II, 412. According to an ironical account by the Colonel of the 2nd Rhode Island (with Sedgwick), "the Sixth Corps' prospect of going to Richmond was remarkably good, but not with arms in their hands." Horatio Rogers, "Personal Experiences of the Chancellorsville Campaign," *Personal Narratives of Events in the War of the Rebellion* (Providence, R. I.: N. Bangs Williams Co., 1880), p. 30.

[95] *O. R.*, XXV, Part II, 418.

[96] *Ibid.*

[97] *Ibid.*, pp. 418-419.

[98] *Ibid.*, pp. 402-421.

[99] Jt. Comm. Conduct of the War, *Report* (1865), I, 77.

[100] *O. R.*, XXV, Part II, 422.

[101] Brooks, *Washington in Lincoln's Time*, p. 58.

[102] Gilmore, p. 103.

[103] Couch, *Battles and Leaders*, III, 171; Jt. Comm. Conduct of the War, *Report* (1865), I, 90.

[104] Stine, p. 392.

[105] Georgeana Woolsey Bacon and Eliza Woolsey Howland, *Letters of a Family during the War for the Union 1861-1865* (1899), II, 517.

[106] Jt. Comm. Conduct of the War, *Report* (1865), I, 90-91.

[107] Couch, *Battles and Leaders*, III, 171.

[108] *O. R.*, XXV, Part I, 508.

[109] Schurz, p. 432.

[110] *O. R.*, XXV, Part II, 432.

[111] *Ibid.*, pp. 433-434.

[112] *Ibid.*, p. 435.

[113] *Ibid.*

[114] Dodge, p. 25.

[115] *O. R.*, XXV, Part I, 171.

## CHAPTER XVI

[1] No attempt has been made to give an exhaustive analysis of the changing positions of regiments, batteries, brigades and divisions on both sides in the complicated battle of Chancellorsville. Only that detail available to Hooker during the campaign has been covered, plus what other information seems necessary to give the story clarity. The most exhaustive report on the entire campaign is John Bigelow Jr.'s *The Campaign of Chancellorsville*. Second in value and foremost in

detail on Jackson's attack is Augustus Choate Hamlin's *The Battle of Chancellorsville, Jackson's Flank Attack.*

The *Official Records* are not complete and some writers believe that Hooker may have withheld reports. If so, they are not included in the Hooker Papers. He made no report and he sent communications to Halleck and Stanton on administrative affairs only, as provided by the Regulations of War. Otherwise he dealt directly with Lincoln. His views on the campaign can be ascertained from his war correspondence, his testimony before the Joint Congressional Committee on the Conduct of the War, and his remarks upon visiting the battlefield thirteen years later as recorded in *Battles and Leaders,* III, 215-223.

Sympathetic accounts of Hooker's work may be found in Samuel P. Bates, *The Battle of Chancellorsville* (Meadville, Pa.: Edward T. Bates, 1882); Tremain, *Two Days of War;* Allaban, *John Watts de Peyster,* and Rusling, *Men and Things I Saw in Civil War Days.* Papers by combatants on either side, for or against Hooker, must be considered in light of the fact that they were almost always written long after the action described and subsequent controversies had brought out personal friction, ax-grinding, and alibiing.

[2] *O. R.,* XXV, Part II, 725.

[3] The drawn battle of Antietam, in September 1862, and the Emancipation Proclamation had effectively ended any probability of intervention.

[4] *O. R.,* XXV, Part I, 192.

[5] *O. R.,* XXV, Part I, 252; Jt. Comm. Conduct of the War, *Report* (1865), I, 92-94.

[6] Had Slocum been permitted to advance that afternoon an overwhelming force of Federals would have confronted less than 5,000 Confederates in the vicinity of the ford.

[7] Hooker's explanation was that he intended to fight on the broad, open fields south of Bank's Ford but that his men were strung out along the narrow roads in the forest where he could not maneuver when he was met by Jackson and two-thirds of the Confederate Army. Being rapidly outflanked, he had to turn back.

[8] General Howard gave little attention to his defenses and then went off with one solitary brigade to take part in Sickles' move against Jackson's trains.

[9] This favorable position separated the wings of Lee's army and was a fine vantage point for a determined thrust against the Confederate flanking column.

[10] Jackson's attack had been daring but, despite the skill and spirit of the movement, it should have ended in failure had it been intelligently met. General Harry Heth, one of Lee's favorites, thought Jackson's corps should have been crushed on May third and the war virtually ended. Stine, p. 396.

[11] As a friend of Hooker's expressed it, he did not hold up his end of the log and the whole weight fell on Sedgwick. J. W. de Peyster in Doubleday, p. 53.

[12] Lee had full intention of attacking on May sixth and it seems probable that he would have gained little and his army would have been further crippled.

[13] Butterfield's testimony in Jt. Comm. Conduct of the War, *Report* (1865), I, 76; Doubleday, p. 54; Hamlin, p. 11; Bartlett, p. 109; Tremain, p. 326. Account of Carleton, a reporter for the Boston *Journal,* printed May 7 and reproduced in

Frank Moore, *The Rebellion Record* (New York: D. Van Nostrand, 1871), VI, 593-597.

[14] Bates, *Battles and Leaders*, III, 223.

[15] A supplemental report followed in 1866 in which General Pleasonton added many remarks but little information.

[16] Jt. Comm. Conduct of the War, *Report* (1865), I, xlix.

[17] Doubleday, p. 32; Meade, II, 169.

[18] Howard admits he was convinced Lee was retreating. Howard, I, 369. Sickles refused to believe the first staff officer sent to bring him back to the battlefield. *O. R.*, XXV, I, 387.

[19] Captain Hubert Dilger, one of the best artillerists the Federals had, made a reconnaissance of his own up the turnpike early in the afternoon of May second. He found the Confederate Army advancing, was chased by cavalry and escaped by a circuitous route. In the late afternoon he reported his experience to one he thought was an officer on Hooker's staff and was told to "peddle his yarn" to his own corps commander. At his corps headquarters he received scant attention. Hamlin, pp. 56-57.

[20] New York *Herald*, May 6 and May 7.

[21] *O. R.*, LI, Part I, 1035.

[22] Jt. Comm. Conduct of the War, *Report* (1865), I, 50.

[23] *Ibid.*, pp. 32, 36.

[24] Jonathan Letterman, *Medical Recollections of the Army of the Potomac* (New York: D. Appleton and Co., 1866), p. 137.

[25] Underwood, p. 78.

[26] Bates, *Battles and Leaders*, III, 221.

[27] Jt. Comm. Conduct of the War, *Report* (1865), I, 22-25, 42, 50, 76.

[28] *Ibid.*, pp. 87-89, 96.

[29] Lee counted heavily on Sedgwick's methodical character which he knew well, having commanded him in the old army.

[30] Jt. Comm. Conduct of the War, *Report* (1865), I, 146. Hooker realized Reynolds' capabilities, and called him his best officer. Bates, *Battles and Leaders*, III, 222.

[31] Bigelow, p. 254.

[32] Jt. Comm. Conduct of the War, *Report* (1865), I, 140.

[33] *Ibid.*, p. xlix.

[34] Welles, *Diary*, pp. 348-349.

[35] Jt. Comm. Conduct of the War, *Report* (1865), I, 1, 5, 31, 37, 84; Meade, I, 365.

[36] From an unidentified clipping in the Huntington collection.

[37] Couch, *Battles and Leaders*, III, 170; Schurz, II, 431.

[38] McClure, p. 348.

[39] Meade, I, 374.

[40] Jt. Comm. Conduct of the War, *Report* (1865), I, xlii.

[41] *O. R.*, XXV, Part II, 505.

[42] Meade, I, 372.

[43] *O. R.*, XXV, Part II, 438.

[44] *Ibid.*

[45] Benjamin, *Battles and Leaders*, III, 241.

[46] *O. R.*, XXV, Part II, 437-448.

[47] *Ibid.*, pp. 439, 449.

[48] *Ibid.*, p. 449.

[49] Benjamin, *Battles and Leaders*, III, 241.

[50] Frederick W. Seward, *Seward at Washington as Senator and Secretary of State* (New York: Derby and Miller, 1891), III (1861-1872), 165.

[51] Gurowski, *Diary*, II, 240-241.

[52] Welles, *Diary*, I, 336.

[53] Washington *National Intelligencer* (Daily), May 18, 1863.

[54] Warren Lee Goss, *Recollections of a Private* (New York: Thomas Y. Crowell and Co., 1890), p. 162.

[55] Ford, II, 14.

[56] *O. R.*, XXV, Part II, 479.

[57] Jt. Comm. Conduct of the War, *Report* (1865), I, 151.

[58] Meade, I, 375. Although Hooker had told Lincoln that he suspected no one, he knew that Curtin had talked to Meade on his recent visit to the army. Jt. Comm. Conduct of the War, *Report* (1865), I, 151.

[59] Meade, I, 376-377.

[60] Letter, Curtin to Hooker, May 23, 1863, in the possession of Dr. Otto Eisenschiml of Chicago.

[61] Meade, I, 379.

[62] Gurowski, *Diary*, II, 228.

[63] Letter, Z. Chandler to his wife, May 20, 1863, Chandler Mss. Collection, Library of Congress.

[64] Letter, Chase to Hooker, May 23, 1863, in the possession of Dr. Otto Eisenschiml of Chicago.

[65] *Ibid.*

[66] Walker, pp. 254-255.

[67] Henry Greenleaf Pearson, *James W. Wadsworth of Geneseo* (London: John Murray, 1913), p. 201.

[68] Meade, I, 385.

[69] John Gibbon, *Personal Recollections of the Civil War* (New York: G. P. Putnam's Sons, 1928), p. 122.

[70] Washington *Daily Morning Chronicle*, May 7 to May 16, 1863.

[71] Washington *National Intelligencer*, daily issues May 8 to May 18, 1863; tri-weekly issues May 9 and May 23, 1863.

[72] New York *Tribune*, May 5 to May 10, 1863.

[73] New York *Herald*, May 8 to May 15, 1863.

[74] New York *Times*, May 9, 1863.

[75] Gurowski, *Diary*, II, 233.

[76] Sacramento *Union*, May 6, 1863.

[77] *Alta California*, May 8, 1863.

[78] Joshua L. Chamberlain, *Antietam to Appomattox with 118th Penna. Vols. Corn Exchange Regiment* (Philadelphia: J. L. Smith, 1892), pp. 226-227.

## Chapter XVII

[1] Present for duty equipped on this day were estimated: 91,000 infantry, 11,000 cavalry, 8,000 artillery. The cavalry estimate was much too high.

[2] *O. R.*, XXV, Part II, 439, 450. A portion of the cavalry under Kilpatrick and Davis had become separated from the main body and had joined the Union forces on the Peninsula.

[3] *Ibid.*, pp. 439, 467.

[4] *Ibid.*, pp. 468-469; *Ibid.*, Part III, pp. 10-11.

[5] Jt. Comm. Conduct of the War, *Report* (1865), I, 140.

[6] *Ibid.*, p. 85.

[7] Schurz, *Reminiscences*, II, 442.

[8] J. W. Schuckers, *The Life and Public Service of Salmon Portland Chase* (New York: D. Appleton and Co., 1874), 467.

[9] *O. R.*, XXV, Part I, 661.

[10] *A Statement of the Case of Brigadier General Joseph W. Revere* (New York: C. A. Alvord, 1863).

[11] *O. R.*, XXV, Part II, 447-449, 461, 465-466, 476-479.

[12] *Ibid.*, pp. 458, 463, 477.

[13] Davis, p. 211; *O. R.*, XXV, Part II, 469-471.

[14] *O. R.*, XXV, Part II, 471-472.

[15] *Ibid.*, p. 473.

[16] *Ibid.*, p. 479.

[17] *Ibid.*, pp. 516-517.

[18] Letter, C. F. Adams, Jr., to his mother, Ford, II, 8.

[19] *O. R.*, XXV, Part II, 509-510.

[20] *Ibid.*, 528-529.

[21] *Ibid.*, pp. 531-532.

[22] *Ibid.*, pp. 504-506, 524, 527.

[23] *Ibid.*, pp. 542-543.

[24] *Ibid.*, XXVII, Part III, 4-5.

[25] *Ibid.*, pp. 7, 12.

[26] *Ibid.*, pp. 12-13.

[27] *Ibid.*, pp. 11-13.

[28] *Ibid.*

[29] *Ibid.*, pp. 8-9.

[30] *Ibid.*, Part I, p. 30.

[31] *Ibid.*, p. 31.

[32] *Ibid.*, pp. 31-32.

[33] *Ibid.*, p. 33.

[34] *Ibid.*, Part III, pp. 15-16, 29.

[35] *Ibid.*, p. 33.

[36] *Ibid.*, pp. 902, 950. Pleasonton had divided his cavalry into two divisions under Generals Buford and Gregg.

[37] *Ibid.*, p. 38.

[38] *Ibid.*, p. 39.

[39] *Ibid.*, Part I, pp. 903-904.

[40] *Ibid.*, Part III, pp. 32, 44.

[41] *Ibid.*, p. 55.

[42] Letter, Sharpe to Hooker, June 9, in the Hooker Papers.

[43] *O. R.*, XXVII, Part I, 34-35.

[44] *Ibid.*, p. 35.

[45] *Ibid.*, Part III, pp. 57-59, 72.

[46] *Ibid.*, pp. 72-73.

[47] *Ibid.*, p. 72.

[48] *Ibid.*, pp. 80-84.

[49] *Ibid.*, pp. 88-89, 95.

[50] *Ibid.*, pp. 86-87.

[51] *Ibid.*, pp. 99-101.

[52] *Ibid.*, Part I, pp. 39-40.

[53] *Ibid.*

[54] *Ibid.*, Part III, pp. 103, 106.

[55] *Ibid.*, Part I, p. 43.

[56] *Ibid.*, pp. 43-44.

[57] *Ibid.*, p. 44.

[58] *Ibid.*, Part III, p. 118; Bartlett, p. 118; Walker, p. 215.

[59] *O. R.*, XXVII, Part I, p. 44; *Ibid.*, Part III, p. 131.

[60] *Ibid.*, Part III, pp. 146-147.

[61] Jt. Comm. Conduct of the War, *Report* (1865), I, 160.

[62] *O. R.*, XXVII, Part I, 45.

[63] Haupt, p. 205. Haupt believed that Hooker at this time wanted to avoid the exercise of any discretion in regard to the movements of the army.

[64] *O. R.*, XXVII, Part I, 45.

[65] *Ibid.*, pp. 45-46.

[66] *Ibid.*, Part III, pp. 148-152. Warren had sent Hooker a detailed report on the crossings of the Potomac and the topography of the countryside near by. This must have been very helpful since Hooker was still using General McDowell's map of January 1, 1862.

[67] *Ibid.*, Part I, p. 46.

[68] *Ibid.*, p. 47.

[69] *Ibid.*

[70] John G. Nicolay and John Hay, *Abraham Lincoln, A History* (New York: The Century Co., 1890), VII, 212.

[71] *O. R.*, XXVII, Part III, 171-174.

[72] *Ibid.*, Part III, pp. 173, 176-177.

[73] *Ibid.*, pp. 174-175. At this time Lee's forces were located as follows: Ewell had one division at Chambersburg, Pa., another at Shepherdstown, W. Va., and another at Winchester, Va.; Longstreet was west of the Blue Ridge Mountains between Snicker's Gap and Ashby's Gap; Hill was at Culpeper; the main body of cavalry was near Middleburg, Va.

[74] *Ibid.*, p. 192.

[75] *Ibid.*, pp. 50-51.

[76] *Ibid.*, p. 210.

[77] *Ibid.*, p. 225.

[78] *Ibid.*, pp. 223-224, 227-228. A. P. Hill's corps had been lost sight of completely. Lee had halted Longstreet while Hill marched north behind him, thereby successfully confusing the Federals.

[79] *Ibid.*, pp. 227-228.

[80] *Ibid.*, p. 228; *Ibid.*, Part I, p. 53.

[81] Schuckers, p. 468.

[82] Welles, *Diary*, I, 329.

[83] George C. Gorham, *Life and Public Services of Edwin M. Stanton* (Boston: Houghton Mifflin Co., 1899), II, 99.

[84] Welles, *Diary*, I, 335-336.

[85] *O. R.*, XXVII, Part I, 54.

[86] *Ibid.*, Part III, 258-259.

[87] *Ibid.*, Part I, 54-55.

[88] Welles, *Diary*, I, 340.

[89] *O. R.*, XXVII, Part III, 271.

[90] *Ibid.*, pp. 279-283.

[91] Butterfield, p. 332. This account of Hooker's prediction of the site of the next battle is given much credence although recorded long after the event.

[92] *O. R.*, XVII, Part I, pp. 55-56.

[93] *Ibid.*, Part III, pp. 279, 382.

[94] *Ibid.*, pp. 284-285.

[95] *Ibid.*, pp. 285-286.

[96] *Ibid.* All of Ewell's advance corps was by now in southern Pennsylvania.

[97] *Ibid.*, pp. 290-292.

[98] *Ibid.*, pp. 301-302.

[99] *Ibid.*, pp. 290-292.

[100] *Ibid.*, pp. 305-307, 319.

[101] *Ibid.*, pp. 306-307.

[102] *Ibid.*, p. 309. When Heintzelman refused to allow one brigade of this division to leave, Hooker vented a loud protest, but Halleck told him that the original order did not include this particular brigade. *Ibid.*, Part I, pp. 56-57.

[103] *Ibid.*, Part III, pp. 311, 313.

[104] *Ibid.*, pp. 314-317. Meade claims that this time Hooker was still keeping his corps commanders in total ignorance of his plans. Meade, I, 389.

[105] *O. R.*, XXVII, Part III, 320-321.

[106] *Ibid.*, pp. 355-358. Halleck claimed that there were only 1,900 men left in the city, including city guards and paroled prisoners.

[107] *Ibid.*, p. 336. Hooker was convinced that Lee had a total of 102,000 men, or almost exactly the number reported to be in the Federal army.

[108] *Ibid.*, Part I, p. 58. This, of course, also meant giving up Harpers Ferry.

[109] *Ibid.*, Part III, p. 349.

[110] *Ibid.*, Part I, p. 59.

[111] *Ibid.*, p. 60.

[112] Grand Rapids *Democrat*, Nov. 1879. Record of a conversation between

Stanton and John C. Ropes dated Feb. 8, 1870, in the possession of the Massachusetts Historical Society.

[113] Benjamin, *Battles and Leaders,* III, 241.

[114] *O. R.,* XXVII, Part III, 60.

[115] *Ibid.*

[116] Jt. Comm. Conduct of the War, *Report* (1865), I, 82.

[117] Welles, *Diary,* I, 348-349.

[118] Gorham, II, 99.

[119] Benjamin, *Battles and Leaders,* III, 241. General Sickles, Hooker's good friend, rode up to Frederick with Hardie but, of course, did not know about the removal order. Stine, pp. 445-446.

[120] Reynolds was not considered for the command, for he had said repeatedly that he would not have it.

[121] Sixteen hours had passed since Hooker had asked to be relieved and he had heard nothing from Washington; he was just beginning to figure that his offer had not been accepted. Benjamin, *Battles and Leaders,* III, 243.

[122] Meade, II, 3. Hooker said that he was gratified at the choice of successor.

[123] Hooker's General Order No. 66, June 28, 1863. *O. R.,* XXVII, Part III, 373-374.

[124] Benjamin, *Battles and Leaders,* III, 243.

## CHAPTER XVIII

[1] Jt. Comm. Conduct of the War, *Report* (1865), I, 175.

[2] Papers of the Military Historical Society of Massachusetts, III, 414.

[3] Jt. Comm. Conduct of the War, *Report* (1865), I, 175.

[4] Noah Brooks, "Glimpses of Lincoln in War Time," *Century Magazine,* Nov. 1894, 461.

[5] Walker, p. 261.

[6] Nicolay and Hay, *Complete Works of Abraham Lincoln* (New York: The Tandy-Thomas Co., 1905), IX, 44-45.

[7] *Ibid.,* pp. 80-81.

[8] Meade, II, 142.

[9] New York *Herald,* July 13, 1863.

[10] *Ibid.,* July 29, 1863.

[11] Welles, *Diary,* I, 349.

[12] New York *Herald,* July 9, 1863.

[13] Lincoln wrote to General McClernand at this time: "I am constantly pressed by those who scold before they think, or without thinking at all, to give commands respectively to . . . Hooker, McClellan, Butter, Sigel, Hunter, Curtis, when no commands are available." *O. R.,* LII, Part I, 438.

[14] William Roscoe Thayer, "Lincoln and Some Union Generals from the Unpublished Diaries of John Hay," *Harper's Monthly Magazine* CXXX (December 1914), 98.

[15] *Ibid.*

[16] Tyler Dennett, *Lincoln and the Civil War in the Diaries and Letters of John Hay* (New York: Dodd, Mead & Co., 1939), p. 85.

[17] *Ibid.*, p. 86.

[18] W. R. Thayer in *Harper's Monthly,* CXXX, 98.

[19] Dennett, p. 88.

[20] *Ibid.*, pp. 87-88.

[21] George A. Thayer, "A Railroad Feat of War," *Sketches of War History, 1861-1865,* ed. by W. H. Chamberlin (Cincinnati: The Robert Clarke Co., 1896), IV, 217.

[22] Frank Abial Flowers, *Edwin McMasters Stanton, the Autocrat of Rebellion, Emancipation and Reconstruction* (Akron, Ohio: The Saalfield Publishing Co., 1905).

[23] Slocum, p. 140.

[24] Nicolay and Hay, *Complete Works of Abraham Lincoln,* IX, 142.

[25] *O. R.,* XXX, Part IV, 49.

[26] Thayer, *Sketches of War History, 1861-1865,* IV, 227.

[27] *O. R.,* Series III, V, p. 524.

[28] Butterfield, p. 135.

[29] Dennett, pp. 93-94.

[30] Villard, II, 178.

[31] *O. R.,* XXX, Part IV, 49.

[32] *Ibid.*, Part III, 904, 928.

[33] Villard, II, 178.

[34] *O. R.,* XXX, Part IV, 71-72.

[35] *Ibid.*, pp. 93-94.

[36] *Ibid.*, pp. 111-112.

[37] *Ibid.*, p. 135.

[38] *Ibid.*, Part II, 712-713.

[39] *Ibid.*, p. 714.

[40] *Ibid.*, Part IV, p. 223.

[41] *Ibid.*, p. 221.

[42] Benjamin F. Taylor, *Mission Ridge and Lookout Mountain with Pictures of Life in Camp and Field* (New York: D. Appleton & Co., 1872), 241-242.

[43] *O. R.,* XXX, Part IV, 466.

[44] *Ibid.*, p. 291.

[45] *Ibid.*, p. 322.

[46] *Ibid.*

[47] *Battles and Leaders,* III, 752.

[48] Ulysses S. Grant, *Personal Memoirs of U. S. Grant* (New York: Charles L. Webster & Co., 1885), II, 18-19.

[49] *Ibid.*, p. 26; O. R., XXX, Part IV, 479.

[50] A Board of Army Officers appointed to settle who originated the plan concluded that Rosecrans should receive the credit. See U. S. War Department, *Report of a Board of Army Officers upon the Claim of Maj. Gen. William Farrar Smith* (Washington: Government Printing Office, 1901).

[51] *O. R.,* XXX, Part IV, 482.

[52] *Ibid.*, p. 454.

[53] *Ibid.*, XXXI, Part I, 43, 47.

[54] Oliver O. Howard, "Grant at Chattanooga," *Personal Recollections of the War of the Rebellion* (New York: N. Y. Commandery of the Loyal Legion of the U. S., 1891), pp. 245-248.

[55] M. A. De Wolfe Howe (ed.), *Home Letters of General Sherman* (New York: Charles Scribner's Sons, 1909), p. 250.

[56] Telegram, Dana to Stanton, Howard, *Autobiography*, I, 459.

[57] *O. R.*, XXXI, Part I, 741.

[58] Shanks, p. 178.

[59] Telegram, Dana to Stanton. *O. R.*, XXXI, Part I, 72.

[60] *Ibid.*, p. 43.

[61] Howard, *Autobiography*, I, 459; Underwood, 159.

[62] *O. R.*, XXXI, Part I, 97.

[63] *Ibid.*, p. 105.

[64] Howard, *Autobiography*, I, 465.

[65] *O. R.*, XXXI, Part I, 94.

[66] *Ibid.*, p. 72.

[67] Howard, *Autobiography*, I, 467. Hartwell Osborn, "Eleventh Corps in East Tennessee," *Military Essays and Recollections* (Chicago: Cozzens & Beaton Co., 1907), IV, 360.

[68] *O. R.*, XXXI, Part I, 98.

[69] The foe were old acquaintances from Virginia—several brigades of Longstreet's corps. Their attack was misdirected by Bragg, the Commander in Chief, on down to the brigade leaders.

[70] Grant, II, 41; Howard, *Autobiography*, I, 470.

[71] *O. R.*, XXXI, Part I, 74-76.

[72] The court heard testimony until February 16, 1864, when Schurz and his brigade commander, Frederick Hecker, were exonerated. Schurz presented a skillful defense and did not spare Hooker's unfair attitude toward the men of the Eleventh Corps. *O. R.*, XXXI, Part I, 137-216. The charge made against Schurz did not reflect credit on Hooker. Villard thought it was instigated either because of malice toward Schurz arising out of Chancellorsville or because of the influence of liquor. The outcome of the trial humiliated Hooker. Villard, II, 228.

[73] *O. R.*, XXXI, Part I, 96.

[74] Underwood, p. 169.

[75] Telegram, Dana to Stanton, October 29, 1863. *O. R.*, XXXI, Part I, 73. Three days before, Grant had suggested that Hooker be assigned to the command of the Twelfth Corps and Slocum relieved for other duty. *Ibid.*, p. 740.

## CHAPTER XIX

[1] Sherman, I, 387.

[2] *O. R.*, XXXI, Part II, 52.

[3] *Ibid.*, Part I, p. 793.

[4] *Ibid.*, Part III, pp. 6, 18.

[5] *Ibid.*, p. 3.

[6] *Ibid.*, pp. 155-156.

7 Grant, II, 49-50.

8 Sherman, I, 391-392.

9 *O. R.*, XXXI, Part II, 314.

10 *Ibid.*, p. 106.

11 *Ibid.*, p. 314.

12 *Ibid.*, p. 392.

13 *Ibid.*, p. 316.

14 *Ibid.*, p. 395.

15 *Ibid.*, p. 317.

16 *Ibid.*, p. 396.

17 *Ibid.*, p. 317.

18 *Ibid.*, p. 398.

19 John Russell Young, *Around the World with General Grant* (New York: The American News Co., 1879), II, 306.

20 *O. R.*, XXXI, Part II, 122, 326, 690, and regimental reports.

21 New York *Herald*, Dec. 2, 1863.

22 *O. R.*, XXXI, Part II, 317-318.

23 *Ibid.*, p. 115.

24 *Ibid.*, p. 319.

25 *Ibid.*, pp. 118, 319.

26 *Ibid.*, p. 320.

27 *Ibid.*, pp. 320-322.

28 Grant, II, 90.

29 *O. R.*, XXXI, Part II, 48.

30 *Ibid.*, p. 120.

31 William Le Barron Jenney, "With Sherman and Grant from Memphis to Chattanooga. A Reminiscence," *Military Essays and Recollections* (Chicago: Cozzens & Beaton Co., 1907), IV, 214.

32 *O. R.*, XXXI, Part II, 70-71.

33 *Ibid.*, p. 325.

34 William F. Smith, "An Historical Sketch of the Military Operations Around Chattanooga, Tennessee, September 22 to November 27, 1863," *Military Historical Society of Massachusetts*, VIII, 245. Smith had his differences with both Hooker and Grant and should be an impartial witness in this case.

35 *Battles and Leaders*, III, 725.

36 New York *Tribune*, Dec. 3, 1863.

37 *O. R.*, XXXI, Part II, 323; *Ibid.*, Part III, 294.

38 *Ibid.*, Part II, 123-124.

39 Underwood, p. 199.

40 Howard, I, 495.

41 Underwood, p. 198.

42 *O. R.*, XXXI, Part II, 256.

43 *Ibid.*, XXXII, Part II, 32.

44 *Ibid.*, pp. 5, 6.

45 *Ibid.*, XXXI, Part III, 339-345. Letter, Hooker to Chase, Dec. 28, 1863.

46 *Ibid.*, XXXII, Part II, 468. Letter, Hooker to Stanton, Feb. 25, 1864.

[47] *Ibid.,* pp. 313, 314.

[48] *Ibid.,* XXXI, Part III, 377.

[49] *Ibid.,* XXXII, Part II, 315.

[50] Letter, Grant to Hooker, Jan. 13, 1864, in the Hooker Papers. Hooker's congratulatory order after Lookout was quite poetic: "The triumphs of yesterday . . . will be remembered as long as the giant peak of Lookout shall be their mute but eloquent monument." *Ibid.,* XXXI, Part II, 117-118.

[51] Meade, II, 160.

[52] The *Spirit of the Times* by March 1864 was almost entirely a "Hooker" journal. Separate attacks were made on Grant, Sherman, McPherson, Schofield and Meade. *Ibid.,* p. 183.

[53] *O. R.,* XXVII, Part III, 857.

[54] The Detroit *Post and Tribune, Zachariah Chandler, An Outline Sketch of His Life and Public Services* (Detroit: The Post and Tribune Co., 1880), p. 244.

[55] *Ibid.,* p. 245.

[56] Meade, II, 179. Letter to Henry A. Cram, Mar. 15, 1864.

[57] Grant, II, 116.

## CHAPTER XX

[1] *O. R.,* XXXII, Part III, 221.

[2] *Ibid.,* pp. 247, 258, 270. At first it was decided to name this command the First Corps. The idea was abandoned for the reason that, although the old First Corps had been consolidated with the Third in the Army of the Potomac, there was the possibility of its being reactivated at a later date.

[3] *Ibid.,* pp. 291, 292, 341.

[4] *Ibid.,* pp. 364-366.

[5] Sherman, II, 23-24.

[6] Henry Stone, "The Atlanta Campaign," in *Papers of the Military Historical Society of Massachusetts* (Boston: The Military Historical Society of Massachusetts, 1910), VIII, 351.

[7] *O. R.,* XXXII, Part III, 470.

[8] Sickles, p. 25.

[9] James R. Burns, *Battle of Williamsburgh with Reminiscences of the Campaign, Vital Experiences, Debates, etc.* (New York: James R. Burns, 1865), p. 52.

[10] Letter, Hooker to Chandler, May 3, 1864, in Chandler Mss., Library of Congress.

[11] *O. R.,* XXXVIII, Part IV, 61.

[12] *Ibid.*

[13] *Ibid.,* p. 70.

[14] *Ibid.,* p. 80.

[15] *Ibid.,* Part II, pp. 114-117.

[16] *Ibid.,* Part IV, p. 71.

[17] *Ibid.,* pp. 113, 116.

[18] Stone, p. 366.

[19] *O. R.,* XXXVIII, Part I, 64.

[20] *Ibid.*, Part II, pp. 27-28.
[21] Howard, I, 516.
[22] John M. Schofield, *Forty-Six Years in the Army* (New York: The Century Co., 1897), p. 141.
[23] *O. R.*, XXXVIII, Part II, 119-120.
[24] Stone, p. 389.
[25] *O. R.*, XXXVIII, Part I, 142.
[26] Johnston, p. 322.
[27] *O. R.*, XXXVIII, Part I, 65.
[28] Stone, p. 408.
[29] *O. R.*, XXXVIII, Part I, 66.
[30] *Ibid.*, Part II, pp. 30, 124.
[31] Stone, p. 414.
[32] *O. R.*, XXXVIII, Part II, 30, 125, 324.
[33] *Ibid.*, Part IV, p. 312.
[34] *Ibid.*, Part I, p. 66; *Ibid.*, Part IV, p. 327.
[35] Butterfield, pp. 146-148.
[36] *O. R.*, XXXVIII, Part IV, 395.
[37] *Ibid.*, p. 420.
[38] *Ibid.*, p. 421.
[39] *Ibid.*, Part I, p. 67.
[40] *Ibid.*, Part II, p. 127.
[41] *Ibid.*, pp. 127-129, 326.
[42] *Ibid.*, Part IV, p. 495.
[43] *Ibid.*, p. 522.
[44] *Ibid.*, p. 559.
[45] *Ibid.*, p. 561.
[46] *Ibid.*, p. 558.
[47] Sherman, p. 57.
[48] Schofield, p. 135.
[49] Kulp's Farm is also referred to as Culp's and Kolb's.
[50] Sherman, II, 59.
[51] *Ibid.*
[52] *Ibid.*
[53] Stone, p. 420.
[54] *O. R.*, XXXVIII, Part I, 68.
[55] *Ibid.*, p. 69.
[56] *Ibid.*, Part V, p. 31.
[57] Johnston, p. 347.
[58] *O. R.*, XXXVIII, Part II, 135-136.
[59] *Ibid.*, Part V, p. 190.
[60] *Ibid.*, Part II, pp. 136-140.
[61] *Ibid.*, pp. 34, 141, 329.
[62] Stone, p. 449.
[63] *O. R.*, XXXVIII, Part V, 228.
[64] *Ibid.*, p. 233.

[65] Joel Tyler Headley, *Grant and Sherman: Their Campaigns and Generals* (New York: E. B. Treat & Co., 1866).

[66] Sherman, II, 59.

[67] Stone, p. 449.

[68] *O. R.*, XXXVIII, Part V, 266.

[69] *Ibid.*, p. 273.

[70] George Francis Dawson, *Life and Services of Gen. John A. Logan as Soldier and Statesman* (Chicago: Belford, Clarke & Co., 1887), p. 511.

[71] Jacob D. Cox, *Atlanta*, Vol. IX of *Campaigns of the Civil War* (New York: Charles Scribner's Sons, 1882).

[72] Shanks, p. 186; Tremain, p. 347; *Society of the Army of the Cumberland, 12th Reunion*, Sept., 1880 (Cincinnati: Robert Clark & Co., 1881), p. 167.

[73] *O. R.*, XXXVIII, Part V, 272.

[74] Howe, p. 303.

[75] *O. R.*, XXXVIII, Part V, 523.

[76] *Ibid.*, p. 793.

[77] Grant, II, 539.

[78] Sherman, II, 58.

[79] Schofield, p. 136.

[80] *Ibid.*, p. 139.

[81] *O. R.*, LII, Part I, 540.

[82] Julian Wisner Hinkley, *A Narrative of Service with the Third Wisconsin Infantry* (Wisconsin Historical Commission, 1912), p. 135.

[83] From a New York *Times* clipping in the Huntington Collection based on a correspondent's story dated Aug. 1, 1864.

[84] Underwood, p. 229.

[85] *O. R.*, XXXVIII, Part II, 407-408.

[86] Hinkley, p. 133.

[87] Undated clipping in the Huntington Collection.

## CHAPTER XXI

[1] *O. R.*, XXXIX, Part II, 515-516.

[2] New York *Times*, Sept. 10, 1864.

[3] New York *Tribune*, Sept. 23, 1864.

[4] *Ibid.*

[5] *O. R.*, XXXVIII, Part V, 857.

[6] *Spirit of the Times*, Aug. 20, 1864.

[7] *O. R.*, XXXIX, Part III, 23-24.

[8] *Ibid.*, p. 694.

[9] *Ibid.*, XLIX, Part I, 716.

[10] *Ibid.*, XLV, Part II, 83.

[11] *Ibid.*, XXXIX, Part III, 551-552.

[12] *Ibid.*, XLV, Part II, 82-83.

[13] *Ibid.*, pp. 42-43.

[14] Cincinnati *Daily Commercial*, Oct. 18, 1864.

[15] New York *Times,* Feb. 23, 1865.

[16] *Ibid.,* Nov. 16, 1864.

[17] *O. R.,* XLV, Part I, 1011-1013.

[18] *Ibid.,* p. 1034.

[19] *Ibid.,* Part II, 282.

[20] Letter, Hooker to Wilson, Dec. 17, 1864; *O. R.,* XLV, Part II, 246-248.

[21] Letter, Hooker to Wilson, Dec. 8, 1864; *O. R.,* XLV, Part II, 109-111.

[22] *Ibid.*

[23] Poore, II, 161.

[24] Letter, Hooker to Nesmith, April 9, 1865, in possession of the Oregon Historical Society.

[25] *O. R.,* XLVI, Part II, 844.

[26] William E. Barton, *President Lincoln* (Indianapolis: The Bobbs-Merrill Company, 1933) II, 735-736.

[27] New York *Times,* June 2, 1865.

[28] This sword is now in the possession of Joseph Hooker Wood of Lancaster, California.

[29] State of California Senate Concurrent Resolution No. 21, March 23, 1863, in the possession of Dr. Otto Eisenschiml of Chicago. Hooker acknowledged this resolution on September 20, 1863, saying, "next to honorable and complete success over the enemies of the Union [I] esteem nothing higher than California's good opinion. . . ." Hittell, IV, 376.

[30] *O. R.,* XLVIII, Part II, 827.

[31] Joel Tyler Headley, *The Life and Travels of General Grant* (Philadelphia: Hubbard Bros., 1879), 238.

[32] Sherman, Halleck, Sheridan and Thomas were also given military divisions. *O. R.,* XLVI, Part II, 1288.

[33] New York *Times,* July 18 and July 26, 1865.

[34] Cincinnati *Daily Commercial,* Oct. 4, 1865.

[35] Shanks, pp. 191-192.

[36] From notes on a conversation between Hooker and the artist, James Edward Kelly, June 30, 1879, in the possession of Dr. George Hope Ryder of New York.

[37] *O. R.,* Series III, Vol. V, p. 1035.

[38] Haynes, p. 323.

[39] Undated clipping from the San Francisco *Chronicle* in the Huntington Collection.

[40] Letter, Hooker to Henry B. Dawson, Nov. 15, 1873, in the possession of the New York Historical Society.

[41] Letter, Hooker to Henry B. Dawson, June 2, 1875, in the possession of the New York Historical Society.

[42] Letters, Adjutant General's Department to Hooker, May 11, 1878, to July 5, 1878, in the Huntington Collection.

[43] *Alta California,* June 27, 1872.

[44] Undated clipping from the San Francisco *Chronicle* in the Huntington Collection.

[45] New York *Times,* Nov. 16, 1864.

[46] Letter, Hooker to Henry B. Dawson, Jan. 4, 1875, in the possession of the New York Historical Society.

[47] John B. Gordon, *Reminiscences of the Civil War* (New York: Charles Scribner's Sons, 1904), pp. 97, 124.

[48] From notes on a conversation between Hooker and the artist, James Edward Kelly, on June 30, 1879, in the possession of Dr. George Hope Ryder of New York.

[49] Unidentified clipping in the Huntington Collection.

[50] *Ibid.*

[51] Sacramento *Union* and *Alta California*, Nov. 8, 1879.

[52] Unidentified clipping in the Huntington Collection.

# INDEX

# INDEX